PELICAN BOOKS

The Popish Plot

John Kenyon has been Professor of Modern
History at the University of Hull since 1962.
Before that he was a Lecturer in History at
Cambridge, and a Fellow of Christ's College. An
acknowledged authority on seventeenth-century
England, his previous works include *The Stuarts*
and *The Stuart Constitution*. He is a regular
contributor to the *Observer*, and is currently
engaged in a study of early eighteenth-century
political thought which will be published under
the title *The Politics of Oligarchy*. He is married
with three children.

JOHN KENYON

The Popish Plot

PENGUIN BOOKS

Penguin Books Ltd, Harmondsworth, Middlesex, England
Penguin Books Australia Ltd, Ringwood, Victoria, Australia
Penguin Books Canada Ltd, 41 Steelcase Road West, Markham, Ontario, Canada

—

First published by William Heinemann Ltd 1972
Published in Pelican Books 1974

—

Copyright © John P. Kenyon, 1972

—

Made and printed in Great Britain
by C. Nicholls & Company Ltd
Set in Linotype Granjon

Contents

List of Illustrations

Preface

I have discussed this book with many of my colleagues and friends over the past five years, and in the process learned a great deal; but I would like to single out for mention a number of younger historians who have very generously allowed me to make use of their work before they could publish it themselves; namely, David Allen, Margaret O'Keefe, John Miller and Peter Roebuck. I am also deeply grateful to Professor Kenneth Haley, who read the book in proof form at very short notice, made some helpful suggestions and corrected several errors.

The Rt Hon. Marquess of Bath kindly allowed me to consult and use the Coventry Papers at Longleat. I must also thank Mrs Nesta Pain for lending me the script of the broadcast discussed in Appendix A, and Professor Keith Simpson and the executors of the late Professor Alexander Kennedy for allowing me to reproduce arguments and theories they put forward on that occasion. I am also grateful to the Librarian of Endsleigh College, Hull, for allowing me access to the Postgate Collection of books on the history of English Roman Catholicism.

The University of Hull was generous, as always, with its research funds, and in the later stages provided me with an assistant, Miss Anne Cantor, who enabled me to complete the work much earlier than I had feared at one time. My wife typed the final manuscript, a daunting task carried out with great good humour, patience and accuracy. She also tidied up the grammar and the spelling.

Lastly, Miss Rachel Montgomery did all that could be expected of a good publisher's editor, and more. In particular, she persuaded me to rewrite the first chapter and in so doing improved it considerably.

J. P. K.
January 1972

xi

Note

As a result of pronouncements made from time to time by the Holy See, several persons mentioned in this book are entitled to be addressed as 'Saint', 'Blessed' or 'Venerable'. I have ignored this convention, though for those who are interested I have set out the position in Appendix C. I have also avoided as far as possible the use of the courtesy title 'Father' when referring to Roman Catholic priests.

All dates in the text are in the English Old Style, ten days behind the Continental New Style, but the year is taken as beginning on 1 January, not 25 March. A few dates are given in the New Style in the notes of reference, where they are distinguished by the abbreviation 'NS'.

There is no want of Summaries, Charges, Defences, besides the very Trials and Examinations themselves, in Print, to divert anyone whose Temper will comport with such phlegmatic Entertainment. I must own that, the more voluminous and dull the Subject is, the greater Art is required to sift and reduce it to tolerable History: And that may be done, far beyond any yet extant, if an able Pen undertakes it ... By this means the Community may gather a just Sentiment of the Times, without turning over and sifting the nasty Rubbish of Narratives, Trials, &c., an Herculean Labour, which, since the Ardour of Zeal, as well as Passion of the People, is spent, few or none will undertake, and yet fewer be able throughout to discern the true from the false, or make such Conclusions as may be drawn from them. And however this may be a great deal, and go far with Persons Inquisitive and industrious, if any such undertake the filthy Analysis, who may thereby obtain some Distinctions of true and false; what is that to the unaccountable Flings of a fyderated Rabble, major as well as minor, when wise Men acted like stark Fools, and honest and good Men like the veriest Fourbs that ever came out of Newgate?

Roger North
(1653–1734)

Abbreviations

The following abbreviations are used throughout the footnotes and in the notes of reference at the end of the book.

Add.	Additional Manuscripts, British Museum.
C.J.	*Commons Journals.*
C.R.S.	Publications of the Catholic Record Society.
C.S.P.D.	*Calendar of State Papers Domestic.*
C.T.B.	*Calendar of Treasury Books.*
D.N.B.	*Dictionary of National Biography.*
D.W.L.	Dr Williams's Library: Roger Morrice's Entering Book (E.B.).
H.M.C.	*Historical Manuscripts Commission* (followed by the name or number of the report).
L.J.	*Lords Journals.*
L.P.	*House of Lords Papers 1678–88 (H.M.C.).*
P.C.	Privy Council Registers (P.R.O.).
P.R.O.	Public Record Office.
Rawl.	Rawlinson Manuscripts, Bodleian Library.
S.P.	State Papers Domestic (P.R.O.).
S.T.	*State Trials,* ed. W. Cobbett and T. C. Howell (34 vols., 1809–28).
V.C.H.	*Victoria County History.*
W.A.(A.)	Westminster Cathedral Archives, 'A' Series.

Other works are cited by a short title, or the name of the author, by which they can be found in the list on pages 314–16.

I

The Catholic Problem

IN the seventeenth century the Englishman's attitude to Roman Catholicism was quite uncompromising. In the words of Andrew Marvell:

Popery is such a thing as cannot, but for want of a word to express it, be called a religion; nor is it to be mentioned with that civility which is otherwise decent to be used in speaking about the differences of human opinion about divine matters,

and the young Lord Russell spoke for most of his countrymen when he told the House of Commons in 1679:

I despise such a ridiculous and nonsensical religion. A piece of wafer, broken betwixt a priest's fingers, to be our Saviour! And what becomes of it when eaten, and taken down, you know.[1]

This was a typical Calvinist reaction to the ceremonial aspect of the Latin mass, which had become even more exuberant and colourful with the Counter-Reformation, and to its central doctrine of transubstantiation, by which the elements at communion were transformed into the body and blood of Christ. Marvell denounced the priesthood as 'jugglers and conjurors', with their 'vestments, consecrations, exorcisms, whisperings, sprinklings, censings and phantastical rites, gesticulations and removals', slaves to 'the infamous transubstantial solecism'. John Tillotson, Dean of St Paul's, was broad-minded enough to remark, 'I doubt not but Papists are made like other men', but even he lamented that they were bound by 'the grossest superstition, so gross that they must forsake their reason, and sense, too, who embrace it'.[2] In the first Test Act of 1673 a simple oath denying transubstantiation was considered enough to separate Catholics from Protestants.

Of course, such attitudes were no more extreme than the Catholic attitude to Protestants in, say, Spain, or Italy, or Bavaria; only in the Netherlands, to a certain extent in France, and in a few of the smaller German states, did members of both sects live side by side in decent amity. If there was any difference, it was that the Protestants' hatred of Catholicism was intensified by fear. The confidently expected victory of Truth over Falsehood had somehow never occurred, and the European rivalry between Catholicism and Protestantism had dragged on into the seventeenth century, with the Catholics steadily gaining ground; first the southern Netherlands had been lost, then southern Germany, and in 1648, when the Thirty Years' War ended, Protestantism had been driven out to the periphery of Europe, where it was precariously lodged in North Germany, Holland, Scandinavia, England and Scotland; all with the exception of Holland poor, thinly populated, second-class nations. Indeed, arguably it owed its survival to the fierce rivalry between the two strongest Catholic nations of Europe, France and Spain, and here the reign of Charles II saw an ominous shift in the balance of power. Spain, exhausted by generations of warfare, and weakened by a backward economy, went down before France. In the 1660s and 1670s the diplomacy and military power of Louis XIV dominated Europe, and for five years, from 1673 to 1678, he held his own against a coalition of Spain, Holland, the Holy Roman Empire and several lesser states. By that time it was also clear that he would not tolerate much longer the existence of the French Protestants, or Huguenots, whose immunity had been guaranteed by the Edict of Nantes in 1598. Moreover, Louis XIV confirmed the assumption of many Englishmen that Catholicism was always to be identified with absolute monarchy, and that it was the aim of the Catholic Church to impose this form of government on the whole world. As Sir Henry Capel put it:

From popery came the notion of a standing army and arbitrary power ... Formerly the crown of Spain, and now France, supports this root of popery amongst us; but lay popery flat, and there's an end of arbitrary government and power. It is a mere chimera, or notion, without popery.[3]

Nor had the Pope ever relinquished his right to depose monarchs; specifically, none of Pius V's successors had cancelled the bull *Regnans in Excelsis* of 1570, which formally deposed Elizabeth I and absolved her subjects from their allegiance to her.* The principal reason why English Catholics were forbidden to take the oath of allegiance was that it contained a clause denying this right.

But since the English had a robust faith in their ability to beat off direct attacks from abroad, it was obvious to them that their Protestant citadel could only be captured by a conspiracy from within. And the danger here seemed a real and urgent one, for English Catholicism was closely associated in the popular mind with a whole series of plots and projected *coups d'état*, some of which had come very near success. There had been the Ridolfi Plot of 1571 to depose Elizabeth I, followed by the assassination plots associated with the names of Throckmorton and Babington, in the 1580s; then the Gunpowder Plot of 1605, one of the best-publicized episodes in English history, which was the subject of a special church service (compulsory, like all church services) on 5 November each year. From 1640 to 1643 another conspiracy was believed to be imminent, a belief confirmed by the outbreak of the Irish Rebellion in 1641. In the winter of 1641–2, as in 1678–9, the country was in the grip of hysterical fear at the prospect of a Catholic uprising – so much so that many landowners put their houses and estates in a posture of defence and turned out the local militia.[4]

The master-minds behind any such rising or conspiracy were, of course, the priesthood, and particularly the Society of Jesus, whose members were credited with fanatical courage, iron determination and a devotion to the Holy See which was the distillation of bigotry. If Catholics were bad, Jesuits were worse, and

*Nor have they down to the present day, though there were hopes that Paul VI would make this gesture to ecumenicism when he canonized the Forty English Martyrs in 1970.

the use in all statutes and proclamations of the term 'priests and Jesuits', as if the two were quite distinct, testifies to their reputation; they were the papacy's elite shock troops, the Waffen S.S. of seventeenth-century Catholicism.

Nor was there any doubt as to what would happen if the Catholics seized control; all good Protestants would burn. The association of Catholicism with combustion had been established, of course, by Mary I, who in her short reign (1553–8) had sent nearly three hundred men and women to the stake. Their fate had been recounted in gory and pathetic detail by John Foxe, whose *Acts and Monuments of these Latter Days*, better known as 'The Book of Martyrs', had been published in 1563 and rapidly emerged as a best-seller second only to the Bible; it was reprinted five times in Elizabeth's reign, and again in 1610, 1632, 1641, and 1684.[5] 'Bloody Mary' was far from being the most popular of English monarchs, but it is a fair guess that she was mentioned in the seventeenth century just as often as her sister Elizabeth, the Protestant Judith, and the persecution she had initiated lurked always in the back of men's minds. In 1679 the Earl of Essex told the Privy Council 'that the apprehension of popery made him imagine he saw his children frying in Smithfield', and a Whig pamphleteer elaborated on this in his macabre picture of a popish London:

Casting your eye towards Smithfield, imagine you see your father, or your mother, or some of your nearest and dearest relations, tied to a stake in the midst of flames, when with eyes lifted up to heaven, they scream and cry out to that God for whose cause they die, which was a frequent spectacle the last time popery reigned amongst us.[6]

Lord Chief Justice Scroggs, who might charitably be supposed to be better educated and better informed than most, summed up the common prejudice against Roman Catholicism when he said of its clergy:

They have, indeed, ways of conversion and conviction by enlightening our understandings by a faggot, and by the powerful and irresistible arguments of a dagger; but there are such wicked solecisms in their religion that they seem to have left them neither natural sense nor natural conscience. Not natural sense, by their absurdity in so unreasonable a belief as of the wine turned into blood; nor natural conscience, by their cruelty, who make the Protestants' blood as wine, and these priests thirst after it.[7]

This paranoiac fear of Catholicism was intensified by the obstinate durability of the Catholic community. Although by the death of Elizabeth I in 1603 it was clearly a minority of the population, it never proved possible to eliminate it entirely, as corresponding Protestant minorities had been eliminated in Spain and Italy, and were to be eliminated in France after 1685, with almost complete success.

There were certainly enough laws on the statute book for this purpose. The criterion was failure to attend the services of the Anglican church once a week, a duty incumbent on all adult Englishmen and women, and take communion three times a year. Those who refused were guilty of 'recusancy', and on conviction were liable to a standing fine of £20 a month or two thirds of the income from their estate, whichever the government preferred. It was high treason to convert another person to Rome, and a felony to be converted oneself; it was also a felony to attend mass, and a serious offence to be found in possession of vestments, pyxes, rosaries, missals, or any other of the apparatus of devotion. Catholic priests were forbidden to enter the country and by a statute of 1585 (the notorious 'Act of 27 Elizabeth') those found there were liable to the death penalty, simply for being priests. Laymen who sheltered or assisted priests were also liable to the death penalty. Enacted between 1580 and 1610, these constituted the 'Penal Laws'. Moreover, the stipulation that all those who held government office, locally as well as centrally, must take the oaths of allegiance and supremacy operated as a stringent bar on sincere Catholics.* They were ex-

---

* The oath of supremacy, instituted in 1559, acknowledged the King as head of the English Church; the oath of allegiance, as revised in 1606, did less violence to the Catholic conscience, but it did deny the Pope's right to excommunicate and depose kings. Despite explicit prohibitions from Rome, some Catholics would take one or the other or both, but usually only under pressure.

cluded in the same way from the Universities and the Inns of Court.

But these laws were never stringently enforced, except for brief periods: from 1605 to about 1612, in the wake of the Gunpowder Plot; under Charles I's personal government, from 1629 to 1637, and then only in certain parts of the country; and in the 1640s, when the Long Parliament passed several new and more stringent edicts against papists.

There are various reasons for this leniency. Some of the laws were so severe as to be self-defeating, particularly the Act of 1585 against priests; witnesses were reluctant to come forward, and when they did juries hesitated to convict. Under James I only twenty-five Catholics were executed (twenty of them priests or lay brothers) and none in the last seven years of the reign (1618–25). Only one perished between Charles I's accession in 1625 and the assembly of the Long Parliament in 1640. Under the Long Parliament, up to 1646, the count was nineteen, but even then no layman was executed for harbouring priests or 'persuading to popery'; the last martyr for this cause was Roger Wrennal in 1616. Rather surprisingly, the Puritan New Model Army, and its leader Oliver Cromwell, were very lenient, and only two more priests were executed between 1646 and the Restoration in 1660. When the Jesuit John Mumford was arrested at Norwich in 1658 there was apparently no thought of indicting him; he was simply 'paraded in his vestments round the city, then sent off to Gt Yarmouth, remanded back to Norwich, and after some months' imprisonment was discharged on bail'. He resumed his missionary work in the same area, and continued unmolested until his death in 1666.[8] Charles II's attitude was even more relaxed, and though at the instance of Parliament he issued a proclamation in 1663 ordering all priests and Jesuits to leave the kingdom forthwith, there was no suggestion that the statute of 1585 be enforced against them.

Laymen were subject to occasional harassment, and no doubt lived in continual fear of it, but after 1603 any planned campaign against them was usually motivated by the government's occasional urge to expand a neglected branch of the public revenue and was never carried through with diligence and efficiency. Like all common law actions, prosecution for recusancy was a time-consuming and protracted business, which could founder at any stage on a technical point. Witnesses had to be found, and persuaded to give evidence, which was not easy when, as so often, it was a case of a lowly constable or churchwarden giving evidence against the local squire. When a judgement was secured, it had to be enforced by the county sheriff, and if he was to be persuaded to act it depended on the local justices of the peace, or the judges of assize, who only visited the county twice a year. The Exchequer found that so much of the money collected at local level stuck to local fingers anyway that it was scarcely worth the effort of intervening; and in any case its powers were only admonitory.

Above all, it is clear that justices of the peace and sheriffs, even though they might vociferously support the persecution of 'papists' in general terms, or papists in other parts of the country, were afflicted by a sudden infirmity of purpose when it came to prosecuting men who were neighbours, friends, even relations by marriage. A comment made by the Northampton justices in 1613 is unusual only in its frankness; it expresses an attitude which was so common as to be almost universal:

> Sir Thomas Brudenell being divers times before us himself, his wife and many of his family, to the number of fifteen recusants, if there had not been too much regard had of him by some of us, there had passed a conviction before this time.[9]

Lord Aston, a wealthy Staffordshire landowner, and an undoubted Catholic all his life, was deeply affronted when a grand jury presented him as a 'suspected papist' in 1675. As he told the Secretary of State in an angry letter:

> Some eminent Justices, my neighbours, assured them I was no such man, nor had they any sufficient ground to suspect me, and I was not by anyone on oath or otherwise presented to be such, and I never declared myself, nor acted or joined with any particular way of worship; I never went to mass, I never was present nor joined in any worship particular to the Church of Rome.[10]

At a humbler level it has been shown how Wiltshire magistrates persistently presented Catholics for three weeks' absence from Church, not four, so that they were liable to a fine of a shilling a week, not £20 a month.[11]

In any case, many heads of Catholic families were 'church-papists'; that is, they safeguarded their position by attending church once a week, and even perhaps taking communion on occasion. In an emergency most of them were also willing to take the oaths. For instance, Thomas Eyre of Hassopp, in Derby-shire, was so notorious a Catholic that when he was made high sheriff in 1621 questions were asked in Parliament, but it was not until 1626 that some of his enemies amongst the local squire-archy presented him at Derby Assizes for recusancy. He promptly took the oaths, then took his accusers to law for con-spiring together to rob him of 'his good name, fame and estima-tion'.[12] The final remedy, though it was strictly forbidden by law, was simply to execute deeds handing over one's estate to Protestant friends or relatives. A striking case in point is that of Lord Vaux of Harrowden, who took refuge in Brussels after the discovery of the Gunpowder Plot. When his mother, Elizabeth Vaux, was arrested in 1611 he rushed home and conveyed the family estates to five of his Protestant neighbours in North-amptonshire, of whom at least one (William Tate of Delapré) was a notorious anti-Catholic. The government arrested Vaux and entered a *praemunire* against his estates, but they could not seize them and after two years he was simply released.[13]

Such instances could be multiplied many times; in fact, out-side the period of the Civil Wars it is difficult to find any Cath-olic family against whom the penal laws were enforced vigorously and consistently. There was a steady dribble of con-versions to the Protestant Church, but this must be attributed not so much to persecution as to the influence of Protestant relatives, especially mothers – many Catholics married Protes-tants, despite the opposition of their priests – and a feeling of social isolation. For the exclusion of Catholics from public life was the one section of the penal laws which was stringently enforced. Under James I and Charles I there were undoubtedly a few Catholic local officials – Thomas Eyre was one – some of them took the oaths, others evaded them. (Usually the oaths were only tendered once, when a man took up office.) But it is unlikely that the numbers were significant, and the Test Act of 1673 finally made such evasion impossible.* Under Charles II the few Catholics found in the government or in Parliament were men who had been converted, or reconverted, after taking the oaths.†

Finally the paranoia of the English Protestants was exacerbated by their understandable misgivings about the religion of their monarchs, which could never be properly established because a man cannot take oaths to himself. But not one of Elizabeth I's successors had been able to convince a suspicious public that he was one-hundred-per-cent Protestant. James I had flirted with outrageous ecumenical schemes involving a summit meeting between himself and the Pope, and done his best to marry his son and heir to a Spanish princess. His fright at the Gunpowder Plot led him to countenance a more intensive persecution of Catholics, but in 1621, to assist his negotiations with Spain, he ordered the suspension of the penal laws, and only reimposed them three years later at Parliament's insistence. Charles I was no better. He escaped from the Infanta of Spain only to marry Henrietta Maria, the sister of Louis XIII of France, an uncompromising bigot who rapidly built up a predominantly Catholic Court circle, expanded in the 1630s by several well-publicized conversions. Charles I himself toyed with schemes for reunion with Rome, like his father, and though this was mercifully unknown to his subjects, they could not fail to be aware of the visits to Whitehall of Catholic luminaries like Gregory Panzani and Daniel Con. The armies he raised against Scotland in 1638 and 1639 included a number of Catholic officers, some of whom were lynched by their enraged troops,

* See p. 18 below.

† Lord Clifford and the Duke of York are obvious examples (p. 18 below). There were also Lord Langdale and Lord Belasyse, Lord Lieutenants of the East and West Ridings of Yorkshire respectively, and Sir Robert Strickland and Sir Solomon Swale, who were elected to the Commons in 1661 and later turned.

and his friendship with Spain, which was at war with Protestant Holland, was regarded with dark suspicion. Throughout the crisis that followed the suspicion that the King was a Catholic sympathizer, perhaps even a secret Catholic himself, did more damage to his cause than any other single factor. The capture of his papers at the battle of Naseby in 1645 revealed that he had been negotiating with the Irish Catholic nobility (the Irish Rebellion of 1641 was known to many as 'The Queen's Rebellion'), and though he died in 1649 a self-styled martyr for the Anglican Church, suspicions lingered and were never entirely allayed.

As for Charles II, a large part of his exile from 1646 to 1660 had been spent at the Catholic Courts of Paris and Brussels, and there had been persistent rumours of his conversion, fostered no doubt by Oliver Cromwell, but not originating with him; an Act of 1661 'for the safety and preservation of his Majesty's person and government' made it a serious offence to 'publish or affirm the King to be an heretic or papist, or that he endeavours to introduce popery'. He was punctilious in his attendance at church, but the rumours continued; on the evidence we now have it must be concluded that he did not join the Roman Church until he was on the point of death, in 1685, but a man who knew him as intimately as Lord Halifax did believed that he had always been a Catholic. Certainly he was in favour of religious toleration on general principles, and he felt a sincere debt of gratitude to the many Catholics, English and foreign, who had helped him during his years of desperate adversity; particularly the West-Country Catholics who had engineered his escape abroad after the battle of Worcester in 1651, and who were exempted from every proclamation and statute made against Catholics from 1660 onwards, even during the Popish Plot.

Indeed, soon after the Restoration he opened negotiations with some Catholic spokesmen for a mitigation of the penal laws, which only foundered at this stage because his Anglican advisers demanded as a prior condition that the Jesuits withdraw their mission from England. In 1662 he showed an alarming tendency to follow in his father's footsteps by marrying a Catholic princess, the Portuguese Catherine of Braganza, and in

December of that year he felt obliged to issue a public Declaration denying, amongst other things, that he was showing undue favour to the Catholics; but this denial was so framed as to excite popular suspicion rather than allay it, especially since it was coupled with a request that Parliament confirm by statute his power to dispense individuals from the provisions of the penal laws.[14]

Fortunately for Charles, all eyes were then on the ex-Puritans, or ex-Cromwellians. It was inconceivable that these powerful elements, which had dominated England for fourteen years and sent Charles I to the block, would remain supine for long. Protestant Plots, not Catholic Plots, were in fashion, and Venner's Rising in 1661 and the Derwentdale Plot in 1663 confirmed that there was a problem to be faced. It was not until 1666, the year which brought Louis XIV into the Second Anglo-Dutch War on the side of Holland, and saw London in flames, that the old fears of a Catholic conspiracy were revived.

The Great Fire of September 1666 destroyed a large part of the old City of London, including St Paul's Cathedral. The suddenness of the outbreak, and the speed with which it spread, at once led to rumours of arson, and no better scapegoat could be found than the conspiratorial Catholic underground, spearheaded by the Jesuits. The more obvious possibilities, that it might be the work of the Dutch, with whom England was, after all, at war, or the Dissenters – 'a hellish contrivance of the French, the Hollanders and the fanatic party' – had remarkably little support. In any case, it was believed by many that the Jesuits were in league with the extreme Dissenters; an unholy alliance later confirmed by Titus Oates.[15] (The other explanation, that it was God's punishment for England's sins, was not at all popular, even with the clergy.)

A nationwide panic seemed likely, and as homeless refugees poured out from London into the countryside they took with them stories of a kind which were to be familiar enough in 1678 and 1679. Lord Maynard at Windsor heard of strange men who had been arrested carrying fireworks at Marylebone, and gave shelter to a man whose servant had actually met them; the same servant reported that a Catholic knight had set fire to the house in which he lodged on High Holborn. Foreigners and Catholics were mobbed in the streets, and one was 'almost dismembered in Moorfields, because he carried balls of fire with him in a chest, when in truth they were only tennis balls'.[16] 'There are thousands of such reports,' wrote Maynard, 'and people know not what to believe.'[17] At Coventry the townspeople were possessed by the idea that the papists were about to rise and cut their throats, and Warwick was thrown into confusion when a small boy saw a man behaving suspiciously at the edge of a ditch, and later found there a 'blackish-brown ball'. There was 'no appearance of anything combustible in it'; nevertheless, the magistrates to whom it was submitted promptly declared it to be one of the dreaded popish fire-balls. Pandemonium broke out; the hue and cry was sent out in all directions, the populace stood to arms, and the militia horse mounted guard on the town all night. Next morning Sir Henry Pickering arrived with a detachment of the county militia, and berated them all for their credulity. 'High words' followed, Sir Henry himself was accused of popery, and there was nearly a pitched battle between the two companies of militia. The Lord Lieutenant, the Earl of Northampton, took such a serious view of the matter that a fortnight later he came in person to Warwick to reprimand the Mayor and Corporation.[18]

Incidents like this were to be commonplace in 1678, and not so easily settled. In 1666 there were even some embryo Oateses about, like Henry Young,

A distiller of hot waters, [who] informed that about April 1661, being in the Jesuits' College in Antwerp, one Powell, an English Jesuit, persuaded him to turn a Roman Catholic, and said that if he intended to save his life and estate he had best turn so, for within seven years he should see all England of that religion. Young replied that the City of London would never endure it. Powell answered that within five or six years they would break the power and strength of London in pieces, and that they had been contriving it these twenty years, and that if Young did live he should see it done.[19]

Also typical of 1678 was the provocative behaviour of some Catholics. It was reported from Warwickshire that the recusant gentry 'are very high, well armed, and have frequent and suspicious meetings'. This was perhaps a natural reaction to the threat of violence, even lynch law, but it is difficult to know what to make of men like Edward Complin of Dorking, who boasted that he was a Catholic, told his neighbours that they would all be Catholics shortly, and asserted that on twenty-four hours' notice he and his friends could raise thirty thousand armed men. A London priest called Carpenter is supposed to have told people that the Plague and the Fire 'were come upon this land and people for their forsaking the true Roman Catholic religion, and shaking off obedience to the Pope, and if they would return to the Church of Rome the Pope would rebuild the City at his own charge'. In the country men were even bolder, and Mr Dormer of Grove Park, Warwickshire, was one of many Catholic gentry bound over by the magistrates for 'dangerous speeches'.[20]

Evidence like this is difficult to assess, interspersed as it is with obvious manifestations of hysteria and such products of the *agent-provocateur* as the notorious doggerel poem '*Cove le feu, ye Huguenots*', which was significantly dated 5 November 1666, 'in the first year of the Restoration of the Church of Rome'.[21] But throughout Charles II's reign there were obviously some Catholics who were culpably loose-tongued. Most magistrates were sensibly content to bind the offenders over to keep the peace, but each such incident added a crumb to a growing mountain of suspicion.

Meanwhile the Fire of '66 had found its Van der Lubbe in Robert Hubert, a half-crazy Frenchman who was arrested in Kent, together with many other foreigners, soon afterwards. He confessed to starting the Fire on the instigation of a mysterious individual called Peidloe, and though he contradicted himself so much on important points that the Privy Council and King's Bench doubted his veracity he did show a detailed knowledge of the topography of Pudding Lane, where the Fire began. In the then state of the law he could not be declared unfit to plead;

instead he was found guilty and hanged.[22] But he never became the popular villain of the piece, in the fashion of Guy Fawkes, and in a year or two his name was forgotten.

Ignoring Hubert, the Privy Council had already investigated the whole affair, and 'nothing had been found to argue the Fire in London to have been caused by other than the hand of God, a great wind and a very dry season'.[23] But this did not prevent the House of Commons appointing its own committee of investigation, seventy strong, on 25 September; and while they ostentatiously refrained from prejudging the matter, only three days later they recommended to the House that the King be requested to enforce the penal laws and issue a proclamation banishing all priests from the kingdom.[24] This Committee presented an interim report on 22 February 1667 – or, it would be more accurate to say, it produced certain evidence; about Catholics who had foretold the Fire, and one or two people surprised in direct incendiary activity or, like Hubert, confessing to it. But most of it was hearsay, and apart from Hubert those accused were not to be found, so the judges were rightly sceptical.[25] In the next session, beginning in October 1667, the Fire Committee was not revived, and though the evidence it had put before the House was printed as a pamphlet the government ordered it to be burnt by the common hangman and all available copies were confiscated. It was not reprinted until 1679, under the title *London's Flames Reviv'd*.[26]

Indeed, the government survived the Great Fire with remarkable ease. But in 1666 the King and the Duke of York were much more popular than they were later in the reign – indeed, their own firm action to contain the Fire enhanced their popularity – and there was no evidence, either, of a plot against the Crown. The government was tougher, and the chief minister, Lord Clarendon, had the self-confidence in this crisis that the Earl of Danby later lacked. All rumours were promptly investigated and their spread stopped, and the House of Commons was not allowed to enjoy a monopoly of public spirit and Protestant zeal. The following year the naval disaster in the Medway, which no one, however lunatic, could attribute to anyone but the

Protestant Dutch, gave the public plenty to agitate about, and the fall of Clarendon in the autumn of 1667 was another distraction.

Nevertheless, the Great Fire at once took its place in the mythology of ultra-Protestantism; it confirmed the belief of the credulous and fearful that the Church of Rome was an organ of international conspiracy, and that the Jesuits were a secret society employing fire, poison and gunpowder for the conversion of England. In May 1668, for instance, a manuscript tract called 'Necessary Queries for these Times' was confiscated and brought to the Secretary of State's office. It asserted – indeed, it accepted as fact – that ever since 1660 Jesuits in their thousands had been flocking to London with direct orders from the Holy See to destroy the Protestant Establishment by fair means or foul, and that they were 'the principal designers and underhand actors in burning the City in 1666', which had been planned originally as the prelude to a general massacre. Plans were now being laid for further fires, and thousands of Catholics in the provinces had been secretly enrolled and armed, ready for a general insurrection supported by the Catholic powers abroad.[27] This belief in the imminence of a general massacre, accompanied by urban incendiarism and a military *coup d'état* by the Catholic nobility and gentry, were to be important elements in the Popish Plot. When the time came, the actuality of the Fire of '66, and its association in the popular mind with the papists, encouraged belief in the Plot, and this in turn confirmed the responsibility of the Catholics for the Fire. In January 1681, when the Plot was running down, the House of Commons solemnly affirmed its belief that the Fire was the work of the Catholics, and that same year the City authorities incised on the Fire Monument the notorious inscription attributing the disaster to 'the treachery and malice of the popish faction'. Erased under James II, restored under William III, it was not finally removed until 1830.

However, in the aftermath of the Fire the Catholics still enjoyed an irritating and perplexing immunity to persecution. In November 1666 Charles acceded to Parliament's request that he issue a proclamation instructing magistrates to enforce the penal laws and ordering priests to leave the kingdom, but in September 1667, again under pressure from Parliament, the Privy Council looked into the matter and found the situation so unsatisfactory that it sent out letters to each bench of justices reminding them of their duty.[28] But again, this had little effect; indeed, the only concrete result was a purge of the Army, initiated by a decree of 15 September ordering all officers and other ranks to take the oaths. Several Catholics who had served Charles II in exile, including veterans who had followed his brother, the Duke of York, from the French into the Spanish service in 1656, were now retired on two shillings a week, though some, ironically, went back to France to join an English regiment being raised for the French Army by Charles's sister, the Duchess of Orleans. (Some of them were to return to embarrass Charles's government in 1678.) As so often, the surprising thing is the number of Catholics revealed by a sudden check like this; more than sixty in the First Regiment of Foot alone, and probably four hundred in all.[29]

The general irritation at such evasion of the law grew more acute over the years 1667 to 1673, as the prestige of the monarchy declined and its involvement with Roman Catholicism became more obvious. In secret, this involvement was now quite deep. In the Treaty of Dover between England and France, signed in May 1670, there was a secret clause in which Charles undertook to announce his conversion, and Louis XIV promised military assitance to suppress the anticipated public reaction. In October the Internuncio at Brussels, Francesco Airoldi, Abbot of Monte Cassino, was ordered by the Pope to visit England, which was technically in the Flanders Province. He lodged with the Venetian Resident incognito, but he had a private audience with Charles, his brother James and the Queen, and 'was made acquainted with the good intentions of the King for the relief of the Catholics'.[30]

The Commons could not be expected to divine knavery like this, but in a revealing Address submitted to the King on 21 February 1671, they complained bitterly of 'the growth of popery'. They pointed out that assize judges and magistrates were grossly remiss in not convicting recusants, that those re-cusants who were convicted were never prosecuted in the Ex-chequer, that popish books and trinkets were freely offered for sale in London 'even in the time of Parliament', that in all large towns Catholic chapels and schools were established with only a token attempt at concealment, that there was even a convent at St James's Palace and a Jesuit College at Combe in Hereford-shire, that Catholics freely sent their children abroad to be edu-cated, and that they were evading the oaths and taking office under the Crown just when it suited them, so that 'suspected recusants are free from all offices chargeable and troublesome, and do enjoy the advantages of offices and places beneficial'.[31] This was an exaggerated picture, of course, but it had elements of truth, and the remarkable thing is that the situation con-tinued. Even the Jesuit college, or residence, at Combe con-tinued undisturbed until December 1678, though its existence was generally known, and Parliament's attention had by then been drawn to it twice. Indeed, in his reply to this Address from the Commons the King introduced a distinction, unknown to the law, between good and bad papists. He undertook to enforce the law more stringently, of course, but he added coolly:

I suppose no man will wonder if I make a difference between those that have newly changed their religion and those that were bred up in that religion, and served my father and me faithfully in the late wars.[32]

The King's leanings were made still more evident in March 1672, when he chose the occasion of his declaration of war on Holland to suspend all the penal laws, against Catholic recusants and Protestant Dissenters alike. Many local magistrates were openly mutinous, the high court judges were dubious, and hatred of the Dutch, which Charles hoped would tide him over a difficult transition, was swamped by fear of England's new ally, France. By now, Louis XIV had slipped into the role of supreme popish bogeyman vacant since the death of Philip II of Spain in 1598. His invasion of the Spanish Netherlands in 1667 had caused great disquiet, threatening as it did the Channel coast nearest to England, and in 1668 the pamphlet 'Necessary Queries' argued that the international conspiracy to exterminate the Protestant heresy was still very much alive; France was to conquer Holland and Switzerland while the Emperor mopped up the German Protestant States and Scandinavia. In the same year the author of 'A Discourse upon the Designs, Practices and Counsels of France' assumed that his readers would accept, 'without dispute, that the French aim at universal dominion'.[33] As Sir Thomas Meres remarked in the Commons, 'Our jealousies of popery, or an arbitrary government, are not from a few inconsiderable papists here, but from the ill example we have from France.'[34]

So it is not surprising that the Anglo-French attack on Holland should rouse the deepest passions, and when Parliament met in February 1673, for the first time since the outbreak of the war, it was in a ferocious mood. On 8 March Charles was forced to cancel his Declaration of Indulgence and issue instead a proclamation ordering the strict enforcement of the penal laws. On the 13th priests were given a month to leave the country, and the Commissary-General was again ordered to tender the oaths to all ranks of the Army. Not content with this, Parliament insisted on a Test Act, which obliged all office-holders to declare their disbelief in the doctrine of transubstantiation, to produce a certificate that they had recently taken Anglican communion, and to take the oaths of allegiance and supremacy in open court. This at once brought the resignation of the Lord Treasurer, Lord Clifford, and, more startling still, that of the Lord High Admiral, the Duke of York.

The public admission that the King's brother was a Catholic confirmed the rumours of months, if not years past, and in view of the Queen's failure to bear children it was infinitely alarming. The religion of the King (the only 'office-holder' not covered by the Test Act) was more than ever in doubt, and the pot was kept on the boil by James's ill-advised marriage, that very summer, to a Roman Catholic princess, Mary of Modena, known to be under French influence. After a brief but disastrous parliamentary session in October, Charles was at last obliged to take serious measures in an attempt to appease public opinion. Catholics were banned from Whitehall (and even St James's Park), magistrates were yet again ordered to enforce the penal laws, and the judges were asked for suggestions how this could best be done.[35] Parliament reassembled in January 1674 amid wild rumours of another Gunpowder Plot, which obliged Charles to order all Catholics who were not householders out of the City for the duration of the session. For once the pressure was maintained, and the Commons found an unexpected ally in the new Lord Treasurer, Sir Thomas Osborne (soon to be Earl of Danby), who was determined to associate the King with a firm Protestant policy at home and abroad.

To this end he had already opened peace negotiations with Holland, and in February 1674 he was behind the introduction of a bill in the Lords to educate the children of the royal family in the Protestant religion.[36] This bill, which was to be reintroduced in a different form in 1677, also barred the marriage of a member of the royal family to a Catholic without consent of Parliament, and this struck more deeply at the prerogative and the personal freedom of the monarch than anything the Commons had yet attempted. Charles could count himself lucky that the Commons were unimpressed, and that the conclusion of peace allowed him to prorogue Parliament on 24 February after a session of less than six weeks.

All the same, a token enforcement of the penal laws would no longer do, and Danby was anxious, too, to exploit every possible source of revenue. In March another minatory proclamation was issued, and the Venetian Resident reported that the Catholics were in a panic, and that many were taking steps to convey their estates to Protestants before they were confiscated. By August, according to him, they were being 'attacked and persecuted daily by the justices', and they despaired 'of saving their property from the grasp of the malignants'.[37] Such facts as we have do not support this gloomy picture, but with another parliamentary session coming in 1675, Charles had to appear to be maintaining the pressure, at least, and in January 1675 he turned for advice to the bishops. The bishops' reply was sensible enough. There was no point, they said, in adding to the existing laws, which ought to be adequate if enforced; the King must induce the Exchequer to proceed against recusants for hard cash; he must give priests a definite date by which they must go abroad, and see that they did; and he must take active measures to prevent the celebration of the mass anywhere in the realm except in the chapels of the Queen and the foreign ambassadors.[38]

Accordingly a new proclamation which went out on 5 February 1675, ordering all priests to leave by 25 March, was more precisely worded than its predecessors; magistrates were ordered 'to forward their transportation before that time, but afterwards to put in execution the laws against them'. But there is no evidence that a single priest complied, nor that any were charged, or even arrested.

On the same day, 5 February, the Council wrote to the Lord Lieutenants ordering them to put pressure on local magistrates to enforce the penal laws against the laity, too, and to notify the Attorney General 'whether any persons of quality who are suspected of being popish recusants have been omitted to be presented'. A fortnight later the Exchequer was ordered to proceed to the sequestration of two thirds of all recusants' estates rather than levy the £20 a month fine, and new Receivers of Recusant Forfeitures were appointed.[39] As a result some Catholics were undoubtedly threatened, and Lord Aston wrote two long letters of complaint about it to Williamson, the Secretary of State.* These suggest that the proceedings in Staffordshire were quite vigorous, and there is similar evidence from Wiltshire and Devonshire.[40] But the significant point is that Aston and some of the Devon recusants were self-confident enough to appeal to the government, and Edward Coleman, Secretary to the Duchess of York, told a correspondent:

We do not find that the commissions sent into the several counties for seizing a recusant's estates meet with the entertainment which was expected, or that the people are half so ready to engage in that business as some believed they would be. There are thirty generally, and in some forty, commission[er]s named for every county, whereof

---

* One of them is quoted above, p. 7.

any three make a quorum and may act, and yet many counties have not been able to get so many to meddle, and so have done nothing. In others where they have sat, as here in Middlesex, they have found their work so intricate and tedious that they have given over again without effecting anything; and in others, where they have made some returns, they are but few, and these either pushed on by private piques or else of some inconsiderable persons.[41]

Whatever the extent of the persecution, it certainly brought no money into the Treasury. On 22 June 1676, a meeting was held at the Exchequer, attended by the law officers of the Crown and the two Chief Justices, where it was reported that the new Receivers were quite ineffectual, and it was decided to fall back on the sheriffs instead.[42] Parliament was understandably sceptical of this whole procedure, and on 19 May 1675 the Commons brought in another bill 'to prevent the growth of popery', aimed at strengthening the Receivers, preventing the conveyance of recusants' estates to third parties, and compelling members of both Houses to take the Anglican sacrament.[43] It passed the Commons, but it was still with the Lords at the prorogation.

The following November there was a public scandal which brought the Society of Jesus further bad publicity. A French priest called de Luzancy, who had been converted to Protestantism and fled to London, appealed to the protection of Lord Holles and Lord Russell, two leading members of the parliamentary opposition, because, he said, the Duchess of York's confessor, the Jesuit St Germain, had put great pressure on him to return to France, even to the extent of threatening his life. Under the name of 'the French Jesuit' de Luzancy at once became a public figure. The Council ordered an investigation, the Commons raved, and St Germain fled to Paris. When it was revealed that de Luzancy's career in the Catholic Church had been distinctly unsavoury he lost his patrons and dropped out of sight. But St Germain was remembered as a typical Jesuit, and the charges against him were probably only slightly exaggerated; excitable priests do strange things on God's behalf. In his correspondence with Edward Coleman St Germain never denied the Protestant version of the affair, and Danby was informed of an Italian merchant in London, specializing in such things, who would have conveyed de Luzancy abroad.[44]

There was a five-week session that autumn, but after the prorogation on 22 November Parliament did not meet again until February 1677. This Parliament had now lasted fifteen years, and the pressure for a general election was mounting. So was hostility to the Duke of York. The author of an unlicensed pamphlet published in 1674 inquired:

Whether it be not more dangerous to have the Crown placed on a Popish head thereafter than to have the office of Admiral of England executed by a papist now; [and] whether therefore it be not high time to consider of settling the succession of the Crown so as may secure us and our posterities from those bloody massacres and Smithfield butcheries, the certain consequences of popish government?[45]

On the other hand, as rumours spread that Parliament might alter the succession, the bolder Catholics grew restless. The King personally ordered an investigation of reports that the papists were gathering arms in Herefordshire, and Thomas Bowyer of Lintlow was thrown into gaol for telling his Protestant neighbours that he would raise a troop of horse for the Duke of York, and 'there would be many bloody noses in England ere it be long'. Calvert Smithson, a fiery Catholic gentleman of the North Riding, was accused of saying:

I have forty men ready to rise at the holding up of my finger, and when I come on the field I will give no quarter. I hope to see five hundred men killed in half a year's time betwixt Allerton and Kipling.

The houses of prominent Catholics were searched regularly for horses and arms, and two priests were arrested in Yorkshire, though there is no evidence of their being exiled or prosecuted.[46]

James's refusal to attend Easter Communion in 1676 publicized his final break with the established Church, and bold words were uttered at a Common Council meeting in the City that July. One speaker said:

Is there any more than the breath of our king between that [popery] and us? If the prospective heir of the Crown be a Roman Catholic, what security can be given that the King shall live eight or nine months?[47]

Nor was there any relief in sight. The marriage between James's elder daughter, Mary, raised as a Protestant, and her cousin William of Orange, in November 1677, was neatly counterbalanced a few days later by the birth of a son to the Duchess of York. True, the young Duke of Cambridge lived only five weeks, but his mother was still under thirty and in good health; it was not only possible but very probable that James would soon have a son to displace the Princesses Mary and Anne in the line of succession.

Yet, paradoxically, the Earl of Danby needed and enjoyed James's support.[48] Despite his religion, the Duke was much more hostile to France than his brother; he not only agreed to the Dutch marriage, he also supported a 'patriotic' Protestant foreign policy of alliance with Holland against France. But the price of his support was the continued prorogation of Parliament and the relaxation of persecution, which indeed died away in 1677. He told Lord O'Brien at this time that 'he would have them [the Catholics] used as Christians, and such who to a man ever stuck fast to the Crown'.[49] The fruits of this alliance were also to be seen in two government-sponsored bills sent down from the Lords in March 1677 as a final settlement of the Catholic problem.

The first bill, 'for the preservation of the Protestant religion and the more effectual conviction and prosecution of popish recusants', was so contrary to popular thinking that the Commons rejected it out of hand, with a curt note that 'it appeared to be much different from the title'. It proposed a distinction between two types of Catholic layman, the loyal and quiet on the one hand, and the disloyal and unquiet on the other; to this end all Catholics who registered themselves as such would merely pay the old fine of a shilling a week for not attending Church, the full penalties of the penal laws being reserved for those who concealed their religion and were detected.

The second bill, though it was more courteously treated, being allowed to expire quietly in committee, roused even stronger passions. Under the innocent title, 'An Act for further securing the Protestant religion by educating the children of the Royal Family therein', it specifically provided for the accession of a Catholic monarch. On the present king's death his successor must comply with the provisions of the Test Act, but if he failed to do so the only penalty was that ecclesiastical patronage was to be removed from his control, as well as the education of his children between the ages of five and fourteen (a proviso not easy to enforce).[50]

To judge by James's later attitude, during the Exclusion Crisis, this represented the limit of concession on his part, and it is reasonable to suppose that the bill had his prior approval. It forced many M.P.s to contemplate for the first time the reality of a Catholic succession, a reality driven home by the French military victories in Europe that spring. The apparent invincibility of Louis XIV, with half Europe against him, was terrifying, and the following winter there appeared one of the most influential pamphlets of the decade: *The Growth of Popery and Arbitrary Government in England*, by Andrew Marvell.[51]

Reviewing recent events, Marvell found in them conclusive proof that:

There has now for divers years a design been carried on, to change the lawful government of England into an absolute tyranny, and to convert the established Protestant religion into downright Popery.

He stressed the unremitting malignity of Rome, and the constant threat she posed to the Protestant establishment, and he closed with this warning:

If under his present Majesty we have as yet seen no more visible effects of the same spirit than the firing of London ... it is not to be attributed to the good nature or better principles of that sect, but to the wisdom of his Holiness, who observes that we are not of late so dangerous Protestants as to deserve any special mark of his indignation, but that we may be made better use of to the weakening of those that are of our religion, and that if he do not disturb us, there are those amongst ourselves that are leading us into a fair way of reconciliation with him.

He never lived to see the confirmation of his fears, and it is surprising that no informer thought to attribute his death in August 1678 to his inveterate enemies.

At this remove in time the only one of Marvell's allegations which calls for serious examination is that the English Catholic community was prospering and growing in numbers. It was a belief he shared with many Protestants, perhaps most of them, and with several prominent Catholics, notably Edward Coleman and Philip Howard. But it was quite untrue; the Catholics were steadily declining in numbers and morale throughout the century.

Clearly the penal laws were not solely responsible for this decline; they were never consistently and strictly enforced over long enough periods. The Holy See itself must take part of the blame, and one Catholic historian characterizes its policy towards the English mission as one of 'chronic dereliction'.[52] The continued failure to appoint an English bishop was particularly disastrous. With the waning of persecution in 1622, Gregory XV had been persuaded to appoint a Vicar Apostolic, William Bishop. He died nine months later, but not before he had exceeded his powers by setting up an English Chapter. His successor, Richard Smith, was even worse; despite repeated prohibitions from Rome he extended the Chapter's powers and activities, he quarrelled violently with the Jesuits, and he embraced the heresy of Jansenism. In 1631 he retired to France, where he survived until 1655 without attempting to exercise further authority over the English mission, but the Chapter persisted, and his ideas were violently maintained by his disciple Thomas White, alias Blacklo.[53]

The antagonism between secular and regular priests* which Smith and Blacklo had provoked, or perhaps merely revealed,

---

*The regulars were those who followed a 'rule', which placed them outside the normal hierarchy of the Church; the Jesuits, the Benedictines, the Franciscans, etc. Only the Jesuits were of real importance in England.

continued. The Jesuits in particular were not prepared to take orders from a secular bishop, and more was involved than comparative power and independence. The seculars, trained for the most part at Douai in northern France, specifically for the cure of souls and nothing else, aimed at the preservation of a distinctly English Catholic Church on pre-Reformation lines; the Jesuits, on the other hand, aimed to draw England into the revitalized Church Universal of the Counter-Reformation which they themselves had done so much to create.

Jesuit pressure may have been behind the continued failure to replace Richard Smith, but ill-luck also entered into it. It was decided in 1665 to appoint the King's cousin, Louis Stewart, Seigneur d'Aubigny, but his patents, and a cardinal's hat, reached him in Paris a few hours after his death on 11 November.[54] Another eminently suitable candidate then presented himself in the Dominican Philip Howard, a younger son of the Earl of Arundel, and Grand Almoner to the Queen. His patents were dispatched to the Internuncio at Brussels in August 1672, but this time the King himself interposed a veto. Howard was thought too extreme and too deficient in judgement and self-control to head the English priesthood at a time of crisis. In 1673 his much-publicized conversion of a Canon of Windsor confirmed these doubts; he was dismissed from Court and the following year retired to Flanders.[55] In 1675 he was made a Cardinal and withdrew to Rome, but he did not succeed Barberini as 'Cardinal-Protector of England' until 1679.

Meanwhile the Chapter provided a sketchy organization; England and Wales were divided into seven districts, each under a Vicar-General, with archdeacons responsible for smaller sub-divisions.[56] But none of these officials, nor the Chapter itself, was recognized by Rome, and they had no disciplinary powers. Yet discipline was essential to an underground church, whose priests, compelled to dress and act as laymen, chronically short of money and lacking any social standing, faced peculiar problems of morale, which were expounded in a long official report to the Holy See as early as 1632.[57] A spectacular minority took to women or drink, but more general and more insidious was the temptation to idleness and virtual laicization. Moreover, since there was no formal machinery for scrutinizing a priest's credentials, England became a refuge for priests manqué, false priests and eccentrics. Even the archdeacons did not know all the priests in their district; the archdeacon of Hampshire in 1692 mentioned a 'Mr Freeman, of what college or standing in the mission I know not, a person of good esteem'.[58] When the Internuncio came to London in 1670 he reported that several French priests with extremely dubious reputations had taken refuge there, including an apostate Capuchin who had married a nun and set up as an innkeeper. He also commented on the large number of Irish priests with no settled occupation, and deplored the fact that many priests were saying mass three or four times a day, contrary to the canons, simply for the sake of the fees. One of Cardinal Barberini's correspondents told him in 1674:

There is no greater obstacle to the freedom which might be given to our religion than the disorder and bad government of our clergy, who go wandering where they please, and hide themselves in London in such great numbers that they crowd the inns and lodging houses. They are uncontrolled and without direction, and none of them stay in the provinces, where the Catholics are more numerous.[59]

The priests who were in the provinces, however, had their own problems, which revolved around money. In the absence of endowments priests were dependent on private charity, which meant that in most cases they lapsed into the role of domestic chaplains, their opportunities for proselytization sharply limited; or they eked out their existence as little more than 'hedge-priests'. The situation was summed up in an archdeacon's report on one Robert Ward, a Yorkshire priest, who

lived a year or two on what he could get at York, where old Mr Salkeld dying, he struck in with the rich and virtuous widow, near Westley, where he has a very happy residence.[60]

In these circumstances, with Rome far away and the patron near, there was every temptation to relax traditional rules, and even ignore express orders from Rome. Many Catholics took the oaths to the government, some got married in Protestant churches, and there is little doubt that they often did so with the tacit approval of their priests. Over and above all this there were not enough priests, even supposing the numbers of the Catholic laity remained static, they were unevenly distributed over the country, and they were insufficiently mobile, with the result that a faith which was probably dwindling anyway dwindled faster for sheer lack of pastoral care.

According to an estimate made by Claudius Agretti, Minister Apostolic in Flanders, in 1669, there were then 230 secular priests in England and at least 255 regulars, including 120 Jesuits and 80 Benedictines, though most of the Benedictines were in London. Of these the Jesuits were obviously the most active and the best organized. England had been made a Vice-Province of the Society in 1619, and a Province in 1625. The first Provincial divided England and Wales into twelve districts, increased to fourteen by 1670, each of which was centred on a 'residence' or 'college', though this did not necessarily imply any permanent physical base, still less any organized teaching activity. Contrary to popular rumour at the time, amongst Catholics as well as Protestants, the Jesuits were not significantly wealthier than their secular colleagues, but they enjoyed a firm Continental base, which allowed a rotation of personnel – in 1678, for instance, there were 128 Jesuits in England and another 160 in the houses belonging to the Province at Watten, Ghent, Liège and St Omers[61] – they were subject to a strict and unquestioned discipline, and they had the constant backing of a great international order.

The number of Catholic laymen in England is almost impossible to calculate with any accuracy. What little evidence we have gives a figure of 260,000; 4.7 per cent of the estimated national population of five million.* Agretti in 1669 put it as low

---

* This is based on the ecclesiastical census of 1676, printed in A. Browning, *English Historical Documents 1660–1714* (London, 1953), p. 413, and on the calculations of Magee, pp. 167–9. Magee's figures have been criticized by W. M. Wingfield in *Theology*, xli (1940), 94, but I see no reason to reject them as a rough working base, though they are undoubtedly not as accurate as he would have us believe.

as 200,000. Certainly it was a very small number to arouse such terror in Protestant hearts. True, the operation of the penal laws, particularly under Elizabeth I, had tended to remove the working-class Catholics, except for those who were servants of the rich and influential, so that a disproportionate number of Catholics were of the landed gentry. It is estimated, for instance, that they constituted 25 per cent of the landowning classes in Yorkshire.[62] Also they made up in piety what they lacked in numbers; a community of not much more than 1,500 adults in the West Riding of Yorkshire produced eighty priests and forty-eight nuns in the course of the century, and it was not uncommon for all the children except the eldest son to enter religion. For instance, the Essex baronet Sir Francis Petre had six sons, of whom five entered the Society of Jesus; so did six out of the seven sons of John Poulton of Desborough, Northants.[63] Sir Henry Bedingfield of Oxburgh had eleven daughters, ten of whom took the veil. Two of Sir Thomas Gascoigne's brothers were Benedictines, another was a secular priest, and two of his sisters were nuns.*

Naturally such families were intensely conservative and inward-looking; one of the most perceptive historians of recusancy has coined the term 'survivalism' to describe their thinkings. Theirs was 'a Catholicism less concerned with doctrinal affirmation or dramas of conscience than with a set of ingrained observances which defined and gave meaning to the cycle of the week and the seasons of the year, to birth, marriage and death'.[64] Though so many children went from such families to be educated in France or Spain, they remained remarkably unaffected by the Continental, ultramontane tradition. This is why Charles II and his brother, whose Catholicism was in that tradition, had so few real contacts with English Catholic society.[65]

This society has yet to be studied as a whole, but its nature is illumined by a number of recent studies made of families like the Stonors of Stonor in Oxfordshire,[66] the Vauxes of Harrowden,[67]

---

* Though I have not tested the hypothesis, it seems reasonable to suppose that this contributed to the decline in Catholic numbers. If the sole non-celibate heir died or proved sterile, then the family died out.

the Brudenells of Deene,[68] the Eyres of Hassopp,[69] and the Constables of Everingham.[70] The Catholics of Wiltshire and Yorkshire have also been examined in great detail.[71] In general terms their relations with their Protestant neighbours were good; they intermarried freely, and, as we have seen, Protestants would often shield Catholics from persecution when necessary. Even in counties like Yorkshire, where the Catholics were a substantial minority of the gentry, there seems to have been no tendency to form an exclusively Catholic social nexus. The general atmosphere was one of permissiveness. Catholic families like the Brudenells continued to exercise their right of presenting to the livings within their gift, a right not removed until 1689. In 1660 Thomas Stonor gave a new bell to Watlington parish church, and in 1666 he endowed a grammar school there. Rowland Eyre of Hassopp buried his parents in Great Longstone parish church under a brass which showed them kneeling before a crucifix and telling their beads. When 'the munificent Lord Aston' died in April 1678 he was buried at St Mary's, Stafford, and a thousand people were said to have followed the hearse.[72]

There were some notorious Catholic enclaves. South Wales was one, where the difficulty of recruiting bilingual Anglican clergy had left the old faith relatively unaffected. The defection of the young Marquess of Worcester to Protestantism in the 1660s left this markedly seigneurial community without a seigneur, but a report made to the House of Commons in April 1678 showed that in Monmouthshire and South Wales Catholicism was practised without much pretence of concealment. Thomas Gunter of Abergavenny told the local vicar roundly 'that in Oliver [Cromwell]'s time of severity he kept a priest, and would keep one now'.[73] Lancashire, too, had a high proportion of Catholics, as in Elizabethan times, though remarkably little is heard of them under Charles II. The returns of 1671 list 5,496 convicted recusants for Lancashire, as against 1,855 for the whole of Yorkshire, 678 for Staffordshire (reputed a strong Catholic community), and – for purposes of comparison – 42 in Devon.[74] Less well known is the strong Catholic enclave in Oxfordshire, headed by the Stonors in the south and the Mildmays of Ambrosden in the north; they and related Catholic families held between them one third of the freehold land in the county.[75] On the other hand in some counties one or two families, with their tenants, retainers and servants, *were* the Catholic community. Returns made in 1603 show that out of twenty-two known Catholics in Leicestershire fourteen were on estates owned by the Brooksby family of Shoby. The role of patron of the Leicestershire Catholics later devolved on the Beaumonts of Grace Dieu and the Carringtons of Ashby Folville, still flourishing under Charles II, and the Gifford family performed a similar function in south Staffordshire. Similarly, Wiltshire Catholicism began and virtually ended with the huge establishment of Lord Arundell in and around Wardour.[76]

Urban Catholicism is something of a mystery. Gloucester for some reason had a strong Catholic minority, which provided two lord mayors in succession under James II. Wolverhampton was once referred to as 'a little Rome', though no doubt with considerable exaggeration. Bath, for no very obvious reason, attracted a comparatively numerous and enduring Catholic element, perhaps because they were excluded from Bristol by the vigorous action of the bishop, the city 'boss', Sir John Knight, and the Lord Lieutenant of the adjoining county, the Marquess of Worcester.[77] Newcastle, rather surprisingly, was credited with seventy-seven Catholics in the returns of 1671, but elsewhere the numbers were trifling, and probably accounted for by the fact that members of certain trades and professions – physicians and wine merchants, for instance – were commonly Catholics, again for no very obvious reason.[78] Reading was credited with only four in the census of 1676, and Birmingham with eleven (out of 2,623 householders). Only twelve people were presented as recusants in Birmingham between 1679 and 1682.* Again, though Lancashire was a centre of recusancy, this does not seem to have affected towns like Manchester and Liverpool.

London, however, contained the largest Catholic community; which is not surprising, since it contained more than 10 per cent

*Also fifteen in Aston and thirteen in Edgbaston, then rural areas; *V.C.H. Warwicks.*, vii, 397–8, *V.C.H. Leics.*, iv, 389

of the whole English population. Agretti was told in 1669 that there were between ten and twelve thousand Catholics in the Capital, and they were particularly numerous in the cosmopolitan 'West End' of the day, between Westminster and the City proper. The returns made to the House of Lords in December 1678 named 606 in the parish of St Martin-in-the-Fields alone, and another 146 in St Paul's, Covent Garden.[79] They were little troubled by persecution – in 1671 the Treasury reported that only fifty-two had been convicted in London and Middlesex since the Restoration – and they were encouraged, directly or indirectly, by the presence of the Court. By the terms of her marriage treaty Queen Catherine was allowed to practise her own religion, and her household included fourteen priests, ten of them English or Irish.* A glance at the registers of her chapel, at St James's until 1671, then at Somerset House, suggests one reason for this; of the 290 marriages solemnized there between 1662 and 1678 all but a handful were those of English couples, many of them from outside London.[80] The Duke and Duchess of York also maintained several priests, though since the Duke was forbidden by his brother to display his religion and the Duchess did not enjoy the protection of a public marriage treaty, less is known of them. But the King himself employed many lay Catholics in specialized posts – painters, musicians, doctors – and even the Protestant champion, the Duke of Monmouth, retained a favourite Catholic barber until September 1679. Then he released the man with great reluctance, and gave him a reference to Fr Stephen Gough, of the Oratory, Paris.[81]

London Catholics also had the advantage that with a minimum of sensible precaution they could always hear mass; at the Queen's chapel, or at the chapels of one of the foreign ambassadors, who enjoyed extraterritorial rights and were expected to maintain English-speaking priests. Also some wealthy Catholic peers, virtually immune from the penal laws, maintained mass centres, if not actual chapels, in their town houses along the Strand, or in the new upper-class suburb of St James's. The Earl

---

* She also had a group of Portuguese Capuchins, between eleven and thirteen in number, who persisted throughout the Plot crisis.

of Powis, Viscount Stafford, Lord Arundell and Lord Aston were all in this category. In any case, as we have seen, London was positively infested with priests of one kind or another, far in excess, no doubt, of the spiritual needs of the population. A report made to Danby in 1676 related that mass was said at Lord Belasyse's house, at Lord Stafford's, and at Signor Brunetti's house in York Garden, he being a 'factor for her Highness the Duchess of York'. Also:

Mr Rose, a Fleming perverted by Father James of Somerset House, has several priests lodge in his house, and lives not far from Sgr Brunetti ... In Duke Street, next Lincolns Inn Fields, lives Father Harcourt, that says mass there every holy day. In King Street, by Long Acre, at the sign of St Paul, at Salvator Winer's, a mountebank, diet a great many renegade priests and friars, that say mass there, and help him to write a book about monarchy ... Price over against the Sun Tavern in Portugal Street lodges several priests.

And so on, and so forth.[82] It is easy to see why the situation in the nation's capital alarmed many M.P.s newly up from the country, as well as permanent residents.

Even so, appearances were deceptive. Hugh Aveling remarks that:

As Catholicism became more intense and definite, as families became more solidly and unitedly Catholic, its diffused influence over a large section of the upper classes faded away.[83]

The greatest enemy was not persecution but boredom; boredom and the frustration of being raised in a class tradition of social service and then denied any chance of following it. Lord Halifax put the predicament of the young Catholic gentleman well when he wrote:

To have no share in business, no opportunity of showing his own value to the world; to live at the best an useless, and by others to be thought a dangerous member of the nation where he is born, is a burden to a generous mind that cannot be taken off by all the pleasures of a lazy, unmanly life, or by the nauseous enjoyment of a dull plenty that produceth no good for the mind.[84]

So conversions amongst the gentry scarcely made up for the defections, and intermarriage with Protestants rarely had the desired effect. The Earl of Danby was only one of many eminent Protestants born to Catholic mothers. Conversely, though daughters and younger sons of landed families sometimes went over to Rome, there is no record of an heir-apparent who could afford this luxury.* Indeed, the traffic was all the other way, and the wealthier and more eminent the family the greater the danger. The 5th Earl of Worcester was one of the wealthiest Catholics in England, and for his financial and military support Charles I made him a marquess in 1643. The 2nd Marquess, who succeeded three years later, was also a Catholic, and married two Catholic wives in succession; but his eldest son, born in 1629, was converted to the established church about 1650, and for a time was even a republican. After the Restoration his devotion to Anglicanism, though often questioned, was in fact unswerving, and in 1682 he was made Duke of Beaufort.

The declension of the Paulets, Marquesses of Winchester, from Catholic loyalism to Protestant whiggery in one generation is even more startling. The 5th Marquess was known as 'The Great Loyalist', and the heroic defence of his fortified manor house at Basing, Hampshire, against the forces of the Long Parliament is a famous episode in the First Civil War. Precisely when his son turned from Rome we do not know, but certainly long before 1678; he supported the Exclusion Bill in 1680, and for his services in the Revolution of 1689 William III made him Duke of Bolton. In the same way the oscillation of the Belasyses of Fauconberg illustrates the conflict between social pressures and family tradition. The first Viscount Fauconberg was a distinguished Catholic loyalist who fought for Charles I in the Civil Wars; but the 2nd Viscount was a Protestant, later a Whig. He held a variety of court offices under Charles II, and was granted an earldom by William III in 1689. His son, the 2nd Earl, reverted to Rome, but his grandson, the 3rd Earl, returned to

---

* The exultation in Catholic circles at the conversion of Charles Manners, younger son of the Earl of Rutland, in 1682 is suggestive in itself. (Foley, v, 88.)

Canterbury. The same pattern is seen in the Digby family. George Digby, 2nd Earl of Bristol, was a convert to Rome, but his son, who succeeded to the title in 1677, was a firm Protestant.

Finally, two of the great Catholic houses of England were eliminated virtually by accident. The 11th Earl of Shrewsbury, the premier earl of England, was killed in a notorious duel with the Duke of Buckingham in 1668, and his young son, the 12th Earl, though he was placed in the care of Catholic relatives, conformed to the established Church before he came of age. He was another renegade Catholic who played a leading part in the Glorious Revolution. A different fate overwhelmed the Howards. In 1660, on the petition of more than ninety members of the House of Lords, Charles II agreed to revive the Dukedom of Norfolk, extinguished by attainder in 1572, and confer it on Thomas Howard, 3rd Earl of Arundel. Unfortunately the new duke was an incurable lunatic, confined at Padua. Charles called Thomas's brother and heir-presumptive, Henry Howard, to the Lords in one of the family baronies, and in 1672 made him Earl of Norwich. But he succeeded to the dukedom in 1677 in the midst of a sordid public quarrel with his eldest son over his decision to marry his mistress Jane Bickerton, and he retired abroad with her in 1677. This same son, who was to succeed him in 1684 as 4th Duke, was converted to the Church of England in 1679.*

It was on the nobility that the English Catholics ought to have been able to lean, and from whom they naturally expected leadership. They alone had a political platform from which to air their views, they had the entrée to the Court, and because of the House of Lords' jealous defence of its privileges they were virtually immune from the penal laws. But in the 1670s an aristocracy already undermined by defection was further weakened by senility and immaturity; in the 1670s a remarkable proportion of its members were either too old or too young. When the first Test Act came before the Lords, on 15 March 1673, there were

*Obviously to save the family estates. He remained a Protestant, but his children were raised as Catholics, and the family is Catholic to this day, though the 9th Duke (1786–1815) was also a Protestant.

only twelve Catholic peers present, and their spokesman was the most recent convert amongst them, the Earl of Bristol, who welcomed the bill with the remark that he was 'a Catholic of the Church of Rome, not a Catholic of the Court of Rome'.[85] Of twelve identifiable absentees we know that four were minors and seven were in their dotage. And though Protestants asserted, and many believed, that the Catholics were a powerful force, politically and socially, it is remarkable that the five Catholic noblemen singled out by Titus Oates in 1678 as the leaders of armed insurrection were all old or ageing men: Powis was fifty-two, Petre fifty-six, Stafford and Belasyse sixty-four, and Arundell of Wardour seventy.

2

James and Coleman

Of course, the most important Catholic nobleman in England was the King's younger brother, James Stuart, Duke of York and Albany. Yet it is significant that James was never the leader of the Catholic community in England, even after his accession to the throne in 1685. Though his upbringing in the chaotic conditions of the Civil Wars does not seem to have been emphatically Protestant, it was certainly not in any way Roman. The influence of his Catholic mother, Henrietta Maria, was removed in 1642, when she left for France; on the other hand his father's death, represented in the circles in which he moved as an Anglican martyrdom, made a deep and lasting impression on him, and he referred to it continually in later life. When he reached France in 1648 he reacted sharply against his mother, and their relations were cool ever after; his preceptor and hero during his years in France was the great Huguenot general, Turenne. Soon after his return to England in 1660 he married the daughter of Lord Chancellor Clarendon, a match which seemed to fix him permanently in the framework of constitutional Anglicanism to which he was accustomed, and he was one of Clarendon's most loyal supporters and defenders.

So his conversion in 1669 was quite unforeseen, and out of character. He was received into the Church by the Jesuit Emmanuel Lobb, alias Simeon, but apart from this we know next to nothing, and the security black-out imposed by his brother was so effective that even Philip Howard seems to have been unaware of it, and the Pope was not definitely informed until 1676.[1] Charles promptly removed his daughters, Mary and Anne, from his care, and expressly forbade him ever to announce his conversion, and though he attended Anglican services with

37

increasing reluctance, finally abandoning them altogether in 1676, James showed no other resentment of his brother's decision, and no disposition to appear in public as a spokesman for his co-religionists, whatever he did behind the scenes.

He retained many Protestant friends, and the two closest were Lawrence Hyde his brother-in-law, and George Legge, firm and ostentatious Anglicans. His entourage at Whitehall was a closed clique, with a strong military flavour (Legge was a professional sailor and later Master General of the Ordnance). The Catholics with whom he was at his ease were swordsmen and rakes, like Henry Jermyn, Bernard Howard, Richard Talbot and Justin Maccarty. (His partiality for Irishmen antedated his conversion by a good many years.) Of the older nobility he favoured the tough old Civil War veteran Lord Belasyse of Worlaby (whose cousin he had once contemplated marrying), and he had some unexpected contacts with other northern gentry, especially those who had military or naval connections, like the Stricklands of Catterick.[2] But the mainstream of the Catholic upper classes, inbred, squirearchal, chauvinistic and unglamorous, passed him by. It is easy to forget how restricted was Court life under Charles II, but a line drawn from Newmarket through Cambridge, Oxford, Winchester, Portsmouth, Sheerness and back to Newmarket defines an area beyond which Charles and his brother very rarely strayed between 1660 and 1679.

The Catholic society James knew best was dominated by the foreign influence of his wife and his sister-in-law, the Queen. He had few known contacts with secular priests, and it was only natural that he should lean towards the Jesuits. One of the aims of the Society of Jesus was to advance the Catholic cause by the conversion of crowned heads, and James was a prince to their liking, who looked for the inauguration of the Catholic millennium by decisive and peremptory state action. In so far as he could ever stomach gradualism – and here the Exclusion Crisis obviously had a sobering effect – it was not in alliance with the English Catholics. His first thought when he came to the throne in 1685 was to consolidate his friendship with the Anglican Church, and even when this alliance broke down he was slow to take on the English Catholics; he never did employ the Earl of Powis, by then the premier Catholic nobleman.

The very existence of the Duke of York as heir-presumptive made the strength or weakness of the English Catholics irrelevant to thinking men. On his own confession he was known as 'a man for arbitrary power', and Shaftesbury's denunciation of him as a man who was 'heady, violent and bloody, who easily believes the rashest and worst of counsels to be most sincere and hearty', is probably a fair expression of contemporary opinion.[3] The revelations made at Edward Coleman's trial in 1678 only confirmed the suspicion that if James wanted to re-establish Roman Catholicism he would do it by violence.

Edward Coleman was the son of a Suffolk clergyman. He went to Trinity, Cambridge, where he took his degree in 1656. His father left him £140 a year, and it is reasonable to suppose that he spent some time abroad between then and 1670, when he reappears as Secretary to the Duke of York and a fanatical Roman Catholic.[4]

He showed himself to be a man of some administrative ability, and he must have wielded considerable personal charm, but he had no common sense, nor sense of proportion. In him the excessive piety and zeal of the new convert was combined with the narrow, blinkered outlook of the habitual courtier and man-about-town with no base in the country. (He must have had Protestant relatives, but nothing is heard of them.) To him the disposition of Father La Chaise, the whims of a Secretary of State or an ambassador, were more important than public opinion, or even government policy. He lived in an unreal world of his own.

He first swung into action in 1673. To an ambitious and able young Catholic like himself the cancellation of Charles's Declaration of Indulgence and the passing of the Test Act were setbacks which it was difficult to accept; they ended his reasonable hopes of a lucrative and distinguished public career, and condemned him to the backstairs for ever. He just had to try to change things.

He already had a useful connection at Paris in Sir William Throckmorton, a Catholic officer in a guards regiment seconded to the French service for the duration, who knew Fr Ferrier, Louis XIV's Jesuit confessor. He and Coleman shared the delusion of all those outside the inner circle of power, that confessors and mistresses were significant political figures — more significant, indeed, than trusted and accredited ministers of state. Apparently on his own initiative, Coleman now warned Ferrier in urgent terms that Charles II would soon make a separate peace with Holland. Louis XIV cannot have been unaware of this possibility, but according to Coleman his warnings were received with incredulity, and when he was proved right, in February 1674, his credit was correspondingly enhanced. He used this credit to support his further argument that unless Charles II could be persuaded to dissolve his present Parliament it would force him back into the war on the Dutch side. His belief that a new Parliament would be pro-French and even pro-Catholic is not one shared by many contemporaries, or by later historians, but it was consistent:

If this parliament were dissolved [he wrote], there would be no difficulty getting a new one which would be more useful, the constitutions of our parliaments being such that a new one can never hurt the Crown, nor an old one do it good.

Apparently James agreed, and Louis XIV was impressed, because in June 1674, through the roundabout mediation of Ferrier, Throckmorton and Coleman, they agreed to work together for dissolution, Louis providing the money to woo Charles II, and James the on-the-spot influence.[5] Of course, this ran counter to Charles's official policy, and though great stress was laid on the 'good understanding' between the brothers, Coleman always presented Charles in a most unflattering light: 'Logic in our Court built upon money,' he wrote, 'has more powerful charms than any other sort of reasoning.'[6] Louis XIV was ill at this time, and perhaps gave Ferrier more rein than usual; anyway, in September 1674 the Jesuit sent Throckmorton to London with a letter pledging Louis's friendship and support for James.[7] In return, Coleman drafted a letter for James in which he pledged his support for the French interest. Whether this letter was ever approved or sent became a matter for controversy later.

Meanwhile in the autumn of 1674 Coleman was also in constant touch with the Internuncio at Brussels, soliciting money from the Pope and the Emperor to prevent the Duke and his brother falling back into the orbit of France. This time James was cast in a more imposing role, as a disinterested mediator between the warring Catholic powers. Predictably, he received lavish assurances of the Pope's sympathy and the Emperor's 'passionate zeal', but no money.[8] The negotiations with France were also delayed by the opposition of the French foreign minister, Pomponne, and the French ambassador to London, Ruvigny, which was sustained until October 1674, when Ferrier's death gave them a breathing-space. Then the prorogation of parliament from November 1674 to April 1675 confirmed Louis and Pomponne in the belief that Charles would preserve his neutrality without financial assistance from them.[9]

James now seems to have withdrawn, and it may have been at this time that Coleman was transferred to the Duchess's household. But Throckmorton returned to Paris in November, and he and Coleman spent the winter working on Pomponne, who was a much tougher proposition than poor, gullible Ferrier. He insisted that his master could not spare the £300,000 required, and doubted if Charles's co-operation was worth bidding for anyway.[10] Louis agreed; in fact Throckmorton admitted, 'He hath so mean an opinion of the King and all his partners, that I doubt he scarce thinks anything they can do worth £300,000.'[11] Negotiations rambled on until 20 February 1675, when Louis finally broke off, and advised James to ally with Parliament, since his brother's debauchery and general bad character were such that national leadership must devolve on him.[12] By April 1675 Throckmorton was talking of renewing his military career, but shortly afterwards he was killed in a duel.

His successor *vis-à-vis* Coleman was an English priest called Sheldon, but he did not have Throckmorton's standing at the French Court, and his position was weakened, paradoxically, as the position of the Catholics in England improved. By August, far from dreading the next session of Parliament, Coleman was positively looking forward to it, and Ruvigny was busy feeling out the Opposition.[13] But here he faced competition from the Spaniards, and eventually Louis ordered Ruvigny to seek an accommodation with Charles instead. He drove a better bargain than Coleman, and in return for a paltry 500,000 *écus* a year, later pared down to 100,000, Charles agreed to dissolve Parliament if it showed itself hostile to France. Promises meant little on either side, but Louis was content for the time being.[14]

St Germain's return to France in November* gave Coleman a new agent as irresponsible and fanatical as himself. But Coleman's position was crumbling; James did not confide in him, Coleman was ignorant of the negotiations between the two governments, and when he approached Louis's new confessor, La Chaise, he met with a cool response.[15] In his first letter from Paris St Germain reported that Louis regarded Coleman as 'a person whose advice is too violent to succeed in the traffic wherein the Duke of York is engaged', and he was dismissed as a man 'of violent counsels', and 'not authorized'.[16] Letters flew to and fro all winter, but both Coleman and St Germain were now clearly regarded as unstable 'ultras', and St Germain's remarkably thick-skinned attempts to reinstate himself with the Duke, and even return to England, did his friend no good. In March 1676 St Germain was advising Coleman to come over in person, but in April he told him resignedly, 'It is wisdom to expect a more favourable conjuncture.'[17]

Coleman probably did go over that summer, but in June and July it was still being reported in Paris that James was angry with him 'for bragging that he made him do what he did', and that he had 'chid him in public'.[18] Then there was a slight thaw: James could never entirely dispense with a servant who knew as much about his activities as Coleman; and on the other hand the worsening relations between England and France led Louis to relent slightly. In June Louis decided to release to Coleman through his London ambassador a small sum of money

* See p. 21 above.

(100,000 crowns) for the purpose of bribing M.P.s, and James was persuaded to write to La Chaise.

The result was another rebuff, though no doubt it was tactfully phrased. In November St Germain wrote with regret:

The King's confessor has answered the Duke of York. But when all is done, the King does not seem to me very eager in your business, and it's said that letters of this nature which come to him from foreign countries are not acceptable to him.[19]

Then at Christmas Charles himself took a hand. Amongst the papers of Henry Coventry, the Secretary of State, are some intercepted letters from the Jesuits Strange and Bedingfield to John Warner at St Omers. Coventry copied them before sending them on, and showed them to the King on 30 December; on 3 January 1677, he showed him copies of another two letters, this time addressed to Coleman.[20] But these were probably not the first, for they contain the information that Coleman had already been disgraced; he had been forbidden the Court and ordered to resign his post as Secretary to the Duchess without reason given. He was then dispatched on an errand to France to get him out of the way, and Lord Arundell commented that in future the Duke and Duchess would not be able to appoint English-born Catholics to confidential positions in their households.[21]

With this the whole intrigue seems to have petered out. The Coventry papers show that the impending session of Parliament in April 1677, the first for nearly two years, produced something of a flutter, and attempts were made to draw in the Earl of Castlemaine, who was then at Liège, but there was no revival of Coleman's influence.[22] He continued to correspond with St Germain up to October 1678, and to receive small sums from the French ambassador to bribe M.P.s, which he later swore he had merely pocketed. He also provided the French ambassador with reports on events in Parliament, and for a while he operated a general newsletter service. Chief Justice North thought these letters were designed 'to misrepresent and misconstrue all the public transactions of state', and denounced them as 'fanatic', and after Coleman's arrest in 1678 Sir Robert Southwell acknowledged to the Duke of Ormonde that:

By your advice I broke off my acquaintance with him as soon as ever it begun, and upon the first receiving of his newsletter, which, when I showed your Grace some daring particulars in it you advised me (considering the station I was in) to knock off, for that he was a man who would certainly run himself into the briars.[23]

It may well have been these indiscreet newsletters that he burnt just before his arrest; but the government – reasonably enough in the circumstances – believed that he had destroyed evidence for a treasonable intrigue with the Court of France extending through 1677 and into 1678, and Sir John Pollock, writing as late as 1903, enthusiastically concurred.[24]

But Pollock had no evidence – he admitted that he was arguing 'from the known to the unknown' – and though he thought general inference was in favour of his theory, this is not so. It is true that James's insistence that he had dismissed Coleman in 1674 or 1675 was disingenuous. He always showed an incapacity to choose good servants and a stubborn reluctance to dismiss bad ones, and there is some evidence that he put up a fight to prevent Coleman's dismissal from his wife's household in late 1676 or early 1677.[25] A new Secretary, a foreigner, was supposed to have replaced him, but Coleman's own papers make it clear that he continued to correspond on her behalf with Cardinal Howard at Rome into 1678.[26] Moreover, in many cases he was clearly writing on her husband's behalf as well as hers.* However, what is important is that in 1675 or 1676 James clearly abandoned the line of policy advocated by Coleman and chose another; and after that his advice on relations with France, and parliamentary tactics, must have been ignored.

Obviously Coleman's was not the only kind of pro-Catholic policy put up to James, and even in Coleman's own correspondence can be heard the echo of dissenting voices, arguing that in view of Charles II's unkingly qualities James should build up his

---

*In his 'Memoirs' James insisted that he had dismissed Coleman from his household altogether (Clarke, i, 533–4), but he was vague as to the date. It is significant that at Coleman's trial, when every effort was made to 'whitewash' James, his dismissal was never mentioned.

own independent interest as heir-presumptive, irrespective of his religion. As early as November 1674 Throckmorton told Coleman that it would be better if James could obtain the money he wanted, or part of it, from the English Catholics rather than the French government.[27] The following February we find Throckmorton arguing that if James made a firm stand, such would be the contrast with his brother's deviousness that he would have 'all the wise, sober, good people, and such as are worth having, as well Protestants as Catholics, on his side'.[28] Indeed, Coleman himself assured La Chaise later that year that 'he makes such a figure already that cautious men do not care to act against him, or always without him'.[29] One anonymous correspondent – perhaps Throckmorton – pointed out the uselessness of trying to bribe M.P.s, for: 'You know those whom money has a power with are the scum of the family, who will promise one thing today and act quite contrary tomorrow.' Sheldon also thought more might be gained for the Catholic cause by conciliating the Protestant interest, or joining with them in an anti-French policy, while Cardinal Howard, following the policy of Innocent XI, also argued strongly against the French interest.[30]

So, pressure from the Catholic side helped James towards a shift in policy which became evident in 1677, leading to an alliance with Danby on the basis of a patriotic, pro-Confederate policy abroad, and some kind of 'national union' at home. This even included government-sponsored legislation which, though for the time being it was abortive, held out hopes of a new deal for the Catholics, and a peaceful accommodation between a Catholic king and a Protestant establishment.*

But in the meanwhile Coleman was not the only impetuous Catholic who was doing his religion no good, and some historians have seen something ineffably sinister in the manoeuvrings of certain Catholic peers at this time.[31] For instance, amongst Coleman's papers were four letters from the Earl of Berkshire, written in the second half of 1674.[32] They offer James support in

* See p. 23 above.

the dark hour of his fortunes, but if this support was intended to be extra-parliamentary this is very far from being made clear. There are a few other scraps of evidence. In July 1676 St Germain thanked Coleman for 'the great packet which Boatman sent me from the Lord Belasyse'. Coleman's steward, Jerome Boatman, confirmed that his master had exchanged frequent visits with Arundell and Belasyse, and that he had visited Arundell the night before he gave himself up to the Council.[33] As for the Earl of Berkshire, he was one of the first to flee abroad in November 1678, together with the Earl of Cardigan; since he had not yet been directly accused, this suggests that he expected the government to find more about him in Coleman's papers than they did. But the decisive piece of evidence against him, a supposed death-bed confession made by him in Paris in April 1679, has now been exposed as a forgery.[34]

Stafford seems to have been a busy, meddling man: the most likely to be mixed up in something rash and shady. He was often abroad, and he visited France in 1678. When he was under sentence of death in 1680 he offered to reveal all he knew of the Catholics' plans in the 1670s – though the implication is that these were not very serious. Unfortunately he was stopped short when he tactlessly mentioned a proposed *rapprochement* between James and Shaftesbury in 1675.[35] On the other hand, soon after his arrest he pointed out to the Privy Council that after a quarrel as long ago as 1654 he had been 'at great distance with the Lord Arundell'. He went on to say:

I may often have spoken of toleration and of possibilities about religion, but I vow to God I do not remember it, and am sure I never spoke seriously of bringing in popery. But when there have been occasions to speak of it in the House of Lords I have ever spoke my mind at the fireside* and to the bishops' bench, that we had no other interest than to be quiet.

As for the gouty Lord Belasyse, he simply said:

* Probably he meant '*to* the fireside'. Charles II sat by the fire when he attended debates in the House of Lords.

Being now in age and living in plenty, and well at ease in my fortune, and impaired for some years past in my health, how can it be thought that I should entertain any desires of change?[36]

They are a pathetic group: Powis, Arundell, Stafford, Belasyse and Petre. But their names are current in the testimony of informers, to the exclusion of other, more likely candidates. If they did entertain some hare-brained scheme, they suffered for it: Stafford was executed, Petre died in the Tower after four years' imprisonment; the other three were not released until February 1684.

Meanwhile, through the spring and early summer of 1678 tension steadily mounted. Much of this tension was associated with the King's sudden decision, in mid-winter, to raise an army. Having resisted pressure from the Commons on this point for more than a year, he at last announced that he was prepared to take the field against Louis XIV – just when the war was obviously drawing to a close. A treaty was hastily patched up with the Dutch, and a small force of twenty thousand men recruited; but it did not begin to disembark at Ostend until early in February, much too late to prevent Louis capturing Ghent on 27 February and Ypres on 15 March, in a lightning attack mounted before the opening of the campaigning season proper. The front then quietened down while both sides waited for the conclusion of the peace negotiations at Nijmegen.

The Commons, not surprisingly, suspected that all this was a ruse on Charles's part to secure a military force which on the conclusion of peace he could use against his opponents in England. The truth is, he was already regretting his own precipitancy, and he had ordered Danby to reopen secret negotiations with France; so both sides, King and Opposition, greeted with some relief the news of an armistice on 23 May. The Commons at once voted £200,000 for the disbandment of the newly raised regiments, but in June this was postponed on the news that France had refused the peace terms offered her, and the session closed on 15 July in the midst of a bad-tempered squabble between the two Houses over the terms of the Disbandment Act itself.[37]

At this stage Charles and Danby took an enormous gamble. They decided to join Holland in exerting pressure on Louis XIV to accept the peace terms, thus enhancing Charles's prestige as a diplomat and arbiter, if not as a war leader. But to do this he had to keep the Army in existence in defiance of the Disbandment Act, and when his gamble failed the consequences were disastrous. Rather than appear to give way to coercion, France came to terms at the last moment, leaving England out on a limb. Charles had no choice but to begin re-embarking his illegal army to England, where its arrival was greeted with alarm and anger. Meanwhile the money voted for its disbandment (not enough, as usual) had been spent maintaining it since June, and it was cheaper to allow arrears of pay and allowances to mount up rather than settle them. So, when Parliament reassembled in the autumn, the King would have to go to them cap-in-hand, ask for more money, and explain as best he could what had happened to the money voted for the same purpose in June.

This partly explains why the government's handling of the Plot, when it came, was so tentative and uncertain, and why the fear of popery was particularly strong in the summer of 1678. Even today some Catholic apologists refer to the Plot as 'Oates's Plot', but this is to flatter him. The King's mystifying foreign policy produced a general feeling of apprehension and instability, and the ebullient self-confidence of his Catholic courtiers and hangers-on accentuated it As Sir Robert Southwell wrote at the time, the Plot was:

A thing [which] could never arise out of the industry or evidence of one single man, and especially a man under the disadvantage of many known failures in his life and conversation, if it were not for other considerations; the first of which I take to be the manifest indulgence which for many years has been extended to the[se] people, and wherein some of them have so imprudently triumphed that it became the grief and scandal of many, and turned itself into so much combustible matter against the day of wrath.

John Evelyn thought much the same 'The truth is', he wrote later, 'the Roman Catholics were exceedingly bold, and busy everywhere since the Duke forbore to go any longer to Chapel.'[38]

On 29 April 1678, the Commons received an alarming report from a Committee appointed to investigate the danger from popery. It dealt mainly with the scandalously open practice of Catholicism in Monmouthshire, but the Commons also heard of the alleged appointment of Catholic J.P.s in Northumberland, despite representations to the Lord Chancellor, and the information provided by the Exchequer gave them no joy. Despite the protests of Catholics in 1675, it now appeared that the sequestration of recusants' estates ordered in that year had not begun until July 1677, and even then had not proceeded very far. No convictions were recorded for Cheshire, Oxfordshire, Northamptonshire, Rutlandshire or the whole of Wales, and the sheriffs of Norfolk, Northumberland, Derbyshire, Leicestershire, Nottinghamshire and Hertfordshire had failed to act at all. The Commons had just heard that Monmouthshire was positively crawling with recusants, but the Exchequer reported that confiscation of a modest £40 had been imposed, and even then the sheriff had only collected £4 13s. 4d., and discharged the rest. London and Middlesex had been assessed at £100 13s. 4d., which was ludicrous enough, but even then only the odd 13s. 4d. had been collected. True, the total income to the Exchequer from recusancy had risen from £78 in 1675 to £535 in 1676, and seemed likely to rise even higher when the sheriff's accounts for 1677 were proved, but no one supposed that this was a tenth, or even a hundredth, of the value of Catholic-owned estates.[39] The Commons had a right to be angry and uneasy. They considered a number of expedients, without adopting any, and in June they brought in another bill to apply the Test to members of both Houses, but it was lost at the prorogation.[40]

Public fear of a conspiracy to establish Catholicism and arbitrary power, perhaps on behalf of the Duke of York, was common enough. Earlier in the year, a pamphlet which listed

Danby's supporters in Parliament alleged that they were 'the principal labourers in the great design of popery and arbitrary power, who have betrayed their country to the conspirators, and bargained with them to maintain a standing army in England, under the command of the bigoted Popish Duke, who, by the assistance of the Lord Lauderdale's Scotch Army, the forces in Ireland and those in France, hopes to bring all back to Rome'.[41] Charles's decision to retain his army of twenty thousand men, half of them in England, confirmed such fears, and as Parliament sweltered on into the summer, Israel Tonge and Richard Greene were at the door with circumstantial tales of a Popish Plot in Herefordshire and the Marches.[42]

Some had a premonition later hailed as miraculous. That summer the Jesuit Provincial, Thomas Whitbread, made a tour of inspection of the Society's seminaries in Flanders. At St Omers he dismissed an unsatisfactory novice of mature years known as Father Ambrose (*vere* Oates), and wound up the tour at Liège on 15 July 1678, when he preached to the text: 'Are ye able to drink of the cup that I shall drink of?' (Matthew 20.22). He warned a shocked audience that though times were now quiet they would not always remain so. 'Can you undergo a hard persecution?' he went on. 'Are you content to be falsely betrayed, and injured, and hurried away to prison? Can you be brought to the bar, and hear yourself falsely sworn against? Can you patiently receive the sentence of an unjust judge, condemning you to a painful and ignominious death?' He answered each question for them. They could.[43]

But August and September were peaceful enough. Whitbread and his *socius* Fr Mico brought back the plague with them from Antwerp, and lay ill at a house owned by the Spanish ambassador in Wild Street, Covent Garden. But Edward Coleman was in Warwickshire most of August, and William Ireland (after Whitbread the most distinguished English Jesuit) was in Staffordshire with patrons and friends like the Southcotes, the Gerards, and the Astons. He attended a horse race at Etching Hill between Sir Henry Gough and Captain Chetwynd, and was often seen on the great bowling-green at Tixhall. It was holiday time; he went fishing with Mr Heveningham of Aston, and caught 'a great pike of a yard long'; next day he hunted buck with Richard Gerard in his deer park at Hilderstone. Then he went on to Boscobel and stayed with the Penderels. A party of twenty or twenty-five gathered at the Royal Oak, partly to view that royalist shrine, and partly to attend a solemn ceremony at which young John Gavan, a local man, took his final vows to the Society of Jesus. They feasted royally on venison, then Ireland travelled on to the home of John Gerard, at Blackladies, and so to Wolverhampton.[44]

Twelve months later Coleman, Gavan, Whitbread and Ireland had all gone to the scaffold, sent there principally by that disreputable novice from St Omers, Titus Oates. Richard Gerard of Hilderstone was dead of the gaol fever in Newgate and Lord Aston was in the Tower. But in the late summer of 1678 Oates was back in London, trudging in his shabby clothes across Lincoln's Inn Fields, cadging off acquaintances at the Pheasant in Fullers' Rents, hanging round the chapel at Somerset House, and begging off the Benedictines in the Savoy next door. As he made notes in his famous 'papers' he was fixing the topography of his outrageous tale; early in September he had reached Lord Danby, and he was in sight of the Privy Council.

3

Titus Oates

OATES's John the Baptist was a crazy clergyman called Israel Tonge, a mental casualty of the Civil Wars. He took his first degree at University College, Oxford, in 1643, and showed considerable promise as a scholar, but the closure of the university in that year drove him out to Chipping Norton, where he languished for five years as a country schoolmaster. Returning to Oxford in 1648, he readily complied with the prevailing Puritanism and was made a Fellow of his old college. In 1649 he was given a rich living in Kent, in 1656 he graduated D.D. and secured a fellowship at the new college founded by Parliament at Durham. Antony à Wood, the Oxford gossip, remembered him as 'cynical and hirsute, shiftless in the world, yet absolutely free from covetousness, and I dare say from pride'.

However, the collapse of Durham College in 1659 terminated his academic career, and on the Restoration of Charles II in 1660 he had to suppress his Puritanism, too. Even then, there were few pickings for an ex-Puritan in the re-established Church, and after a year as chaplain to the Dunkirk garrison he had to settle for a small country living, at Leintwardine in Herefordshire. In June 1666, however, a new and important career opened before him when he was presented to the living of St Mary Stayning in the City of London. But less than three months later he saw his church, and most of his parish, go up in flames in the Great Fire. The experience permanently unhinged him.

Israel Tonge went back to the Army, and spent two years as chaplain to the Tangier garrison, but he had at least one important patron in Sir Richard Barker, a City physician who may have obtained St Mary's for him in the first place, and who certainly installed him at St Michael's, Wood Street, on his return from Tangier. The addition in 1672 of the rectory of Aston in Herefordshire put him beyond serious financial difficulties, and since he was now a widower with a grown-up family he settled down in Sir Richard Barker's household in the Barbican.

But he had been left with a settled persecution complex of psychopathic proportions, focused on the Society of Jesus, which according to him was responsible not only for the Great Fire but the Great Rebellion and the execution of Charles I. Extraordinary as it may seem to us, this was an 'alibi' commonly put forward by old Puritans, but he seems genuinely to have believed it. In 1671 he undertook a translation of certain Jansenist tracts under the title *Jesuits' Morals*, but the first two parts had such a disastrous sale that publication of the third was stopped. It is just possible that he was hampered by official disfavour, as he claimed, but in any case his style was at once incoherent and turgid, even by the standards of the age, and this in itself would account for the book's failure. But he thought he had been 'unreasonably decried and vilified and disserved, without any just reason'.[1]

He then settled down to compose a wild and wonderful History of the Jesuits, though he could not find a publisher for it until 1679. He had always been convinced of the existence of a Popish Plot in general terms, but according to him the first he heard of a specific conspiracy to assassinate the King was from a man called Richard Greene, in Herefordshire in 1675.[2] The following year, at Sir Richard Barker's, he also fell in with Titus Oates.

Oates was another casualty of the Civil Wars, though indirectly. His father, Samuel Oates, had been a chaplain in the New Model Army, and an Anabaptist. This self-taught ex-weaver was luckier than Tonge, the ex-don, for in 1660 Sir Richard Barker presented him to the living of All Saints', Hastings. Titus was born in 1649, went to Westminster School, then Merchant Taylors', from which he was expelled, and on to Gonville and Caius College, Cambridge, in 1667. He was expelled after two terms, cause unknown, and transferred to St John's. But he went down without a degree in 1669, after a petty dispute with his tutor over a tailor's bill. Allowance must be made for retrospective bias, but the only significant qualities his Cambridge teachers were willing to allow him were 'plodding industry and unparalleled assurance'. He never mastered Latin, the basis of all seventeenth-century education and scholarship, and his tutor at St John's dismissed him as 'a great dunce'. However, he did have a good memory.

Despite his lack of a degree, and the heterodox opinions he had imbibed from his father, he took holy orders soon after leaving Cambridge, and was presented to a curacy at Sandhurst in Surrey, apparently through the good offices of Lord Howard, a Roman Catholic.* In March 1673 he was further presented to the living of Bobbing, in Kent, by the local squire, Sir George Moore, of whom little is known. But his stay there was short; his parishioners accused him of drunkenness, drink brought out his father's Anabaptist teachings, and he was heard to use 'some very indecent expressions concerning the mysteries of the Christian religion'. Before the end of the year he was ejected from the living, and took refuge in Hastings. There he eagerly joined in his father's quarrel with a prominent local family, the Parkers, but he made the mistake of accusing young William Parker of sodomy and his father of treasonable words. The elder Parker's case went up to the Privy Council, which exonerated him, and the local magistrates dismissed the case against his son, who at once brought an action for £1,000 damages. Oates was bound over to Quarter Sessions on a further charge of perjury, and in May 1675 he hastily signed up as chaplain on the frigate *Adventure,* bound for Tangier.

It was a trifle strange that Oates should have left two public schools and one Cambridge college in a hurry; it is also strange that he should accuse young Parker of sodomy when there was absolutely no case to answer. The probable reason appeared when the *Adventure* docked on its return from Tangiers. Oates was dismissed for homosexual practices, and he was lucky not

---

*Usually referred to as 'the Duke of Norfolk', though he did not succeed to this title until 1677. He was in fact Baron Howard of Castle Rising (1669) and Earl of Norwich (1672). See p. 35 above.

to be tried for his life. The fact that Oates was an active and practising homosexual had always been known, but historians have evaded one obvious conclusion; that this explains the astonishing ease with which he was admitted to certain Catholic circles which one would have supposed barred to a disreputable Anglican clergyman with heterodox leanings.

For instance, on his return to London early in 1676, he was often in the company of Matthew Medburne, 'actor and comedian', who 'picked him up in the Earl of Suffolk's cellar at Whitehall'. (Suffolk was another member of the Howard family, but of the Protestant branch.) With Medburne he frequented a low club in Fullers' Rents, Holborn, which was the haunt of many Catholics, and may have had other specialized attractions. It was about this time that he met Israel Tonge, but their friendship did not prosper, mainly because of the hostility of Sir Richard Barker, who had now disowned the Oates family. Early in 1677 he was appointed chaplain to the Earl of Norwich's London household, presumably to minister to its Protestant members, but again, he was dismissed in mysterious circumstances three months later. Immediately afterwards, on 3 March 1677, he was received into the Roman Catholic Church.

This is one of the strangest episodes in a strange career. He afterwards insisted that his conversion was insincere, which is not difficult to believe; what is difficult to understand is why he did not turn when he was in the household of Lord Norwich, a distinguished and influential Catholic. His subsequent explanation was that he wanted to infiltrate the Society of Jesus and discover more about the conspiracy in which Tonge believed. However, he said nothing of this to Tonge, who was baffled by his sudden disappearance from his old haunts. Typically, he was admitted to the Church by a spoiled priest called Berry, who had been converted from Protestantism to Catholicism, and back, and back again.[3] He was generally regarded as insane; certainly he was the last man to assist Oates in his new life, and for his first few weeks as a Catholic he was almost starving. Then he was introduced to Richard Strange, the English Provincial of the Society of Jesus, no less, who at once arranged for him to go to the English College at Valladolid for further study, with a view to entering upon the novitiate.

The new novice was a strange, not to say alarming figure. The description left by the Jesuit historian John Warner is naturally lacking in charity, but it can be confirmed from other sources. He had, says Warner:

> the speech of the gutter, and a strident and sing-song voice, so that he seemed to wail rather than to speak. His brow was low, his eyes small and sunk deep in his head; his face was flat, compressed in the middle so as to look like a dish or discus; on each side were prominent ruddy cheeks, his nose was snub, his mouth in the very centre of his face, for his chin was almost equal in size to the rest of his face. His head scarcely protruded from his body, and was bowed towards his chest.

And so on.[4] But what Warner does not explain is why the elite Society accepted this bizarre creature so readily.

Strange was a man of sixty-six, with a distinguished but unremarkable career in the Society behind him. He escaped to the Low Countries early in 1679, and was adviser to John Warner, who had taken over as Vice-Provincial after Whitbread's arrest. In the remaining three years of his life he was not reappointed to any office in the Society, but by this time, of course, he was an old man. Was he already senile in 1677? When every excuse is made – the most usual being the difficulty of checking a man's professional credentials in this era – his prompt and expansive credulity is astonishing. It is even more astonishing when we remember that all the instruction at Valladolid was given in Latin or Spanish, neither of which languages Oates knew, and he was setting off in May, when the college was about to close until the late autumn. Yet Strange must have financed his passage out of Jesuit funds and given him a subsistence allowance of some kind – certainly he was not short of money in Spain. Were Strange and Oates, and perhaps Lord Norwich, members of some Catholic 'homintern', pledged to mutual assistance in adversity? This may seem an insulting and unfair reflection on a man held in reverence by his church and his order down to this day. But the facts call for some explanation.

Anyway, Oates arrived at Valladolid just as classes were ending, and hung around until October. Then his ignorance of
Latin was discovered in a matter of days, and he was sent back
to England. He reached London again at the end of November,
with a sketchy knowledge of the Spanish Jesuits which was to be
useful later. Apart from this, his only useful experience was an
encounter with two accomplished con-men, 'Captain' William
Bedloe and his brother James, who were posing as an English
peer on the Grand Tour with his valet. The elder Bedloe, with
his dark good looks and imposing presence, looked the part, and
he relieved Oates of ten pieces of eight before passing on.

Strange does not appear to have been upset by Oates's sudden
return, or the waste of money involved. Oates remained in touch
with him and other Jesuit fathers, and adopted the pseudonym
of Fr Ambrose, though he was not in Catholic orders. But he
turned for a minimum subsistence to Israel Tonge, who was
encouraged to hope for his speedy conversion. However, by the
end of 1677 Oates was tired of this situation, or Tonge was tired
of him, and he approached Strange again. This time Strange
gave him letters of introduction to the College of St Omers, in
northern France. There he presented himself, under the alias
Sampson Lucy, on 10 December 1677.

Tonge later pretended that Oates had gone under his patronage, as a spy, a story Oates was to concoct to explain his activities, but at the time Tonge did not even know he had left
England. Moreover, if Oates wanted evidence of Jesuit plotting,
he was much more likely to find it at the seminaries of Watten
or Liège than at St Omers, which was a boarding-school and
nothing more. However, the ostensible motive for his going is
clear enough; his elementary education was deficient, and it was
not unknown for St Omers to accept adults who had a late voca-
tion.* If one accepts Oates as a suitable candidate, the rest follows.

Of course he was not a suitable candidate, and this soon became apparent. No school would have welcomed a new pupil of

---

*Foley (vii, 20) mentions the case of Herbert Aston, brother of the 2nd
Lord Aston, who entered St Omers in 1684, when he was over thirty.
But the practice certainly could not be described as common.

his age, and especially one so bizarre. His personal appearance was grotesquely unprepossessing. His conversation was often bawdy and blasphemous, and on this count alone he was no fit company for small boys. But worse was to come when the authorities divined his peculiar sexual tastes. The fact that he was not expelled after a few weeks speaks volumes for Strange's influence.

As for Oates himself, he had to put up with a great deal of schoolboy 'ragging', which he accepted with a very ill grace; nor did he take to the regime at St Omers, which obliged him to rise at five and go to bed at nine, to study long hours on very inadequate food, and to speak nothing but Latin under pain of punishment.* Not surprisingly, he was anxious to proceed with the novitiate, and he was sent to the seminary at Watten for an interview. The Rector formed a very poor opinion of him; in fact, if later testimony is to be believed, he was the first Jesuit to suspect that he was not what he pretended to be, 'but sent as a spy by some enemy to religion'.[5] On his return to St Omers his conduct deteriorated further, but by now his patron Strange had given way to Thomas Whitbread as Provincial, and when Whitbread reached St Omers in June 1678 on a tour of inspection he had no hesitation in expelling him forthwith. By the end of the month he was back in London, begging his bread as best he could.

It was at this stage that Oates took up again with Tonge, who in the session of Parliament just ended had made an unsuccessful attempt to bring home to the public the dangers of the Popish Plot.[6] He was almost insane with frustration and alarm. Oates possessed what he conspicuously lacked, detailed firsthand knowledge of the English Province of the Society of Jesus, and especially its European base. He even pretended that he was still associating with the Jesuits in London. So Tonge asked him to put down in writing all he had heard and seen in his travels, and all he knew about the Jesuits, apparently expecting just a list of names and facts.

*For a detailed account of the school at this time, see Beales, *Education Under Penalty*, pp. 158–73.

58

But Oates, consumed with malice against the Jesuits, and desperate to re-establish himself with someone, if only this crazy old clergyman, used the information stowed in his capacious memory to construct a detailed story of a specific conspiracy to assassinate the King and raise a rebellion in all three kingdoms. On or about 1 August he appeared at Tonge's lodgings in the Barbican, and tried him out with a brief statement, which he read aloud. Tonge was electrified, especially since he himself appeared with flattering prominence in the list of those to be killed off. His interest was titillated still further by Oates's refusal to allow him to keep the document, or even read it.[7]

There followed a comedy of errors and misunderstandings, occasioned partly by Tonge's neurotic fears of assassination, partly by Oates's reluctance to commit himself too far. According to Warner, at this stage Oates offered to sell his manuscript to the Jesuits, and certainly some of the London fathers seem to have been forewarned. (They refused to buy, of course.[8]) But in any case, bearing false witness was a serious crime, and misprision (or concealment) of treason still more so, and this alone could explain Oates's coyness. And when Oates did start looking for Tonge again he could not find him; in fact he had gone to stay with his friend Christopher Kirkby at Vauxhall without leaving an address. However, they were in touch by 10 August, because next day, by prior arrangement, Oates left his account of the Plot, now set out in forty-three numbered paragraphs, 'under the wainscot at the farther end of Sir Richard Barker's gallery in his house at the Barbican, near to the Doctor's chamber door', where Tonge pretended to find it. Tonge dimly appreciated the absurdity and danger of this procedure, because he asked Oates to disguise his handwriting by using the Greek alphabet, a suggestion Oates ignored (no doubt because he knew no Greek). For greater security, therefore, Tonge copied it all out himself. He then decided that the King himself must see it as soon as possible.

Here Kirkby was useful, because his amateur experiments in chemistry had brought him into personal contact with King Charles. Also he shared his friend Tonge's delusions about popery, and made no difficulty about acting as go-between. But he hung about Whitehall all day on 12 August without finding an opportunity to speak to the King alone. So that evening he and Tonge drew up a brief note requesting a private audience on a matter of urgent public importance. Next morning Kirkby was at Whitehall early, before Charles came down for his usual morning walk in St James's Park. He handed the King the letter in the outer gallery, he read it as he walked downstairs, and at the bottom, at the entrance to the Park, he called Kirkby to him and asked him to elaborate. Kirkby replied that there was a plot against his life, and he might be in danger that very morning, in the Park. 'How?' said Charles, and Kirkby replied, 'By shot.' Charles replied that he would see him alone in his bedchamber on his return.

When Charles returned he did see Kirkby alone, and heard how a Benedictine, Thomas Pickering, and a Jesuit lay brother, John Grove, had vowed to shoot him, and if this failed Sir George Wakeman, his wife's physician, was to poison him. The King asked for the source of his information, and Kirkby offered to produce Tonge, though it is not clear that he named him. The King said he would see them both that evening between eight and nine, and at that hour they returned on the river from Vauxhall, landed at the Privy Stairs, and were eventually shown into the Red Room, at the top of the stairs leading from the Privy Garden.

Tonge read out the more important of Oates's forty-three articles, including those which bore on the assassination, and handed him the rest to peruse. Charles said he had no time for this, and requested a verbal precis. Tonge told him that on his death the plan was to raise the three kingdoms against his brother, after which they would be subjugated piecemeal by the French. (This summary bears little reference to what Oates had in fact written, though it later appeared as an appendix to his published *Narrative*.) Charles

did not contradict the danger his brother might incur by his untimely death, but expressed himself as not giving any credence to what was pretended either of the papists or the French king seeking his life, alleging that if the papists attempted anything against him they would be knocked on the head themselves, and that the French would have worse neighbours of them who would succeed him and his brother, whom he admitted to be ruined by his fall.

He was sceptical about Wakeman's part in the affair, and asked what other 'persons of quality' were involved. Tonge answered that he had heard of none except Lord Petre, and even he was not privy to the assassination, for 'he had a very particular love and tenderness towards his Majesty's person'. Charles then inquired searchingly after the author of these accusations, but he appeared satisfied with the explanation that the man wished to preserve his anonymity because he was still mixing with the Jesuits in London and might be able to make further discoveries in the course of the next few weeks.

Charles is usually represented as listening to all this with some impatience. This may be so, but, as he told Burnet later, 'among so many particulars he did not know but there might be some truth', and no seventeenth-century ruler could afford to ignore assassination threats.[9] After all, in 1673 the Secretary of State, Henry Coventry, had spent a great deal of time and trouble, without result, trying to get at the truth of a supposed plot by a man called Edmund Everard to murder nobody more important than Charles's illegitimate son, Monmouth.[10] Nor did men have to threaten the King's life to bring them to the attention of a Secretary; in June 1677 Coventry was looking for one David Walker, who had said that Charles 'would live no longer than himself, being born under one planet', and in March 1678 he received information against the wife of the town gaoler at Newcastle, who amongst much else said 'that the King got the curse of many good and faithful wives such as she was for his bad examples', and if he 'went to heaven let none care what he did'.[11]

Charles was sufficiently concerned at the mere mention of assassination to grant two obscure men the privilege of at least twenty minutes' conversation with him alone: something often denied to Cabinet ministers. He now offered to turn the matter over to the Earl of Danby, Lord Treasurer and chief minister, who would interview Tonge and Kirkby, read their papers, and make further recommendations to him at Windsor, where he was going next day. It is especially significant that, at Tonge's request, he agreed to keep the matter from his brother. James came in as they were leaving, and inquired what was the matter. Tonge heard the King reply that 'it was a base business', but it is clear that James learnt nothing more until the end of the month.

Before he left for Windsor next morning Charles sealed up Tonge's papers and sent them round to Danby's lodgings in the Cockpit by the hand of a Gentleman of the Bedchamber, Lord Plymouth. After kicking their heels half the day in the great man's ante-room, Tonge and Kirkby got an interview with him about four o'clock. Danby's reactions are difficult to assess, but in the beginning he seems to have been favourably impressed. The manic copying and recopying which Tonge was now indulging in, and his reluctance to divulge all he knew to Kirkby, make it difficult to decide what precisely Danby was given, but it seems to have been substantially the first forty-three articles of Oates's 'Narrative', as sworn before Sir Edmund Berry Godfrey.

Oates's story had venerable antecedents; in general concept it had echoes of 'Habernfeld's Plot' in 1643, and it has been pointed out that it owed much to the Fifth Monarchy Plots of the 1660s, with Papists substituted for 'fanatics'.[12] Nor is this surprising. The 'Captain Oates' who was executed at York in 1664 for his share in a misty 'Presbyterian' Plot was almost certainly a relative of Titus Oates, just as the Fifth Monarchy man, Thomas Tonge, who was executed for a similar crime in 1662, was a relative, perhaps a brother, of Israel Tonge. His background of left-wing religious fanaticism coloured all Oates's evidence and set him off from the other informers who followed him. At St Omers he had shocked the seminarists and their teachers by the irreverent, even destructive way in which he spoke of the monarchy and the royal family; they accused him of trying to bring down the monarchy by indirect means, and there was some truth behind this theory.

On the other hand, his evidence has been too easily dismissed as obvious nonsense, and those who believed it arrant fools.* Its very incoherence and planlessness, the way accusations of high treason were thrown carelessly amongst items of trifling gossip, added to its apparent veracity; why invent what were misdemeanours at the most? It was as lucid as the subject-matter would permit, and its matter-of-factness was chilling. Most important, it gave the names and functions of scores of Jesuits of the English Province, their movements and actions; this gave it a ballast of fact which few such narratives could claim. Once it was accepted that such men would, half a dozen at a time, put their hands to letters detailing their treasonable plans, and consign their secrets to an ex-Anabaptist homosexual, then the rest followed. It must be remembered that Englishmen's hatred for the Jesuits was equalled only by their ignorance of them, and if they had behaved with astonishing folly, this was the ill-luck that attends a bad cause.

Oates's evidence opened with plans for a rebellion in Scotland, a mainstay of Nonconformist plots. But this time it was the Jesuits at work, and Oates had carried word of the plan to Valladolid in 1677. There he learned for the first time, he said, that the English Jesuits, led by Keynes and Conyers, were planning to assassinate Charles II; on 20 July Strange, William Ireland, Thomas Whitbread and four other Jesuits wrote to report the first of many misfires, 'their man Honest William† being faint-hearted'. The Jesuits of the Spanish Province at once offered £10,000 to hasten the good work, but when Oates reached London with this news in November he found that Father La Chaise, Louis XIV's confessor, had offered the same sum. Thus fortified, Strange and his colleagues decided to have the King stabbed, or if that failed, poisoned. Oates was sent with this news to St Omers, in a letter which he opened on the way, and went on to Paris to thank La Chaise on the Jesuits' behalf.

In December 1677 Thomas Whitbread succeeded Strange as

---

*Pollock gives it two pages (*Popish Plot*, pp. 11–12). Lane (pp. 91. ff.) analyses it by subject, but this destroys its impact.

† A pseudonym for the lay brother John Grove.

Provincial, and this provoked a fresh wave of activity, chiefly epistolary; Oates's Jesuits were certainly mightier with the pen than with the sword. One of Whitbread's first acts was to get twelve of his colleagues to sign a letter to St Omers announcing that they would murder James as well as Charles, 'if he should not appear to answer their expectations' – one of many statements absolving James. For instance, he also gave a circumstantial account of a conversation in the library at St Omers with Edward Nevill and Thomas Fermor, on 3 January 1678. They told him 'that they would not let this black bastard go to his grave in peace'. (Charles II was supposed to have been fathered on Henrietta Maria by 'a black Scotsman' – another 'fanatic' fantasy.)* Oates asked, 'What if the Duke should prove slippery?' and the answer was that 'his passport was ready whenever he should fail them'. In the midst of the Jesuits' busy attempts to stir up trouble for Charles with the Stadholder William III and the Emperor Leopold I came bad news from London; Pickering, one of their Benedictine allies, had tried to shoot the King in St James's Park, only to be frustrated by a loose flint in his pistol.

The next few articles descend into trivialities; denigration of Charles I, vague talk of risings in Ireland, and so on; but on 10 February, Oates continued, the Rector of St Omers abruptly wrote to Whitbread urging him to hasten his assassination plans, 'and if his Royal Highness should not comply with them, to dispatch him too'. The reply from London was that:

Although the Duke was a good Catholic, yet he had a tender affection to the King, and would scarcely be engaged in that concern, and if they should once intimate their designs and purposes to him, they might not only be frustrated of their design but also might lose his favour.

Similarly, after some discussion, it was agreed not to bring in the secular clergy, who were as sentimental as James, 'men inclined to live in peace and obedience to their prince'. However, the Jesuits pressed on alone, and it was the accidental failure of

*Art. 3. Later (Art. 20) Oates was told that Charles I was also a bastard, the son of Anne of Denmark's tailor.

several successive attempts at assassination in March – attempts so abortive that they went completely unnoticed – that led the Provincial to summon a Consult to London the following month.

This famous Consult, held on 24 April, was in fact one of the regular triennial business meetings attended by the seniors of the Province, and usually held on the Continent. Oates gave the attendance as about fifty; Whitbread later admitted it was forty. After a preliminary meeting at the White Horse Tavern in the Strand,* Oates said, they broke up into small groups, accommodated at various houses in the neighbourhood, and their deliberations lasted four days. Oates carried messages from one group to another.

Of course, there *was* a Consult in London at that time, but it was held in the Duke of York's apartments at Whitehall. This made the Jesuits' defence much more difficult later, but the secret was well kept. Oates certainly never knew it – it would have been a pearl without price in the 'Exclusion' years of 1679 and 1680 – and he consistently minimized the Duke's part in the Plot. For instance, he goes on to say that Whitbread arrived at St Omers on 1 June, on his way to Germany, and remarked to the fathers there 'that he hoped to see the fool at Whitehall laid fast enough'; but after further pleasantries of this nature Whitbread added that 'if the Duke should set his face in the least measure to follow his brother's footsteps, his passport was made out to lay him asleep' – the same metaphor as Nevill and Fermor had used. But lesser game was in view as well, and two days later Whitbread approached Oates and asked him if he would assassinate Israel Tonge for £50, the proposal (if not the price) being an obvious sop to Tonge's vanity. There was talk at the same time of killing the brilliant young Anglican divine Edward Stillingfleet, and Matthew Poole, an erudite but harmless biblical scholar.

* Strangely enough, no proceedings were apparently taken against the proprietress, who even appeared to give evidence on behalf of the Jesuits' lawyer, Langhorn (14 June 1679, *S. T.*, vii, 463–4, and p. 187 below). The House of Lords ordered Scroggs to interrogate her on 1 December 1678 (*L.J.*, xiii, 331), but nothing seems to have come of it.

At this stage, in real life, Whitbread ordered Oates's expulsion from St Omers; but in the imaginary world of the 'evidence' he was ordered express to London on 13 June, taking only two days over an action-packed journey. But it is significant that he does not give the reason for his mission. In fact, cast off by Catholics and Protestants alike, he was living in lonely poverty, so the last eleven of these first forty-three Articles are certainly invention. According to them, he learned when he reached Jesuit head-quarters in London that Sir George Wakeman was to poison the King, and Whitbread had already sent over his fee of £10,000, presumably from La Chaise. (Rather incongruously, he also found that the Jesuits were plotting the assassination of Herbert Croft, Bishop of Hereford, 'a forward man against the Cath-olics', but hardly a man of prime importance.) To pad things out he included a long conversation with Richard Strange (Article 34) in which the ex-Provincial described in detail how he and his Fifth Monarchist allies had fired London in 1666, in-formation undoubtedly deriving from Tonge, who was an auth-ority on the Fire. Meanwhile Father Richard Ashby, who was in charge of the Scottish sector, retired to Bath to nurse his gout and at the same time alert the Jesuit mission in Somerset.

Ashby's visit to Bath was to acquire new importance when it came to building up a case against Wakeman, but as it stood it was tame stuff. So Oates took advantage of Whitbread's con-tinued absence in Germany to bring in more incriminating letters. On 4 August he caught a glimpse of a letter from Whit-bread to the Jesuit John Fenwick, authorizing him to offer Wakeman £15,000 if he balked at £10,000, and on the 19th a further letter urged them to get Wakeman moving as soon as possible. A few days later came another letter, even more im-prudent, in which Whitbread said that 'if poison would not take the King away, fire should', and hinted broadly at the burning of Westminster and Whitehall.

But by now Oates was really scraping the bottom of the barrel, and he closed with a rag, tag and bobtail of information; Jesuits off to Scotland disguised as Dissenting ministers to stir the people to revolt, and some stale hearsay stuff about a 'commotion' the Jesuits were going to raise in England and Wales, vaguely hooked to some letters which Oates could not date with his usual precision – 'in August', he thought. But he was precise about the Jesuits' wealth; he credited them with capital of £100,000, presumably in land, and an income from all sources of £60,000 a year. Of course, this was wildly imaginary; the income of the English province was nearer £6,000 than £60,000*; but it set the government off on a long wild-goose chase, and helped bring the Jesuits' lawyer, Richard Langhorn, to the gallows.

Danby's reaction to this was much the same as Charles's. Contemporaries assumed that the Lord Treasurer encouraged Tonge, whom he knew to be mad, so as to seize a tactical advantage when Parliament met. There is some truth in this. But in any case no officer of state could possibly have ignored such a document; indeed, whatever verbal message he may have sent by Lord Plymouth, Charles's action in referring the matter to him left Danby with little choice.

Of course, there was insufficient material for a prosecution, even an arrest, and Danby agreed that Tonge's informant should remain anonymous while he tried to dig out more information. This information was to be sent to Danby as it came in, and so as not to arouse suspicion Danby lent him one of his servants, Lloyd, as a link man.

The first requisite was to identify and shadow the Jesuits who were potential assassins – Keynes, Conyers, Pickering and Grove. But Tonge did not know any of them by sight, and Oates dared not reveal that he was not still on good terms with them. So Oates lay low, under plea of security, and tried to direct Tonge, Kirkby and Lloyd by letters left in a prearranged hiding-place. After many farcical manoeuvres, Keynes and Conyers were identified, and either Tonge or Kirkby even made a clumsy approach to them. It is perhaps significant that these two were the only leading Jesuits who escaped.

* Figures are difficult to come by, but in 1645 the income of the Province, on the Continent as well as in England, was £3,915 (Guilday, p. 156).

Meanwhile from day to day Oates was feeding Tonge, and indirectly Danby, with further false information which was to form the second part of his 'Narrative'.* Danby went to Windsor at intervals, and may have shown some of it to the King. Oates was alert for any suggestions, and as soon as Danby remarked that 'Coleman must needs be busy in the plot if any were' Coleman duly appeared.[13] Charles was kept informed of the more important developments, but Danby could not get enough hard evidence to justify even a search warrant. To remedy this, he suggested to Tonge that the Jesuits' correspondence be intercepted at the Post Office. This called Oates's bluff, and in desperation he or Tonge or both of them forged five wildly incriminating letters to Thomas Bedingfield, the Duke of York's Jesuit Confessor, and sent them to him at Windsor on 31 August. (Apparently Bedingfield was chosen simply because he was the only Jesuit whom they definitely knew had left town with the Court.) Danby was warned, and they should have been intercepted in London, but his creatures in the Post Office let him down. Bedingfield received the letters on 1 September, and found their form and content so sinister that he at once showed them to James.

This is not surprising. Four of them purported to be from Whitbread, Ireland, Fenwick and Blundell, another Jesuit, though they were not in their handwriting, of course, nor anything like it. The other purported to be from William Fogarty, who had the ill-luck to be Oates's doctor; it is unlikely that Bedingfield even knew him. Being framed so as to confirm Oates's story in a general way, without going into detail, they were oracular and threatening to a degree; also they were barely literate, and even Bedingfield's name was misspelt![14] But the fact that they were obvious forgeries only strengthened James's determination to get to the bottom of the matter, and on the face of it he was right. They were intended to incriminate the recipient, and whoever harmed his confessor harmed him. At this stage James was still ignorant of Tonge's revelations to the

*Arts. 44–76 correspond to the rough notes made by Tonge for Danby in S.P. 29/409, 49 ff.

King, but if he had been aware of them it could only have confirmed his desire to have the whole matter thoroughly ventilated before the Privy Council.

But Charles appreciated, as James did not, that whatever the outcome of a Council investigation it could not be to the advantage of the Catholics. He probably suspected that Tonge was mad (if he had consulted his Secretary of State, Williamson, he would have confirmed this); it was even doubtful whether his anonymous informant existed. Moreover, the Council could not proceed on mere copies of documents made by Tonge, and Danby, perhaps acting on Charles's instructions, continued to press for hard evidence. Also, prompted by Tonge, he ordered the interception of any further suspicious letters in the London post house, but with no result whatsover, and Tonge, who had not seen Oates for two or three weeks, grew desperate. However, on 2 September Oates came to one of Tonge's services at St Mary Overy and was immediately grabbed. Tonge took him back to Kirkby's house at Vauxhall, and though Oates returned to London next day Tonge now knew where he was to be found.

By this time Oates was rattled. When he made up his tale to ingratiate himself with Tonge he never expected it to go up to the King and the Lord Treasurer. Meeting his old schoolmaster William Smith a day or two later, he asked him for a crib to some Latin verses on the Saviour and the Virgin Mary, saying he was hoping to get a post as a tutor to a Catholic family.[18] However, on or about 4 September something happened which severed Oates's last weak connection with the Jesuits, and indeed the Catholics in general. His story that Whitbread sent for him and beat him, accusing him of having betrayed the Society, can be discounted – he was simply not in touch with the Provincial at all, who was in any case gravely ill on his return from Europe. But by this time Keynes and Conyers had been warned indirectly, and one of Danby's servants may have leaked the secret, too. Oates may have received threats, and his tale of going in fear of his life from then on may have had some slight foundation of truth. It is noticeable that right up to 4 September he had been markedly evasive with Tonge, almost playing fast and loose with him; then he suddenly agreed to give up his London lodgings and return to Vauxhall, and on the 6th he took the decisive step of swearing to the first part of his evidence before a Justice of the Peace. The next three weeks he spent copying and recopying the second part.

Of course, the decision to go to a Justice of the Peace was fraught with significance for the future. The subsequent murder of that Justice, Sir Edmund Berry Godfrey, casts a retrospective shadow.* But Tonge's motive was quite straightforward and he explained it to the Privy Council later.[16] In going to the King and Danby he had put himself out on a limb, and Oates's recent conduct led him to fear that he would renege, leaving him to face ridicule and perhaps, with James on the warpath, worse. But if Oates could be made to swear to it all before a magistrate Tonge would be protected, and in his new mood of docility Oates was nothing loath.

Tonge's first thought, on the evening of the 4th, was Sir Joseph Williamson, after the Lord Chancellor the premier magistrate in England. But Williamson was out, and when Tonge went round next morning he met with 'a rude repulse'. Williamson knew him, and thought him mad.[17]

According to Tonge's own account,[17] he was now at a loss, since he did not know any other J.P. in the area (the implication being that he did not know one well enough to trust him). He therefore 'advised with some very honourable friends', who 'after some consideration' recommended Godfrey. Who these friends were we do not know, but if they were friends of Tonge's they can hardly have been pro-Catholic. Yet Godfrey had many Catholic friends, including Edward Coleman, which lent colour to the later story that he took Oates's narrative straight to Coleman, who took it to James. In any event, it was a strange choice.

It was Tonge's misfortune always to make simple matters complicated, and when approached Godfrey at once made difficulties. Yet it was only reasonable that he should; he was being asked to take a deposition containing the most serious allega-

*See Appendix A, p. 302 below.

tions of high treason, with only Tonge's verbal assurance that the matter had been reported to the King. There were earnest discussions between Tonge and Godfrey before he consented to see him and Oates next day, 6 September.

What Oates swore to is not entirely clear; certainly the first forty-three articles, plus other 'information' gathered since, but not yet assembled in its final form.* It was not expected of Godfrey that he should read it all, for it was accompanied by an affidavit which stated that all the matters contained therein were treasons or felonies. Godfrey asked what the felonies were, and Tonge airily replied, 'Firing houses and towns'. Under this broad heading they discussed the fire at Southwark in 1676, which Oates attributed to the Jesuit lay brother Grove. Godfrey said he knew Grove well, and he had been active in suppressing that fire, but despite this difference of opinion they parted on good terms, and Oates returned to his old lodgings. However, it was now time to be done with the Jesuits, and later that day he took refuge with Tonge, at the Flying Horse in the Strand, on the grounds that he had overheard Whitbread and Mico conspiring to kidnap him. A day or two later he fled to Vauxhall for good.

Meanwhile Charles was so irritated by the incident of the forged letters that he refused to have anything further to do with the matter. Kirkby went to Windsor on 6 September, and stayed overnight, but Danby refused even to speak to him. On the 9th Tonge managed to see Danby in London, but he too was rebuffed. On the same day Kirkby saw the King, but had the same treatment. Tonge's last hope was Henry Compton, Bishop of London, an old acquaintance of his, but he was absent on a visitation in Essex. Compton returned to town on the 13th, at the same time as Danby, and Tonge's journal records a whole series of apparently fruitless visits to both, on the 14th, 16th, 17th and 19th. At last Tonge had a meeting with Compton and Danby together, on the 20th. This time he had a further shred of proof. On the 18th there had been a fire at Limehouse Hole which had been forecast, though very vaguely, by Oates in the deposition submitted to Godfrey a fortnight before.[18]

* See, however, the footnote to p. 304 below.

On the 21st Danby rejoined Charles at Windsor, and the next day the Privy Council decided that the coming session of Parliament should be postponed from 1 to 21 October because of the situation in Europe. Danby was still cautious, and Tonge noted that he and Compton 'did both observe a prudent reservedness, and show little countenance either in the Privy Council or other public place'.[19] On 24 or 25 September Tonge turned in desperation to Gilbert Burnet, a young Scots clergyman in good standing at Court and firm on the subject of popery. Burnet was 'amazed' at his revelations; at first he thought he was insane, then he suspected a plot to implicate him in misprision of treason. But when he sent a friend to Williamson's office, the reply was that they knew all about it, and Tonge was just after a deanery. Burnet's friends in Parliament dismissed it as another trick of Danby's, though Halifax did remark that 'considering the suspicions all people had of the Duke's religion, he believed every discovery of that sort would raise a flame, which the Court would not be able to manage'.[20]

However, it seems to have been James himself who now persuaded the King that the matter must come before the Council before he left for the autumn meeting at Newmarket on 28 September; when he returned there would be little time left before the assembly of Parliament. The matter was broached at a meeting of the Committee for Foreign Affairs* on the evening of the 27th. Tonge was sent for, but by the time he arrived the committee had risen, having referred the matter to a special meeting of Council next morning, Saturday the 28th.[21]

On the Friday Tonge had sent Danby an affidavit calling for the arrest of the leading Jesuits, and with it the final version of Oates's deposition, the original forty-three articles having now been extended to eighty-one. The thirty-eight new articles covered Oates's activities in London in August and September – or his peculiar version of them – and with accustomed inconsequentiality they opened with an account of an intelligence agent

---

*The most confidential committee of Council, the ancestor of the Cabinet. It usually comprised the King, the Lord Chancellor, the Lord Privy Seal, the Lord Treasurer and the two Secretaries of State.

for the Jesuits called John Smith, 'who daily lurked about Whitehall, and in Parliament time about Westminster Hall and the lobby' in search of confidential information.

Oates had to be very careful from now on not to say anything which might be disproved, for he was dealing with events in London. He used an imaginary letter from Whitbread on 9 August to incriminate Wakeman a little further; the Provincial wrote that Wakeman was now definitely engaged, though this did not mean that Pickering and Grove should abandon their plan to shoot the King. There was much loose talk about Charles I's bastardy, about the Southwark Fire in 1676, about killing dissident priests; and on the 11th letters from St Omers spoke of the assassination of the Duke of Ormonde in Dublin and risings in Scotland and Ireland. The Jesuits talked freely of their plans for a Catholic England, and one of them remarked that by Christmas 'one that was a Catholic should play such a game as never was played since the Conquest'. When Oates asked what they meant, Fenwick replied, 'The Duke of York' – which was as near as Oates came to incriminating James.

Several more articles were little more than gossip and chat, but Oates took the opportunity to incriminate his old friend Matthew Medburne, and the other Catholics who frequented the club at Fullers' Rents. Clearly this reflects some recent quarrel, but his account of the 'treasonable and detestable' words spoken there from time to time may have some truth in it. By this time it was 13 August, and the assassins were completing their arrangements at Windsor, where the King now was; Keynes and Fenwick had reached the stage of going round telling their friends to leave London, lest God destroy them 'with the sins of that city'. In fact for men engaged in a desperate mission the Jesuits seemed strangely reluctant to come to the point, but Oates could use the delay to good effect, to drag in the London Benedictines, who had a house in the Savoy. Hitherto the only Benedictine involved was Pickering, who had turned Oates away that summer when he came round begging. It had been enough to give him a leading role in the plot. On 17 August, according to Oates, the Prior, Fr Howard, came to see

Keynes and offered him £6,000 to further the great work. However expressed doubts as to whether it was wise to kill Charles unless his brother and successor was prepared to absolve them:

To which the said Keynes replied that the Duke was not the strength of their trust, for that they had another way to effect the setting up of the Catholic religion; for when they had destroyed the King they had a list of 20,000 Catholics in London, that were substantial persons and fit for arms, that would rise in twenty-four hours and less; and if James did not comply with them to the pot he must go also.

This not only served to clear James, it was the only indication in all these articles how the actual rebellion, as distinct from the assassination, was to be effected.

After the Benedictines the Dominicans came in, or all those that Oates happened to know by name, and further news arrived from Dublin of Ormonde's impending assassination, which was to be planned and directed by Fogarty. But Fogarty was also interested in Charles's assassination, and on 22 August, irritated by all the delays, he offered the Jesuits four unnamed 'Irish ruffians' who would do the job. They were given their expenses and sent off to Windsor. Fogarty happened to mention to Oates about now that Edward Coleman had been present when Wakeman had agreed to poison the King; but at this stage, there was no suggestion that Coleman had agreed to it, or that he had anything to do with Fogarty's ruffians – that was to be an afterthought. Oates was now cramming in anyone he could think of; for instance, he threw in the information that Charles's ambassador to Madrid, Sir William Godolphin, was a convert to Rome, and in league with one Heirom Swiman, who held the mysterious title of 'Procurator for the Jesuits of the Kingdoms of England and Ireland'.

From then on Oates provided what was almost a day-to-day diary. On 22 August Fenwick left for St Omers with a party of new boys he was taking over, but before he left he showed Oates a letter he had written to Bedingfield, and others addressed to the same person. These were the notorious forged letters, of course. That evening, strolling in Gray's Inn Walks, he was surprised to run into Conyers, whom he had thought in Windsor. Conyers told him he was held up because his horse was lame, and if Oates thought it strange that a Society which had an income of £60,000 a year should be short of a horse he did not say so. When he asked him how he proposed to kill the King Conyers showed him 'a dagger, or knife, two-edged with a very sharp point; and it was broader and broader towards the haft, which was of buckthorn, and was a foot long in the blade, and near half a foot in the haft'; he had bought it specially, he said, from an old cutler in Russell Street. Oates asked him how he would get away afterwards, to which he replied that he 'doubted not to obtain a pardon, if he were not knocked on the head upon the place'.

From Gray's Inn Oates went on to meet Tonge for a drink at the King's Head Tavern, and coming away about nine he ran into Blundell with a bag full of fire-balls. A few days later, on 30 August, Blundell explained in great detail how he and his accomplices were going to set fire to London, beginning at Bugbies Hole, or Limehouse Hole, in Wapping, where in fact a fire did break out early in September. Blundell also showed him a papal bull, dated the previous November or December, in which the English sees were all allotted to various Roman priests, beginning with Cardinal Howard as Archbishop of Canterbury, and the Benedictine James Corker as Bishop of London. On 2 September he saw various letters bearing on the conspiracy in Scotland, which was going well.

But the next confidential letter Oates saw was his last. It was from Whitbread, who was now 'somewhere in England', and had written urgently to Blundell warning him that their plans had been betrayed to the King. (In fact, Whitbread had gone straight to the Spanish ambassador's at Wild House, seriously ill.) However, according to Oates Whitbread reached London from the country late in the evening of 3 September, and sent for him early next morning. He then accused him of betraying the Society and administered corporal punishment on the spot. (A strange episode, this, and it clearly reflects Oates's private fantasies.) Amazingly enough, these bloodthirsty and reckless men were not prepared to kill him on the spot; instead they proposed to send him back to St Omers as soon as possible. But he overheard them planning to torture a confession from him as soon as he was safely out of the country, and when he made a brief visit to his old lodgings late the following day, 7 September, several friendly Catholics warned him that the Jesuits were looking for him. Notwithstanding this, he decided to stay the night, only to be terrified out of his wits by an attempt to assassinate him (in fact, a rowdy brawl involving some entirely innocent but very drunken fellow-lodgers). Next day he fled to the protection of Tonge and Kirkby, and there his narrative ends.

This is what Danby put before the Foreign Affairs Committee on 27 September, but there was only one copy, and no one seems to have sat down and perused it overnight. Tonge rose early next day and took Oates down to see Godfrey again, where he swore to the truth of all eighty-one articles. Tonge feared the Council would turn against him, and he had good reason; he had written Danby a highly injudicious letter requesting that Secretary Williamson and Lord Chancellor Finch be excluded from the investigation because of their hostility to him, their partiality to the Catholics, or both, and Danby had put this before the Committee, too. The King opened the proceedings at ten with a brief account of his dealings with Tonge so far, after which Williamson presented the Bedingfield letters. These 'being looked upon, and examined by several of the lords, the writing in most of them seemed to be forced, and by the ill-spelling of names, and other suspicious marks, [it was] thought to be a counterfeit matter'.[22]

At this inauspicious moment Tonge was brought in. He was well known to many present and 'altogether smiled at', but in any case he proved a most unsatisfactory witness. After importuning Danby for six weeks to bring the matter before the Council, he now had the gall to say that 'he was sorry the affair was disclosed so soon, and that it would have been much better, and more would have been discovered, if the business had been kept concealed some time longer'.[23] Several councillors asked him for a digest of the very complicated material before them, but he replied that he could not give it without unavoidable distortion. He then named Oates, and it was decided to adjourn until the afternoon and send for him.[24]

The King then left for Newmarket, with his son the Duke of Monmouth, and the Earl of Ossory and Lord Berkeley. They were all absent in the afternoon, and so was the Lord Privy Seal, Anglesey. However, the Bishop of Durham and two other councillors who had not been present in the morning (the Earls of Strafford and Oxford) did turn up in the afternoon, and the fact that Tonge was offered an apartment in Whitehall suggests that the King and the rest of the Council were not so indifferent as they seemed.

In the afternoon James made a statement about Bedingfield's receipt of the forged letters; then he left to join his brother at Newmarket. He must have been furious at being kept in the dark so long.[25] Then came Titus Oates.

Oates's performance was masterly. He found the Council in some confusion. In the chair was Prince Rupert, the King's cousin, an ageing man of action racked by syphilis, and never noted for subtlety of thought or ratiocinative powers when fit. Of the ministers present, Danby was willing to be convinced, and if the Lord Chancellor, Heneage Finch, had doubts he did not air them; the Duke of Lauderdale, High Commissioner for Scotland and another rather seedy man of action, impatient of debate, was fiercely prejudiced against Rome. The Chancellor of Exchequer, Sir John Ernle, was very much a junior minister. This left Williamson, the Secretary of State, who had already shown himself sceptical; but he was the only minister who was, and the two clerics present, Sancroft, Archbishop of Canterbury, and Crewe, Bishop of Durham, were both weak men, principally anxious to vote with the majority. With them sat seven rather undistinguished peers. Two of them, Craven and Oxford, were professional soldiers; the rest had no experience of government except at the Council Board itself.

This weak and heterogeneous body had before them Oates's

eighty-one articles, which in longhand must have covered thirty or forty pages and would have taken a quick-witted man an hour or two to master. In fact, there was only one copy, which had been handed to Williamson the night before 'rolled up'; it is doubtful if he had unrolled it before the morning, and the King's brief introductory speech had not been of much help. We have seen them in the morning almost pleading with Tonge to give them a verbal summary, or at least put the contents of these papers in some sort of logical order.

To this confused body of men Oates came almost as a saviour. First he insisted on taking an oath, braving any subsequent prosecution for swearing false information. Then he launched on a fairly full summary of his deposition, referring specifically to certain articles from time to time, and submitting to questioning as he went along.* (Perhaps the loose sheets were passed around the Board, or the clerks read out certain sections of them.) From the start the Council was impressed by the fact that his oral testimony, delivered without notes, coincided so exactly, even in names, dates and places, with the written deposition before them; they did not allow for the fact that he had been copying and recopying it for weeks. Also, in this deposition there was a strong basis of what might be called neutral fact; the Jesuits he named did exist, and he knew most of them; usually they had been at the places he named at the relevant dates. The club at Fullers' Rents did exist, so did the White Horse Tavern and a score of other places. He had been to Valladolid, and he had been to St Omers. In almost every instance he could produce circumstantial details which added colour and plausibility to his narration. For instance, the cutler in Russell Street, who had sold Conyers his assassin's dagger, now emerged as 'an old papist named Wood', and it did not take the Council long to confirm his existence. The fact that when the man did appear

---

* The brief account in the Council Register, P.C.2/66,393, is supplemented by Williamson's notes, *C.S.P.D. 1678*, p. 427. These notes confirm the supposition that Williamson had not read the deposition, because many of them are verbatim reproduction of certain passages, no doubt taken down while Oates was speaking.

before them days later he stoutly denied the whole affair and produced proof that he was a Protestant scarcely mattered.[26]

One of his excursions was to have far-reaching results. In his deposition Edward Coleman was only mentioned twice, and in the first instance only incidentally, as one who supplied the informer Smith with Court news. According to Fogarty he had also been present when Wakeman agreed to poison the King.* But this was very indirect, and useless as evidence. Oates was now questioned hard about Coleman and Wakeman, presumably because of all those accused they were nearest the royal family, and under cross-examination he added that Coleman was a friend of La Chaise's and the money sent by the French Jesuit to bribe Wakeman had passed through his hands.[27]

Sir Robert Southwell, the Clerk-in-waiting, thought the issue was still in the balance:

> It went on for two or three hours very doubtful to his credit, though the Board, in a question of the King's safety, and to see his prodigious memory, confidence and unexpected answers at several turns, were in great pain and surprise.

The turning-point came at the weakest point in Oates's evidence, the forged letters to Bedingfield.

> At last [wrote Southwell] thinking to confuse him by the said five letters, which contained such palpable matters of forgery as well from the treason so grossly disguised in them as from the handwriting all appearing to be counterfeit, I was commanded there in their Lordships' view to show him those letters one by one, to see if he knew the hands. Which I did as much to his disadvantage as I could, by folding and exposing only a line or two of each; but he at a glance could name all the hands.[28]

Nothing would have been easier if he had composed and written them all. But this was the Privy Council; the letters were addressed to the King's brother's confessor; would a penniless renegade clergyman have the nerve to make the whole thing up? Their doubts were set at rest by the next exchange. When it

* And this has almost certainly been included after a hint from Danby. See p. 68 above.

was pointed out to him that the writing bore no resemblance to these men's usual hands, Oates replied with his usual assurance that the Jesuits commonly wrote a disguised hand. This simple answer, still compatible with Oates having written the lot, was a turning-point — according to Southwell, 'this very thing took like fire, so that what he said afterwards had credit'. The Council was 'amazed', and 'strangely perplexed'. 'They were very much changed in their opinion, and began to apprehend that there was some danger and mischief contrived against His Majesty.'[29] Warrants were issued for the arrest of Fogarty, Grove, Pickering, Conyers and Fenwick — that is, those directly concerned in the projected assassination of the King at Windsor — and they were all rounded up that night, with the exception of Conyers, who escaped and was never taken. Oates joined Tonge in Whitehall Palace, and an urgent message was sent to the King, asking him to return for an emergency meeting next day, Sunday, the 29th. Sir George Wakeman was also summoned.

At this meeting, held in the afternoon, Charles resumed the chair, and Williamson's notes suggest that Oates was questioned rather more rigorously than before. He now mentioned Lord Belasyse and Lord Arundell, perhaps in response to the reasonable inquiry, how was the whole country to be subdued after his assassination? Charles told him at once that he could not accept accusations against loyal subjects like these 'unless the proofs against them were very clear', to which Oates hastily replied, 'he did not say they knew it, but were to be acquainted with it' — though four weeks later he was to 'remember' that they had accepted commissions from the Pope. Any improvisation on his written articles was dangerous, as he discovered when he casually mentioned that he had met Don John of Austria at Madrid. Charles asked him to describe him, but his description differed markedly from the King's remembrance of Don John. Oates could have pointed out that it was twenty years since the King had met Don John, but he replied instead 'that it was one they called Don John, and he could say no more than as he was told'. Similarly, he was caught out on the topography of Paris, where he had never been, and he found it difficult to explain why he spelt La Chaise's name 'LeShee', though he had carried letters addressed to him.[30] Still, warrants were issued for the arrest of Whitbread, Keynes and six other Jesuits, together with the mysterious John Smith.

Naturally he was again pressed hard on the involvement of Coleman, Wakeman and the Duke of York. On the two latter he stuck to his written deposition, which exonerated the one and contained no definite evidence against the other. But on Coleman he was willing to elaborate; this was safer game; and he

testified much touching the activity and concern of Mr Coleman in these matters, and particularly of his corresponding with Mr La Chaise, confessor of the French King, and that if his papers were well looked into there would appear that which might cost him his neck.[31]

This was an amazingly lucky shot, but it can have been no more than that; for if Oates had had an inkling of what Coleman's papers did in fact contain he would surely have given him more prominence in his deposition. Events were to show that he did not even know him. Of course, Oates was playing for time; he hoped that if enough of the Jesuits' papers were seized some evidence would come to light which could be twisted his way. He had a narrow escape, for apart from Coleman's letters the government drew a blank; hundredweights of paper were found in the Jesuits' lodgings, but only one or two items could be used in evidence against them.

The Council gave orders for Coleman's papers to be seized, and then adjourned. That night most of the remaining Jesuits named by Oates were picked up, though Keynes and one other, named William Morgan, escaped. (It is ironic that Keynes and Conyers, according to Oates the two greatest villains, escaped scotfree.) Next morning, the 30th, with the King still in the chair, they began to examine the prisoners.

The proceedings did not go well for Oates.[32] John Smith, the Jesuits' so-called intelligence agent, hotly denied Oates's accusations, and melted back into the obscurity from which he had emerged.* William Ireland denied writing the forged letter to

* An interesting case. Why did the Council hear him first, when he was accused of a mere misdemeanour, instead of proceeding with its other

Bedingfield, he sneered at its illiteracy, and wrote out a specimen of his own handwriting. Oates retorted that the illiteracy was deliberate, and all the Jesuits could disguise their writing 'with a great deal of art'. Ireland then produced an alibi for 3 August, when he was supposed to have been plotting in London; it involved Lord Aston and another very respectable Staffordshire Catholic, Sir John Southcote. (He had been arrested at Southcote's London house.) At this stage Oates retired for a few hours, on the plea that he had been up for two nights supervising the search for the men he had accused, and it is easy to believe that he was truly exhausted. But before they rose for dinner the Council ordered letters to be sent to the Lord Lieutenants to disarm all papists in the provinces.

When they resumed in the afternoon they found that the ripples of the Plot were spreading fast. Monmouth produced two soldiers from his regiment who testified that a certain John Wilkes of Romford had told them that Lord Petre had offered to pay all his debts if he turned Catholic, and that he had arms for three hundred men 'lodged in a vault'. The matter was not pursued.

John Fenwick was then examined. He denied Oates's accusations of treason, but had to admit to the truth of several comparatively innocent episodes in his deposition. Next came Doctor Fogarty, who admitted that he had the misfortune to be Oates's physician, but denied the rest. A Lieutenant Stevens – perhaps from Monmouth's regiment again – testified to hearing Fogarty utter mildly seditious words – probably true enough.* Then came another interruption; the lawyer William Williams (to be Speaker in 1680, and Solicitor-General to James II) reported a man called Netterville for talking sedition in St James's Park the previous afternoon – 'that the Parliament men were a company of fellows that voted for bread', and much more. Netterville followed Williams to the Council Chamber, had a dispute with

---

prisoners charged with treason? This, and the failure to proceed further against him, suggests that he had powerful friends.

* Watching a troop of guards go by, he had exclaimed, 'There go our masters! Will these times never change?' (P.C.2/66,404).

him outside, and was hustled in. There 'he used some very undecent expressions towards the King' and was sent to cool his heels in Newgate, with the ominous annotation that he was 'under an ill name, for a very insolent and liberal talker in state matters'.

By this time the proceedings had become almost clownish, but Oates's return, and the entry of Fr Thomas Jenison, restored sobriety. Jenison was a comparatively young man, a convert, and he seems to have been the first to turn on Oates — 'with passion, crying out, what is this fellow, that brings in question the lives of so many men?' Confusing him with his father, he accused him of being a former chaplain of Okey, the regicide major-general, and he concluded with 'other passionate words of warning to the Board, and particularly the Lord Chancellor, to take care how they did proceed, for all must be answered at the day of judgement'.

Then came Wakeman. He was still the Queen's physician, the King was watching, and he was not in custody. The Board handled him with care, telling him

that although there were no charges that could be particularly laid home by proof against him, yet 'twas his misfortune to be named in a very unhappy circumstance and 'twas wished there might be no fire where there appeared smoke.

But Wakeman was bullish. First he demanded to see his accuser. He then gave the Board a résumé of his past life, one of unstinted loyalty to the House of Stuart, asked them if this was compatible with the atrocious crime of which he was accused, then demanded reparation. They were all taken aback. 'It was insinuated to him that he ought with more concern to express his innocence, and detestation of the matter in question, but he withdrew.'

He was followed by Coleman, another voluntary witness. He too faced up to the Council with great boldness, and at the same time displayed that levity of mind which was to bring him to the gallows. He was much too conceited to deny any connection with an illustrious man like La Chaise, though he insisted it was just a casual acquaintance. He admitted, too, that he had recently been to Paris without a pass, 'about the disorder that had happened about M. St Germain' – not an auspicious errand.* Then 'he was asked if he used not cyphers; he said he did, and supposed they were all taken, and if not he would send them in'. His papers had been seized the night before, and we can only assume that he had genuinely forgotten what he had written three or four years before. (Until he was shown the letters themselves, in Newgate on 28 October, he denied corresponding with La Chaise.[33])

Oates testified that he had in fact carried letters from Coleman to La Chaise, and he had been told that Coleman had also supplied five of the fifteen thousand pounds needed to bribe Wakeman† By this time the Council was tired and confused, and Coleman 'made so voluble and fair a defence, and urged so strongly his voluntary appearing to manifest his innocency, that the Board did as he requested', and committed him to the care of a messenger instead of sending him to Newgate with the rest.[34] Charles then departed once more for Newmarket, leaving the further investigation of the Plot to a secret committee of Council, consisting of Prince Rupert, the Lord Chancellor, Danby, the Bishop of London (who had been absent hitherto), and Henry Coventry, Secretary of State.

There was little else he could do until the evidence had been processed and he had received the opinion of the law officers on it. Before he left he had a long talk with the French ambassador, and told him frankly that 'he did not believe the accusation had any foundation in truth', and Oates was 'a wicked man'. But it must be investigated thoroughly and 'with great circumspection' if they were to arrive at the truth, especially in view of the fact that Parliament was about to sit. As Sir Robert Southwell remarked, 'What should herein be omitted at the Council Board will infallibly be taken up at the House of Commons.'[35]

* See p. 42 above.

† Oates did not recognize Coleman, but *at this stage* this did not matter; he had not claimed that he knew him personally. So those who build this up into an occasion of high drama (e.g. Lane, p. 114) are exercising their imagination to no purpose. Exactly the same considerations apply to Wakeman.

Oates's antecedents and character were an obvious bar to belief. Charles commented dourly on the fact that he had changed his religion twice, and James dismissed him as '*un scélérat*'. Henry Coventry, who saw him for the first time on 30 September, commented:

> If he be a liar he is the greatest and adroitest I ever saw, and yet it is a stupendous thing to think what vast concerns are like to depend on the evidence of one young man who hath twice changed his religion – if he be now a Protestant.[96]

But Oates himself was cock-a-hoop, and had no thoughts of failure now. Burnet was revolted by him when he met him at Whitehall a day or two later: 'He broke out in great fury against the Jesuits, and said he would have their blood.' As for Tonge, he was 'so lifted up that he seemed to have lost the little sense he had.' John Evelyn, who also waited on this precious pair, thought Oates 'a bold man, and in my thoughts furiously indiscreet'.[37]

However, the case against the prisoners could never go to a court of law in its present state. Even in the seventeenth century men could not be convicted of treason on the evidence of one witness, and much of that evidence hearsay. The only other evidence at present forthcoming were the letters to Bedingfield, and whatever the Council on reflection thought of their authenticity they came too near the Duke of York for the government's liking. Another witness might come forward; the Jesuits had been careless enough with Oates to encourage that hope; but the Council's main expectations rested on the wealth of documents now in their possession, including all the account books and papers of the English Province, discovered in Ireland's lodgings.* Southwell had had to buy a new iron chest weighing 356 pounds to hold them all, and Henry Coventry was sure 'there

---

*Foley, vi, 395. They have disappeared, with virtually all the other Council papers for the seventeenth century; perhaps in the Whitehall fire of 1698. Fenwick's papers were retained by Sir George Treby (see *H.M.C. Fitzherbert*, pp. 115–17), and Grove's were so innocuous that they were returned to him.

will be many things appear that will administer matter for noise'.[38] But he was disappointed. As the Lord Chancellor caustically remarked a few days later:

Amongst the many bags of papers that have been seized there doth not appear one line relating to this matter; so that all depends upon what one witness will swear he saw, or heard read, without any concurrent circumstance to confirm his testimony.[39]

The only fact which emerged was that Richard Langhorn, a wealthy Catholic lawyer practising in London, had been the Jesuits' attorney and steward in England, and on 4 October the Secret Committee accordingly dispatched him to Newgate, though there was no evidence of treason against him.

But the Committee was shocked by what it found in Coleman's papers — 'Little as to the present question,' Coventry told the King,

But so much presumption in treating with the Most Christian King's Confessor and Ministers for the altering of Religion and Government, with such characters upon your Majesty's Royal Person, his Royal Highness and all your Ministers, that I believe never any age produced a man placed in no higher a post than he is, nor of so indifferent quality, that had the confidence to adventure on so many extravagant crimes at one time, nor so little care as to leave such papers to be seized after so fair a warning.

As soon as Charles returned from Newmarket on 16 October the Lord Chancellor gave a more considered report, in which he declared that many of the letters were clearly treasonable. Coleman was at once removed from the messenger's custody and sent to Newgate.[40]

But as for the Jesuits, although the evidence against them 'was set off to its utmost advantage', Charles, who 'had judgement to penetrate', was not impressed. Moreover, he had probably seen a paper by the Lord Chancellor which is not reported in the Privy Council Registers, with the ominous heading, 'The discovery made by Oates is liable to many exceptions'. Finch shared to the full Charles's doubts about Oates's character, the feasibility of his story, and the plausibility of his actions, and like him he was convinced the letters to Bedingfield were forged.[41] Sir William Jones, the Attorney-General, was much more sanguine, but he agreed with Finch that one witness to high treason was not enough. Moreover:

His Majesty was not willing to have these men hurried off, or their blood taken in a case so improbable; and because if without more circumstance they were left to the mercy of a jury he foresaw what must happen.[42]

The Council was now at a stand; with Parliament due to meet in three days it was important that the government seem to be prosecuting the plotters with the utmost vigour, and the Committee during Charles's absence had even hoped to appoint a commission of oyer and terminer before the new session opened. Instead Charles sought the advice of the high court judges. The question was put to them whether a single witness was enough. They confirmed that it was not; 'but if one witness', they added, 'swear fully to the point, with one or more other witnesses concurring in material circumstances to the same fact, it is sufficient' – a remarkable prevision of the role William Bedloe was later to play. When asked a supplementary question, whether there was 'any evidence against these particular persons besides the single testimony of Mr Oates', they hedged, obviously unwilling to discuss the letters to Bedingfield, though they were the only independent evidence corroborating Oates's deposition. They replied that they could not answer 'otherwise than in a judicial way', but they added darkly, 'in which judicial way of proceedings many things may arise to enforce the evidence.'[43]

Finally, Sir William Jones was ordered to draw up indictments against the Jesuits in prison not later than Christmas. Here is no evidence of stampede; and the King, the Lord Chancellor and the Judges were not the only ones with doubts. But by now it was 23 October, the body of Sir Edmund Berry Godfrey had been found, and while the Council was still sitting Oates was giving evidence at the Bar of the House of Commons.

4

Godfrey's Autumn

THE magistrate to whom Oates had confided his first depositions was an unusual man; this much is clear from the patchy evidence. He was a wealthy wood and coal dealer, of Kentish gentry stock, born to a family which had a tradition of public service as Justices of the Peace. He was an intelligent and well-read man, who had travelled abroad; no doubt the later description of him as the best Justice of the Peace in England is a pious exaggeration, but certainly he was a man of repute. He was a friend of the Attorney-General and the Lord Chancellor on the one hand, and of Edward Coleman and other Court Catholics on the other. He also had some acquaintance with rising young Anglican divines like Gilbert Burnet and William Lloyd, Rector of St Martin-in-the-Fields. He was a bachelor, and a man of austere and melancholy disposition.

It is only appropriate that Godfrey's name should have been linked with Coleman's. For the murder of Godfrey, and the discovery of Coleman's letters, provided the solid basis of fact for the lies of Oates and the other informers who followed him, and made it impossible for the government to 'lay' the Plot. As Serjeant Maynard told the Commons in November:

What ground was there for Godfrey's death? Nothing, but in relation to Mr Oates' information. How many lies and stories were made, to persuade the world about it? But when the murder was discovered, the world was awakened.[1]

Godfrey left his house on the morning of 12 October, 1678. He was last seen alive that afternoon in St Martin's Lane. His body was found on the evening of the 17th in a ditch at the foot of Primrose Hill. From the start the medical evidence presented difficulties, and it still does. But it must be accepted that he had been strangled several days before, and subsequently run through with his own sword. He had been brought to Primrose Hill by covered transport, for his clothes were dry despite recent rain, and the valuables left on him showed that it was not just a common murder for gain.

The mystery of Godfrey's death has never been solved, and it is now highly unlikely that it ever will be.* But the mere fact of his death was political dynamite. Oates's story was already going the rounds, within the week he gave it to the House of Commons; it was known that he had originally made his deposition before Godfrey. A coroner's jury brought in a verdict of wilful murder by some person or persons unknown, but for this formula the popular mind substituted two words, 'The Papists!' While Godfrey's corpse was brought back for an elaborate lying-in-state which lasted ten days, London was gripped by the kind of panic not seen since 1666.

The King had returned from Newmarket at last on 16 October, and the following evening, while Godfrey's body was being dragged from the ditch on Primrose Hill and carried to the local pub, the Committee of Intelligence met to discuss the coming session of Parliament. The Council had already discussed Oates's evidence, for what it was worth, the previous day. Williamson made a gloomy note: 'What like to be the humour of the Houses, uncertain.' Next day, the 18th, James wrote to William of Orange that Godfrey's death was already 'laid against the Catholics', and even he, never the most realistic of men, feared that 'all these things happening together will cause a great flame in the Parliament'.[2]

This Parliament, which met for its eighteenth session on 21 October, was a tired jade. It had been elected in 1661, when it had been known as the Cavalier Parliament, a parliament of young men, and Charles II had fulfilled his jocular promise to keep them until they grew beards. Of course, the erosion of death and retirement had scoured away 338 of the original Members, and much of the initiative now lay with the 'patriotic'

*See Appendix A, p. 302 below, for an account of the various theories.

opposition, the Country Party, led by Lord Russell and Sir Thomas Meres in the Commons, and in the Lords by a vocal minority of ex-ministers, notably the brilliant, combative and unscrupulous Anthony Ashley Cooper, Earl of Shaftesbury; 'the false Achitophel' of Dryden's famous poem, or, in the rolling periods of the Jesuit Father Warner: *'regiae auctoritatis pestis, regiae familiae flagellum, gentis totis pernicies.'** The King could not keep this Parliament for ever – it was now approaching the record set by the Long Parliament of infamous memory – and, since 1677 at least, each session had opened and closed in tense expectation of a snap dissolution. But Charles had never quite achieved the outstanding success in war or diplomacy which would have allowed him to go to the country with any hope of improving his position, and now he had another fiasco to explain away. The European powers had made peace without him; an expensive army of twenty thousand men had been wasted; and worse still, that army was still in existence, in barefaced disregard of solemn assurances made only three months before. Parliament must regard the continuance of the Army with neurotic suspicion, yet it would jib at paying for its disbandment all over again. The government was weak, discredited, unpopular and unsuccessful, and in no state to face an internal crisis of the dimensions of the Popish Plot.

There was some virtue in making a clean breast of it, and the Lord Chancellor, in his formal opening speech to Parliament, admitted that the Peace of Nijmegen was 'very far from such a peace as his Majesty would have wished', and that:

> You find the King involved in difficulties as great, and without your assistance as insuperable, as ever any government did labour under.

His audience was waiting for more. Oates's information was supposedly confidential to the Council, but there is no record of Oates himself being sworn to secrecy; and in any case the sudden arrest of the London Jesuits, plus Richard Langhorn and

---

* 'Plague of the royal authority, scourge of the royal family, bane of the whole nation' (Warner, ii, 320).

Coleman, could not go unnoticed. As early as 1 October news-letters were going out to the provinces containing garbled but recognizable versions of Oates's evidence.[3] Moreover, the Order in Council issued on 30 September for the disarming of the papists, without reason given, was a disturbing, though not strictly accurate, indication of the government's fears.* By 17 October the authorities in Bridlington, in Yorkshire, were deeply disturbed by reports from London,

That daily carts are loaded with arms found in papists' houses and carried to the Tower, and that an absolute change of govern-ment was intended if it [the Plot] had succeeded, and that a model of that intended government was found among Coleman's papers.[4]

So the Members of both Houses expected bloodcurdling and aweful news, and they were disappointed. Lord Finch spoke oracularly, and with the prophetic accuracy of experience, but he did not mention the Plot:

There is so strange a concurrence of ill accidents at this time, that 'tis not to be wondered at if some very honest and good men begin to have troubled and thoughtful hearts; yet that which is to be in-finitely lamented is that malicious men too begin to work upon this occasion, and are in no small hopes to raise a storm that nothing shall be able to allay.

Charles was brisker, as was his wont; he did speak of 'a design' on his life by the Jesuits – 'of which I shall forbear any opinion lest I may seem to say too much or too little' – and he added casually that he intended to 'leave the matter to the Law'.[5]

This attempt to sweep the matter under the carpet was politic-ally maladroit, especially since Charles knew there was as yet no case to go to law. He may have been irritated by Danby's desire to make political capital out of the Plot; certainly he was more worried about the Army and foreign affairs; yet only the even-ing before, the Committee of Intelligence had been obliged to interrupt its deliberations to draw up a proclamation offering a

* There is every reason for regarding this as premature, and likely in itself to cause a panic. Monmouth, as Lord Lieutenant of the East Riding, waited until 8 October before issuing instructions to his Deputy Lieutenants (*C.S.P.D. 1678*, p. 451).

reward of £500 for the capture of Godfrey's murderers. The failure to mention this event, which had all London in turmoil, and the subsequent failure of any of the King's ministers to lay before Parliament the information in their possession on the Plot, obliged Parliament to go in search of information itself, and in so doing to seize the initiative. At the same time it fostered the suspicion that men in high places – notably Danby and the Duke of York – were trying to smother the investigation. In the House of Commons:

> Many of the country gentlemen were much scandalized to see none of the other side speak a word, but all the agitation of this matter left to them, though it concerned the King's security. One of them, a principal man, pressing to have the cognizance of this affair brought before them, enlarged into the rumour of other things intended, and said these could not be the doings of a little Secretary, but persons of other note, that must be inquired after.[6]

The Lords' first move was to request a day of solemn fasting and repentance. The Commons briskly agreed, but at once moved to more positive action. As soon as they returned to their own chamber after the King's Speech (for which they pointedly omitted the usual Address of Thanks) they chose a strong committee, with a Country Party majority, to consider means of providing for 'the better preservation and safety of his Majesty's person'. The first fruit of their labours was an Address asking the King to banish all papists from a radius of twenty miles round London, which went up two days later. Charles issued the desired proclamation on 30 October; but by that time the City was in a panic and chains were being placed across the streets, something not seen since 1660. The City Chamberlain, Sir Thomas Player, justified this order with the classic remark, 'He did not know but the next morning they might all rise with their throats cut.' On the 21st the Commons also appointed another committee to investigate Godfrey's murder and the Plot, the former being given, if anything, greater prominence.[7]

The Lords, meanwhile, had requested more information from the King direct. He replied by ordering the Clerks to the Council to turn over to them all the papers they had – another act of doubtful wisdom at this juncture, especially since the material was largely unsorted. On the 23rd a Lords Committee began this task, and by the 25th they had clearly decided to concentrate for the moment on Edward Coleman. But this was altogether too leisurely and oblique for an impatient House of Commons, and on the 23rd they sent for Titus Oates. After a deal of play-acting, calling for an armed guard and the like, the great man arrived, to find a credulous and admiring audience, which absorbed his lengthy narrative without demur or question. As soon as he withdrew, orders were given to arrest the Benedictines in the Savoy, and to bring in the usual panacea, a bill to exclude Catholics from both Houses. It was given its first reading there and then, and its second the next day.[8]

Then in the afternoon Oates reappeared at the bar, to make the first significant addition to his testimony. He told the House that in the summer, in London, he had seen a number of commissions which had been signed by the General of the Society of Jesus, on the authority of the Pope, appointing officers to command a popish army in England, and ministers of state in a new popish government.* Oates had either delivered these personally, or seen evidence in writing that they had been accepted; and for good measure the wealthier recipients had made substantial donations on the spot to the fund to finance the King's assassination. They were: Lord Arundell (Lord Chancellor), the Earl of Powis (Lord Treasurer), Sir William Godolphin (Lord Privy Seal), Viscount Stafford and Edward Coleman (Secretaries of State), Lord Belasyse (Captain-General), Lord Petre (Lieutenant-General), Sir Francis Ratcliffe (Major-General), John Lambert (Adjutant-General), Sir George Wakeman (Surgeon-General) and Richard Langhorn (Advocate-General). In addi-

---

* This evidence was given to the Lords on 31 October (*L.J.*, xiii, 327–8), but not to the Council previously, though in the government's papers (P.R.O.S.P. 29/409) there is a rough draft of these commissions, with one of the original drafts of the eighty-one articles. The depositions made on 23, 24, and 28 October are separated out in Rawl. MS A. 136, ff. 243–52. Oates later published an outline of them as an Appendix to his *Narrative; S.T.*, vi, 1468 ff.

tion he named some Catholic gentry who had accepted ordinary commissions in this ghost army – notably the Irish Lord Baltimore, Sir Henry Tichborne, Thomas Howard, and John Caryll of West Grinstead. But here Oates's knowledge and powers of invention began to falter – he had never moved in respectable recusant society – and he had to drag in his one-time friend Matthew Medburne, the comedian, as a rather implausible army captain, and 'one Penny', of the 'Pheasant' in Fullers' Rents, whose sister was a servant to the Queen; presumably another pathetic crony of former days who knew too much.

Who, or what, prompted Oates to this step we do not know. Tradition names Shaftesbury, but it is difficult to see what Shaftesbury had to gain by it; his prime targets were James and the Queen. It is more likely that Oates was puffed up by his excellent reception that morning, and dazed by public acclaim. He did not want to lose momentum, and he was beginning to realize that the Jesuits, plus a few laymen of the professional classes, like Wakeman and Coleman, could not possibly have taken over the whole country once Charles was killed; there had to be some sort of military backing and upper-class support. Moreover, by now he was probably aware that the Jesuits' papers had yielded scarcely any supporting evidence; perhaps with the Catholic peers he would be luckier.

The nature of the men he named strengthens this hypothesis. Why not the Duke of Norfolk, the premier Catholic peer and probably the wealthiest, or the Earl of Berkshire, another prominent member of the same family? Amongst the gentry he probably named those whom he knew or knew of, and promptings of memory caused him to reappear before the Commons on the 28th and accuse two substantial Sussex landowners, Sir William Goring and Sir John Gage; we know that by then Oates's father had come up from Hastings (in Sussex) and was often with him. On the same day something or someone also prompted him to name the King's ex-mistress, the Duchess of Mazarin, as a French spy – an accusation tactfully ignored, even by the House of Commons. But the psychotic mind of Oates is most evident in the attempt to resurrect John Lambert, the great Cromwellian general, who had been in close confinement since 1660, and whose mind had given way under the strain. His was still a name to conjure with, and the alliance of Jesuits and Cromwellians was no joke to contemporaries, but in this case Williamson soon confirmed that Lambert was still in his island prison in Plymouth Sound, that he had received no suspicious correspondence, and that he was indeed still simple-minded.[9] Though at the time this was slurred over, it was a substantial break in Oates's testimony. If he could be so absurdly wrong about one man, was he right about others?

But the Commons' first reaction was one of frenzy. The Lord Chief Justice was sent for posthaste, the doors were barred and no one allowed to leave, though by now it was well on into the evening.* In Sir William Scroggs the Commons were delighted to find at least one member of the government alive to the danger that menaced them all. He readily issued the required warrants, and the House of Lords assembled next morning to find that five of its members were already in the Gatehouse prison without their being even consulted. Three of them – Powis, Stafford and Petre – were members of the Lords Committee on the Plot.[10]

On 26 October Tonge gave evidence to the Commons on his favourite topic, the Great Fire, and when they resumed on Monday the 28th they were not surprised to be told that there were rumours of another Gunpowder Plot, and a deputation was sent off at once to search the cellars. The Lords were just as rattled; they ordered the Lord Chamberlain to remove some combustible timber stored in the old Court of Requests next door. (All this is the more comprehensible if it is remembered that the Houses formed part of the old Palace of Westminster, a crazy warren of buildings, outbuildings and cellars, many of them let out to private persons.) On 1 November both Houses neurotically appointed committees to investigate 'a noise of knocking and digging' heard between midnight and three o'clock the

---

* *C.S.P.D. 1678*, p. 480. In the seventeenth century the House sat at nine or ten in the morning and rose at dinner-time, two or three in the afternoon. Five o'clock was a late hour.

previous night in Old Palace Yard, and the Commons ordered a census of all papists living in the vicinity. It found, in fact, that the only solution was to clear all these buildings completely, and mount guards. This decided, they were then informed by Sir Christopher Wren, the King's Surveyor, that the roof of the Houses, the Lords 'readily and unanimously' agreed. There had down in the next high wind. Further excitement was generated by the discovery that a French papist called Choqueux was storing gunpowder in the next street; an excitement not substantially allayed by the discovery that he was the King's firework-maker. On 20 October a regiment of the London Militia was mobilized, and on 4 November the troops were ordered to challenge all funeral processions and search the coffins for concealed arms.[11]

On 31 October Sir Edmund Berry Godfrey was finally taken to the grave followed by an enormous procession, with seventy-two clergymen at its head. The sermon was preached by William Lloyd, to the text of 2 Samuel 3.33–4, 'Died Abner as a fool dieth ?', with sentiments that can well be left to the imagination. To protect him from assassination he was flanked by two brawny curates.* That evening Oates came to the Lords' bar to repeat the evidence he had already given to the Commons, and on his departure 'humbly desired that he might have a guard, in regard it is late, and dark, and that he goeth in danger'.[12] That same night, after listening to a reading of some of Coleman's letters borrowed from the Lords, the Commons resolved, *nem. con.*,

That upon the evidence that has already appeared to this House, that this House is of opinion that there hath been and still is a damnable and hellish plot contrived and carried on by the popish recusants for the assassinating and murdering the King, and for subverting the government, and rooting out and destroying the Protestant religion.

The following afternoon, at a conference between the two Houses, the Lords 'readily and unanimously' agreed. There had

---

* As Roger North flippantly remarked, 'Three parsons in one pulpit! Enough of itself, on a less occasion, to excite terror in the audience!' (*Examen*, p. 205). The printed version of the sermon was a best-seller; there are nine copies in the British Museum.

been some tension between them hitherto, and their committees had been wastefully and often confusingly pursuing separate investigations into the same things; also the Lords were ill pleased with the bill to exclude Catholics from Parliament, which had come up from the Commons the day before. However, they now agreed to sit morning and afternoon, and to 'suffer nothing to be wanting on their parts which may preserve a good correspondency between both Houses.'[13] The nearest precedent for such unanimity was in 1640 and 1641.

In this situation of terrible danger and confusion the King's well-known carelessness and informality were a real cause of anxiety, and on 28 October an Address from both Houses requested him to dismiss all papists from Court, paying special attention to guards and cooks; and furthermore, to restrict 'the great concourse of mean and unwarranted persons frequenting your Majesty's privy galleries and privy lodgings'. They asked that the Officers of the Household 'wait in their proper stations', and that all locks be changed, also that the doors which gave directly from the Palace on to St James's Park be walled up. Charles did not take this interference with his leisure very well, and he replied rather coolly that 'he had done most of the things already; [as for] the rest, he will do what shall be convenient'. But Parliament's requests were really common sense; the ease with which Kirkby and Tonge had been able to approach him in the Park, and even on the Privy Stairs,* showed that there was a security problem, and on 31 October Wren was ordered to put the work in hand.[14]

But concern for the King's person was also prompted by suspicion of his brother, which was accentuated, of course, by the revelation of Coleman's intrigues. 'The discovery of Coleman's papers', says Roger North, 'made as much noise in and about London, and indeed all over the nation, as if the very Cabinet of Hell had been laid open ... People's passions would not let them attend to any reason or deliberation on the matter ... so as one might have denied Christ with more content than the

* See p. 60 above.

Plot.'[15] It was fortunate that there was no time to sort through Coleman's papers thoroughly, and that many of them were in cypher, others in French, others undated. In the first week of November they were being passed to and fro between Lords and Commons, and it was not long before two of Throckmorton's letters were found to be missing. These turned up, but 'four or five bundles of letters addressed to the Duchess of York', which reached the House of Commons, have never been found since. On the other hand, the four damaging letters from the Earl of Berkshire were noticed much too late, in the third week of November; Berkshire had left for France on 19 November with a pass from the Secretary of State's office.[16] An elaborate check and double-check instituted by the Lords Committee for Examinations only increased their bewilderment, and revealed the awkward fact that Berkeley, captain of the guard which had searched Coleman's house, had been persuaded by Mrs Coleman to give up to her a large bundle of what she insisted were private papers. (Mrs Coleman, from this and other instances, was obviously a woman of considerable charm and address.) The Lords Committee was harassed, too, by the plaintive denials of James himself, who with his usual doubtful taste insisted on sitting in with them. The Commons were clamouring for instant publications, and there was also the Attorney-General, impatient to prepare his case. Meanwhile, the discovery of a new-laid pavement in Coleman's house, and the information that his sister had removed a trunkful of papers on 7 or 8 October, gave promise of even more revelations.[17]

In this hurly-burly, no exact or logical reconstruction of Coleman's activities could be attempted, but this scarcely mattered. The basic fact was that in 1674 and 1675 Coleman had been seeking money from Louis XIV and the Pope to bribe the King to dissolve Parliament; worse still, in 1675, 1676 and perhaps later, he had received French money to bribe Members of Parliament. In fact, when examined by a Commons delegation Coleman admitted as much, though he insisted he had pocketed the money.[18]

The name of the Duke was associated with most of these

intrigues, of course, and letters like this could only inflame existing suspicions:

> If we can advance the Duke's interest one step forward, we shall
> put him out of reach of all chances for ever; for he makes such a
> figure already that if he could gain any considerable new addition of
> power, all would come over to him as the only steady centre of our
> government. Then would Catholics be at ease, and his most Chris-
> tian Majesty's interest secure with us in England.[19]

James stuck to the story that Coleman was acting without his
knowledge and using his name without permission. But Coleman on his first examination by the Commons was still labouring his innocence, and he did not hesitate to admit that James
and Lord Arundell knew all his plans. This was confirmed by
two letters he had drafted for James's signature, one to La
Chaise, the other to Oliva, the General of the Jesuits. At the
crucial point these disappeared, to the general rage and suspicion, and the one to Oliva was never found.* However, in the
one to La Chaise, which *did* turn up, James firmly associated
himself with Coleman, and pledged support for the French
interest.[20] Moreover, a letter of St Germain's in August 1676
revealed that James had written to La Chaise again, and though
Coleman said he had drafted the first letter on his own initiative,
and James had rejected it – the story he gave at his trial – he
admitted that the Duke 'was acquainted with his correspondence with Ferrier and St Germain; not perhaps with every
letter, but in general', and that he was also 'acquainted with
the sum and substance' of his correspondence with the Internuncio. Asked why he had requested an interview with the
King and James, he replied 'that it was to know how he should
govern himself as to naming the Duke'.[21]

Nor was James the only prince to appear in an unflattering
light in Coleman's papers; his portrayal of Charles II savoured
strongly of *lèse-majesté*, if not worse. According to him,
Charles's debauchery had made him 'odious to all the nation

---

* The Lords Committee for Examination had it on 28 October, when
they showed it to Coleman in Newgate. Coleman said it was drafted for
the Duchess (*L.J.*, xiii, 307).

and the world'; in politics he had given so many signs of weakness that he was no longer to be trusted; and he was motivated solely by a love of the 'glistering metal'.[22] Moreover, in Coleman's correspondence with Cardinal Howard and John Leyburn, his secretary at Rome, Charles as well as James appears in the role of a good Catholic prince, son of the Pope. Charles and James order Howard to support the French interest in the Conclave of 1676, and send congratulations to Innocent XI on his election. James writes to the Pope to excuse his elder daughter's marriage to a heretic, and discusses his younger daughter's marriage to a Medici prince. James and his Duchess are gratified by a present of personal rosaries from the Pope 'with ample indulgences' – and so on.[23] When the Committee of Secrecy presented these letters to the House of Commons in May 1679 they tipped the balance in favour of Exclusion. It was also embarrassingly obvious from this Roman correspondence that Coleman was still acting as the Duke's secretary as well as his wife's as late as 1677.

Finally, what of Coleman's aims? He told the Commons that he had never intended to subvert the established religion or bring in popery; but he was tactless enough to add that

He observed every session of parliament the growth of popery complained of, notwithstanding all their endeavours against it, and believed the Catholic religion to be the true one, and the Protestant the false, and therefore only proposed a toleration, as concluding that if the Catholic religion stood upon equal ground it would prevail.

But the hysterical phraseology of his own letters told against him. In August 1674 he had told the Internuncio:

We have in agitation great designs, worth the consideration of your friends [the Pope and the Emperor], and to be supported with all their power, wherein we have no doubt but to succeed, and it may be to the utter ruin of the Protestant party.[24]

Coleman insisted that this referred to the Protestant party in Parliament, but it did not seem likely, and the following passage could admit of only one interpretation:

We have here a mighty work upon our hands [he told La Chaise]; no less than the conversion of three kingdoms, and by that perhaps the subduing of a pestilent heresy which has domineered over a greater part of this northern world a long time. There were never such hopes of success since the death of Queen Mary, as now in our days.[25]

By 10 November Coleman had come to his senses, and he told the Lords Committee:

I am ready to confess all the follies I have been guilty of concerning the state. I have already confessed that which will destroy myself.

But it was too late for him to shield James, when he had told La Chaise that the Duke was 'converted to such a degree of zeal and piety as not to regard anything in the world in comparison of God Almighty's glory, the salvation of his own soul, and the conversion of our poor kingdom'.[26] Against such terrible words not even the testimony of Titus Oates could prevail. Making the best of a bad job, Oates came to the House of Lords on 30 October at his own request, and reinforced the picture of the Duke's innocence that he had given in his original deposition; he said the Jesuits had forged James's signature and seal.[27] But this did not prevent Shaftesbury putting forward a motion three days later that the Duke be removed from his Majesty's presence and counsels; and though he would not court defeat by pressing it to a division he received an alarming amount of support, including that of two Privy Councillors and five bishops.[28]

The government capitulated at once. Next day, 3 November, despite considerable opposition from conservatives like Williamson, who cited Charles I's warning that his sons should never be separated, it was decided that James should cease to attend the Privy Council, its Committees, 'and all places where any affairs of the nation were agitated'.* On the 4th this was announced to

*H.M.C. Ormonde NS, iv 227; C.S.P.D. 1678, p. 503; Clarke, i, 524–5. The Commons put the obvious point that since James had not taken the Test he had no business on the Council anyway. His name never appears on the Registers, and he presumably attended as an observer. Coventry explained that he came to the Admiralty Board as Lord High Admiral of Scotland and Ireland, which countries were not covered by the Test Act (Grey, vi, 141).

both Houses as a voluntary act on James's part, though in fact he had taken it with a very ill grace; but it was too late to prevent Lord Russell from introducing a motion similar to Shaftesbury's in the House of Commons. Many speakers now called for James's removal from Court, or even from England – which his brother had hoped to prevent by the concession already announced. James had powerful support, but the general concern was obvious, especially in view of Coleman's letters. One sturdy squire exclaimed:

The Duke has houses in the country, and loves fox-hunting; I would have him retire to some of them, to be out of the influence of those damned Jesuits!

Others, like Sir Robert Sawyer, a Tory lawyer, put the obvious point that the Duke's religion had encouraged the Plot:

I can assign no other cause for this dismal attempt [he said] but the hopes the papists have of the Duke's religion.[29]

But back came the counter-argument, so powerful in 1680: 'If you turn the Duke thus away, you put him at the head of twenty thousand men'; and it was finally decided to adjourn the debate until Friday.

Next day was 5 November, an occasion for bonfires everywhere and hell-fire sermons in the City. But the Lords and Commons each heard a remarkably temperate sermon on the same text: 'The Son of Man is come not to destroy men's lives, but to save them' (Luke 9.56), preached by Thomas Lamplugh, Bishop of Exeter, and John Tillotson, Dean of Canterbury, respectively. Tillotson, though he could not avoid some discussion of the iniquities of the papists, hastened to add:

I speak not this to exasperate you, worthy patriots, and the great bulwark of our religion, to any unreasonable or unnecessary, much less unchristian, severities.

Both preachers were royal chaplains, and perhaps had been warned by Charles. Certainly on 9 November, the day before the Commons were due to reopen their debate on James, Charles intervened directly, and with more skill than he had recently shown. He came down to Westminster to thank both Houses for their concern for him and for the Protestant religion, and to assure them of his willing co-operation.

And therefore [he went on] I am come to assure you that whatsoever reasonable bills you shall present to be passed into laws, to make you safe in the reign of my successor, so as they tend not to impeach the right of succession, nor the descent of the Crown in the true line, and so as they restrain not my power, nor the just rights of any Protestant successor, shall find from me a ready concurrence.[30]

He further encouraged them 'to think of some more effectual means for the conviction of popish recusants', and offered to do 'anything that may give comfort and satisfaction to such dutiful and loyal subjects'. Next day, as an earnest of his good intentions, he issued a proclamation ordering all papists to retire to their homes and not travel more than five miles thence under the penalty of total confiscation of property.

Some, like Sir Robert Southwell, found this speech bewildering. Clearly Southwell had heard no talk of excluding the Duke from the succession, and thought it dangerous to put the idea into men's heads. As it was, the Members for the City of London gave such a garbled report to their constituents that many of them broke out into premature rejoicing because the King had legitimized his bastard son the Duke of Monmouth. These celebrations went on for hours, 'with shooting and outcries' and 'there were drunk healths to the King, the Duke of Monmouth and the Earl of Shaftesbury, as the only true pillars of our safety'; the first indication of Monmouth's candidature for the succession.[31]

But in Parliament the King's speech had its desired effect. The Commons voted thanks *nem. con.*, and again adjourned their debate on James. Much now depended on the Lords' attitude to the bill before them to exclude Catholics from both Houses, which had been before them since 30 October. To the Commons the important thing was that it would drive the Catholics, including James, from the Court as well as Parliament, for it contained a proviso that none could come into the King's presence unless he had taken the oaths and made the new anti-Catholic declaration, which was much more elaborate and 'watertight' than the one hastily drawn up in 1673. But the Lords saw it as an attempt to tamper with the membership of their own House, which had been left untouched even in 1559, when the oaths of allegiance and supremacy had been imposed on the Commons. The Catholic peers were a small and not very influential body, but they were inoffensive and generally respected, and the argument that their exclusion would pave the way for the exclusion of other categories of men was difficult to counter. The bill's progress was painfully slow, and further delays were imposed by arguments as to whether it should extend to the Queen's servants and if so, to how many. Then two of the bishops decided that the new declaration was doctrinally unsound, and voted against it. Meanwhile the House decided rather provocatively that not only the Catholic peers themselves but also their wives and even their widows could stay in London notwithstanding the proclamation of 30 October.[32]

Such delays infuriated the Commons, of course. On 7 and 11 November they sent up special messengers, 'some of them numerously attended, to show their impatience for the bill, not sparing in their discourses to reflect on the Duke in plain terms, even to wish that never such a curse may befall the nation as to have a popish prince', and to compound James's embarrassment they again proposed that some of Coleman's letters be published. James spoke against it 'with the most advantage imaginable', and he won his point; but the only result was the publication of a much more tendentious version the following month.* On the 12th the allegations of a second witness, William Bedloe, gave the Commons another line of attack, and they at once requested that the oaths be tendered to the Duke, together with all members of the royal household, and menial servants. The King agreed in principle, but in his reply he failed to mention his brother, and the matter was not pressed. On the 16th the Commons took the unusual step of sending a Secretary of State, Henry Coventry, to hasten the Lords' deliberations, and they even considered sending the Speaker; meanwhile, as a threat

*See p. 141 below.

and a measure of insurance, the adjourned debate on James's removal from Court was postponed week by week but not abandoned. But when the bill finally came down at last on 21 November, it was found to contain a special proviso exempting the Duke, which had been inserted at his personal request only the day before.[33]

Naturally the debate which followed was impassioned; the hot-headed Sir Jonathan Trelawney was sent to the Tower for striking another Member in the lobby; and it seemed doubtful sense to divide the legislature in this way and put the Duke's prestige and influence to the test. But, as was to be apparent again and again in the next two years, James's support was much stronger than his enemies and even some of his friends imagined. Sir Charles Wheeler appealed to common sense – 'If the Duke remains in the Lords' house he cannot singly and solely, on his own vote, stop any business' – and Secretary Coventry was only one of those who harped on the danger of civil war – 'If this prince should go into another place, it must cost you a standing army to bring him home again.' The Opposition chanted 'Coleman's Letters! Coleman's Letters!' but the proviso had caught them by surprise, and they were short of logical arguments. The temper of the Lords was such that if the proviso were removed they would probably refuse to pass the bill at all – some peers may have voted for it with this in mind – and then all else would be lost. Sir Edmund Jennings told them roundly:

You have not yet made any steps towards the safety of the kingdom. It is not removing popish lords out of the House [that will do it], nor banishing priests and Jesuits, nor removing the Duke from the King; but it must be removing papists from the nation. As long as such a body of men are here you must never expect that the Pope, with his congregation *de propaganda fide,* will let you be at rest. Till you do that, you do nothing; when that is done you need not trouble yourself with the succession.

To the amazement and horror of the Opposition, the proviso was finally accepted by two votes – 158 to 156.[34]

James was lucky, and if the House had had time to look into the Coleman affair at leisure its decision might have been different. As it was, Coleman was to be tried as soon as possible, and on 10 November the King had agreed that if he made a full confession he would be pardoned; if he did not, and was tried and found guilty, then he would die. But the murder of Godfrey roused more public concern, and there the government was at a stand. Oates still enjoyed great public prestige – had not the Lords grandly 'recommended to the Duke of Monmouth, to take care of the safety of his person, and to the Lord Chamberlain of His Majesty's household, for better accommodation of lodgings, and to the Lord High Treasurer of England, for supplying him with necessaries' ? – but he knew nothing about Godfrey's death, and it was now too late for him to pretend that he did.[35] All he could do was to fill the gaols to bursting with people who could not be sent to trial for want of a second witness. This witness now appeared in the person of William Bedloe, who wrote from Bristol on 27 October to say he had new information on Godfrey's death.

Bedloe was a professional criminal, a robber, highwayman and a confidence trickster. Indeed, his record was so well known that he chose to glory in it rather than suppress it. When he first appeared at the Bar of the House of Commons he said:

Mr Speaker, I have been a great rogue, but had I not been so I could not have known these things I am now about to tell you.[36]

Henry Coventry met his first advances coolly, but the other Secretary of State, Williamson, was more accommodating, and he was brought up from Bristol at the public expense. He came before the Council on the evening of 7 November, and the next day Danby produced him to the House of Lords. He told them in general terms that he had been converted by the Jesuits two years before, and some of his Jesuit associates had murdered Godfrey in Somerset House, under the general direction of Lord Belasyse. He also confirmed some of Oates's testimony, that Belasyse, Arundell and Powis had commissions from the Pope, and that Coleman was 'a great agitator' in the design to kill the King.*

While Bedloe wrote down his testimony in greater detail, Somerset House was searched at the Queen's anxious invitation. On the 12th he appeared before the Lords again, to give them the full story, which he handed over in writing.[37] He said that two Jesuit fathers, 'Charles Walsh' and 'Le Fevre', had offered him £4,000 to help them kill Godfrey. With the usual inconsequentiality of such encounters they then went and killed Godfrey themselves; but, meeting Bedloe by chance in a pub (much of the action took place in pubs, like the Palsgrave's Head and the King's Head in the Strand, and the Greyhound in Fleet Street), they took him back to Somerset House to view the body. After a desultory chat over the corpse, they then asked Bedloe to help them dispose of it; then they changed their minds again, removing it themselves by night in a sedan chair. Bedloe was told that the murder had been ordered and planned by Belasyse, and executed by unnamed servants of his.

On the Plot in general he now had much more to tell. Like Oates, he had been an express messenger for the Jesuits, and a personal servant to Fr Harcourt†. In the winter of 1677–8 at Douai he had heard details of a planned Catholic *coup d'état*. The king was to be deposed and put in a convent (!), and 'there should be a tender made to one of the Crown, if he would acknowledge it from the Church; but they did not believe he would accept it; and then the government should be left to some lords the Pope would appoint.' Predictably, these lords were soon revealed as Arundell, Belasyse, Petre, Stafford and Powis. Belasyse, who had been unlucky enough to employ Bedloe years before, was to engineer a rising in the north, with Sir Francis

---

*L.J., xiii, 343. It is established that Bedloe only told the Council of Godfrey's murder, and added the rest, in corroboration of Oates, next morning. On this point Pollock, *Popish Plot*, p. 110, is corrected by John Gerard, *The Popish Plot and its newest historian* (1903), pp. 22–4. So Charles II was almost certainly right in his assumption that Bedloe was 'tampered with' overnight (Burnet, ii, 160–61).

†In the absence of a first name, this could be either Thomas Ireland or William Barrow, who both used the alias 'Harcourt'.

Ratcliffe and a Mr Thimbleby of Ernham. They were to seize the arsenal at Hull to equip ten thousand men from Flanders who were to land in Bridlington Bay. A parallel rising in the West, under Powis and Petre, was described in great detail. It centred on Charles Price, steward to the Marquess of Worcester, the Marquess's cousin, Mr Milborne Vaughan of Monmouth, two other Vaughans, of Courtfield and Upper Ross respectively, Charles Winter, and other marcher papists who were less precisely designated. Chepstow Castle, already garrisoned by crypto-papists under its governor, Captain Francis Spalding, would be surrendered to the rebels, who would then march down to Milford Haven, to meet an army of twenty or thirty thousand men from Spain, made up of 'religious men and pilgrims'. Meanwhile, Lord Stafford, Ireland and Coleman had promised forty thousand men from the Home Counties, and unlimited funds.

By the time all this had been worked out it was the summer of 1678, and the unlikely idea of imprisoning the King had been abandoned. Instead he was to be assassinated by the Jesuits Conyers and Keynes at Newmarket, on his early morning walk over the Heath, and the Earl of Shaftesbury and the Dukes of Ormonde, Monmouth and Buckingham would be killed with him. But the whole plan had then been torpedoed by Oates's decision to confess. After hanging around London for a week or two in fear of his life, Bedloe had fled to Bristol.

This was a remarkable feat of the imagination. In many ways it was more sophisticated than Oates's story; for instance, Bedloe was not so silly as to bring in people like John Lambert. On the other hand, though Bedloe's plot and Oates's plot had common features and certain similarities, it was difficult to make them coincide. The huge numbers of men involved, increasing as the narrative progressed – ten thousand from Flanders, twenty to thirty thousand from Spain, forty thousand in the London area – were a strain on any sober man's credulity, especially if it is remembered that the English Army establishment then was less than ten thousand, and that William of Orange only brought twelve thousand to England in 1688. Also, though Bedloe did provide a military and political 'back-up' to

Oates's conspiracy of priests, his emphasis was rather eccentric. He took pains to exonerate Lord Worcester completely, but his steward Price, a disguised priest, was 'one of the principal persons in contriving the design, and one whose wise counsels were the most observed in England'; even Lord Belasyse, the overall commander, deferred to him. As for the gaggle of marcher gentry surrounding this unlikely Solomon, they seemed altogether too poor, isolated and uninfluential for such vast designs. It is significant that when he appeared before the Commons on 18 November he 'remembered' that weightier men like Lord Carrington, Lord Brudenell and his father the Earl of Cardigan were also involved.* Similarly, his idea that Shaftesbury and Buckingham were to be killed with the King was unlikely, to say the least, though his motive for including the leaders of the Opposition in this context were obvious. As for Ormonde, even Oates knew that he had been in Dublin the whole year.

When we turn to Godfrey's murder the situation is even worse. The motive given for the crime – that the Jesuits wanted Godfrey's original copy of Oates's depositions so that they could confound him in the witness box by pointing out the alterations he had subsequently made – casts a strange light on one informer's opinion of another, but it also shows an ignorance of the law. In the Courts of Common Law sworn depositions could not be brought in as evidence by either side; the witness had to tell the tale afresh. The sum of £4,000 offered him (perhaps as much as £40,000 in our money) was ridiculously generous. Bedloe stated that Godfrey was smothered, which contradicted the clear medical evidence that he had been strangled. Moreover, though every one of the Jesuits mentioned by Oates could be shown to have existed, there is not the least trace, then or now, of 'Charles Walsh', Bedloe's principal villain.

The first reaction of the Marchioness of Worcester, at Badminton, was to hope that Bedloe would be 'safe kept'. The Marquess replied ruefully, 'You have not a right apprehension how things go here, for he is at this time a man of that extreme

---

* On the 14th he also 'remembered' a plan to seize the Channel Islands. (*L.J.*, xiii, 363; Grey, vi, 199.)

credit that he may point out whom he pleases to be safe kept.'
His wife replied:

> I cannot but lament the unhappy age we live in, when a man
> whose whole life hath been nothing but villainy and pageantry, and
> whose word would not have been taken for sixpence, shall now have
> it in his power to ruin any man.[38]

True, but to imagine that any government in November 1678
could afford to ignore evidence like Bedloe's is to miss entirely
the current atmosphere of strain and tension. Every day which
passed without an arrest for Godfrey's murder was a serious
blow to the government's credit, and particularly that of Danby,
who was already being most unfairly criticized for 'the con-
cealing of this horrid plot for six weeks'.[39] Coleman's papers
were still being sorted in conditions of mounting confusion; further revelations were expected there; and to cap it all, on 14
November it was discovered that another London magistrate
who had taken depositions from informers, one John Powell,
was missing from home. During the week that followed, several
broadsheets and pamphlets were published describing how
Powell had been murdered, or kidnapped and taken abroad.
What is remarkable is that the House of Lords at once assumed
his death too, and brushed aside the King's proposal that a
proclamation should be issued not for his murderers but for
him. It was not until the end of the month that he was found at
Worcester, the victim of some kind of nervous breakdown.[40]

It must be remembered that none of Oates's evidence was
published before the following April; until then it was locked
up in the confidential records of Council and Parliament. All the
general public had to go on were rumours filtering down from
above, and the overt acts of the government; the disarming of
Catholics, the order for the arrest of all priests, and so on. These
strongly suggested a crisis situation, and the public accepted the
reality of this crisis because it had been bred in an atmosphere of
continual plotting, or imagined plotting, not only by Catholics
but by 'fanatics', 'levellers', Dissenters and such-like scum, with
whom the Jesuits were freely believed to be associated. The

belief in a 'continuous conspiracy' lasting over generations was axiomatic, and even amongst the educated this engendered a curious logic, which was expounded by Roger North.

It was not safe [he said] for anyone to show scepticism. For upon the least occasion of that sort, What, replied they, don't you believe in the Plot? (As if the Plot were turned into a creed.) Then, if one was not straight converted, the word was, do you believe there is a *Plot*? That must be admitted, that the papists ever since the Reformation have had designs by all means possible to bring in their persuasion again, and so have the rest of the sectaries, not one of which are quiet a moment in their Plot to subvert the Church and Monarchy, and to introduce their model in Church and State. But what is all that to Oates? Nay, said they, if you will allow there is a *Plot*, we will make no doubt but this is it. And this sort was the reasoning at that time even amongst the better sort of people who should know better.[41]

Naturally, the Catholics were under intolerable pressure. Pickett, a papist at Temple Bar, was reported for having a new handle put on a dagger. Mr Burdett, of Holborn Court, had his house searched twice simply for entertaining 'an unusual concourse' of people – 'for what purpose is not known, but suspected'. People heard the strangest things in the street, perhaps in their own heads, perhaps not. For instance, a French girl called Marie Grenier, walking at ten at night in a side street near Covent Garden, heard a man say to his companion in French 'that he would have the courage to thrust his sword into the King's body, the other answering, "Take care what you say in the street."' The City was patrolled every night by a regiment of the trained bands in arms (2,500 men in an area of two square miles), and even in the daytime there were so many guards challenging passers-by that it took the Marquess of Worcester's footman an hour to get from Ludgate to the Post Office in Bishopsgate. The House of Lords was in deep anxiety about London's fresh water supply, and recommended that those in charge of the conduits be screened for popery; it also recommended the banishment from the City of papist cutlers and armourers.[42]

Nor did all Catholics behave with the tact which common prudence should have dictated in these circumstances. Taking their cue from the King and the Council, whose views were widely known or suspected, they dismissed Oates as a criminal liar, and decried Godfrey's murder as a Protestant trick – if it had not been carried out by Oates himself or the Country Party. Tillotson, in his Gunpowder Plot sermon, referred to 'the continued and insupportable insolence of their carriage and behaviour, even upon this occasion', and the Secretary of State's office received a stream of reports about boastful and intemperate papists. For instance, an honest soul called Ely Thomas, returning from an afternoon's dalliance with 'an hairy girl', had an unnerving experience at the Salutation Tavern in Moorfields, where he was accosted by a drunk who admitted to being a Dominican, and was tentatively identified later as a secular priest called Hale, supposedly converted to Protestantism by the Dean of St Paul's. Obviously the conversion had not 'taken', for he swore horribly, said Oates was a rogue, and asked the terrified Thomas what he would do 'if swords should come into fashion'.[43] In this atmosphere public frustration and tension soon exploded, and when it did, it engulfed William Staley, the young son of a wealthy Catholic banker in Covent Garden.

On the morning of 14 November Staley went into the Black Lion in King Street, with an old Frenchman named Fromante, and called for a pot of ale and a slice of roast beef. He and Fromante talked in French, and Staley, getting more and more excited, was heard to say, 'The King is a great heretic', and 'I would kill him myself.' (There was more, but these are the material words.) He was overheard by two witnesses who both understood French. He was arrested next day, and brought to trial on the 20th in King's Bench, for high treason, in that he had 'compassed' or 'imagined' the King's death.

The haste with which he was brought to trial suggests popular pressure, and a certain hysteria on the Government's part. Certainly the Attorney-General in his opening speech found it difficult to explain why this young coxcomb was in the dock, and not Coleman or Ireland. But the sympathy of Catholic hagiographers is wasted on Staley, who was almost certainly guilty as charged*; criticism should be directed at the state of the law, which permitted a man to be executed for careless words spoken in drink. His attempt to explain his words as 'I would kill myself' was plausible neither in French idiom nor in circumstantial fact – 'What Jesuit taught you that trick?' sneered Scroggs. But the trial was fairly conducted by the standards of the time, the prisoner called two witnesses in his defence, and Lord Chief Justice Scroggs warned the jury, 'When it is the case of a man's life I would not have any compliance with the rumours and disorders of the times'.

But it was 'the disorders of the times' that had put Staley where he was, after all, and Scroggs's summing-up was far from impartial.

> Excuse me if I am a little warm [he said], when perils are so many, their murders so secret, that we cannot discover the murderer of that gentleman whom we all know so well; when things are transacted so closely, and our king in so great danger, and religion at stake. It is better to be warm here than in Smithfield.

The jury found Staley guilty without leaving the box, and he was hung, drawn and quartered the following Tuesday, the 26th. But even then the episode was not over. His conduct in prison was exemplary – there is some suggestion that he confessed – and the King agreed that his body be handed over to his family. It is eloquent of the tactlessness, and at the same time the self-confidence, of the Catholic community that his family and friends arranged a lying-in-state at their house, with a series of requiem masses without attempt at concealment, followed by a magnificent funeral at St Paul's, Covent Garden. The Privy Council, enraged, ordered the body to be exhumed and the head impaled on London Bridge and the quarters on the four gates of the City, in accordance with the usual practice.[44]

All this time government and Parliament were not only living

---

*Too much has been made of Burnet's attack on the credibility and reputation of one of the witnesses, William Carstares. Burnet is least to be trusted when discussing fellow-Scotsmen, and particularly political opponents (Burnet, ii, 163–4). For the opposing case, see Warner, i, 220–21.

in a state of anxiety and tension, they were working without ceasing. For the more prominent men what little time was left over from the actual service of Parliament or Council was spent in committees or sub-committees, sifting papers and taking depositions. For from under the feet of the major witnesses had risen a whole swarm of petty nuisances, vindictive, unhinged or just plain terrified: bricklayers who had found priest-holes in London houses years before; other bricklayers who had hidden arms in the houses of eminent papists like Lady St John and Lord Rivers (one, wilder than the rest, had even hidden two hundred muskets, he said, in the Bishop of Winchester's house in Chelsea); men who had seen a man baptize a child at the Golden Dragon in Great Queen Street 'about six or seven years since'; men who had found popish books, beads and chalices in the house of one Edward Billington, in Silver Street, Bloomsbury; and so on, day after day.[45] As for the investigation of major depositions, like Bedloe's, this went on for over a month at full pressure, and after him came Prance, and after Prance, Dugdale.* The Marquess of Worcester found it 'a very wearisome life here, with little satisfaction in it; we either sit morning and afternoon, or the whole day without adjourning for a dining time'. Committees were squeezed in at ungodly times like nine in the morning or, worse still, late in the evening. Yet a week later Worcester remarked, 'I must not be absent even for an hour when the Council and Parliament are sitting, or something happens to make me repent my being away.'[46] As for the Justices of the Peace, they were run off their feet, especially in London; searching for priests, taking down informations from every Tom, Dick and Harry until their arms ached, and coping with informers who were not only malicious but aggressive. One hard-pressed Justice called Hoare, relaxing with friends over a bottle or two of wine, unluckily used the term 'blunderbuss' for a type of large wine-glass. A notorious informer called William Smith happened to be passing with a constable; he called Hoare 'a great rogue' and a papist, and offered to arrest him on the spot. The Lords Committee for Examinations had to leave

*For Prance and Dugdale, see pp. 150 and 157 below.

more important matters in order to probe this ridiculous affair in depth, but after hearing evidence that the egregious Smith 'was much in drink, and had like to have fallen in the fire, and he had broken his knuckles and was all dirty', they sent out word to the doorkeeper to discharge them all.[47]

In the provinces, where communications were slow and rumours difficult to kill, the hysteria was if anything worse. As early as 17 October an itinerant ostler called Richard Warren, rambling through Kent, was arrested at the Plough Inn at Deal for refusing the King's health, saying that 'he wished him neither health nor wealth'. By November things were warming up; it was said that priests were disembarking from every ship, some with papal bulls, some not; and there were arms everywhere. Two cartloads of arms had been taken by night to Lord Teynham's house near Faversham, in Kent; in the Marches there was 'unusual travelling of strangers well horsed and armed', and 'quantities of new arms' were reported 'to have been lately bespoken at Ludlow, Bridgnorth, and besides what is suspected to be concealed in rooms underground'. (Underground rooms play a great part in the mythology of the Plot.) The Red Castle of Lord Powis was searched again and again, with mounting frustration, and while it was still considering all this the Privy Council was distracted by events in Hampshire, where 'great knocking' had been heard in Tichborne Church at night. The lord of the manor was a notorious papist, Sir Henry Tichborne, now in the Tower, but his servant had recently borrowed the key of the church, and the Council ordered a strict search of the whole building, 'particularly in the aisle belonging to the family of the Tichbornes, and in the tomb there, and in the vault under the said aisle'. In Sussex 'a great light' was burning every night in the house of a reputed papist near Chichester, and three ships lay off the shore 'under pretence of fetching oysters, which have been seen several times to go on and off without any'. As for outposts like Whitby, in north Yorkshire, they were particularly prone to hysteria, and on 15 November the town was agitated by the news that 'forty horsemen armed were heard and seen to march through Skelton and

Brotton in the dead of night', and a twenty-four-hour watch was placed on the ships in the harbour.[48]

The 'night riders' would make an interesting study in crowd hysteria or mass hypnotism, for the horsemen who troubled the people of Whitby were active all over England. In Wiltshire they were seen riding north every night between twelve and two, in parties of twenty or thirty men, over the bridges at Hannington, Castle Eaton and Cricklade. The Council took notice, and alerted the Lord Lieutenant. On 14 November the House of Lords heard of them in south Yorkshire, too, and by the 20th they were in Buckinghamshire. Sir John Ernle, the sober Chancellor of Exchequer, told the Commons they had been seen in Gloucestershire, and it was debated whether the government should be asked to confiscate papists' horses as well as their arms. By the 26th, with reports flooding in from every county, the situation was serious enough for the Captain General to order the regular garrisons throughout England to mount night patrols.[49]

Bedloe's testimony justified such hysteria and even encouraged it. As for the House of Commons, its neuroses reflected those of the nation at large, and the opposition did not scruple to play on them. On 12 November the veteran Colonel Titus produced a pair of manacles found in Somerset House; 'I know not what use they are for,' he said darkly, 'neither do I desire to try.' The evocative name of Smithfield was mentioned far more often than was healthy, and Sir Edward Dering warned the Commons on the 16th that unless something was done quickly, 'nothing remains but to make our graves and lie down in them'. We have already seen that on the 21st two Members came to blows, and in the same debate another Member burst into tears. The way in which Bedloe strung out his revelations generated further tension, and he let it be understood that if he had his pardon he could inform 'of some who have his Majesty's ear'. The Commons, 'being curious and desirous to have the handling of some of those jewels that hang so near his Majesty's ear', supported him. The King, naturally, held back. Even Lord Chief Justice Scroggs entered into the general mood. Called down on the evening of the 18th to take further information from Bedloe on oath, he said, 'Mr Speaker, you shall find me the same man, and nothing on my part shall be wanting. When a knife is at my throat, I will pluck it away.'[50]

The obvious step was to bring in the Army, but not the highly suspect standing army of King Charles. On 11 November the Lords asked the King to mobilize one third of the national militia, but at the same time they asked him to move three regular Scots regiments stationed in Hertfordshire farther north. On the 18th, when they had heard Bedloe's evidence, the Commons seconded this request, and their feelings can be imagined when the Opposition spokesman William Sacheverell then told them that Secretary Williamson had been issuing commissions to Catholic army officers ever since the assembly of Parliament a month ago.[51]

These were officers withdrawn from the service of France earlier in the year at Parliament's own request. It had been decided to send them to Ireland to join a new regiment being raised by Colonel Thomas Dongan and intended for Flanders. Those still in London when Parliament met were dispatched to Dublin with all speed, equipped with new commissions in the Irish Army, signed by Williamson, but on 8 November one of these officers, Colonel Justin Maccarty, was found strolling outside the House of Commons, brought in and questioned, and sent out of London. (He was then arrested at Barnet by over-zealous magistrates, and had to be released by Council order.)[52] On the 10th Charles felt in a strong enough position to offer a reward to anyone who could name a Catholic still serving in the guards, but when some Irish officers were detained at Chester and their commissions inspected the scandal broke, and it was made worse when it was discovered that these men had been excused not only the Test but the oaths. Williamson tried to throw the blame on Monmouth, but 'the Protestant Duke' could look after himself, and in any case he was not as accessible as the Secretary, who went to the Tower forthwith.

The 'Cabinet Council' was summoned that evening, the 18th, and sat late; the Privy Council met early next morning under conditions of strict secrecy, and when it broke up, the King ordered the Commons to meet him at the Banqueting House, Whitehall. There he gave them the official line: that all the offenders concerned were destined for the French Army, that they 'had not convenient time' to take the Test, and that it had been decided to grant them Irish commissions long before Parliament met, though by administrative oversight they had not been issued until 27 October. In conclusion he told them that he had ordered Williamson's release.[53]

The Commons wasted the rest of that day, well into the evening, debating the pros and cons of Williamson's release, and ended by rejecting the King's right to order it. Williamson went free, of course, but he did not resume his seat that session, and Danby's organization in the Commons was seriously weakened as a result. But this only made the Opposition's defeat on the proviso to the Test Bill two days later harder to bear, and when the House met on 22 November to take the King's Speech of the 9th into belated consideration, several Members questioned the feasibility of protecting the Protestant religion for the future if they could not alter the succession. Eventually the Speaker, Edward Seymour, intervened decisively for the government.* He proposed that each M.P. compile a list of recusants or suspected recusants for his own constituency, and that these men should be declared Catholics by act of Parliament and forfeit four fifths of their estates unless they took the Test. The forfeitures thus obtained were to be assigned to the augmentation of poor livings. Seymour further proposed an act to deny a Catholic monarch control of the Army, the revenue and all appointments in church and state, and another to ensure that Parliament remained in being on the King's death instead of being automatically dissolved. In personal conversation he even spoke of a regency.

The Speaker was a crown official, and though Seymour had quarrelled with Danby he was far from being *persona non grata* at Whitehall; moreover, the proposals he made had much in

---

* The House was in Grand Committee, in which circumstances the Speaker reverted to being an ordinary Member.

common with the scheme of 'Limitations' sponsored by Charles in the next Parliament. Certainly he carried with him many of the uncommitted Members. In Southwell's words:

There was at first some despair thrown out of ever being able to patch up things, without all were sound at the bottom; but what Mr Seymour said seemed to surprise many with the hopes of obtaining things of considerable magnitude.[54]

The proposals were accepted more or less as they stood, and bills ordered to be drafted and brought in.

But the irreconcilables of the left were not so easily won over. Since the King would not raise the militia himself, they brought in a bill for that purpose. They nagged away about Coleman's letters, and began to ask embarrassing questions about his correspondence with John Leyburn, Cardinal Howard's secretary in Rome. Having found papists in the Army, they naturally started looking for them in the Navy, too, and when they found none at first glance they began to inquire why the Army had not been disbanded, anyway. The Army was now a desperate source of embarrassment, in more ways than one; on 15 November Williamson noted: 'Troops in Flanders; their pay wholly out this day. No subsistence, no bread.'[55] When the Militia Bill was introduced on the 23rd, the Army naturally came under discussion in the Commons. The result was indecisive. The House was determined not to grant further money without novel safeguards, but when Sir Nicholas Carew argued that men in arms in contravention of an act of Parliament for their disbandment were not soldiers but rioters this was altogether too much for many patriotic gentry, not to mention the professional soldiers present. The question was shelved to preserve unanimity on the Militia Bill, which was given its first two readings that day, its third on the 26th, and was then passed by the Lords, apparently with little debate. But the King sent his Attorney-General to Westminster on the 29th to inspect it, and next day he vetoed it, on the grounds that it took the control of the militia out of his hands, in contravention of the Militia Act of 1661, and this he could not allow, 'though it were but for half an hour'. At the same time he passed the second Test Act, and stressed his magnanimity in so doing, for 'it might hereafter be of ill consequence'. In return he expected them to get about their proper business and trust for their security to him.[56]

The remarkable thing is that the first week or ten days of December did mark a turning-point, and the hysteria of 'Godfrey's Autumn' began to die down. The rejection of the Militia Bill was a shock in more ways than one; many men were dismayed at the unforeseen parallel with the Militia Ordinance of 1642 – the words in which Charles refused it were in fact an echo of his father's then. The Test Act *was* a considerable concession – many had thought that it would never pass both King and Lords – and though James was still in Parliament he was the only Catholic who was.* Similarly, though the King put up a tough fight to save his wife's Portuguese servants, guaranteed by her marriage treaty, the rest had to go. Her Secretary, Sir Richard Bellings, and her Master of Horse, Sir John Arundell, left for overseas on 29 November, followed by her Surgeon, David Power, and a motley collection of equerries, ushers, dressers, pages and grooms, including several under-servants from the chapel at Somerset House. Presumably her priests left more discreetly, as did some of the Duchess of York's. Other members of the Court followed suit: the Duchess of Mazarin sent back two of her French servants, and another royal mistress, the Duchess of Portsmouth, released five English and Irish Catholics; the Earl of Sunderland sent back his French butler, and the ⁀uchess of Cleveland one of her footmen. Even Borgomaniero, the Spanish ambassador, sent away two English Catholics from his household. The only exception recorded was in favour of Antony Verrio and his assistants, plus a French gilder, a Flemish stonecarver and two Flemish woodcarvers, assistants to Grinling Gibbons, all of them 'employed in painting and adorning Windsor Castle'.[57] No doubt there were other exceptions – we have already seen that the Duke of Monmouth kept his

---

* Rather surprisingly, James continued to attend the House of Lords almost every day up to the end of the session.

Catholic barber another ten months – but if the Court had not been entirely cleansed of popery, it had certainly been thoroughly purged.

Indeed, though it suited the House of Commons to maintain the contrary, Charles showed himself willing to meet any of their reasonable requests and even some which he thought unreasonable. The basis of his policy was established in a proclamation of 17 November, which ordered all constables to draw up a list of papists and suspected papists in their parish and hand it to the nearest Justice of the Peace, who would send for those listed and tender the oaths to them. Those who refused were to be disarmed, and unless they entered into recognizances for their appearance at next Quarter Sessions, where they could be prosecuted for recusancy, they were to be imprisoned. Three days later, on the 20th, came a proclamation for the immediate seizure of all priests and Jesuits in the kingdom; the usual period of grace was not offered, nor the alternative of deportation; they were to be imprisoned 'in order to their trial'. These five simple words launched the whole vicious pogrom against the priesthood which was to continue for two years, and they went beyond the recommendations of Parliament itself. Two days later, obviously in ignorance of this proclamation, a Lords Committee simply recommended that the law against the priesthood be put in operation 'after a day to be set for their departure'.[58]

Indeed, both Houses seemed unaware of what the King had done. As we have seen, on 22 November the Commons debated how to strengthen the law against the Catholic laity, and on 4 December they sent up an address requesting the King to take recognizances from popish recusants for their good behaviour. At no stage did they show any awareness of the proclamation of 17 November, of which their proposals of 4 December were a weaker version.[59]

Furthermore, on 27 November Charles made a notable surrender to parliamentary clamour by issuing a proclamation offering a reward of £200 and a free pardon for further information on the Plot or Godfrey's murder, though he doubted the wisdom of dangling further temptation before rogues and criminals.

On 6 December, again at Parliament's request, he agreed that the oaths be tendered to papists residing in the Universities and the Inns of Court, or belonging to the College of Physicians. On the same day the Secretaries wrote to the foreign ambassadors in London to say that it was the King's expectation and desire that they should not keep more than four priests, whose names were to be registered with the government, 'to the end that they may be permitted to enjoy the privileges and immunities which justly belong unto them' – a clear hint that the others would not.[60] A proclamation was also issued warning Englishmen that if they frequented embassy chapels they ran the risk of being arrested coming out and taken before a magistrate, who would tender the oaths to them.

Meanwhile, parts of Bedloe's testimony had been seriously undermined. The Marquess of Worcester advised his steward, Price, to surrender himself, but it could not be proved that he was a priest or even a Catholic; still less did he seem a conspiratorial master-mind. Another man accused by Bedloe, John Vaughan, was released by the Lords on bail as early as 3 December, followed by Walter James two days later; they were both relatives of Lord Worcester. Captain Spalding, of Chepstow Castle, admitted that he had not taken the sacrament for five years, and this was enough to keep him behind bars for a while. But he took the oaths and the Test at once, and Worcester was able to collect affidavits showing that every officer and soldier in the Chepstow garrison had done likewise, and that Spalding had administered the castle with Puritan fervour, holding regular chapel services and fining absentees.[61] Bedloe had made the mistake of involving himself in a pre-existing quarrel between the Marquess of Worcester and a consortium of ultra-Protestant gentry headed by John Arnold and Herbert Croft of Croft Castle, Bishop of Hereford, who was a local landowner in his own right and a lapsed Catholic.* (As such, Oates's Jesuits had him marked for assassination.) But Worcester, despite his damaging association with the local recusant gentry, proved able to take care of them as well as himself. Not only was he a rock-

* See p. 244 below.

steady Protestant and a member of the Lords Committee for Examinations, but he had married a sister of Arthur Capel, Earl of Essex, an active and influential Privy Councillor with un-impeachable royalist qualifications and close connections with the Opposition. Despite Shaftesbury's trouble-making, and Captain Spalding's choler and indiscretion, Worcester and Essex succeeded in burying the Welsh and marcher section of Bedloe's testimony completely. All the marcher gentry arrested on his word were quietly released that winter, and Charles Price even resumed his stewardship of Worcester's estates.[62]

In the same way Samuel Atkins, a young Admiralty clerk accused by Bedloe of complicity in Godfrey's murder, had a powerful patron in his chief, Samuel Pepys, Secretary to the Admiralty Commission. By 21 November Pepys had constructed a watertight alibi for Atkins, and his trial had to be postponed into the New Year.[63] As for the rest, though Bedloe had implicated some of Oates's favourite peers, Oates showed no signs of returning the compliment, and though men like Carrington and Brudenell remained in gaol for the time being there was no prospect of bringing them to trial either. Brudenell was not bailed until June 1679, but Carrington received permission to retire to his Oxfordshire estates as early as 2 December and did not return to prison.[64]

Finally, the public hysteria provoked by Bedloe reached a climax early in December with the great Purbeck invasion scare, and this was so manifestly ludicrous that it brought on a distinct relaxation of tension. 'A great body of men both horse and foot' glimpsed on the Isle of Purbeck on the night of 9–10 December started a powerful rumour of a French invasion. The local militia found not a thing, but by the following day the news had reached Bristol, and the mayor asked the Marchioness of Worcester to call out the militia (her husband, the Lord Lieutenant, being in London). In a state of 'horrible fear' she did so. By the time the news reached London denials were coming in, but rumours continued to sweep north as far as Yorkshire, where a week later a group of jurymen on horseback pacing out the boundaries of some estates near Hull threw the whole area into a state of alarm.[65] But a reaction was now setting in, and one Tory J.P. from Leeds told Williamson:

> On the breaking up of the great Popish Plot the crack and noise filled us with great visions and the apparition of armed men assembled and riding by night, on which strong, strict watches were set, our militia drawn out, all popish houses searched, and all in great rumour and expectation for ten or twelve days; and I, hearing of such rides, made my best inquiries, but could not find one word of truth in any of these reports, nor persons nor thing of danger met with, no arms of danger nor ammunition in any popish house.[66]

He was right, of course. The disarmament of Catholics had been carried out with rigour – Sir Richard Astley, of Pattishall, Staffs., had to take the oaths and go right up to the Privy Council to retrieve his duelling pistols – but the results were pitiful. In Westmorland, for instance, the Justices took:

From Sir Thomas Braithwaite, 1 rapier, 1 carbine.

From Mr John Pickering, 1 large gun.

From Mr Peter Mowson, 1 little gun.

From Mr Stephenson, I old sword.

From Mr Anthony Duckett, back, breast and head piece,* 2 fowling pieces, 1 musket with firelock, 1 great sword.

From widow Platt, 1 old gun.

From Mr John Wilkinson, 1 Scottish side pistol.

From Sir Thomas Strickland, back, breast and head piece,* 1 case of pistols, and holsters, 1 silver-hilted rapier.

From Walter Kendall, 1 large fowling piece.[67]

This was typical. Of course, depositions by the score pointed with great authority to substantial caches of modern arms all over the country, but though every such deposition was followed up, and some more than once, not a single one was ever substantiated. As for the Catholic freeholders and gentry who were supposed to carry these arms, most of them had by now realized the virtue of tact and discretion, and many who could afford it had taken passes and gone abroad.† Williamson's correspondent

---

* Armour. Perhaps Civil War relics.

† See Chapter 7 below for a discussion of the state of the Catholic community at this time.

in Leeds found the situation somewhat ludicrous, and Parliament's agony over the loss of the Militia Bill quite unnecessary. 'For every single papist,' he wrote, 'we are ready to set out a thousand men.'[68] Even in London the tension lessened with the reappearance of the missing magistrate, John Powell, on 6 December. Clearly the man had had a nervous breakdown, but his name was in some papist 'black book', and he was considered important enough to be brought before the King in Council. Far too many people were chattering about this non-existent 'black book'. Charles 'advised him to go home to his wife, and trust to him for keeping him, and the rest of the kingdom, in peace and safety'.[69]

But what weakened Oates and Bedloe more than anything else was their insane decision to accuse the Queen of complicity in the Plot. What prompted them to this step is still a mystery. The King blamed Shaftesbury, of course, but this will not hold water. True, Shaftesbury was known to favour the King's divorce and remarriage, and convicting the Queen of high treason was one way of effecting it, but as an experienced politician and a member of the House of Lords since 1661, he should have been able to estimate the Queen's popularity, and foresee the 'backlash' which in fact occurred. Gilbert Burnet told the King as much.[70] No, both informers had advice, of course, but not necessarily from the best quarter; Oates relied a great deal on his legal adviser, the shady barrister Aaron Smith. They were rivals, too, and their attempts to out-lie each other, encouraged by the government as much as anyone, led inevitably to competition between them. Oates's original deposition, in September, had come very near the Queen, in the person of Wakeman, her physician, and when he came before the Lords on 31 October to exonerate James, they told him that if others were involved 'of whatsoever quality they be, the House expected he should name them'. But Oates stuck to his denial, explaining later that he thought the question was confined to members of that House.[71] However, Bedloe's information brought the Queen further into the limelight by placing Godfrey's murder in Somerset House, and on 13 November Charles summoned Oates to a private audience with the two Secretaries present, and cross-examined him about her connections with the Society of Jesus. Oates said he had seen letters to her from the last two Provincials, thanking her for her favours, which included a gift of £4,000 for the general purposes of the Society; but this had nothing to do with the Plot. Nor did the Portuguese Jesuits in her household have much contact with members of the English Province.[72]

Charles made a mistake in sending for Oates; it may even have encouraged him. He gave the man the strong impression that he was worried about Catherine, that she was his weak flank, and he may even have conveyed the impression that he was encouraging him to attack her in the hope of getting rid of her; certainly he thought afterwards he had.[73] But Oates needed little invitation; he had to keep ahead of the egregious Bedloe, and re-establish himself as Public Informer No. 1.

So, on Sunday, 24 November, he requested another audience with the King, and told him that in July last he had seen a letter from Wakeman to Richard Thimbleby (alias Ashby), the Jesuit, in which he said that his mistress would assist in the King's murder; and later that month, on a visit to Somerset House, he had heard a woman in the next room, demonstrably the Queen, 'say that she would not take these affronts any longer that had been done unto her, but would revenge the violation of her bed'. What she was to do was never made clear, but the £4,000 she had given to the Society had now crept up to £5,000, and was earmarked for the murder – presumably as part of Wakeman's fee. Henry Coventry, who was present, took all this down in writing, and at a meeting of the Privy Council early next morning Oates added only a few details.

The Council then submitted him to the most searching and hostile cross-examination he had so far faced, and one which ranged over the whole of his evidence to date. Had he known Bedloe before? He denied this, but the Council was clearly puzzled that they had not met, since they were both such trusted servants of the English Jesuits. He was also asked, with obvious reference to the Bedingfield letters, how many different hands he could write. On the matter in hand a sustained attempt was made to pin him down to the exact day on which he had over-heard the Queen talking treason, and he was sharply reminded of his former precision in such matters. He was asked (as he ought to have been asked long before) why it was necessary for Wakeman to poison Charles when Pickering planned to shoot him and Conyers to stab him – was not this over-insurance? Why had he not revealed this very strong evidence against Wakeman at his first examination before the Council? This was the next question, for which Oates fell back on his stock answer, 'that he was at that time faint and weak, and had been up two nights together'. And of course, he was pressed hard on why he had concealed this vital information, so closely affecting the King's personal safety, for nearly two months. To this he could only reply 'that he had much distrust within himself in his own judgement about the discovering it', and wanted a private inter-view with the King (which he had in fact had as recently as 13 November).[74]

Then, without time to think, he was rushed straight to Somer-set House under guard, with the Earls of Ossory and Bridge-water, and asked to point out the rooms in question. He knew the porters' lodge all right, and the guard room, but after that he was lost; he roamed in and out, upstairs and down, out into the garden and back in; there was great talk of a certain un-mistakable flight of stairs and large folding doors; but though he was given the run of the palace and unlimited time he had to admit defeat.[75]

Charles II was as angry as he had ever been, and Oates was left in no doubts to the gaffe he had committed. He was confined to his rooms in Whitehall under guard, a soldier con-stantly with him; his papers were seized, his correspondence was censored; he was allowed to see no one, not even his father, without permission of the Council, and then in the presence of one of its Clerks. The King told Burnet that the Queen 'was a weak woman, and had some disagreeable humours, but was not capable of a wicked thing; and considering his faultiness towards her in other things he thought it a horrid thing to abandon her'. Indeed, he showed no sign of doing so. On the morning of the 26th the Council met again. None of them doubted that Oates had been 'tampered with', but for the moment he was invulnerable; to prosecute him for misprision of treason would imply that the Queen was guilty, and before he could be charged with perjury she would have to be tried and acquitted; but if Bedloe came forward to support Oates, as he well might, this could be infinitely dangerous. 'Wherefore,' it was decided, 'all that could be done at present was to hasten on the trials depending, wherein he was to be an evidence, which being once over, there might be more room left to consider of him.' Coleman would be in the dock next day, and here was one man the government was happy to make an example of. Meanwhile 'some principal lords were deputed to acquaint the Queen hereof, and to express the concern of the Board'.[76]

But even while the Council was sitting, Bedloe had gone down to the House of Commons and offered to make new revelations if his pardon was extended in time up to the present day and in scope to include misprision of treason. An immediate request was sent to the King, who replied that he would consider it. The House pointedly adjourned until three for a further answer, and Charles equally pointedly summoned another Council meeting for that hour. He expressed 'his resentment of these proceedings; that Bedloe was tampered withal, and might accuse the Queen or he knew not whom, without any grounds'. Eventually he returned the answer that if Bedloe had committed some fresh crime since 1 November (the date his present pardon expired) he ought to know what it was before he pardoned it, and a pardon extending to midnight that night, as the Commons demanded, implied a pardon for crimes not yet committed, which was not good in law. The Commons were 'so perfectly incensed' that they seriously debated whether they should adjourn forthwith, some Members 'saying that if the Plot must be smothered it was to no purpose to do anything else'.[77]

But wiser counsels prevailed on both sides. The Commons went on to other business, and the following evening Bedloe appeared before the Council. Coleman's trial and conviction earlier in the day* had lightened the atmosphere a little; Charles thanked Bedloe for his evidence, and assured him of his pardon. Bedloe then gave further evidence, 'newly recollected', that on 11 May 1678 he had been at Somerset House with Charles Walsh, his fictitious Jesuit, and waited in an ante-room while the Queen presided over a meeting in the next room between Coleman, Belasyse, Powis and various priests. (There were two other persons of quality, but he saw them only from the back.) Coleman told him afterwards 'that the Queen wept at what was proposed there, but was over-persuaded to consent'. A week or two later, in France, the Jesuit Stapleton opened a letter from England, and having read it, said, 'Well, I am glad they have brought her to it.'[78] It was by no means clear to what the Queen had consented, or whether she was identical with the 'she' mentioned by Stapleton, but that was typical of Bedloe's method. Also he had to tread carefully; he wanted to get in on Oates's act, but he was probably in some doubt as to what Oates had actually said; and the treatment meted out to Oates was not encouraging. Though it was a stroke of genius to tie in Coleman, by this time a convicted traitor, his evidence was much less direct and damaging than Oates's, and after one or two questions – including the pertinent one, had he not been in gaol at the time of these events? – he was dismissed.

Next morning he appeared before the House of Commons, and gave them his evidence behind locked doors. There was one important addition. Asked by one excited M.P. if the two persons with their backs to him in the Queen's consult 'were not the Duke of York and the Duke of Norfolk', he answered airily, 'for anything he knew they might be'. This was soon transformed by the House into a positive statement to this effect, and Bedloe had some awkward explaining to do when he went to see Williamson about his pardon.[79] The Commons then sent for Oates, who arrived in a perfect fury at being beaten to the draw by Bedloe. 'He began by ripping up all the hard treatment he has suffered at Whitehall, taunting and reviling the hardship

*See p. 131 below.

thereof,' and he rather pettishly refused to give evidence until he had been freed from restraint, and given his own quarters at Westminster, near Parliament. But Oates found he had earlier overreached himself in depicting the dangers of popery; it was clearly felt that he should remain under guard for his own protection, though the House at once drew up an address to the King requesting him to mitigate the petty restrictions which had been placed on him.

With this assurance Oates returned to the bar, and, 'after preambling something about his pardon' in an inaudible voice, he uttered the famous words 'I do accuse the Queen for conspiring the death of the King.' The Commons heard his story with uncritical horror and after a brief debate it was agreed to seek the Lords' support for an address requesting the King to banish his wife and her household from London forthwith.[80]

But the Lords were not to be stampeded. After sending a delegation to meet representatives of the Commons, they adjourned until nine the next morning, when they ordered Oates and Bedloe before them. Unlike the Commons, they were not impressed by what they heard. They also had the advantage over the Commons in that they had a record of the informers' interrogation by the Council, and Ossory's and Bridgewater's report on their visit to Somerset House. They were in a better position to know the King's mind, and most of them knew the Queen personally, sympathized with her, and liked her. Not only was there a recognizable 'Queen's party', but she had the general support of the House.

They went upon the virtues of the Queen [ran one report], and though the witnesses were ever so good, yet this evidence is short and defective. And therefore, considering the dignity of the person, it was not fit to proceed but upon plain and palpable demonstration.

The issue was so much a foregone conclusion that many left before the end, and only five voted for the motion, though three of them – Shaftesbury, Clare and Paget – distinguished themselves by entering their dissent in writing.[81]

The Commons acquiesced with remarkable docility. Even

Colonel Titus admitted, 'I do not think that we are ready yet for impeaching the Queen', and short of this there was little they could do. Oates's evidence at Coleman's trial had been rather frail, and Charles wisely agreed to extend his pardon to 28 November and give him the freedom of Whitehall and St James's Park, with 'a convenient allowance for all things necessary for him'. When he appeared at the House on 2 December, still grumbling, 'his reception was not so cheerful there as formerly it has been, and seeing so many of the Lords were favourably inclined towards the Queen it is very possible that matter may sink and vanish'.[82]

Next day, 3 December, Edward Coleman was executed at Tyburn. This eliminated the slight chance that he might yet make further revelations damaging to James, and proved that the King would let the law take its course, even against a member of his own Court. Though some witnesses thought Coleman was expecting a pardon, even on the scaffold, it did not come.[83]

Coleman's was the first of the great Plot Trials, and in many ways the easiest to follow. Sir John Pollock and Sir James Stephen have both outlined the state of the criminal law at this time,[84] but the procedure in these trials is so baffling and unpleasant to a modern reader that some further effort must be made to explain it and set it in context.

Coleman was tried in Westminster Hall – then the seat of the high courts of justice – by a special commission of oyer and terminer. Presiding was Sir William Scroggs, Chief Justice of King's Bench, assisted by three other prominent judges, and the young Recorder of London, Sir George Jeffreys. The usual jury of twelve was empanelled by the sheriff of Middlesex. The prosecution was in the hands of the Attorney-General, Sir William Jones, the Solicitor-General, Sir Francis Winnington,* and two of the King's serjeants-at-law, Pemberton and Maynard. There was no defence counsel.

* Both had strong Opposition sympathies, and were dismissed or resigned the following year.

This was because treason was so heinous a crime, implying the overthrow of the whole body public, and so difficult to detect with the means at the government's disposal – the amateur Justices of the Peace, the dogberry village constables, a few government messengers – that any man who was detected and accused could not be allowed the least advantage in a court of law; he must be convicted. Nor was English practice in this respect unique; it was Cardinal Richelieu who said:

Although in the course of ordinary cases justice requires authenticated proof, it is not the same with those which affect the state, because in such instances what appears to be circumstantial conjecture must at times be held sufficiently convincing, since plots and conspiracies aimed at the public welfare are ordinarily conducted with such cunning and secrecy that there is never any persuasive evidence of them until they strike, at which time they are beyond prevention.[85]

Indeed, a seventeenth-century treason trial was not an attempt to ascertain the truth or administer justice, except in a punitive sense. It was a morality play, staged as a demonstration of government power, an affirmation of kingly authority, and a warning to the unwary. This is evident in the awesome and explicit words of Coleman's indictment, which told how he,

Having not the fear of God in his heart, nor duly weighing his allegiance, but being moved and seduced by the instigation of the Devil, his cordial love and true duty (which true and lawful subjects of our Lord the King ought to bear towards him, and by law ought to have) altogether withdrawing and devising, and with all his strength intending, the peace and tranquillity of this Kingdom of England to disturb, and the true worship of God within the Kingdom of England practised and by law established to overthrow, and sedition and rebellion within this realm of England to move, stir up and procure, and the cordial love and true duty and allegiance, which true and lawful subjects of our Sovereign Lord the King towards their Sovereign bear, and by law ought to have, altogether to withdraw, forsake and extinguish, and our Sovereign Lord the King to death and final destruction to bring and put, did . . . [etc.]

So, the prisoner was not allowed counsel, except on strict points of law; he was not allowed a list of the jury, nor a list of the witnesses against him, nor a copy of the indictment; in other words, he came into court with no knowledge of the case the prosecution was to put or the charges they were to make, except in the most general terms. He was not allowed to *subpoena* witnesses in his defence, and if any did come forward they could not be put on oath. Moreover, in dealing with the prosecution witnesses he was hampered by two conventions which applied to all criminal trials: there was no objection to hearsay evidence as such, and the evidence of accomplices was regarded as perfectly acceptable, even in some cases particularly valuable. It was fortunate for Oates and Bedloe that this was so.

If the prisoner required assistance on a point of law it was for the judges to provide it. This was one reason why the judges took a much more direct and positive part in these trials than a modern judge, cross-examining witnesses at considerable length, summarizing the state of the evidence at intervals, and in general relegating the prosecuting counsel to a secondary role. The bullying manner they frequently adopted, and their cod oratory, was conventional, and is to be explained in terms of social psychology rather than moral assumptions. Not all judges indulged in it, but many did, and in part it arose from the fact that the position of the jury as neutral judges of fact had not yet been stabilized; a verdict was a corporate act by the judges as well as the jury, and if the jury could not be persuaded to accept the judges' verdict as to fact they must be coerced. But the social background of judges had something to do with it, too. Like the Church, the Law either bred its own recruits or drew them from the lower classes; each was a profession apart. Their manners were rough because they were rough, and the perusal of a large number of state trials suggests that their conduct in court, though degrading and disgusting by modern standards, was very much taken for granted.

Of this breed Sir William Scroggs, the Chief Justice of King's Bench, was but too typical. He was a protégé of Danby's, who had promoted him to be Lord Chief Justice of England earlier in the year because he knew him as a staunch church-and-king man. Unfortunately, the discovery of the Plot so unmanned him that from then on he ran with the Opposition.[86] In the words of Roger North:

He was a man that lay too open; his course of life was scandalous, and his discourses violent and intemperate. His talent was wit; and he was master of sagacity and boldness enough, for the setting off of which his person was large and his visage broad. He had a fluent expression, and many good terms of thought and language, but he could not avoid extremities. If he did ill, it was extremely so, and if he did well, in extreme also.

In him the popular prejudice against popery achieved its highest, or its lowest, expression, and from the start he 'ranted for the Plot, hewing down Popery as Scanderbeg hewed the Turks'. But North admitted that 'the other judges were passive, and meddled little, except some that were takers also', and with the tide of opinion flowing as it did it is unlikely that Scroggs's worst antics seriously influenced the verdicts he obtained.[87]

In Coleman's trial, as in no other, the government was firmly behind the Chief Justice, but Scroggs faced peculiar difficulties. Coleman's letters, given the circumstances in which they were written, could obviously be put forward as proof of guilt. But if the jury would not accept them as such, the Crown would have to rely on Oates, whose 'evidence' posed difficulties, and on Bedloe, who was even less reliable. But if Coleman did get off, not only would the government have suffered a disastrous defeat, but the Duke of York would have been exposed to evident danger to no purpose. As it was, James's responsibility for Coleman was slurred over as much as possible. 'The prisoner had an employment here amongst us, by which he gave La Chaise instructions how to proceed' – this was how Serjeant Maynard chose to describe Coleman's position as Secretary to the Duke.[88] He went on to say that James, on oath before the Committee for Examinations, had disowned Coleman, and offered to produce proof of this, but Scroggs was careful to see that the offer was not taken up. As few of Coleman's letters as possible must be submitted to the court, and every emphasis placed on his actions instead.

After Maynard and Jones had opened the case for the Crown,

Coleman made the usual request that Scroggs advise him, and added that it was impossible for a Roman Catholic to have a fair trial in the present circumstances. Scroggs told him:

You shall find we will not do to you as you do to us, blow up at adventure, kill people because they are not of your persuasion; our religion teacheth us another doctrine, and you shall find it clearly to your advantage. We seek no man's blood, but our own safety. But you are brought here from the necessity of things, which yourselves have made, and from your own actions you shall be condemned.

But only Oates and Bedloe could testify to Coleman's actions, and Oates's accusations made in September had been flimsy enough, and based on hearsay; in October he had merely added the 'fact' that Coleman had received a patent as Secretary of State, which he had never used, of course. Oates's own position was now somewhat peculiar, and the solitary confinement in which he had been placed must have shaken even his massive self-assurance; when he told the Commons next day that it was a short step from Whitehall to Newgate for once he was probably not exaggerating. Now he had to face ordeal by cross-examination, not at the hands of amateur councillors, but a professional judge. Nor did Scroggs spare Oates; he gave him a thoroughly unpleasant time, and if he did not press the attack it was because he was afraid of ruining the Crown's case and perhaps provoking Oates into dragging in the Queen – which he showed a disposition to do more than once. The idea that Scroggs, or any other judge, treated Oates with rapturous credulity is an interpretation by later historians for which there is no support in the records of the trial. Suspicion there undoubtedly was, and a great deal of impatience, though this did not imply a lack of confidence in the guilt of the accused. A man could still be guilty, even if the evidence against him was defective.

But it was a close thing. As soon as Oates began it was obvious that Coleman, hitherto on the periphery of the assassination plot, was being brought down to the centre. Oates deposed that in November 1677 he had carried a letter from Coleman to La Chaise, and seen La Chaise's reply, in which he offered £10,000 to finance the King's assassination. This was valuable, because it covered the period on which Coleman's surviving correspondence was silent, but when pressed on details Oates was vague. La Chaise had asked after some gentleman with a French name; he thought he meant Coleman, but when he was pressed again he had to admit, 'I could say little to this.' Under further pressure from Scroggs he remembered that he had in fact asked La Chaise if he meant Coleman, but he went on to say, feebly, that he had forgotten his answer.

There can be little doubt that Oates was making up a great deal of this as he went along, and this explains his uncertainty; he had to remember not to contradict his previous testimony, and try to weave the new material into that testimony as far as he could. Also, he does not seem to have been 'briefed' by any of the Crown lawyers, for he clearly did not understand which 'facts' would constitute legal proof, and which not. The former had to be wormed out of him, often with great difficulty.

However, the Attorney-General then moved him on to the famous Jesuit 'Consult' of April 1678, which had planned the assassination. Here Oates repeated the evidence he had given originally, with the important addition that immediately after the Consult the Jesuits went to communicate their decision to Coleman. He also invented another letter, from Coleman to William Ireland, in which he said he would do all he could to bring in the Duke. Scroggs was on to this in a flash – 'What was the substance of the letter?' Oates airily replied, 'Nothing but compliment, and recommendations, and that all means might be used for trepanning the Duke.' The word 'trepan' was much better from the Crown's point of view, it conjured up visions of an unconscious James being skilfully operated on; but the judges still could not get what they wanted, which was a fact definitely tying Coleman into the assassination plot. Oates was willing, and anxious to please, but clearly he did not realize that the fact that Coleman knew about the plot, from La Chaise or the Jesuits, only made him guilty of misprision of treason. Scroggs was getting nowhere, and Mr Justice Wild took Oates back to the meeting between Coleman and the Jesuits after the Consult. 'Did you hear him consent to it?' he asked. Oates got the point at last, and replied in a low voice, 'I heard him say, he thought it was well contrived.' Both Scroggs and Jeffreys made sure the jury had heard this before they allowed the Attorney-General to shunt the interrogation on to the safer ground of Ireland.

For Coleman had interests in Ireland, too; it now appeared that he and Dr Fogarty had been deeply involved in the Jesuits' plans for a bloodthirsty armed rebellion there. This was almost routine; Irish plots were bread and butter to any self-respecting informer, and Oates was on the subject for fifteen to twenty minutes before Sir William Jones moved him smoothly on, via Fogarty, to the plan to assassinate the King at Windsor in August. (In his original deposition Oates could never quite make up his mind whether this was to be done by George Conyers, or by four Irish ruffians recruited by Fogarty, but for the moment the Irish ruffians had it.) He now added that Coleman had contributed towards the Irishmen's expenses, though, he not understanding the law, it took some time and effort on the judges' part to establish that Coleman had paid a guinea over the table out of his own pocket, thus committing an overt act of treason. This confirmed, it was not strictly necessary to pull Coleman into the parallel or alternative scheme to poison the King through Wakeman; but Oates now did so. For good measure he also said that Richard Ashby had brought over some general instructions to the conspirators, drawn up at St Omers, which Coleman had copied out in his own hand and distributed far and wide. This obviously strained Scroggs's credulity to the limit, especially since Oates could not name a single recipient of these instructions, but he did not press the point.

Jeffreys interrupted this line of questioning to examine Coleman's commission as Secretary of State. This was straightforward enough, if you accepted the conventions of the Oatesian world, but it involved the court in an irrelevant discussion of the Catholic lawyer Richard Langhorn, in the course of which Scroggs, Oates and one of the other judges, Dolben, got into an almost inextricable tangle over dates. Oates had by now invented so many different incidents that he was hard put to it to fit them all into his personal schedule for 1677 and 1678, which included long periods of comparative inaction at St Omers. However, this was cleared up somehow, and the prosecution rested.

But Coleman was now allowed to ask his own questions, and the trouble really began. His first question was why Oates had told the Council on 30 September that he had never seen him before in his life, when he now claimed an intimate acquaintance with him. Oates hastily replied, 'I then said, I would not swear that I had seen him before in my life, because my sight was bad by candlelight.' Scroggs brushed this aside: 'The stress of the objection', he said, 'lieth not upon seeing so much, but how came you that you laid no more to Mr Coleman's charge at that time?' Oates replied that he was then only giving general information, and that he had accused Coleman of corresponding with La Chaise, which was true – indeed, the Privy Council minutes say that he 'testified much touching the activity and concern of Mr Coleman in these matters'.* But Scroggs still demanded why he had suppressed Coleman's part in the Windsor assassination plot, not to mention the Wakeman poison plot, and when Oates pleaded that by the evening of 30 September, after two days' interrogation and two nights out in the streets organizing the arrest of those he had accused, he could hardly stand, he was reminded that the Council had been on the point of letting this dangerous traitor go free that night. To which Oates hastily replied, 'No, I never apprehended that, for if I did, I should have given a further account.' But by a further series of questions, relentlessly stripping aside all Oates's evasions, Scroggs and Mr Justice Wild then elicited the fact that Oates had never subsequently given this 'further account' to the King and Council, but only to Parliament. Scroggs was incredulous, 'Mr Coleman being so desperate a man as he was, endeavouring the killing of the King.' Oates took refuge in loss of memory; he had not recollected the precise nature of Coleman's involvement until he had consulted his famous papers again, some time later. Scroggs went on hammering at him until he got him to admit that he had concealed this dangerous information from every-

* See p. 81 above.

body for over three weeks, from 30 September to 23 October; then he left it.

But Coleman at once returned to his original question; why had Oates not recognized him? Oates took refuge in talk of periwigs, though it is not clear whether Coleman had donned or discarded a periwig to come to Council; then he resorted to outright lying, saying he had never been asked the question. At this Scroggs was very impatient, and he pointed out that it contradicted what he had implicitly admitted himself only a few minutes before. Coleman then appealed to one of the Clerks to the Council, Sir Thomas Doleman, who was in court. Doleman testified that Oates had said 'that he did not well know him'. ('Did he add that he did not know him well by candlelight?' sneered Scroggs, not waiting for an answer.) He also disposed of Oates's other excuses, but Oates was obstinate, and it may well have been in hopes of squeezing him further that Scroggs then appealed to another Clerk to the Council, Sir Robert Southwell, whom he noticed in court.

But, quite unexpectedly, Southwell's testimony restored the situation. He admitted that Oates had given 'so large and general information to the Council that it could not easily be fixed', but he was positive that Oates had in fact accused Coleman of contributing £5,000 towards the Wakeman poisoning project. He could not be shaken, and he was quite right.* Everyone else, including Oates, had forgotten what he did say at Council. This shifted the responsibility on to the Council, whose shoulders were broad enough, and Scroggs was happy. He let Oates stand down at last.

After this Bedloe was by way of light relief. At the beginning Scroggs had to stop him reading from a prepared script, but he managed to confirm Oates's testimony that Coleman had received treasonable letters from La Chaise, and accepted a com-

---

*P.C.2/66/406. Three years later the conscientious Southwell, who loathed Oates, was still defending himself against the charge that he had been 'pushed on by the judges impudently to affirm that Oates had before declared what Oates then at the trial confessed he had not said before', (22 November 1682, Add. MS 38015, f. 278.)

mission as Secretary of State. He had also heard Coleman say that.

If he had a hundred lives, and a sea of blood to carry on the cause, he would spend it all; and if there was an hundred heretical kings to be deposed, he would see them all destroyed.

This was a bit strong, even for Scroggs, and he questioned him sharply as to circumstances; when and where had Coleman said this? But he let him go, and Coleman contented himself with affirming that he had never seen the man in his life.

On the whole the Crown witnesses had put up a feeble exhibition, and the Attorney-General was happy to move on to Coleman's letters, with the remark 'his own papers are as good as an hundred witnesses to condemn him'. The Clerk of the Crown then read out Coleman's letter of 29 September 1675 to La Chaise, outlining the whole course of the negotiation to date; then La Chaise's brief answer: then a draft declaration dissolving Parliament drawn up by Coleman in 1674 or 1675. Also presented was the notorious letter drafted by Coleman for James's signature, though the judges were careful to stress, again, that James had disowned it and that Coleman while in Newgate had admitted this. But it was this third letter which did the damage, and especially the famous passage, printed in black-letter in the contemporary accounts of the trial:

We have a mighty work upon our hands, no less than the conversion of three kingdoms, and the utter subduing of a pestilent heresy, which hath for some time domineered over this northern part of the world, and we never had so great hopes of it since our Queen Mary's days.

There the Crown rested its case, but subsequently Scroggs became involved in an argument with Coleman whether these letters constituted evidence of treasonable intent, and for a moment it seemed that Coleman was going to drag James in neck and crop. Scroggs told him:

You were carrying on such a design, that you intended to put the Duke in the head of, in such method and ways as the Duke himself would not approve, but rejected.

Coleman replied:

Do not think I would throw anything upon the Duke, though I might (in the beginning of it) possibly make use of the Duke's name. It is possible; they say I did.

And he went on, more obscurely:

But can any imagine that people will lay down money, £200,000 or £20,000, with me upon the Duke's name, and not know whether the Duke be in it; and consequently nobody will imagine the Duke would ever employ any sum to this King's prejudice or disservice.

Scroggs dismissed all this in haste:

What a kind of way of talking is this [he said]! You have such a swimming way of melting words that it is a troublesome thing for a man to collect matter out of them. The thing these letters do seem to import is this, that your design to bring in popery into England, and to promote the interest of the French king in this place, for which you hoped to have a pension, that's plain. The Duke's name is often mentioned, that's true; sometimes it appears it is against his will, and sometimes he might know of it, and be told that the consequence was not great.

He declared that Coleman's arguments were all 'vain, inconsequential discourses', and cut him off forthwith. But it is not surprising that within a week or two the letters read at the trial were illegally published with the tendentious title page: *Mr Coleman's Two Letters to Mr La Chaise, with the Duke of York's letter to the said Monsieur La Chaise, which sheweth what Mr Coleman wrote to him was by his special command and appointment.*[89]

But in his summing-up Scroggs felt he must continue to emphasize the letters, rather than Oates's and Bedloe's lame testimony. He put his finger on the weak point in Coleman's case, that if his negotiations with France had been designed only to achieve general toleration in England, why was he so sure that this would produce the triumph of Catholicism? 'There must be more in it,' he growled, and indeed, he proved to his own satisfaction that the only way to convert England was by torture and massacre, devices which came readily enough to the popish priesthood. 'Our execution shall be as quick as their gunpowder,' he warned them, 'but more effectual.' He then descanted on the impossibility of anyone of normal instinct and intelligence being converted to Rome, in terms scarcely calculated to mollify the Duke of York, especially when he turned for support to James's martyred father, Charles I.

Have we so soon forgot our reverence to the late King [he thundered], and the pious advice he left us? A King that was truly a Defender of the Faith, not only by his title, but by his abilities and writings. A King who understood the Protestant religion so well that he was able to defend it against any of the Cardinals of Rome. And when he knew it so thoroughly and died so eminently for it, I will leave this characteristical note, that whosoever after that departs from his judgement had need of a very good one of his own, to bear him out.

He concluded with a brief sideways glance at Oates and Bedloe, in two sentences:

For the other part of the evidence, which is by the testimony of the witnesses present, you have heard them. I will not detain you longer now the day is going out.

Mr Justice Jones quickly interposed: 'You must find the prisoner guilty, or bring in two persons perjured.' But the jury had no doubts, and after a brief interval they returned and found the prisoner guilty. Sentence was delivered next morning.

Sympathy is wasted on Coleman. The perjured evidence of Oates and Bedloe was irrelevant, except as a technical device which allowed the government to bring the trial on. His letters revealed that he had been planning to alter the balance of the religious establishment (to put it no worse), and though to classify this as high treason was perhaps a strained construction on the statute of 1661, it was a perfectly natural one. But even if his meddling with religion were overlooked, he had still plotted to bring about a dissolution of Parliament. Strafford had been accused of high treason in 1641 for coming between the King and his natural advisers in Parliament, and though this construction had not been completely accepted it had not been rejected out of hand either. And Strafford *had* gone to the block, Father Warner regarded Coleman as a martyr for religion, and this has remained the official policy of the Roman Church; he was even beatified by Pius XI in 1929. But some contemporary Catholics had other views. When a French translation of his trial appeared in Paris, the English *chargé d'affaires* noticed 'that those who not long ago did canonize Mr Coleman do now acknowledge his execution to have been a just punishment'.[90]

However, Coleman's trial had seriously undermined the standing of Titus Oates. The government already had grave doubts of his credibility; now his technical reliability was in question. In his first appearance in the witness box under cross-examination he had fared so badly that without a great deal of assistance from the court he would have been lost. Coleman had quoted back at Scroggs one of his own pronouncements, 'that it would much enervate any man's testimony as to the whole if he could be proved false in any one thing', and Oates was certainly 'enervated' in this sense. Could the government let him take the stand again?

But the answer is, they had to. The fact that the Jesuit fathers, principals in a crime to which Coleman was really only an accessory, were still untried nearly three months after they had first been accused was prime ammunition in the hands of those who accused the government, and particularly Danby, of trying to 'smother' the Plot. And Danby knew by now that Ralph Montagu was planning a quite separate attack on him in the House of Commons. So, on 17 December the Jesuits Thomas Whitbread, William Ireland and John Fenwick, with Thomas Pickering and John Grove, were put up at the Old Bailey on a charge of high treason, in that they had plotted the King's death in April 1678 and again in August.

The result, again, was a qualified fiasco.[91] True, Oates gave his evidence well, despite continual interruptions from the dock, and Scroggs was pleased with him. Moreover, under cross-examination both Grove and Fenwick had to admit that they knew Oates, though they denied knowing him intimately. This was the first 'hard' evidence corroborating Oates's story, and the prosecution also produced a letter from Fr Edward Petre, seized with Harcourt's papers, which independently confirmed that a Jesuit Consult had been held in London on 24 April 1678. Ironically, Scroggs ruled that this, the only valid piece of evidence produced by the government in all these trials, could not go to the jury, but it made its impression. (No one asked the prisoners if they had been at a Consult in *London* in April 1678, only at the *White Horse Tavern,* as Oates insisted; this gave them a welcome chance to prevaricate.)

But Bedloe, judging by the printed record, was even less effectual than he had been at Coleman's trial. He was rambling and inconsequential; he tried to drag in his pet hates, the Vaughans of Monmouth; he hinted broadly at the Queen's complicity; and he had to be pulled up by Scroggs more than once. When he stood down the prosecution felt it advisable to put James Bedloe in the box to testify that his brother had known the Jesuits at all. Worse still, he would not corroborate Oates's evidence against Whitbread and Fenwick, and on the completion of the prosecution evidence Scroggs ordered them to be returned to prison. 'It will be convenient from what is already proved', he told the jury, 'to have them stay until more proof may come in.' But it was not convenient at all that the government could not clinch its case against Whitbread, the English Provincial, who had figured in Oates's testimony as the *fons et origo* of the whole Plot.

As in Coleman's trial, there is little evidence that the prosecution had prepared their case, and when the remaining prisoners came to make their defence, further difficulties arose. Ireland and Whitbread had already offered to send for sworn depositions that Oates had been at St Omers the whole of April 1678, when he was supposed to have been in London, but Scroggs ruled these to be inadmissible. Ireland now swore that he himself had been out of London, at Sir John Southcote's house near St Albans, at Lord Aston's at Tixall, and at Mr Charles Gifford's at Wolverhampton, for the whole of August, when he was supposed to be plotting the King's assassination in

London. To support this he produced not only his mother and his sister, but Sir John Southcote's coachman, Harrison, who had conveyed him from St Albans to Tixall, and Charles Gifford himself. Scroggs ruled that these witnesses (presumably counting Mrs and Miss Ireland as one) were counterbalanced by Oates, Bedloe, and Sarah Paine, a servant-girl who swore she had seen Ireland at Grove's house on the relevant dates. But he must have been worried lest Southcote himself appear, or Lord Aston, whose evidence could not be so easily 'counterbalanced', and he committed himself to the extraordinary proposition that:

If it should be a mistake only in point of time, it may go to invalidate the credibility of a man's testimony, but it does not invalidate the truth of the thing itself, which may be true in substance, though the circumstances of time differ.

But there was worse to come than mistakes in time. Ireland now suggested that Oates's character would not stand up to close examination, and he produced Sir Denny Ashburnham, M.P. for Hastings, with a record of the perjury indictment against Oates in 1673. Ashburnham, who had been persuaded to appear by Ireland's womenfolk, was pitiably embarrassed. He admitted that he had known Oates all his life, and 'that when he was a child he was not a person of that credit that we could depend upon what he said'. But he added that in view of the support Oates's testimony now had he saw no reason to doubt his word in this particular case. In fact, the only support for Oates's word was Bedloe, and Scroggs was badly rattled. If the Crown's case collapsed he would bear the brunt of the blame. He got rid of Ashburnham quickly enough, but the Attorney-General seemed disposed to read out Oates's record for perjury, saying it was of no account. Scroggs refused point-blank, but Jones tactlessly persisted. However, he was suppressed at last, and Scroggs turned to the summing-up.

Without necessarily accepting in full the rhapsodies of Catholic hagiography, it is reasonable to suppose that these Catholic priests, earnest, sober, dignified and devout, made a better impression on the court and jury than the general run of defendants at the Old Bailey; and the jury was composed of quite substantial men, including a knight and two baronets, and eight others entitled to the superior title 'esquire'. This is probably why Scroggs throughout the trial laboured the point that any priest could get a dispensation to lie, and therefore the defendants' solemn denials must be ignored; and why his summing-up was little more than a long tirade against the Catholic priest-hood, which was blatantly unfair since he had taken pains to assure the court at the beginning that these men were not on trial simply as priests.

When they have debauched men's understandings [he roared], overturned all morals, and destroyed all divinity, what shall I say of them? When their humility is such that they tread upon the heels of emperors, their charity such as to kill princes, and their vow of poverty such as to covet kingdoms, what shall I judge of them?

What indeed? — and in his peroration he delivered himself of the famous accusation: 'They eat their God, they kill their King, and saint the murderer!'

The verdict was 'guilty', of course, and the sentence 'death'; and Scroggs commended the jury in these remarkable words: 'You have done, gentlemen, like very good Christians; that is to say, very good Protestants.' But the way the verdict had been obtained did not inspire confidence; and the problem remained what to do with the other priests accused by Oates and not by Bedloe. There were also the Catholic lords still in the Tower. A peer of the realm could not be stampeded to the gallows in a cloud of cod oratory and bad law, and early in December the House of Lords forced the issue by making preparations for a speedy trial in the usual way — that is, by the House itself. The Commons responded by impeaching all five in an effort to retain control of the proceedings.

In fact, this may have saved four of the lords, for they could now only be tried during a parliamentary session, and except in the case of Viscount Stafford this never proved possible to arrange. But the incident precipitated a serious quarrel between the Houses which had been brewing for some time. (Indeed, in this reign they were on bad terms more often than not.) The

Lords never had reconciled themselves to the second Test Act, and when the Catholic peers took their leave on 30 November there was an emotional scene. The Duke of Norfolk magnanimously pointed out that if some peers did not take the oaths and the Test at once the House could not reassemble on the Monday as a legally constituted body, and they were 'moved to take notice of the good services of the Duke of Norfolk herein, before his withdrawing, which their lordships took very well from him'. Then Lord Audley, a distinguished but impoverished soldier, took leave of the House with a speech expressing 'his great duty to his Majesty, and the welfare and peace of this kingdom, to the great satisfaction of the whole House', and their conscience prompted them to write in fulsome terms to the King, recommending Audley to his bounty. It was a moving occasion.[92]

The reduction of the royalist majority in the Upper House by twenty or so could have had serious implications,* if the Lords had not by this time become thoroughly disenchanted with the Commons. Their bad taste in prejudging the Queen was the least of their follies; they seemed intent on fighting the Civil Wars all over again. On 2 December they held a wild debate on the state of the nation in which several speakers irresponsibly compared the present situation to that in 1641, and the heads of an address they drew up to the King, warning him 'of the dangers that have and may arise from private advices, contrary to the advice of his Parliament', was certainly reminiscent of some of the pronouncements of the Long Parliament.[93] The Lords even preferred to draft their own legislation against popery, and they cannot have been pleased to see their new bills receiving extremely dilatory treatment below.† Their temper was shown by their decision to wind up the Lords Committee for Examinations on 12 December and hand back their papers to the Council.

In fact, the week before, the Council had already appointed its own committee again, 'to consider of all informations relating to

---

* For an estimate of the Catholic peerage, see Appendix B.

† This abortive legislation is discussed in Chapter 7 below.

the Plot and Popery', as well as the murder of Sir Edmund Berry Godfrey, of course. At the outset it was a small and not very distinguished group, consisting of the Lord Privy Seal (Anglesey), Secretary Williamson, and Lords Bridgewater, Ailesbury, Fauconberg and Maynard. But on the 12th it was stiffened by the addition of Danby, the Duke of Ormonde,* the Lord Chamberlain (Arlington) and the other Secretary of State (Henry Coventry). Other important peers, like Clarendon and Essex, attended regularly, and it was ordered to meet every morning except Sunday at nine.[94] The government thus regained control for the moment of the investigation of the Plot.

Meanwhile the differences between the two Houses came to a head with the impeachment of the Earl of Danby. Since the beginning of the session he had been fighting an all-out battle for survival, with mixed success. After a dispute lasting over a fortnight, the House of Commons agreed on 16 December to vote a further £200,000 to disband the troops in England. But in view of the fact that the money they had voted that summer for the same purpose had been misapplied, they ordered that this money be paid into the Chamber of the City of London, who would control its expenditure. The Lords rallied to the King and his chief minister, and removed this and other tendentious clauses. The Commons furiously denied their constitutional right to amend a money bill – there had been a dispute on the same point in the summer – and the result was complete deadlock.

At this stage the government got wind of a plan to unseat Danby by means of evidence in the hands of Ralph Montagu, the former Paris ambassador, who had been recalled in disgrace that July. Montagu was now in league with Shaftesbury and with the French ambassador, Barillon, and he had entered Parliament at a by-election for Northampton, thus securing the protection of parliamentary privilege. On the 19th Danby decided not to wait for Montagu to attack him, and got in first by accusing him of trafficking with the Papal Nuncio in Paris. But this only provoked Montagu to produce in the House itself let-

* The Council Order says 'Lord Steward', which was certainly Ormonde, though he was in Dublin.

ters he had received from Danby in 1677 and 1678, which showed that while Danby had been posing as the champion of a Protestant, pro-Dutch policy he had been negotiating with Louis XIV for a secret treaty and a financial subsidy.

The House was in an uproar, and a wild speech from William Harbord reflected the hysteria of the hour:

> I believe, if the House will command Mr Montagu, he will tell you more now. But I would not press it now upon him, because poisoning and stabbing are in use. As to the danger to the King's person, there is something much more extraordinary. But I will not name him yet – the thing has taken wind – a witness has been taken off with £300 and denies his hand. I protest, I am afraid that the King will be murdered every night. A peer, and an intimate of the Earl [of Danby], said, 'There would be a change in the government in a year.' He has poison both liquid and in powders. But I would ask Montagu no more questions now.[95]

What these ravings were about we do not know, but if Montagu's letters were genuine (which they were), then the House need ask him no more. They promptly impeached Danby for high treason, and articles of impeachment were drawn up, one of which asserted:

> That he is popishly affected, and hath traitorously concealed, after he had notice, the late horrid and bloody Plot and conspiracy contrived by the papists against his Majesty's person and government, and hath suppressed the evidence and reproachfully discountenanced the King's witnesses in the discovery of it, in favour of popery.[96]

They were approved on the 23rd, and taken up to the Lords, who after debating them at leisure and hearing Danby in his own defence gave the Commons another slap in the face by refusing to commit him to prison.[97] By this time it was 27 December. Time was necessary to prepare Danby's defence, and to see if he could be dispensed with. Also it was clear that in their present mood the two Houses were not likely to achieve anything constructive – even the new penal statutes were hanging fire. On the 30th Charles came down to Westminster and prorogued them until 4 February, with the petulant remark, 'I think all of you are witnesses that I have been ill-used.'[98]

5

The High Tide of the Plot

ANOTHER factor may have prompted Charles's decision to prorogue Parliament: the fact that the first 'break' in the Godfrey case had come at last.

Miles Prance was a Catholic silversmith in Covent Garden, who had done work for the Queen and the Society of Jesus, and knew Whitbread, Ireland, Fenwick, Pickering and Grove. After their trial he was foolish enough to remark publicly that they were 'very honest men', and two Protestants who lodged with him remembered that he had been missing for three days about the time of Godfrey's murder. (This was afterwards shown to be a mistake, or a lie, but by then it was much too late.) They denounced him to the authorities on 20 December, and next day he was arrested and taken to Westminster to be examined by the House of Commons Committee for the Plot. After a long wait he and his guards adjourned for dinner to a nearby eating-house called 'Heaven', where they ran into Bedloe, who at once pointed him out as one of the men he had seen standing by Godfrey's bier in Somerset House.

Denying everything, Prance was hustled before the House of Lords Committee for Examinations. After a fruitless cross-examination they dispatched him to Newgate, where he was placed in a particularly unpleasant cell known as 'Little Ease'. Sunday he spent in this condition, and on Monday he sent word to the Lords that if he had the King's pardon he would make 'a true and perfect discovery'. The Lords at once sent a deputation to Whitehall, where Charles gave them a verbal assurance on this point, but Prance still hung back. The King now intervened, and next day, 24 December, Prance made a full confession before a special meeting of the Council.[1]

By way of preface he revealed conversations he had had with Fenwick, Ireland and Grover about a military rising to be led by Lords Belasyse, Petre and Arundell; but after this rather perfunctory nod at Oates and Bedloe he launched into a detailed and circumstantial account of Godfrey's murder which coincided with Bedloe's only occasionally. According to him, the murder had been instigated by a priest called Girauld, Gerald or Fitzgerald, of the household of the Venetian envoy, because Godfrey had been harassing or persecuting him in some way. (Like all accounts of Godfrey's murder, Prance's evidence breaks down on the question of motive.) With the assistance of Lord Belasyse, Gerald had recruited two lay Catholics; Robert Green, a cushion-layer in the chapel at Somerset House, and Lawrence Hill, servant to Dr Gauden, Treasurer to the Chapel. (Though the government did not realize it, Gauden was also head of the English Chapter of the secular clergy.) On the evening of 12 October, after stalking Godfrey through the streets all day, Green and Hill caught up with him in the Strand, and lured him down a narrow passage leading to the watergate of Somerset House. There, with the assistance of one of the palace porters, a Protestant called Berry, they strangled him and broke his neck. They lodged the body in Hill's room at Gauden's house, which was part of the palace, for twenty-four hours, then brought it back. On Wednesday the 16th they smuggled it out in a sedan chair, transferred it to a hearse in Soho, and then took it out to Primrose Hill, where one of them ran a sword through it.

This is by far the most lucid and circumstantial account of the murder we have, and it meets most of the medical evidence. It differs markedly from Bedloe's tale, particularly as to time and persons, though in view of Bedloe's character this was perhaps a recommendation. Also, when Prance was taken to Somerset House he knew his way around (unlike Oates and Bedloe), and the only room he could not identify was the room 'towards the garden' whither the body had been temporarily removed on the Monday. However, it was in this room that Bedloe was supposed to have seen Godfrey lying in state, and Prance probably invented this whole incident to bring his testimony into line with the senior informer's.

Sir John Pollock was most impressed by Prance's narrative.[2] Without accepting the elaborate conjectures he built upon it, we may allow that Prance probably did know something about Godfrey's death. Bedloe may also have known a little, too; the most unscrupulous and inventive liar does not build elaborate stories on nothing at all. Bedloe's account of a Plot in the Marches and Wales was based on personal knowledge, and so perhaps was his account of the murder. He was an experienced member of a London underworld of which we know next to nothing. Also, circumstances suggest that the confrontation between Prance and Bedloe in 'Heaven' was prearranged in some way, perhaps by the two men, John Wren and Joseph Hale, who had denounced Prance in the first place. On the other hand Bedloe almost certainly did not know Prance well, if at all. He made the error of deposing in the beginning that he had seen Prance in a periwig at Somerset House; even he never dared withdraw this categorical statement, but it was subsequently very difficult to prove that the silversmith ever owned a periwig, which was an expensive upper-class affectation.

So somebody, perhaps Wren or Hale, tipped Bedloe off to the fact that here was a habitué of Somerset House who had gone missing at the right time; a humble, defenceless man with no friends in high places, who might crack if he was leaned on hard. Which he did. The fact that Bedloe did not know if Prance had an alibi or not is beside the point; Ireland's case had shown that it was extremely difficult for an accused Catholic to prove even the best alibi. When Prance did crack he had an impressive tale to tell, but he had had forty-eight hours to think it up, in conditions which must have concentrated his mind wonderfully and he could have been more intelligent than is generally supposed; a silversmith was a highly skilled man, and Prance was obviously a very good one, patronized by royalty. Green, Berry and Hill were undoubtedly innocent – they were the first victims of the Plot to be completely exonerated – but to suggest as Pollock does that Prance named them to shield others is mere speculation. He could just as easily have been activated by petty spite.

Prance recanted completely in the next reign, and blamed his perjury on Shaftesbury. But Shaftesbury was dead by then, of course, and a convenient whipping-boy. It is suspicious that on 21 December Bedloe hustled Prance before the Lords, when he had been awaiting the Commons' pleasure, but it is important to remember that after that it was the Privy Council Committee for Examinations, not the Lords Committee, which piled the pressure on. It was they who put Prance in irons, and denied him light and fire in the coldest month of the year, and it was they who sent an Anglican clergyman, Dr William Lloyd, to pester him day and night. It was the Lord Chancellor, usually a mild enough man, who at one stage threatened him with the rack.

Indeed, the Opposition leaders could have had no motive for wilfully and deliberately ending a situation which reflected discredit on the government; and only the government would profit if Godfrey's assassins were brought to justice. But Prance strained the Council's patience to the utmost. Summoned before them again on the 29th, he insisted on seeing the King privately, with only Chiffinch, the Keeper of the King's Closet, and Richardson, Keeper of Newgate, in attendance. He then recanted, and denied all knowledge of the Plot or Godfrey's murder. 'Upon your salvation, is this so?' said Charles. 'Upon my salvation,' he replied, 'the whole accusation is false.' Next day he repeated his recantation before the Council; when he returned to Newgate he first withdrew the recantation, then reaffirmed it. The Council ordered that he be deprived of fire or light, and on 8 January he was put back in irons. When William Lloyd came to see him he found him on the point of death. Lloyd thawed him out in front of the fire, and on 11 January he finally confirmed his original testimony, and this time stuck to it.

The government now had a good witness, it seemed, and with Parliament prorogued it had a chance to regain control of the investigation of the Plot. On 31 December the King had enlarged the membership of the Privy Council Committee for

Examinations, and committed it particularly to the care of Anglesey, the Lord Privy Seal, the Earl of Bridgewater and the Earl of Essex, tough men with impeccable Protestant reputations who were not involved with the Earl of Danby. It was ordered to go on meeting at nine o'clock every morning except Sunday, and its first act was to appropriate all the papers on the Plot still in the hands of the Clerks to the Parliaments.[3] Momentarily the government had the initiative.

Charles's first proposal was to try the five Catholic lords by ordinary process of law, which, Parliament not sitting, meant that they would appear before a select group of peers nominated by a High Steward appointed by the Crown. However, this ran into strong opposition on the Council, and he agreed to consult the judges. The opinion of the judges was confused – certainly the surviving record of it is – but it is probably safe to sum it up in the words of Lord Chancellor Finch: 'Whatever the law be, it is not prudence to proceed.' This only strengthened Charles's mounting resolution to dissolve Parliament, on the assumption that all existing impeachments would then lapse.[4]

The other outstanding problem was whether to reprieve Ireland, Grove and Pickering. It was unusual for as long as a fortnight to lapse between sentence and execution in cases of treason. The London mob was agitated, it was proposed to censure Jeffreys, Recorder of London, and Charles was under pressure from the Lord Mayor as well as from Danby and Finch. But on the other side he was under pressure from many Catholics who knew Ireland had been in Staffordshire that August, when he was supposed to have been plotting treason in London. Mrs Jane Harwell, a prosperous widow at whose house in Wolverhampton he had stayed on the key dates 4–7 September, sent an express direct to the King demanding a retrial. He told the Council

that he had no manner of satisfaction in the truth of the evidence, but rather of its falsehood, and that when they were so busy in revenging the innocent blood of Godfrey, it was hard for him to consent to the shedding of more, and that he well remembered what his father suffered for consenting to the Earl of Strafford's death.[5]

All he would agree to do was to hear the judges, and then he insisted on hearing the bishops, too, 'to assist his Majesty as to the point of conscience in this matter'. The judges waited on him on 3 January, but they took the matter no further. They were ready enough to expound the law, but they deferred to the King on matters of conscience. Ireland's alibi was explored at great length, pro and con, without any firm conclusion being reached. Scroggs insisted that Ireland had had the opportunity to bring what witnesses he liked, but he dismissed the evidence of those he had brought as 'all arguing'. Williamson noted parenthetically, 'It's according to argument that they are condemned, but 'tis not fit to be said so at this board, lest the witnesses should be invalidated.'[6]

What the bishops said we do not know, but Charles still hung on, against the advice of almost all his ministers. Agitation was mounting steadily with every day that Ireland remained unhanged, and Charles told the French ambassador that his life as well as his throne were in danger. Henry Coventry, not a man easily ruffled, told the Duke of Ormonde on 4 January:

> The nation and the city are in as great a consternation as can be imagined. If the Fleet and Army come into as deep a discontent miracles only can preserve us and nothing else.

As for the other Secretary, Williamson, he was cowed by the hammering he had received from Parliament the previous session, and the King was furious to find that he had given orders for Somerset House to be searched on his own initiative; he told him, 'in great anger, that he marvelled at his effrontery in ordering his own house to be searched, that his head was turning, and that he did not wish to be served by a man who feared anyone else but him'.[7] (Williamson was dismissed early in February 1679, and replaced by the Earl of Sunderland, a bold and adaptable young courtier.)

Yet moral courage was not lacking. The execution of Ireland continued to be held up, and early in the New Year orders were going out from the Privy Council to provincial mayors and magistrates to stop sending priests or suspected priests to London unless there was good reason to suppose that they had been involved in the Plot, and a start was made on clearing the London prisons, which were all unpleasantly full. Oates and Bedloe were sent on a tour of these prisons looking for plotting priests, but they could only identify the Jesuit Anthony Turner (and that was a mistake), the Benedictine William Marshal, and a secular called Loomis.[8]

Oates and Bedloe were still popular heroes, but their prestige had sunk badly, especially with the advent of Prance. The fact that the King totally rejected the evidence they had given against Ireland, Grove and Pickering was well known at Court. Oates was not allowed before the Council to argue his case for a larger allowance, and all the Committee for Examinations would offer him was £10 a week with free board. They were unmoved by his threats 'to take care for himself', though they later produced another £2 a week for incidental expenses. He was still something of an oracle, casually re-enlisted for such tasks as composing a list of all prominent Englishmen in foreign seminaries, but when in return he sought permission to peruse the 'blue book' of depositions kept by the Committee he met with a brusque refusal. Moreover, in the new term the Judges proved willing to bail Catholic laymen against whom only he or Bedloe alone had sworn information, beginning with the Earl of Castlemaine on 23 January. Oates still regarded himself as a clerk in holy orders, and was in great demand as a preacher in City churches; he affected a mode of dress which was not only clerical but episcopal – 'silk gown and cassock, great hat, satin hatband and long rose scarf' – which he perhaps deemed appropriate for the holder of a Doctor's degree in Divinity from Salamanca (a spurious qualification he claimed with increasing insistence at this time). But he was offered no preferment in the Church, though according to him Archbishop Sancroft had given him an undertaking to this effect.[9]

Bedloe was even more obviously disreputable. Early in February he got drunk and criticized the Duke of York in public, and Daniel Archer, a Catholic merchant, complained to the Committee for Examinations that after a search of his premises by Bedloe 'and his company' a large amount of jewellery could not be accounted for. On another occasion he was soundly abused by a mettlesome Catholic while sitting on a privy behind a public house. Since December at least the government had been in possession of evidence supplied by the Bishop of Hereford that Oates and Bedloe had known each other in Spain in 1677, but it did nothing with it. Attempts were still being made to resurrect the old perjury charge at Hastings, and the Committee for Examinations did not seem averse to hearing about it. On the other hand, Oates's and Bedloe's complaints that their evidence had been misrepresented in the printed accounts of Coleman's trial were ignored – or, at least, no identifiable second edition was ever issued.[10] No doubt the government, even those members of it who believed in the Plot, would have liked to discard both informers, but Godfrey's supposed murderers had still to be brought to justice, as well as Whitbread, the Jesuit Provincial. However, at this stage a much more impressive witness at last appeared.

Stephen Dugdale was arrested at Stafford early in December as a notorious Catholic, and on the 21st he made a deposition to the local justices. They forwarded it to the Earl of Essex, who laid it before the House of Lords on the 28th. The Lords sent for him, but in the meanwhile Parliament was prorogued, and on 4 January the Committee for Examinations took over; Essex was ordered 'to prevent all persons from coming to him or tampering with him, and to send him immediately on his arrival to be examined by them'. He came before the Committee on the 8th, and they were so impressed that they asked the King to hear him personally.[11]

Dugdale had been land steward to the Catholic Lord Aston, a wealthy Staffordshire landowner.* It was later discovered that he had a weakness for gambling, and had used his employer's money for the purpose; the young Lord Aston, who had succeeded to the title in April, had called him to account and suspended him. But all this was still unknown; a land steward to a large estate was a man of good social standing, and Dug-

* See pp. 7 and 30 above.

dale was a superior example of the breed. His speech and bearing were those of a gentleman, and his record – apart from his Catholicism – was one of blameless respectability. According to Burnet:

He was a man of sense and temper; and behaved himself decently; and had somewhat in his air and deportment that disposed people to believe him; so that the King himself began to think there was somewhat in the Plot, though he had very little regard either to Oates or Bedloe.[12]

He not only confirmed the existing 'evidence' against the convicted Jesuits, thus salving Charles's conscience, he also produced much firmer evidence against Lord Stafford, and to some extent Lords Belasyse and Arundell. Charles always found it much easier to believe in an aristocratic *coup d'état* than in a conspiracy of ageing priests wielding pistols, or hiring anonymous Irishmen to do so.

From the very first, Dugdale's story had a certain internal consistency, and though in successive examinations and depositions he developed some aspects to an extraordinary degree, until Parliament met he avoided Oates's and Bedloe's mistake of trying to tack on to it wholly new incidents.[13] The skeleton was outlined in his first deposition, at Stafford on 24 December. He then swore that at Tixall (Lord Aston's home) in September Lord Stafford had told him broadly of a conspiracy to bring in the Catholic religion, and on the 20th had invited him to join. He had then been turned over to a new villain entirely, Francis Evers,* Aston's Jesuit chaplain, who confirmed that the plan was to shoot the King and the Duke of Monmouth. Dugdale had subsequently received a host of incriminating letters on Evers's behalf in his absence, and had helped him collect money from the local recusant gentry to finance the plan. He also said, rather inconsequentially in this context, that he had heard Evers discuss the letters sent to Bedingfield at Windsor the previous September. Five days later he made a further deposition, adding a few details. £500 was the sum he had been offered for his part in

* His real name was 'Eure', but he was always known to contemporaries as 'Evers'.

the assassination; this and more had been collected locally on the pretext of financing the school at St Omers, under the general direction of John Warner and a Harcourt. (The Committee naturally identified this Harcourt with Bedloe's former patron, but they were disappointed. Two Jesuits used the alias 'William Harcourt': William Barrow and William Aylworth; while Thomas Whitbread, the Provincial, was also known as 'Thomas Harcourt'. The confusion between Whitbread and Harcourt persisted.) Most suspiciously, Ireland now made his first appearance, as the master-mind behind Evers.

When Dugdale appeared before the King and the Committee for Examinations he did not have much to add, but he gave a frank and manly account of himself and his past circumstances, and he made a considerable impression. He agreed that Ireland was at Tixall in mid-September, but he was positive that he was not there the first half of the month. He admitted that he had heard of Oates and Bedloe in Jesuit circles, and confirmed that there had been a Jesuit Consult in London the previous April, for Evers had gone up to town for it. He had no knowledge of Pickering, but Pickering's nephew George North, a fellow servant of Lord Aston's, was in the Plot, and had told Dugdale that 'the King deserved such an execrable death as was intended him, because of his whoring and debauchery'. But Charles was most impressed by his evidence against Lord Stafford. Stafford's words:

It was sad that they were troubled for that they could not say their prayers but in a hid manner, but suddenly there would be a reformation to the Romish religion,

were perfectly in character, and many lesser Catholics had been charged with similar statements in recent years. The King told the Committee that his evidence 'was very sober, and came home to Lord Stafford'; he ordered him to be kept a close prisoner, with no visitors, and that afternoon he sent a deputation of Councillors to the Tower to warn him 'that the King had received such full testimony as to himself that nothing could be doubted'. He was offered a full pardon if he would confess — 'otherwise he need not expect it hereafter'.[14]

Stafford, of course, refused the offer, protested his complete innocence, and demanded a speedy trial. But Dugdale now had his sights aligned; in a series of depositions extending into February he developed his testimony along three main lines: the conspiracy of the Catholic peers, not only Stafford but others; the associated Jesuit conspiracy, where he could link up with Oates; and the sub-plot in Staffordshire, involving the local Catholic gentry.

Under re-interrogation on 11 January Dugdale's Plot began to take shape. The master-mind was Ireland in London, and his lay coadjutors were Belasyse and Arundell of Wardour, whom he had described as 'the loyallest men of trust and counsel of any in the world'. (According to Evers, Arundell was particularly important, 'for he was a very wise man, and much in favour with the Duke of York'. The Duke's confessor, Bedingfield, had taken a prominent part, too, and it was perhaps a blessing that he had died in Newgate the previous month.) Other leading spokesmen in London were Edward Petre, William Vavasour, Edward Levison and Whitbread. At the Staffordshire end Evers was the leader, of course, assisted by a younger Jesuit, John Gavan, and several secular priests.

Dugdale's main weakness was that he could not explain how the assassination was to be achieved; Ireland and Stafford had promised to summon him to London for an exact briefing nearer the time, but before that the whole plan was blown sky-high by Oates. Nor could he explain how the rising was to take place; he admitted on 17 January that there had been no arms stockpiled in Staffordshire, but he had been told 'there was provision made beyond seas'.

But his superior intelligence and sophistication enabled him to make the general concept of the Popish Plot much more credible. For instance, when they asked him why on earth Monmouth was to be killed with Charles, he said it was to prevent a Protestant succession; and though he was not ready yet to incriminate James, he had prepared the ground. He was so self-confident that on 23 January he threw his mantle over Oates, and explained that the letters sent to Bedingfield at Windsor were deliberate forgeries, designed to discredit the Plot in the King's eyes.

Charles seemed disposed to accept this, especially since Prance had suddenly remembered on 13 January that Belasyse and Powis had paid a 'messenger' to carry out the assassination. Sir Robert Southwell pointed out as the cross-examination proceeded that the evidence was now clear against Ireland, and later that day, the 13th, Charles told Williamson that he was 'full satisfied'. He might not have been so satisfied if he had heard the evidence of a priest called John Parsons, recently arrested, who said he had seen Ireland at Standon on 4 August last. But no one had the responsibility of collating or comparing the hundreds of depositions now in the hands of magistrates, secretaries of state, Clerks to the Council and Clerks to the Parliaments. Preparations were made for the execution of Grove and Ireland, Pickering's being held over, and Belasyse and Arundell were closely questioned. Belasyse would admit to knowing only two or three priests and one Jesuit – but the Jesuit was called Vavasour.[15] (In fact, Belasyse's Vavasour was almost certainly William Vavasour, of the Suffolk District, whereas Dugdale's was Peter Vavasour, Procurator of the Staffordshire District, whose real name was Gifford. This is not the only case in which the Jesuits' obsession with aliases told against them and their friends.) On 15 January a proclamation was issued offering a reward of £100 for Evers, and £50 for Gavan, Vavasour, Edward Levison (another Jesuit) and a secular priest called Broadstreet. Francis Evers was never taken, though there is no suggestion in the records that he left England, and Vavasour (Gifford) was not arrested until April 1681, when the authorities, even if they made the connection, were not looking for martyrs. Edward Levison also led a charmed life; there is no record of his leaving England, though he may have transferred from the Stafford to the Oxfordshire district. Only John Gavan was arrested, on 29 January at the Imperial embassy, on the point of leaving for Flanders.[16] Edward Petre had already been denounced by Oates, and had been in Newgate since the previous September. On the 19th, to judge by Williamson's brief notes, the government considered reissuing a general proclamation against priests, then thought better of it – 'The proclamation against priests,' noted Williamson. 'If we order the penalty of the laws pass on them.'[17]

On the other hand, from time to time the government showed astonishing zeal. For instance, for reasons which are not apparent, it was extremely anxious to capture Anthony Turner, the Jesuit Superior of the Worcestershire District, and he was sought by three King's Messengers in three counties, the hunt ending at Holbeck, Notts., early in March, with the arrest of a man who was soon identified as Edward Turner, a secular priest. Meanwhile, Anthony Turner had fled to London, and whether from starvation, desperation or an itch for martyrdom, had voluntarily given himself up to the authorities.[18]

Some issues were still in considerable doubt. On 19 January the Committee of Intelligence again debated what to do with Parliament. Danby could not be allowed to go to trial, yet the King was anxious to deal with the Catholic lords, especially since there were now two firm witnesses against Stafford, Arundell and Belasyse. There was also some doubt about Lord Aston. Dugdale had so far declined to accuse him directly; all he would say was that he had overheard Stafford talking to him in a way which suggested that he had at least some idea of what was going on. On the 20th, Aston was confronted with Dugdale before the Council, but the results were inconclusive. However, he was sent to the Tower for the time being.[19]

Tixall House was searched from top to bottom, of course; in fact, it was searched twice, but nothing was found of the many papers Dugdale had seen there, including a notorious 'wallet' of Evers's.[20] (The government's disappointment at not finding such incriminating evidence seems very naïve.) On the other hand, the Council seemed reluctant to proceed against the Staffordshire gentry, who according to Dugdale had been pouring money into the coffers of the Jesuits. Mr Fowler of St Thomas, he said, had even been excommunicated for refusing, and on 17 January he handed in a list of similar gentry for Worcestershire, Derbyshire and Nottinghamshire.

As a result several Staffordshire gentry were sent for by the

Committee for Examinations; Sir James Symons, his father-in-law, Mr Heveningham, Robert Howard of How-Cross and Mr Fowler of St Thomas. They were confronted with Dugdale and interrogated by the Committee. They were quite frank about their patronage of various priests and Jesuits, and admitted that they had given money from time to time for St Omers (though this was a serious offence in law). They also admitted quite freely that they and about twenty other recusant gentry had gathered at Boscobel the previous August, but declined to accept Dugdale's sinister interpretation of the meeting. They had met to view that royalist relic, the Royal Oak, to feast on venison, and to attend the open-air service at which John Gavan had taken his final vows to the Society of Jesus. They denied all knowledge of the Plot, and were incredulous to hear of the large contributions they were supposed to have made to Jesuit funds. The seventy-year-old Heveningham told the Committee he 'never but once saw such a sum as two thousand pounds', and

He admires much that any great sums should be imagined to come from him, and that his fortune is strait, and that money and he hardly meet, and that therefore should hardly part.

The Committee dismissed him 'with respect, for that he behaved himself with great sobriety'; they also took a fancy to Fowler, another crotchety veteran, who admitted criticizing the Jesuits often enough, but denied coming to any harm by it – when asked if he thought Evers was honest, 'he said if Jesuits can be honest men Evers may be so too'. They elicited the fact that Sir James Symons's brother was a Jesuit, but were tactful enough to inquire no further (he had, in fact, fled to the Continent). Finally, they recommended to the Council that these men be dismissed to their homes without even being asked for recognizances, and two days later the Council concurred. On 12 February Dugdale made a further deposition, in which he incriminated Symons and Heveningham directly in the Plot, but apparently this was just ignored.[21]

In May, with Parliament sitting, it was another matter. Symons and Heveningham were arrested, and spent at least twelve months in prison,* and when another Staffordshire man, Richard Gerard of Hilderstone, came to town to provide Lord Stafford with an alibi, it was enough for Dugdale to name him as one of those present at the Boscobel meeting. The Lords threw him into the Gatehouse prison on 13 May, and he died there in March 1680, though the evidence against him was no stronger than against many of his neighbours.[22]

The King ordered Ireland and Grove to be executed on 24 January, though they were to be hanged until they were dead, instead of being cut down and disembowelled alive. That morning he told the Committee of Intelligence that he had decided to dissolve Parliament and summon another for March. He added, in the broken phrases of Williamson's notes:

No advice asked, because he found everybody more afraid to displease Parliament than him. If could have an equal debate, &c. would, &c.[23]

The perils of such a step were obvious enough then, more so in retrospect. But Charles was relying on a promise from the moderate wing of the Opposition, which had broken away from Shaftesbury, that they would not pursue Danby's impeachment in a new Parliament. In return Charles would sacrifice the Catholic peers, who were deeply suspect anyway. Also the government had a trump card in the person of Miles Prance; at least it would be able to meet Parliament claiming to have solved the Godfrey case.

The trial of Green, Berry and Hill opened on Wednesday, 5 February, but after the prisoners' pleas of not guilty had been entered it was adjourned for no obvious reason until the next day. In fact, the day before Bedloe had been reported to the Council for declaring in his cups that the Duke of York was 'a rogue and a rascal'. He appeared before the Council that evening, and when the Court reassembled next morning the prosecution asked for another adjournment, this time until Monday, 10

---

* In fact, I can find no record of their arrest. But they were certainly in prison in June 1680, when it was proposed to put them on trial with Lord Aston (D.W.L.: EB1/261,262).

February, 'that the King's evidence might be the more ready'. However, the government decided that it could not afford the luxury of dealing with Bedloe as it would have liked at the risk of letting the men accused of Godfrey's murder go free, and on the 10th the trial proceeded.[24]

Prance gave his evidence clearly and well, and unlike Bedloe and Oates he did not present a continuous narrative, but allowed the facts to be drawn out of him by cross-examination – in other words, he behaved like a true witness. The defendants could do little with him, except show that he had retracted his evidence once (they did not know he had done it twice). Oates had little to do; he could only testify that Godfrey was in fear of being murdered by the Catholics, and Bedloe, not having mentioned Prance, Green, Berry or Hill before, had some difficulty weaving them into his previous narrative. More impressive was the evidence of Godfrey's former maid, that Green and Hill were known to her master. Nor could they deny knowing a priest called Gerald.

Gauden's niece Mary Tilden appeared in Hill's defence: a bold thing to do, considering her uncle's position in the English Chapter. She testified that Hill had not been out after eight o'clock on the night of the murder, and that their apartments were so small that Godfrey's body could not possibly have been hidden there for three days without her knowing it. But she was a Catholic, it was her testimony against Prance's, and her evidence might well be held to incriminate her with Hill. (Scroggs had other ideas; he suggested that she must have been in bed with Hill, to be so sure he had not gone out all that night.) It was the same with another Catholic, Mistress Broadstreet. Mr Justice Wild pointed out that if she insisted that nobody could have lived in the house for more than a few hours without falling over Godfrey's body, then suspicion must turn against her. Mr Justice Dolben agreed, adding, 'It is well *you* are not indicted.' Her standing as a witness declined even further when the Attorney-General elicited the fact that her brother was the priest Broadstreet recently accused by Dugdale, for whom there was a proclamation out.

Hill called a few witnesses in an attempt to establish an alibi, but without success. Green, however, produced his landlord and landlady, both Protestants, to swear that he had been in all evening on the night of the murder. They were not very intelligent, but Scroggs could not shake them. Similarly, the sentry who had been on duty at Somerset House on the night of 16 October declared that no sedan chair had gone out; but since he was not obliged to challenge those going out, only those going in, the jury was left to reflect how he remembered that one night out of so many.

The Attorney-General then said he would curtail his closing address to the jury, because:

In truth, the King's evidence did fall out much better than I could expect, and the defence of the prisoners much weaker than I could foresee.

Nor was this unreasonable. Of the defence witnesses, only Green's had been at all impressive, and none of them was on oath. Bedloe had been kept well in hand. He still had a penchant for melodrama and literary flourishes, but he was not allowed to ramble or digress. Prance, as we have seen, was a model witness. At this stage it seemed incredible that all the King's witnesses should be lying, and when Mrs Hill cried out from the well of the court, with prophetic insight,

He [Prance] knows all these things to be as false as God's true, and you will see it declared hereafter, when it is too late,

Scroggs replied incredulously, 'Do you think he would swear three men out of their lives for nothing?'

After this Scroggs's summing-up was comparatively moderate. This trial, technically, had nothing to do with the Plot; it was murder, not treason; and the accused were laymen, who did not rouse his fury like the priests. But he showed not the least doubt of their guilt, and when the jury brought in a verdict of guilty he told them:

Gentlemen, you have found the same verdict that I would have found if I had been one with you; and if it were the last word I were to speak in this world I should have pronounced them guilty.

R. White ad vivum   delin et Sculp.

TITUS OATES.
Anagramma
TESTIS OVAT.

This is the true Originall taken from the Life,
done for HEN. BREME and RIC: CHISWELL. All others are Counterfeit.

1. Titus Oates, 1679.

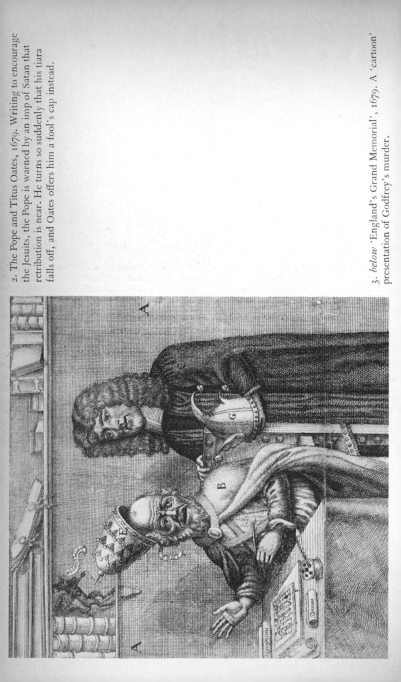

2. The Pope and Titus Oates, 1679. Writing to encourage the Jesuits, the Pope is warned by an imp of Satan that retribution is near. He turns so suddenly that his tiara falls off, and Oates offers him a fool's cap instead.

3. *below* 'England's Grand Memorial', 1679. A 'cartoon' presentation of Godfrey's murder.

The discoverers of the plot and Treasonable Plotters.   Fires and Massacres Romish Mercies.

1678 ☙ SP EDMUND-BURIE-GODFREY THE KINGDOMS MARTYR

The first Account of their Damnable & horrid Plot.

Certainly this is the day that they looked for, &c.
Whose Innocent Blood yet Cryes Vengeance, Vengeance!

Dr Oates.   Mr Bedloe.   Mr France.   Mr Dugdale.

Fig: 2.   The Hellish Councell of the Whole Plott.

Fig: 3.   Mr Oates   and   Dr Tongs Information.

Justice Godfrey Drawne into Coleman: field.
A Pretended Quarrel betweene Berry and Kelly.

Fig: 4.

Printed for Tho: Danks the twn: of the 5 Inthlmans. 1679

Fig: 6.

Green missing his neck about.

Justice Godfrey Carried before Hills.

Girald   Kelly

Fig: 8.   Iust Godfrey begin pe to the wall of his house   Girald   France   Kelly

Fig: 7.

Fig: 9.

Sir Edmund Burie Godfrey Anstrum Ilf and murder ed by Rogues.

Kawn out Justice Godfrey Sword thorow him.

Gerald   Hill

Fig: 10.

Murdered Justice Godfrey

Fig: 11.

4. Playing cards of the Plot. These are often useful on points of detail, such as the kind of sled on which traitors were drawn to Tyburn.

5. Sir William Scroggs, by an unknown artist, 1678.

Rome's *Scarlet* whore doth here in *Tryumph* Ride,
And Spurns off *Soveraign* Crowns in Aeight of Pride
Poor *Christians* and *brave* Citties too shee Burns
And Stabbs and Poisons daily serve her Turns.

6. *left* 'The dreadful Apparition; or, The Pope Haunted with Ghosts', 1680. The Pope haunted by the victims of the Plot, Catholic and Protestant. Left to right: Coleman is introduced by the Devil, and Godfrey, transfixed by three swords, by a female angel attired as a Roman soldier. Then come Whitbread and Harcourt, watched by a horrified cardinal. Godfrey exhorts the Pope to repent and join him in Heaven by and by; the others reproach him for the fact that they are in Hell.

7. 'Babel and Bethel; or, The Pope in his Colours', 1679. A diptych contrasting the Pope with Charles II, the latter portrayed as the Church of England's protector. On the far left London is in flames, and below that Wakeman is offering the King poison while Godfrey lies dead. On the right-hand side, the traitors go to their just deserts.

Behold our Church (like Esther here doth tender
Her Supplications to the Faiths Defender
In vain Rome Plots, while Charles's Sceptre Sways
May Sled and Gibbet end all Traitors Days.

8. Sir George Jeffreys, attributed to W. Claret, c. 1679.

Green replied, 'God bless the King, and I desire all good people to pray for us'

Green and Hill were executed on 21 February. Berry was reprieved for a further week; he was a Protestant, and there was some hope of a confession, but none came. Contemporary Catholics argued that in his last days he was received back into the Catholic faith from which he had reneged, but there seems no truth in this.

The trial which immediately followed undid Bedloe again. In November he had rashly identified Samuel Atkins, a young Admiralty clerk, as one of Godfrey's murderers, present at Somerset House the night of the crime. He was backed up by a cashiered naval officer called Captain Charles Atkins. Why the government did not back down when it learned, as it soon did, that Samuel Atkins had a cast-iron alibi it is impossible to say; it is part of the general confusion and ill-organization typical of the government prosecutor's department under Sir William Jones. Scroggs saw the danger, and tried to have the trial postponed to the following term, but it came on the day after that of Green, Berry and Hill, 11 February.[25] In the event Charles Atkins's evidence was so thin and implausible that even Scroggs could not stomach it. When the defendant tried to rebut it, Scroggs told him it was 'nothing to the purpose', 'you need not labour your defence as to anything he says'. Bedloe himself decided to hedge; he was not so sure now that the man he had seen standing by Godfrey's bier was Samuel Atkins – 'he had a more manly face than he hath, and a beard'. Scroggs remarked, 'You do well to be cautious.' The Attorney-General concurred, and when Scroggs had heard evidence that Atkins was a loyal and zealous Protestant he told him, 'Call a couple of witnesses to prove where you were that Monday night, the 14th of October, and you need not trouble yourself any further.' This was easy. Atkins promptly produced Captain Vittles, of the King's ship *Katherine,* who had entertained him on board that night off Greenwich. He testified that Atkins had been taken off, much the worse for wear, at ten-thirty at the earliest, and deposited at Billingsgate Steps at eleven-thirty; and this was confirmed by his boatswain. Drunk or sober, it was quite clear that Atkins could never have been at Somerset House between nine and ten. The trial petered out in an atmosphere of unwonted geniality, with Scroggs advising Atkins and Captain Vittles to split another bottle between them.

Before a formal verdict of 'not guilty' was brought in, the Attorney-General anxiously sought an assurance from the bench that 'here is no disproving the King's evidence'. Scroggs replied that Bedloe's evidence had never been direct enough to convict, even without Atkins's fine alibi. Again the question arises, why bring the trial on at all? It may have been intended simply to humiliate Bedloe and warn him that he and his underworld cronies like Captain Atkins must refrain from attacking members of the government, even if they were only clerks. Later that same day Scroggs, sitting in King's Bench, bailed a whole string of lay Catholics named in Oates's and Bedloe's original confessions, including Charles Price, Sir William Goring and Sir John Page, though he dismissed other applications with the remark that 'one positive single witness against a plotting Papist was sufficient to keep him in prison'.[26] The implication was that neither Oates nor Bedloe was a positive witness.

As Bedloe's star fell, Dugdale's rose. True, ugly tales were flying around about his financial defalcations in Staffordshire. But these could be dismissed as papist libels. From the beginning he had frankly admitted that he was in debt, and clearly the man still had the power to charm; on 31 January the Committee for Examinations stamped him with its seal of approval as 'a witness of untainted credit'.[27] His accusations against the Staffordshire gentry had not stuck, but his evidence on the Jesuits was clear, unambiguous and plausible; moreover, it was to some extent confirmed by one of his former accomplices, Dr Robert Needham, who was arrested early in February and confessed.[28] The fact that most of the priests he named were either dead or could not be found was of scant concern to the government, especially since he was so positive about Lord Stafford. The Committee for Examinations could not hear enough about this, and on 21 February he gave them an improved version of a conversation between himself, Stafford and Evers the previous September, in which the old loyalist peer explained in terms which were only too plausible 'the reason of his dissatisfaction against his Majesty':

Towards whom he had long carried himself with all sorts of loyalty as he had towards his father, but that he and others had thereby had their families ruined. And in particular, that the old Lord Aston had been a great sufferer, and his father the ambassador had spent £30,000 out of their own estate, but that there was no hopes of any recompense, for he saw plainly as anything fell to be given it was rather disposed of to rebels and traitors and those who had served against the King, rather than those who had been loyal. And therefore those things had wrought with him, and were sufficient to change his mind towards the King, [even] if there were not the matter of religion in question.[29]

At this stage he also turned against Lord Aston at last, perhaps in response to accusations from him. On 24 February he told how Lord Aston had made every effort to prevent his making his original deposition in December, and revealed for the first time that Aston had been due to go over to Paris the previous October, in circumstances that pointed to his involvement in the Plot. This nailed Aston, and prepared the way for a final, positive accusation against him a month later, when Parliament had met.[30]

There was now enough evidence to convict Whitbread and Fenwick, remanded from December, but Pickering had not yet been executed, and the government was not anxious to hold further trials before Parliament met. Williamson was dismissed on 12 February, and with his going we lose an important witness to cabinet discussions. But the government had an excuse for delay in that it had not yet found Evers, one of the chief villains, or Harcourt. The multiplicity of 'Harcourts' was still causing trouble. William Aylworth, alias Harcourt, probably the man intended by Dugdale and certainly by Oates, had gone underground. William Barrow, alias Harcourt, was not found until 7 May, in London, where he had been all the time; in the meanwhile the Council amused itself with Valentine Harcourt, a secular priest brought up from Shrewsbury for their inspection.[31]

However, when the new Parliament met in March its primary concern was with Danby and the Duke of York. From the first it was clear that the elections were going against the Court. The Popish Plot apart, the government had under-estimated the natural reaction inevitable in the first general election in eighteen years. The country voted for a change. The government also under-estimated the damage done by Ralph Montagu's revelations, coming hard on Oates's; in the majority of constituencies the electors voted consciously against the Court and against the Lord Treasurer, and only a Member who could demonstrate his previous opposition to both had much chance in a marginal seat. On 8 February, with the campaign only just beginning, Edward Seymour warned Williamson:

> I evidently foresee a violent shock, that will press the government, and will call upon all our courage and prudence to withstand it. God avert it, and preserve those that endeavour to preserve it.[32]

All the same, there was a tendency to exaggerate the extent of the disaster. The French ambassador hysterically declared that the supporters of the government were reduced to thirty, but Shaftesbury drew up a list just before Parliament met which credited his opponents with 158 seats, and this proved fairly accurate. On 11 May, after two months of bitter contestation, the government minority on the second reading of the Exclusion Bill was still 128. Ormonde, in Dublin, remarked:

> The elections are not so bad as we feared, nor so good as some hoped. I think monarchy will not be struck at the root, but I fear it will be very close lopped.[33]

What *had* collapsed was Danby's parliamentary organization, his family connections and his ministerial allies, and Charles's decision to retain him was an act of doubtful wisdom, though in the long run it proved a diversion which kept Parliament from more important or more damaging matters.

One of these was obviously James. So far he had led a charmed life; none of the informers had directly implicated him in the Plot, and Oates had gone out of his way to exculpate him. He had been excepted from the second Test Act, and he probably still had a majority of the House of Lords behind him. The chief count against him was Coleman's letters, and only three of those had yet been printed officially – in the record of the trial, which the government had recalled in January on Oates's plea that his evidence had been misrepresented. A report drawn up for Shaftesbury shortly before Parliament met suggests that the emotion James aroused in the Opposition was fear rather than hatred:

He is every way a perfect Stuart, and hath the advantage of his brother only that he hath ambition and thoughts of something he hath not, which gives him industry and address even beyond his natural parts. Yet his conduct, courage, judgement and honour are not much to be confided in ... His religion suits well with his temper; heady, violent and bloody, who easily believes the rashest and worst of counsels to be most sincere and hearty ... His interest and design are to introduce a military and arbitrary government in his brother's time.[34]

In these circumstances it was unwise for Charles to yield to Danby's advice that he send his brother into exile on 3 March, three days before Parliament met. It confirmed that James was a liability, and that the government could not defend him. It was just as unwise for James on his part to take himself off to the Spanish Netherlands, which was notoriously the headquarters of the Catholic English Missions, and even sillier of him to demand from his brother a public denial that he had ever been married to Monmouth's mother. This must encourage in Monmouth ambitions which at this stage only his close friends took seriously.

Charles's opening speech on 6 March was moderate and sensible. He stressed the concessions he had made, particularly in passing the second Test Act and sending his brother from his side; he reminded them of the offenders already convicted and executed; he undertook to implement the penal laws against Catholics with the utmost vigour, and to pass any new penal laws Parliament cared to present to him. He told them that they could be 'a healing parliament', and closed with a statesman-like appeal for national unity, later to be strengthened by close alliances with Protestant states abroad.

In fact, so far as the Plot was concerned, this Parliament was less obstreperous and effective than its predecessor, partly because many of its members were inevitably new, and inexperienced in obstruction, partly because of the distractions offered by Danby and James. But of course, the Commons could not help but be affected to some degree by the prevailing hysteria in London, which had been at boiling-point since January, when the New Year had been ushered in by 'Black Sunday'. (Freak weather conditions plunged the City into darkness at eleven in the morning.) On 17 January the militia had been ordered to search papists' houses on a regular rota every ten days, and on the 26th there was a large fire at the Temple, which was the first of a series which brought back fears of 1666, and provoked the publication of pamphlets like *London's Flames Revived*. In March there were four more fires, in the shops around St Paul's Churchyard, in St Clement's Lane, Creed Lane and Fetter Lane; it was also rumoured that St John's College, Cambridge, had been burnt down 'by the malice of the Jesuits'. On 10 April another fire in Fetter Lane was traced to a servant girl called Elizabeth Oxley, who admitted acting under the orders of a papist called Stubbs. When Stubbs was arrested he in his turn implicated a priest called Guilford, who had told him that the King would be killed before the middle of June, and six thousand French troops were ready to land.[35]

The assembly of Parliament also restored Oates's and Bedloe's prestige as saviours of the nation. They both appeared before the House of Commons, to go through their evidence again for the benefit of new Members, and Prance and Dugdale also came before the Lords Committee for Examinations, which had taken over from the Privy Council again. It was difficult now for Oates to enlarge on his testimony, but on 21 March he accused two Members of the Commons of impugning his evidence, and had one of them, Edward Sackville, expelled, and on 15 April he published his *Narrative*. This was the gist of what he had testified the previous September, with insignificant alterations, though as usual he promised a 'larger account and journal, in which the whole mystery of this hellish plot shall be more fully laid open'.[36] It was dedicated to the King, without permission, with a new introduction which declared that James I had been murdered (a theory maintained by the Long Parliament), and attributed the Great Rebellion and the death of Charles I to the Jesuits. He also criticized the King for his prevous indulgence to the Catholics. The Commons backed his demand for a larger allowance from the Crown, while the Lords helped him frustrate Francis Norwood, who was still trying to revive the old perjury indictment against him at Hastings; he threatened Sir John Robinson, the Governor of the Tower, and even administered a public snub to the Queen – though there were limits, and he had to swallow a reprimand from the Speaker for declaring 'The King holds his crown by the same title I hold my liberty.'[37]

Even Bedloe was prospering. The Commons successfully backed his demand of £500 reward for discovering the murderers of Sir Edmund Berry Godfrey (to be shared with Prance and others), and he succeeded in 'improving' his previous evidence. On 3 April in the Commons, Sir Henry Capel 'chanced in the nick of time to surprise and amaze the House' with a cry of 'Strangers'. The stranger proved to be Nathaniel Reading, a lawyer who often pleaded before the Commons in election cases, and had also been engaged by prominent Roman Catholics from time to time. Bedloe promptly accused him of suborning his evidence in previous trials, and he was indicted for a misdemeanour. He was tried in King's Bench on 24 April, when Bedloe accused him of bribing him to swear that he had no evidence against Whitbread and Fenwick the previous December. He was found guilty and sentenced to the pillory, and this cleared Beldoe to give evidence against the two Jesuits when they were next arraigned.[38] The fact that Bedloe was now a self-confessed as distinct from a suspected perjurer seemed to trouble no one, least of all opposition leaders like Capel. Oates's conduct towards the Queen showed that that issue was far from dead, and like him Bedloe pretended to have some evidence still to come. He told the Commons, 'My full discovery of all things cannot be expected till the Lords' trials.'[39]

Certainly the Commons were still deeply committed to a belief in the Plot, and as sceptical as ever of the King's ability or willingness to investigate it to the depths. On 20 March they elected a new Committee of Secrecy with a majority of old Opposition spokesmen. It was the same with the Lords Committee for Examinations, though after 21 April, when Shaftesbury became Lord President, the full weight of the Privy Council was thrown behind it. That same day orders went out to the Provinces for several priests condemned at the spring assizes to be brought to London for interrogation. They all resolutely denied any knowledge of the Plot, of course, though there is a strong tradition (and a plausible one) that Shaftesbury offered them pardons if they turned King's evidence. On the scaffold in August the Welsh Jesuit David Lewis said, 'When I was examined in London last May a certain nobleman of high rank openly told me that I must die unless I betrayed the secret of the Plot, or else accommodated myself to the reformed religion.' Lewis was the only one of these provincial priests whom Oates 'recognized' – as a member of the Jesuit Consult of 24 April 1678.[40]

In fact, though Members were very ready to assert that this parliament was much better than the last – 'This brings their interest with them; the last came to make an interest here' is a typical comment – its record of achievement on the Plot was poor. It could only attract one new informer, Sidway, who wildly accused the bishops of Bath and Wells, Ely and Gloucester of being in league with Cardinal Howard, and was promptly and predictably clapped in the Tower. Meanwhile the Jesuits remaining in the London prisons had not been put on trial, nor had Richard Langhorn and Sir George Wakeman, though they had been arrested the previous October. Parliament's solitary success on this front came when the Commons sent up an address demanding the execution of Pickering, who had been sentenced to death more than three months before. Even then Charles hesitated; he sent back a message saying, 'I have always been tender in matters of blood, which my subjects have no reason to take exception at.' But after another week he gave way, and Pickering was executed on 9 May.[41]

Meanwhile, the credit of the existing Plot witnesses was crumbling, and each new day brought the possibility of some revelation which would blow their credit to rags, even in the eyes of a credulous public. This is what Charles hoped, and Shaftesbury feared. On 25 April Oates produced a man called Lane before the Lords Committee for Examinations to support a tale he was now peddling that Danby had tried to suppress his evidence. But instead Lane denied all knowledge of that matter, and

fell to arraigning Mr Oates himself, as one that spoke the basest and most contemptible words of the King imaginable, as if he associated himself with none but whores, rogues, pimps and panders, and that Mr Chiffinch* was a pimp, the son of a pimp, and that the King never went sober to bed; and thence proceeded to such beastly, bawdy discourse that the Lords stopped his mouth and would hear him no further nor believe him so far.

Indeed, Lane had gone too far, and given Shaftesbury an excuse to silence him. But Charles let it be known that he was extremely displeased that his private life should be discussed at a Lords' Committee, and he ostentatiously released Edward Sackville, whom the Commons had sent to the Tower for presuming to cast doubt on Oates's truthfulness.[42] By this time Parliament had slowed down almost to a walking pace. This was largely because of procedural difficulties, and disagreements between the Houses, but how far these were natural, or created by the government, it is difficult to say. At the very beginning of the session a week had been lost because of a three-cornered struggle between Charles, Danby and the Commons over the choice of Speaker. Then Danby resigned. The Commons decided to deal with him at once, even though this meant keeping the Catholic lords in abeyance. On 23 March, on the King's orders, Danby went into hiding, and another three weeks passed while the two

---

* William Chiffinch, Keeper of the Closet and confidential servant to Charles II.

Houses argued whether he should be banished or attainted. The Commons got their way, but not until 14 April, on which day Danby surrendered himself, and the whole process restarted. When he produced a retrospective pardon from the King, this at once occasioned further long arguments.[43]

Next, on 21 April Charles brought things to a halt again by announcing a signal concession. He dismissed his Privy Council *en bloc* and appointed a new one limited to thirty members, including the principal leaders of the Opposition in both Houses: Sir Henry Capel, Henry Powle, Essex, Halifax and Shaftesbury himself, who was also made Lord President. This threw the Opposition into some confusion. The new Councillors had much greater power over the administrative machinery of government, for what this was worth, but they were still excluded from policy-making discussions, and they were promptly accused by their old associates of having betrayed their cause. The immediate result was to divert the Opposition into an attack on the Duke of York, which Shaftesbury probably regarded as premature.

James had never lived down his association with Coleman, and his retreat to Flanders was suspicious in itself. Oates and Bedloe had never dared put forward evidence directly implicating him in the Plot, and it was now too late for them to do so, but Dugdale, who had kept his options open, began to develop and 'improve' his evidence as soon as Parliament met. On 21 March he gave the Lords Committee for Examinations evidence tying Evers with Godfrey's murder; on the 25th he strengthened and elaborated his previous evidence against Lord Stafford and Lord Aston; and finally on the 26th he dragged in James; almost casually, but perhaps in answer to a direct question:

Mr Evers told me about July 78 the Duke of York had promised he would establish the Romish religion, and I saw it written in a letter from Mr Bedingfield the same, and I even understood he would accept it under the Pope.[44]

Shaftesbury seems to have held back this information, even after he rejoined the Privy Council on 21 April. But at the end of that week his friends in the Commons persuaded the House to sit on Sunday the 27th, 'to consider how to preserve the King's person from the attempts and conspiracies of the Papists'. This debate generated more heat than light, except for the fact that members of the Committee of Secrecy now brought forward the rest of Coleman's correspondence, still unpublished, and especially his correspondence with John Leyburn at Rome.* Sir Thomas Player said:

> Some time ago I saw considerable papers and transactions betwixt the Duke and the Pope. I did scarce believe it till I saw it. Some from his Highness to his Holiness gave him occasion of so great joy (and surely they must be considerable letters that made his Holiness so merry) and yet they made the old man weep; and that bespeaks excess of joy. Some time before there was notice given of such letters coming, but they gave great trouble at Rome that they came not, but when they were received, his Holiness returned the Duke a most kind and obliging answer, and her Highness the Duchess was presented from the Pope with a holy token of consecrated beads, and other fine things, which I do not understand, and I hope never shall.

This alarmed even the moderate Members, and it threw the hard-line Opposition spokesmen into a veritable frenzy:

> If we do not something relating to the succession [said Lord Russell], we must resolve, when we have a Prince of the Popish Religion, to be papists or burn, and I will do neither. We see now, by what is done under a Protestant Prince, what will be done under a Popish. This is the deciding day betwixt both religions.

Finally it was resolved *nem. con.* 'that the Duke of York's being a papist, and the hopes of his coming such to the Crown, has given the greatest countenance and encouragement to the present conspiracies and designs of the Papists'; and Russell at once took this up to the Lords, further debate being adjourned until Wednesday.[45]

In fact, the Lords made no move to second this resolution, then or later, and on Wednesday, 30 April, the day to which the Commons debate stood adjourned, the King dropped another bombshell. He came down to address both Houses, and after a

* See p. 100 above.

brief speech calling, tongue in cheek, for the more vigorous investigation of the Plot, he gave way to the Lord Chancellor, who announced that to meet the fears expressed by Parliament the King was willing to sanction statutory restrictions on the authority of his successor. The next king, if he was a Catholic, would have no say whatsoever in ecclesiastical appointments, and no power to dismiss judges, officers of the armed forces or members of the Privy Council, and Charles was willing to discuss further concessions along these lines, provided they did not infringe James's hereditary right to the throne.

This *démarche* again disorganized the Opposition for a few days, some Members being willing to accept it at its face value.[46] It was not until 11 May that the debate on the Duke was renewed, and his exclusion from the succession proposed. An Exclusion Bill was introduced on the 15th, but its second reading was postponed until the 21st, and then the division (207 : 128) revealed an unexpectedly large minority against it. It was also obvious that the Lords would have nothing to do with it, and in any case the two Houses were still in a deadlock over the trial of Danby. The Commons had alienated the Lords by insisting that the earl be condemned on his attainder, without further trial, and it was not until 11 May that this was resolved in the Lords' favour. At once another dispute broke out as to whether the bishops could vote in capital cases. So bad was the situation that Sir Thomas Clarges told the Commons, 'The whole manner of the Lords' proceeding since the Plot seems extraordinary, and I despair of justice from them.'[47]

All this time the trial of the five Catholic peers had been held up, though the crimes of which they were accused were much more serious than Danby's, and popular fury against them much more intense. Their impeachment was renewed on 7 April, and when they were brought by water to Westminster two days later to enter their pleas, a hostile mob 'flocked into boats, showing them halters and making of gallows, and such a noise was raised at their landing near the House of Lords that the House issued orders to the Lord Mayor to suppress such tumultuary courses'. On 6 May, perhaps under pressure from Court, the Lords finally fixed their trial for that day week, but it was then successively postponed until 23 May, while the Commons obstinately struggled to bring Danby's trial forward. On the 23rd the Lords finally voted to adjourn the proceedings against Danby for the time being, and fixed yet another date for the trial of the Catholic lords, on the 27th. But the Commons protested angrily, and it was doubtful if they could or would appear on that day to lead the prosecution. 'We are almost run aground,' said one M.P., and Charles was justified in his view that there was no purpose in prolonging the session. Therefore on 27 May, without taking the advice of his new Privy Council, he came down to Westminster and prorogued Parliament until 14 August. 'All parted in a mist of surprise.'[48]

It was a drawn game. Parliament had done nothing constructive to deal with the Plot or the Catholic problem. Danby had been reprieved, and so had the Catholic lords. Orders had gone out on 28 April for the immediate execution of all priests lying under sentence of death in provincial gaols, but a combination of languor on the part of the government and obstruction by local authorities had done much to mitigate the effects of this.

However, the trials of further Jesuits could not be postponed indefinitely. The sudden outbreak of the Covenanters Rebellion in Scotland, while in some ways providing a distraction, certainly heightened public agitation and encouraged a sense of instability. In the third week of May another serious fire, this time in Holborn, was again attributed to the Catholics, and Salvetti, the Modenese Resident, admitted that he was shaken.

Whether these insane tales are true or false [he wrote] I do not presume to decide, but so many persons of quality, moderation and intelligence affirm them to be true that I am confounded in my thoughts, and it is surprising (considering the temper of this nation) that they have not risen and massacred all those suspected of such crimes, and I have heard it said by several people, that all the Catholics deserve to be killed.[49]

So, in the first week of June the Lord Chancellor was instructed to issue a special commission of oyer and terminer and gaol delivery for Newgate, and preparations were made for the speedy trial of Whitbread and Fenwick, together with three other Jesuits arrested since the beginning of the year, John Gavan, William Harcourt and Anthony Turner, plus a Dominican, James Corker. Edward Petre, S.J., an intimate of the Duke of York's who was accused by Dugdale as well as Oates, and had been in prison since the previous October, was significantly omitted, perhaps on the plea that he ought to stand trial with Lord Aston and the other Staffordshire conspirators. The inability of the government to find a second witness against Aston held this up indefinitely, of course.

The trial opened at the Old Bailey on 13 June, and it is significant of the importance attached to it by the government that on the bench there sat not only Scroggs and the King's Bench judges, with the Recorder of London (Jeffreys), but also the Chief Justice of Common Pleas (Francis North), the Attorney-General (Jones) and the new Solicitor-General (Heneage Finch). Cresswell Levinz led for the Crown.[50]

The opening exchanges were courteous enough. Whitbread accepted Scroggs's ruling that it was lawful for him and Fenwick to be tried again, after the fiasco of the previous December, and in turn Scroggs accepted a challenge to one of the jurymen on the grounds that he had served in previous trials. Corker was even allowed to stand down, on the thin plea that he had not had time to prepare his defence; he was lucky enough to be tried with Wakeman the following month.[51] The truth is, the bench was feeling its way. At the end of April Sir William Waller had arrested five schoolboys from St Omers, part of a larger group which had come over 'at the instigation of the Superior of the College, as likewise the desire of several Roman Catholics in England for the justification of the Roman Catholic cause, and in relation to Mr Oates'. They had come to swear that Oates had been at St Omers in April 1678, when he was supposed to have been at the Jesuit Consult in London, yet the government put no obstacles in their way. After interrogation they were released, and so was Nicholas Blundell, the Jesuit father who had escorted them over, though Oates had specifically charged him with a plan to burn London. He afterwards returned with the boys to

St Omers, where he died peacefully the following year.[52] On his side Oates had anxiously been collecting witnesses in rebuttal, but it was not clear what the jury's attitude would be, and certainly when he took the stand he was nervous.

He made a bad beginning. He had to explain why he had not accused John Gavan at the earliest opportunity, the previous September, and why he had not recognized him when they both appeared before the Privy Council in January. This was the Coleman case all over again, and again Oates took refuge in talk of periwigs. When asked directly if Gavan had been at the White Horse Tavern on 24 April 1678, he hedged – 'Among forty men I cannot particularly say he was there, but I saw his name signed as to the King's death, but I cannot say I saw his person.' Asked if he knew Gavan's handwriting, he said he had seen it in letters written from Staffordshire in June and July 1678. Scroggs tried to secure more definite proof from him, and more detail, but in the end he dismissed him with the impatient remark, 'I perceive your memory is not good.'

Then Oates had to face a stream of questions from Gavan, some of which jolted him. Gavan was a comparatively young man, not yet forty; he was exceptionally able, and he had not suffered the privations of prison for very long. It is clear from the records that he dominated the trial and took over the direction of the defence from his seniors, who seemed for the most part to be passively resigned to their fate. (Whitbread was sixty-one years old, Fenwick fifty-one, Harcourt, sixty-nine and Turner fifty.) Oates was upset, and at one stage peevishly demanded that Gavan direct his questions to the court, 'for they are nimble in their questions, and do a little abuse the evidence [*sc.* the witnesses]. They put things upon them that they never say.' Mr Justice Pemberton told Gavan to comply with this, and the Jesuit answered, 'I would do so, my lord, in whose honour I have more confidence than in whatsoever Mr Oates says or swears.' Scroggs seemed disposed to ignore this (as he had ignored Oates's protest), and it was left to Chief Justice North to issue a reproof: 'Do not give the King's witnesses ill words.'

Whitbread then questioned Oates about certain details in his published *Narrative*, which it appeared he had forgotten. Scroggs observed, 'Perhaps a man will venture to write more than he will swear,' adding hastily, 'Not that he does write what he does not believe, but that he knows he ought to be more cautious in his oath than in his affirmation.' Fenwick's remark that Oates *had* sworn to the truth of his *Narrative* was brushed aside; it was not an oath relevant to this court at this time.

Dugdale now took the stand, and turned in another polished performance, his first in public. Scroggs was charmed. 'You deliver your testimony', he said, 'like a sober, modest man, upon my word' – perhaps a reflection on the previous witnesses; certainly he had never spoken of Oates or Bedloe in such terms. The fact that Dugdale's eyesight was fully as bad as Oates's – he had not recognized Harcourt when he was presented to him in Newgate – was offset by the new evidence he had to offer linking the Jesuits with Godfrey's murder. Scroggs dwelt lovingly on this. However, it soon appeared that he had little to offer against Whitbread, only a letter from him to Evers, 'in which he gave Mr Evers a caution to choose those that were very trusty, it was no matter whether they were gentlemen or no, so they would be but stout and courageous'. Pressed, he simply repeated this in slightly different words, but the judges continued the attack:

ATKINS, J.: What were they to do?

DUGDALE: For the killing of the King.

LORD CHIEF JUSTICE: What was in Whitbread's letter?

DUGDALE: Mr Whitbread wrote those words. They were in the letter.

WHITBREAD: Was that very word in the letter, for killing the King?

DUGDALE: It was, that they should be stout and courageous persons.

LORD CHIEF JUSTICE: For what end?

DUGDALE: It was for taking away the King's life.

LORD CHIEF JUSTICE: I ask you to recollect yourself, was it by way of description of some design or plot, that those persons were to be chosen out? Or was it in downright words, for killing the King?

DUGDALE: To the best of my remembrance those were the words.

Having practically forced the words into the witness's mouth, Scroggs rather perversely remarked, 'It was much he would write such words in a letter', and inquired if it had been sent by ordinary mail. It had.

As so often in these trials, we are astonished at the lack of preparation in the Crown witnesses. Dugdale was an accomplished liar, and he was testifying to the contents of a letter which no one expected him to produce. All he need do was to insert the phrase Scroggs required and testify that it had been sent by messenger. (Gavan was an obvious candidate for that task.) Was Dugdale in fact twisting the actual words of a letter he had really seen? Whitbread's solitary interjection, and the fact that he did not deny the letter in general terms, suggests that this was the case.

However, after Dugdale came Prance, who could only testify that Fenwick, with Grove and Ireland, had talked treason to him the previous September in London. Bedloe followed, and made the best job he could of explaining his previous refusal to testify against Fenwick and Whitbread. To make amends he was now willing to testify against Harcourt, too. Harcourt denied it all, but admitted under cross-examination that he *had* used Bedloe to carry letters for him between London and the Continent in 1675. This made an impression, and so did Edward Petre's letter of 23 February 1678, confirming the plans for a consult in London in April, and using the fatal word 'design'. This had been referred to in previous trials, but it was now put up as evidence in chief, together with another letter, of 5 February 1678, containing a reference to 'patents', which were construed by the prosecution as being the famous 'patents' or commissions seen by Oates in Langhorn's study, for appointments to the new Catholic army and administration. Whitbread's explanation, that it referred to his 'patents' of appointment as Provincial, was not likely to be accepted by the jury. At this point the prosecution rested, with a vigorous protest from Fenwick:

I have had a thousand letters taken from me; not any of these letters had anything of treason in them. All the evidence that is given comes but to this; there is but saying and swearing.

Then the defence produced sixteen witnesses from St Omers to testify that Oates had never left the college for the first six months of 1678. Scroggs told the jury 'to take great heed of what they say, and to be governed by it according to the credibility of the person and of the matter', and reminded them that if they were not on oath this was only because it was not permitted, not because they were unwilling to swear. But the attitude of the audience, which was by now markedly unruly, was not conducive to impartiality; a great shout went up when the first witness admitted that he was a Catholic, and Pemberton told him, 'Be not ashamed of your religion, do not deny that; your Provincial there can give you a dispensation for what you say.' Certainly, as witness succeeded witness, each telling the same tale in much the same way, a degree of rehearsal was obvious, and Scroggs, losing his temper, told the jury that they were clearly 'instructed'. At another point he told the prisoners their witnesses were nothing but 'a fry out of your own schools'. When Cresswell Levinz then brought up four witnesses, including an old Dominican friar Matthew Clay, to testify that they had seen Oates in London in April 1678,

The whole court gave a shout of laughter and hallow, that for almost a quarter of an hour the criers could not still them. Never was a bear-baiting more rude and boisterous than this trial.[53]

Gavan, who had already irritated Scroggs to no purpose by demanding trial by ordeal, which had gone out of use centuries before, irritated him still further by a long speech in justification, which he delivered, despite interruptions, 'with a countenance wholly unconcerned, and in a voice very audible, and largely and pertinently expressed'.[54] The Lord Chief Justice, who was not accustomed to such harangues from the dock, then began his summing-up with the remarkable statement:

Gentlemen of the Jury, here hath been a very long evidence, and a very confused one, and you cannot expect that it should be wholly repeated to you. For it is almost impossible for anyone to remember it; neither would I if I could, because a great deal of it is impertinent [*sc.* irrelevant] and vainly to be repeated.*

As in previous trials, he left it to the jury, quite legitimately, to decide on the validity of the witnesses. But he strongly hinted that the seminarists from St Omers had been drilled to an unusual degree, though he did not attempt to impugn their evidence further – for instance, by suggesting, as Pemberton had done, that they had received dispensations to lie. But on Dugdale he waxed eloquent, and he especially welcomed his new evidence on Godfrey's murder which gave him, he said, 'the greatest satisfaction of anything in the world in this matter'. This led up to a long and largely irrelevant peroration on Godfrey, and his usual intemperate tirade against Catholicism in general. The jury only retired for fifteen minutes before returning with a verdict of 'guilty' against all five prisoners. They were remanded for sentence.

Next day, Saturday 14 June, the same court reassembled to try the rest of the prisoners before it; Corker again, two other Benedictines, Marshal and Rumley, the lawyer Richard Langhorn, and Sir George Wakeman. But they were a heterogeneous lot, and it was decided to begin with Langhorn separately.

The proceedings were so casual that Scroggs himself arrived half an hour late (the trial had opened at 8.0 a.m.). Dugdale and Prance came first to offer general 'proof' of the existence of the Popish Plot. (This was a waste of time, and it had not been done in previous trials, but it would be unwise to assume that this indicated a growth of scepticism.) Oates then took the stand, and unblushingly proceeded to extend the evidence he had given against Langhorn in his original depositions and *Narrative*. Not only had Langhorn received and distributed the Pope's com-

---

*For reasons which are not clear, judges in criminal cases did not take notes of the evidence and had to sum it up from memory. It should also be remembered that however long the case there was no break for meals; after Wakeman's trial, which lasted nine hours, John Evelyn dined with the judges – 'or rather indeed supped, so late it was' (*Diary,* iv, 175).

missions to the putative leaders of the Catholic revolt, including one for himself as advocate-general to the Army, he had participated in the now famous Consult of April 1678 and specifically approved the King's assassination. With much prompting from Levinz and Scroggs, who were perhaps influenced by the fact that they had three Benedictines to try soon, he also brought in the Benedictine community in London who, he said, had given Langhorn £6,000 to be transferred to the Jesuits' assassination fund.[55]

In reply, Langhorn adopted what was to prove a consistent policy, of attacking the witnesses' character rather than their evidence. His questions about Oates's conversions and reconversions made him squirm, but in themselves they were pointless, everybody knew the kind of man Oates had been, and the court had already heard much worse about him, and probably knew more.

Bedloe, when his turn came, was troublesome and not very effective. He began by pointing out that the Marchioness of Worcester,* the wife of his arch-enemy, was sitting in the gallery, taking notes. Scroggs told him irritably, 'A woman's notes will not signify much, truly; no more than her tongue.' Moreover, his evidence, when he could be induced to give it, did not amount to very much. On the strength of letters he had read he was able to tie Langhorn into his favourite conspiracy for a rising in Wales and the Marches, but all he knew of his share in the Jesuit Plot to assassinate the King was from conversations he had overheard by chance. Mr Justice Atkins intervened to dismiss this as hearsay, and Scroggs rather surprisingly agreed. (Apparently hearsay was only hearsay at third hand.) Trying harder, Bedloe then said that he had seen letters from the accused to La Chaise mentioning a certain design, which from a subsequent conversation between Langhorn and Coleman obviously referred to the Plot. This time the evocative names of 'La Chaise' and 'Coleman' were enough to remove any imputation

* The text (*S.T.*, viii, 436–7) says 'Winchester', but clearly Lady Worcester was meant. The Winchesters are known to have been travelling abroad, anyway.

of hearsay, but Langhorn understandably thought otherwise. He observed jeeringly, 'My lord, ask whether this be all that he charges against me'; to which Bedloe brazenly replied, 'Things may occur to my memory hereafter which do not now.' But Atkins hastily intervened to assure the jury that the conversation between Langhorn and Coleman was of the greatest importance – 'This rivets the whole,' he said.

When the time came for him to reply Langhorn again attacked the character of the witnesses, and argued that as accomplices, who had also received substantial rewards from the government, they were not to be trusted. He then called the same witnesses as had appeared the day before, to testify that Oates had been at St Omers, and not in London, in April 1678. Unfortunately, a second performance in twenty-four hours did not increase their confidence, especially since the crowd was even more abusive and violent than it had been the day before. In the middle of the proceedings Lord Castlemaine boldly appeared before the court to protest that these witnesses were being mobbed and even manhandled as they left the hall; Scroggs expressed anger and dismay at this, but if he issued any orders on the matter they were not recorded. Moreover, when he suddenly asked one witness a question about June 1678, not April, he was lost. He finally admitted that he could not answer offhand, 'because the question, my lord, that I came for, did not fall upon that time'.

Scroggs was delighted, and it now signified little that a lodging-house keeper called Mrs Grove, whom Oates said he had stayed with in April 1678, denied the fact, or that the proprietress of the White Horse Tavern testified that her private rooms would only hold twelve people. Women of her class and type were of no account, and in any case several men at once rose in court to argue with her, and assert that she could accommodate at least forty.

Oates then called the same witnesses as the day before, to prove he *had* been in London in April 1678, and Scroggs proceeded to his summing up. Again, he made some effort to be fair to the St Omers witnesses, but it must be doubted if the jury paid him (or them) the least attention. Nor did they heed the emphasis he laid on Oates's testimony in his final peroration, or his caveat against shedding innocent blood.

Here is a gentleman that stands at the bar upon his life on the one hand, but if Mr Oates says true, all our lives and liberties, our king and our religion, are at stake upon the other hand. God defend that innocent blood should be shed, and God defend us also from popery, and from all popish plots, and from all the bloody principles of papists. You cannot blame us to look to ourselves.

The jury retired at 7.0 p.m., and 'after a short space' returned with the usual verdict. The five Jesuits were then brought up to be sentenced with Langhorn, and Scroggs, as was usual, retired in favour of the Recorder, Sir George Jeffreys. This was to be the last of the great Plot trials, though no one knew it, and Jeffreys was to go on to make an even less savoury reputation than Scroggs's. So parts of his speech to the court are worth quoting.

His imprecations against Catholicism show that he had nothing to learn from his chief:

What a strange sort of religion is that [he said], whose doctrine seems to allow them to be the greatest saints in another world, that can be the most impudent sinners in this! Murder, and the blackest of crimes here, are the best means among you to get a man to be canonized a saint hereafter. Is it not strange that men professed in religion, that use all endeavours to gain proselytes for heaven, should so pervert the scripture (as I perceive some of you have done) and make that justify your impious designs of assassinating kings and murdering their subjects? What can be said to such a sort of people, the very foundation of whose religion is laid in blood? Nay, lest you should not be able so easily to persuade them so cleverly to imbibe those bloody principles, you do absolve them from all the obligations that they remain under, of obedience to their sovereign; you do therefore from the pulpits publicly teach, that the oaths of allegiance and supremacy signify nothing. It is a strange religion, that applies everything to these wicked and detestable purposes.

What he had to say about the King's evidence was later remembered, in 1685, when he presided as Lord Chief Justice at the trial of Titus Oates for perjury:

Your several crimes have been so fully proved against you, that truly I think no person that stands by can be in any doubt of the guilt; nor is there the least room for the most scrupulous man to doubt of the credibility of the witnesses that have been examined against you.

A more sincere Christian than Scroggs, he closed by offering the defendants the services of a Protestant divine in their last days – 'Gentlemen, with great charity to your immortal souls, I desire you, for the love of God, and in the name of his Son Jesus Christ, consider these things; for it will not be long ere you be summoned before another tribunal about them, and great and dreadful is the day of judgement, at which you and all men must appear.' To speed them before that tribunal he then pronounced the usual sentence of death, 'after which there was a very great acclamation'.

At this stage the special commission of oyer and terminer under which the court sat expired, with Wakeman still untried. But public pressure for his trial was mounting, and it was now fixed for the early days of the next London and Middlesex sessions, in mid-July. Apart from any other consideration, this sealed the fate of the condemned Jesuits.

There is no reason to disbelieve Queen Catherine's testimony that in later years, whenever the King entered her boudoir, where the portraits of these martyrs hung in state, he 'would turn towards them, and kissing their hands would beg their forgiveness in the most humble manner'. In all except outward observance Charles was now a Catholic himself; on his death-bed he was not only formally reconciled, he handed his brother a crucifix containing a piece of the True Cross which he had taken from the iconoclast Waller in 1679 and worn ever after concealed on his person. He had held up the execution of Ireland and Grove, and then that of Pickering, when he believed – and quite plausibly, too – that he was endangering the regime by so doing. He was now so angry and disgusted at the reports he received of Whitbread's trial that for a day or two he declined to issue the death warrants. But another long delay was unthinkable; the Queen was in danger, and the right line of the succession; as for the people, as Salvetti remarked, they were so saturated with lies that all they would do was howl, 'Crucify them !' He gave way; from now on he would follow the cynical advice of Lord Halifax, promoted to an earldom that same month, 'that the Plot must be handled as if it were true, whether it were so or not'.[56] But shame and frustration contributed much to the marked air of indifference with which he rode out the rest of the crisis, arousing wonder and horror in those around him, and the bitterness so evident in his declining years.

It was the same with the priests condemned to death at the spring assizes, though they were not even guilty of positive treason, only an infraction of the statute of 1585. Because it was hoped that they might confess to a knowledge of the Plot, five of them had been brought up to London for examination in April, and the rest temporarily reprieved. Even before the end of the session this gave rise to unfavourable comment, and in a moment of forgetfulness Shaftesbury berated the government for culpable indulgence. When he was sharply reminded that he had issued the orders himself, as Lord President, he replied lamely that 'if he had any fault it was tender-heartedness'. So, on 30 May, and again on 11 July, the Privy Council issued orders for their execution with all convenient speed. In some quarters this roused consternation and, according to Barillon, 'several members of the Commons are saying that they had only proposed that they be banished', which was certainly true of the previous Parliament; but in the circumstances of June 1679 it was difficult to see what alternative there was; the mistake, arising from the government's hasty action the previous November, in advance of Parliament, was to have put them on trial at all. The best Charles could do, by another Council order, dated 4 June, was to forbid the execution of any priest tried and condemned thereafter under the statute of 1585 until his further pleasure was known. None condemned after that date were in fact executed, though the government's intentions were not clear for some time, perhaps least of all to itself.[57]

However, the five Jesuits were hustled to the scaffold on 20 June, though they were allowed to die by hanging, the drawing and quartering being a formality. Langhorn was only reprieved for a time in the hope that he would crack; he was old, his health was poor, and he did not want to leave his children's upbringing to his Protestant wife. In fact he did produce a list of Jesuit property in England,* and he was the only one of the martyrs, apart from Staley, to avail himself of the services of the Protestant chaplain of Newgate. But he purged his offence by composing some long and somewhat sentimental meditations, and went to the scaffold on 14 July, only four days before Wakeman's trial, with the same fortitude as the priests who had gone before.[58]

The King's next step was to confront the witnesses direct, to see what evidence they intended to give against the Queen, and to inhibit them from enlarging on it further. The situation was complicated by the need, if possible, to preserve them for future use. As Sir Robert Southwell put it:

How to prevent these reflections [on the Queen] without taking a course which might blast their evidence and consequently save the Lords in the Tower is the great point under consideration, and his Majesty seems extremely concerned herein.[59]

So on 24 June Oates, Prance, Bedloe and Dugdale were brought separately before the Privy Council, and asked if they could add anything to their previous evidence against the Queen. Oates had learnt sense by now, and he had little to add, and all of it hearsay. All Prance could swear to was some treasonable talk by a servant of the Queen's confessor, which did not even implicate the confessor. Bedloe added several further details about Wakeman, and confessed that he was building up his case against him, but he had nothing to add directly implicating the Queen. Dugdale had heard Evers say that the Queen knew all about the plot to murder her husband, but that was all. The law

* Supposedly with the Provincial's express permission, though since he and Whitbread were both close prisoners, and Whitbread was executed on 20 June, it is difficult to see how this could have been obtained. In *Hatton Correspondence* (i, 188), there is a hint that he was tricked into believing that Whitbread had given his permission, though this would damage the Society and be of benefit only to Langhorn personally.

officers gave their opinion that a case could not be made out, and the King was 'much at his ease'.[60]

Another advantage of bringing the informers before the Council was that the government could test the nature of the case against Wakeman, and even, perhaps, help him prepare his defence.[61] How far the Lord Chief Justice was taken into Council's confidence we do not know, but the general assumption that he would drive hard for Wakeman's conviction can be seen in retrospect to be unwarranted. Now the Jesuits were safely out of the way the immediate danger was passed, and the opportunity was there for deeper prejudices to rise again to the surface. Scroggs had always been a firm Church-and-King man, hostile in the 1670s to the parliamentary opposition, and it could have been foreseen that his working alliance with them would not survive indefinitely. Like Jeffreys after him, he had always taken pride in being 'clamour-proof', and he was certainly not lacking in courage. How far his attitude towards the Plot from November 1678 to February 1679 had been encouraged or even dictated by his patron Danby we do not know, but Danby's fall must have given him pause. As we have seen, Oates and Bedloe had always needed considerable support from the Bench; would that now be forthcoming? It was doubtful, especially since the establishment was now in clear and obvious danger; and if he had any serious doubts of the King's wishes they must have been settled by his sudden decision to dissolve Parliament on 10 July and summon another for the autumn.[62] Such a decision, taken flatly against the advice of the new Privy Council, was a sure sign that Shaftesbury's influence was broken and the lists were reforming.

The trial[63] opened two days late, on Friday, 18 July, perhaps because of the uncommon delay in executing Langhorn. With Wakeman in the dock were three Benedictine monks, William Marshal, William Rumley and James Corker, the latter left over from the Whitbread trial the previous month. Dugdale was first put up to prove the general existence of a Plot, but even in this comparatively modest role he put up a poor performance. He was getting careless. When he remarked casually that after the

King's assassination, 'All Protestants they intended to cut off', it was too much even for Edward Ward, the prosecution counsel. '*All* Protestants?' he said incredulously. 'Yes,' said Dugdale. The prisoners then questioned him sharply and pointedly, and Corker accused him of lying without bringing down any reproof from the Bench. Dugdale withdrew somewhat battered, and Prance took his place, to give in some hearsay chatter which neither the prosecution nor the defence seemed to take very seriously.

But the third of these preliminary witnesses was a quite different character. Robert Jenison was a lapsed Catholic from a well-to-do family, whose elder brother Thomas, a Jesuit, had been in Newgate since the previous October. He had agreed to give evidence on condition that his brother was spared, and the government complied (though in fact Thomas died, still in Newgate, that September).[64] Jenison's sole function now was to disprove Ireland's alibi, which had caused Scroggs more trouble than anything else in these trials. Charles had allowed Ireland to go to the scaffold on Dugdale's information, but since then Dugdale's credit had sunk so much that he was not even called to testify on this particular point. Jenison now testified to seeing Ireland in London on 19 August 1678, which clinched part of Oates's testimony. Scroggs crooned delightedly, and expounded the whole matter again at some length in his summing-up, though he admitted that it had nothing to do with the present case.

The evidence proper began with Oates, at his most circumstantial and detailed. He deposed that in August 1678 he had seen a letter in Wakeman's hand containing a medical prescription for the Jesuit Richard Ashby, alias Thimbleby, who was going to take the cure at Bath. The rest of the letter was devoted to a discussion of the assassination plot. He then gave his evidence on the conduct of the Queen at Somerset House, and her complicity (which was not mentioned again in the whole course of the trial), and said he had seen an entry in the Jesuits' ledger book kept at Wild House, Covent Garden, of £5,000 paid to Wakeman, in account of £15,000 owing. This was the first mention of this ledger. Finally, he deposed that he had seen in Langhorn's office a commission from the Pope appointing Wakeman physician-general to the Army.

As soon as he had finished Wakeman briskly asked him why he had not even recognized him when he was brought before the Council on 30 September 1678 ? Oates replied lamely that the candlelight had been in his eyes, and Wakeman remarked triumphantly, 'This was just Coleman's case.' He then asked why his testimony against him on that occasion had been so slight that he had been allowed to go free until Parliament met. Oates said insolently, 'I am not bound to answer that question', only to be pulled up sharp by Scroggs, who told him ,'You must answer his questions, if they be lawful.'

Oates *had* no answer, and this was when Scroggs turned. Exactly the same question had arisen at Coleman's trial, as Wakeman reminded him; but the issue was now much more serious. Oates had let a man go free who (he now said) was committed to poisoning the King and had every opportunity of doing so. It was almost constructive treason in itself.

However, for the moment Oates was allowed to proceed, and give his testimony against the other prisoners. He swore that Corker was the President of the English Benedictines, and in that capacity he had authorized the payment of £6,000 to the Society of Jesus in August 1678, knowing it was to help finance the King's assassination. Marshal and Rumley were also implicated in the same transaction. Marshal promptly asked on what day in August this had happened. In previous trials various defendants had asked similar questions about the month of August, a very crowded month in Oates's time-table, but with no success, and he answered loftily, 'It is a great privilege that I tell you the month; it was between the first and the middle of August.' But this time Scroggs remarked with a sneer, 'It is in his breast, whether he will or no, to tell you the exact day.' Nettled, Oates said it was the day before or the day after the Feast of the Assumption; that is, 14 or 16 August. Pressed for the date of another treasonable consult, he gingerly committed himself to 21 August, 'if it were a Wednesday'. His evidence done, he begged leave to retire, because he was 'not well'. Scroggs told him to stay.

Bedloe then appeared, and gave an artistic account of various treasonable conversations he had overheard between Wakeman and the Jesuit Harcourt. Corker, he said, was closely associated with Keynes, the leader of the assassination plot, and the mythical Jesuit LeFevre, who had master-minded Godfrey's murder. As for Marshal, he knew him as a messenger who had carried confidential letters down to the provinces, notably one from La Chaise which he took to show Sir Francis Ratcliffe. Unfortunately, the third Benedictine, Rumley, was a stranger to him. When he had finished Scroggs made the shattering observation:

I do not find by the strictest observation that I have made that Mr Bedloe, who is the second witness, does say any great thing, any material thing, against any one of them.

Sir Robert Sawyer, chief prosecution counsel, promptly repeated a remark of Harcourt's to Wakeman which he said Bedloe had given in evidence: 'If we should miss to kill [the King] at Windsor, or you miss in your way, we will do it at Newmarket.'

Where is all this? [roared Scroggs] Pray Mr Bedloe, stand up again. We are now in the case of men's lives, and pray have a care that you say no more than what is true upon any man whatsoever. I would be loath to keep out popery by that way they would bring it in; that is, by blood and violence. I would have all things very fair.

Chief Justice North now told Bedloe to repeat his evidence, which he did, with the addition provided by Sawyer. Scroggs growled, 'He says now quite another thing than he said before', but North, Jeffreys and Sawyer all contradicted him, and for the moment the matter rested. Wakeman, to whom this new and outrageous fiction had come as a complete surprise, said to his companions in the dock, 'There is my business done!'

But he rallied almost at once, and summoned on his behalf one Chapman, an apothecary from Bath, a former Mayor of that city, and, of course, an unimpeachable Protestant. Chapman testified that Ashby had given him a prescription from Wakeman, certainly, and it was followed by a letter; but the letter had contained nothing treasonable. He agreed with Wakeman that Oates's account of the prescription – a pint of milk night and morning and a hundred glasses of Bath water a week – was ridiculous; the veriest tyro knew that the water would curdle the milk and induce vomiting.* After him came Wakeman's assistant, Hurst, who testified that he himself had written this particular letter at Wakeman's dictation, so it could not have been in Wakeman's hand. Oates's only reply to all this was that there must have been two letters from Wakeman to Ashby; he had seen one, and Chapman the other. Two of the judges, Atkins and Pemberton, seemed disposed to swallow this story, but Scroggs's only comment was 'Mr Oates stands with the jury, how far they will believe him.'

Then Wakeman returned to Oates's strange conduct before Council the previous September, and called Sir Philip Lloyd, one of the Clerks of the Council who had been present. Lloyd said that on 30 September the Council had examined Wakeman, but he denied everything so hotly and the testimony against him was so thin that they had sent for Oates again, and asked him if he knew anything more. Oates's answer had been: 'No, God forbid that I should say anything against Sir George Wakeman, for I know nothing more against him.'

Oates could only put forward the same excuse as he had at Coleman's trial; that he had been examined by the Council for two days continually, and up to two nights arresting priests, and 'by reason of my being hurried up and down, and sitting up, I was scarce *compos mentis*'. But this time it would not do.

What? [bellowed Scroggs] Must we be amused with I know not what, for being up but two nights? You were not able to give an answer; that when they call and send for Mr Oates again to give a positive charge; and then you tell me a story so remote. What, was Mr Oates just so spent that he could not say, 'I have seen a letter under Sir George Wakeman's own hand'?

Chief Justice North then tried to take the heat off Oates by asking Wakeman to call his next witness, but Scroggs would not

---

* Milk was rarely taken by the upper and middle classes except for medicinal purposes.

be denied the last word. He pointed out to the court that Oates's failure 'to charge him home' had left Wakeman at liberty from 30 September to 26 October. Goaded beyond all discretion, Oates replied, 'To speak the truth, they were such a Council as would commit nobody.' Scroggs told him, 'You have taken a great confidence, I know not by what authority, to say anything of anybody.'

After this triumph Wakeman sustained a check. The court, adhering to a rule laid down in previous trials, would not let him produce the manuscript Journal of the House of Lords for 28 November, when Oates had admitted he did not know Wakeman's handwriting. At this stage he could have asked Lloyd for an account of the Council meeting of 26 November, when Oates had given the same evidence, but he was rattled, and asked instead for an account of the meeting of 24 June, when Oates had given evidence against the Queen. This was ruled out of order.

Wakeman then rested his defence, and Sawyer brought up another Clerk of the Council, Sir Thomas Doleman, to testify that Oates had indeed been in a state of exhaustion on the evening of 30 September. The court did not seem interested, but Doleman's remark that Wakeman's conduct before the Council had been unexpectedly aggressive gave him an excellent opportunity to repeat at length the statement he had then made detailing his father's, his brother's and his own eminent services to the Crown, particularly in the Civil Wars and the Interregnum.

Corker then began his defence with a long, well-reasoned speech attacking the whole structure of the evidence at these trials:

My lord, it is a well-known general maxim, that a positive assertion is as easy to be made, as to prove a negative is oft-times hard, if not impossible. Men may easily devise crimes and frame accusations against innocent men in such a manner that the contrary cannot possibly be demonstrated. No mortal man can tell where he was, and what he did and said every day and hour of his whole life. Therefore I think it is not only positive bare swearing, but it is probable swearing, that must render a man guilty of a crime.

He went on to argue that far from being probable, it was basic-ally improbable that men of eminent respectability, 'men of good and virtuous lives and unblemished conversations before this hour', should have been engaged in this kind of conspiracy. Scroggs was sufficiently relaxed to essay a joke: 'Ay, ay,' he said, 'I am of that opinion, if thou canst but satisfy us and the jury that there is no Plot, thou shalt be [ac]quitted by my consent.' But after a few more minutes he lost patience and forced Corker to the point – which was that Stapleton, not he, was the President of the English Benedictines. He further sub-mitted that he had been in the same room when Oates came with a posse to arrest Pickering on 29 September 1678; why had he not arrested him, or even accused him, until the New Year?

The question then arose whether Oates had recognized Mar-shal, either, the first time he saw him in the Gatehouse prison. Marshal called Sir William Waller, who had been present on that occasion; but predictably Waller chose to support Oates. However, he then produced another witness, Ellen Rigby, the Benedictines' former housekeeper at the Savoy, and obviously an imposing woman, for although she was a Catholic the court treated her evidence with the greatest respect. She deposed that when Oates came to the house on 29 September he saw not only Corker, but also Marshal and Hesketh,* another Benedictine who had not been arrested until early 1679. She also confirmed that Stapleton was the President of the Benedictines, and had been for years. As for Oates, she said, the only time she had seen him before was once that summer, when he had come begging for bread. Afterwards Pickering, normally a charitable and sweet-tempered man, had ordered her 'never to let that man come in again'.

At this point Marshal and Corker nearly threw their advan-tage away. First Corker tried to persuade Scroggs to remand him for a few days so that he could bring witnesses up from the country to support his alibi. Scroggs was highly impatient, and for once with some reason; he pointed out that he had had since 13 June to do this. Then Marshal threw oil on the fire by point-

* See p. 248 below.

ing out that 'Every judge is as much obliged to follow his conscience as any formality in law.' 'Pray teach your own disciples,'
snarled Scroggs, 'don't teach us.' Marshal then launched forth
into a long, florid speech, which he must have prepared beforehand, in which he argued that the speeches made on the scaffold
by the five Jesuits were proof of their innocence, and proof that
there had been no Plot. This was too much even for Lord Chief
Justice North, and Mr Justice Pemberton told him he was
affronting the court. Jeffreys warned him, with some reason,
'You abound too much in the flowers of rhetoric.' Then
Scroggs, who had been ominously quiet, had his say:

I was loath to interrupt you, because you are upon your lives, and
because it is fit you should have as much indulgence as can be allowed. Your defence has been very mean, I tell you beforehand; your
case looked much better before you spoke a word in your defence,
so wisely have you managed it.

Notwithstanding this, Marshal tried to continue, and brought
down upon himself a thunderous oration, in which Scroggs
reviewed the history of popery in England since the Reformation, culminating in a devastating tirade on the Gunpowder
Plot[65]; this was stirring stuff, and the audience 'gave a shout'.
When Marshal still tried to argue that Catholics could not receive absolution for lies uttered in the face of death Scroggs told
him he did not know the doctrines of his own church – 'We
have a bench of Aldermen have more wit than your conclave,
and a Lord Mayor that is as infallible as your Pope.' Even then,
Marshal was undeterred, and continued the same argument
with Pemberton, frustrating an attempt by Scroggs to begin his
charge to the jury; the trial had now been in progress more than
eight hours. When he did begin he was in a black bad temper.

First he directed the jury to acquit Rumley, against whom
there was only one witness. He then dwelt irrelevantly and at
some length on Jenison's evidence, pointing out that it made
nonsense of Ireland's alibi, and therefore of his protestations of
innocence on the scaffold. Glancing at the prisoners, he remarked:

You are not going, according to your own doctrine, so immediately to hell; I hope you suppose a purgatory, where you may be purged from such peccadilloes as this, of dying with a lie in your mouths.

But then he turned to the actual evidence, and all was changed. He began by casting doubt on Oates's assertion that he knew Wakeman's handwriting. He did not refer to the evidence of Wakeman's assistant on this point, but he solemnly warned the jury:

We would not, to prevent all their plots (let them be as big as they can make them), shed one drop of innocent blood; therefore I would have you, in all these gentlemen's cases, consider seriously and weigh truly the circumstances and the probability of things charged upon them.

Turning to Bedloe's evidence, he described it as 'discourses of doubtful words, but whether they be plain enough to satisfy your consciences, when men are upon their lives, I leave to you'. The only serious issue was whether Harcourt had spoken the words: 'If we should miss to kill [the King] at Windsor ... etc.' This he left to the jury, with no comment on its probability either way.

He went on to point out that Oates's evidence against Corker was very thin, and remarked that Bedloe had proved 'rather less than what Oates had to say'; and if Corker was *not* President of the Benedictines then much of the case against him dropped to the ground. As for Marshal, the case against him was even weaker.

Then he turned back to Oates's refusal to testify against Wakeman before the Privy Council, and declared his excuse 'a very faint one'. He went through the events of that September evening again in some detail, and for the third time pointed out that for Oates to give decisive evidence against Wakeman would have required very little effort, mental or physical. He also admitted to the jury that it was 'strange indeed' that Oates had not recognized Marshal and Corker when he came upon them in the Savoy. This part of the summing-up was dead against Oates, but the rest of the defence he dismissed with contempt, as 'improper for the court to hear, and them to urge'.

But he went on to warn the jury again:

I will discharge my own conscience to you; it lies upon the oaths of these two men. Though there was a Plot in general proved, yet that does not affect these men [the accused] in particular.

This gave him another chance to affirm his own belief in the Plot, and the monstrous iniquity of the Catholic priesthood. Then he briefly returned, for the fourth time, to Oates's conduct before the Council in September 1678, and told the jury to 'weigh it well'. 'Let us not be so amazed and frightened with the noise of plots', he said, 'as to take away any man's life without reasonable evidence.' For the fifth time he reverted to Oates's conduct before the Council, and again mentioned his failure to recognize the Benedictines; for good measure he threw in a reference to Oates's begging for bread, as if he saw no reason to disbelieve it. His closing words were clear enough:

These men's bloods are at stake, and your soul and mine, and our oaths and consciences are at stake; and therefore never care what the world says, follow your conscience. If you are satisfied these men swear true, you will do well to find them guilty, and they deserve to die for it. If you are unsatisfied, upon these things put together, and they do weigh with you, that they have not said true, you will do well to acquit them.

Bedloe protested from the well of the court, 'My lord, my evidence is not right summed up.' 'I know not', said Scroggs awfully, 'by what authority this man speaks.' The jury retired, and so did the judges, leaving the faithful Jeffreys and a few J.P.s to take the verdict. The jury returned after an hour, and asked if they could give a verdict of 'Guilty of misprision of treason'. Jeffreys said, 'No, you must either convict them of high treason, or acquit them.' 'Then take a verdict,' said the foreman. It was 'Not guilty' against all four accused.

6

The Tide Ebbs

THE popular fury at Wakeman's acquittal knew no bounds, and Scroggs was naturally the villain of the piece, those who did not pay him the compliment of supposing that he had succumbed to well-concealed religious convictions preferring to believe him bribed. Point was lent to these tales by the incredible folly of the Portuguese ambassador in waiting on him next day to thank him – though in the Marquez d'Arronches's defence it must be said that he had only arrived in England the previous month. As late as March 1681 men were still being prosecuted for peddling tales of Scroggs and his bag of Portuguese doubloons, and a host of contemporary lampoons maintained the sad tale of justice forefeit:

> His Holiness has three grand friends
>   On Great Britain's shore
> That prosecute his (and their own) ends
>   A Duke, a judge and a whore.
>
> The Duke is as true as steel
>   To the Pope, that infallible elf;
> Therefore no friend to the commonweal
>   Nor no friend to himself.
>
> The judge is a butcher's son
>   Yet hates to shed innocent blood;
> But for ten thousand pounds has done
>   The Pope a great deal of good.
>
> He that villain Wakeman cleared,
>   Who was to have poisoned the King;
> As it most plainly appeared,
>   For which he deserves to swing.

Rumley was found to be a lay brother, but the other two Benedictines were promptly rearrested on a charge of being priests, and Wakeman thought it wise to retire to Brussels, where he was 'much caressed' by the governor and the people. The jurymen had to flee from their homes in fear of the mob.[1]

As the Lord Chief Justice left London for the Oxford Circuit the day after the trial a dead dog was thrown into his coach, and everywhere on circuit he was greeted by derisory cries of 'A Wakeman! A Wakeman!' On at least one occasion he was publicly affronted in open court.[2] But this merely roused Scroggs's violent and combative spirit. He departed boasting 'that he had condemned Coleman against the will of the Court [at Whitehall], that he had acquitted Wakeman against the will of the City, and he would keep his office against the will of the Devil'.[3] It was a stormy circuit indeed. At Monmouth Assizes on 31 July he told Bedloe to his face that he was 'a perjured person', and had given false evidence against Langhorn. When his fellow judge, Atkins, pointed out that 'he had given judgement on his evidence', he took it out on him, too.[4] His temper was not sweetened by having to acquit the seminary priest Walter Jones, against whom only one witness appeared, and William Pugh, a Benedictine. However, he remanded Jones in custody without bail, and had the satisfaction of ordering the speedy execution of the famous Jesuit David Lewis, who had been condemned at the previous assizes, in March. He went to his death on 27 August at Usk.[5]

Waiting for him at Hereford on 4 August he found John Kemble and William Lloyd, two secular priests also condemned at the last assizes. Kemble's execution was carried out on the 22nd, but Lloyd died in prison a week beforehand.[6] When Charles Carne (or Kerne), a secular priest, stood trial on 6 August three of the four witnesses against him broke down; this, and the fact that he was one of the few priests known to have taken the oaths, disposed Scroggs to mercy, and he told the jury: 'I must leave it with you as a tender point on both sides; I would not shed innocent blood, neither would I willingly let a popish priest escape.'[7] They took the hint, and brought him in 'Not guilty'. But when he reached Stafford on the 12th he was back in his old form. He warned the sheriff to empanel 'a good jury', and when the sheriff admitted that one juryman had conscientious scruples about condemning men to death simply as priests Scroggs remanded him in custody until he could produce sureties for his good behaviour, and removed three others whom he regarded as 'popishly affected'. Awaiting trial were Andrew Bromwich, a secular priest, and the veteran Jesuit William Atkins. Atkins was seventy-eight years old, so weak that he had to be carried into the courtroom, and so deaf that he could not follow the proceedings at all: but this did not prevent Scroggs treating him as an immediate menace to the security of church and state:

It is to these sorts of men [he thundered] we owe all the troubles we are in, the fear of the King's life, the subversion of our government, and the loss of our religion. It is notorious by what they have done that they have departed from the meekness and simplicity of Christ's doctrine, and would bring in a religion of blood and tyranny amongst us; as if God Almighty were some omnipotent mischief that delighted [in] and would be served with the sacrifice of human blood.[8]

A cowed jury had no difficulty in consenting to further human sacrifices, but both men were in fact reprieved, Bromwich because he had taken the oaths, and Atkins because of his advanced age, though he remained in prison until his death in March 1681.[9] Finally, at Worcester Scroggs found waiting for him John Wall, one of the most distinguished Franciscans of his generation, who had been condemned on 15 April, when the presiding judge, Littleton, had told him, 'I do not intend you shall die, at least not for the present, until I know the King's further pleasure.' Scroggs was now the bearer of the King's further pleasure, and he was executed on the Red Hill at Worcester on 22 August.[10]

On other circuits the autumn harvest was thinner, but this was probably because fewer priests had been tried the previous spring. On 7 August Nicholas Postgate, a gentle old secular priest of eighty, was executed at the Knavesmire, York; the date of his trial is uncertain, but he had been arrested the previous December, so it is reasonable to suppose that he had been tried and condemned in the spring.[11] John Plessington was executed at Chester on 10 July, before the assize judges came down, and Philip Evans and John Lloyd at Cardiff on 22 July. Evans was a Jesuit, the others secular priests, John Lloyd being a brother of the William Lloyd who died in Hereford Gaol in August. They had all been tried and condemned the previous winter.[12] But the most shocking case was that of Charles Mahoney (or Mihan), an Irish Franciscan who had been shipwrecked off South Wales on his way to or from Ireland in June 1678. The date of his trial is unknown, but he was executed at Ruthin on 12 August. His plea that he had not acted or intended to act as a priest in England was not accepted, though it was in the case of other Irish priests – such as John Dowdeswell and Thomas Eustace, who were forced into Haverfordwest in May 1679. In fact, in the summer of 1680 King's Bench decided in the case of *Rex v. O'Cullen* that an Irish priest shipwrecked at Minehead on his way from Cork to Bordeaux did not come within the scope of the Act of 1585 and ordered his release. Another such case was that of Alexander Lumsden, the Scots Dominican spared by the King's Bench in January 1680.[13] But all this was too late to help Mahoney.

This was the great holocaust of the Plot. Between 20 June and 27 August 1679, and including those tried in London, fourteen Catholics were executed; one layman, two Franciscans, four seminary priests and seven Jesuits. To these must be added two reprieved for special reasons, and one who died in prison before execution, as we have seen. To the Catholics it must have seemed that the reign of terror would henceforward mount in intensity, engulfing at least those priests still in prison. John Warner remarked: 'The Catholics living in England lurked in the obscurity of prisons, or shut up in their homes; the Protestants, completely at a loss, were doing nothing.'[14]

But the whole process was self-defeating. Shaftesbury himself is credited with the statement that hanging so many at one occasion had been a mistake, because now that the popular mind was pacified, it would be impossible to stir it up again without a great expenditure of careful effort over a long period of time.[15] But there was more to it than that. It would be going too far to say that the nation was sated with blood – it took a great deal of blood to sate the seventeenth-century English public – but there is some evidence that the steady denials of those convicted were beginning to take effect. According to a Catholic eye-witness of the execution of the five Jesuits at Tyburn on 20 June, a huge crowd stood in perfect silence for more than an hour while each man in turn made a long speech solemnly denying his part in the Plot; then John Gavan led them all in an act of contrition.[16] In the provinces, where the victims were notable local figures, and were being executed not for specific treason but merely for being in orders, feelings were even stronger. The attitude of the jurymen at Hereford Assizes was typical, and it was often impossible to secure the two prosecution witnesses required by law. The death of men like Francis Wall, John Kemble and David Lewis did no one any good except the Catholic community, which was strengthened by their sacrifice. There is a tradition that the crowd at Wall's execution wept, even the sheriff, and that some cried out, 'Is this the way to destroy popery? This is enough to make us all papists!' As for the nonagenarian Kemble, a Catholic chronicler remarks of him: 'His very enemies – at least, those of a contrary judgement – have been found to say that they never saw one die so like a gentleman.' The sheriff of Monmouth (James Herbert of Coldbrook) postponed David Lewis's execution as long as he could, then stayed away from it; the large crowd, predominantly Protestant, of course, would not allow the victim to be cut down alive, and with the under-sheriff at their head they escorted his body afterwards to honourable interment in the local churchyard.[17] In fact, it is significant that at most provincial executions the priest was merely hanged, not hanged, drawn and quartered as the law required, and they were almost invariably buried with some solemnity in the local churchyard.*

---

*In fact, Catholics were usually buried in 'Protestant' graveyards. Coleman and the five Jesuits were buried at St Giles'-in-the-Fields, and

Particularly damaging was the decision to publish the last speeches of the accused, beginning with the five Jesuits on 20 June. The government itself may have authorized this step, on the assumption that it would discredit the authors – the truth is surprisingly difficult to discover – but the opposite was the case. The appetite of the public for works of piety was insatiable, and Catholic piety did as well as any other. It soon became *de rigueur* for every prospective martyr to compose a long farewell speech protesting his innocence and justifying his Catholic faith; even William Lloyd composed one, and had it printed, though he died in prison. Veterans like Wall and Postgate, who were unequal to the task, felt obliged to apologize for the omission; Richard Langhorn even composed lengthy meditations in verse. The government made no effort to interfere; after the lapse of the Licensing Act that spring it never felt strong enough to prohibit any publication that did not libel the King or his immediate family, and only the most daring of those. But the concern of the Church of England is shown by the haste with which many clergymen, led by the Bishop of Lincoln, rushed into print to rebut them, stressing the fact that Catholics could secure a dispensation for lies uttered in the face of death. Burnet commented:

Many thought that what doctrines soever men might by a subtlety of speculation be carried into, the approach of death, with the seriousness that appeared in their deportment, must needs work so much on the probity and candour which seemed rooted in human nature, that even immoral opinions maintained in the way of argument, could not then resist it.[18]

The intrinsic value of these scaffold speeches must depend on one's faith, and one's taste in such things; they have an important place in the English recusant tradition. Their extrinsic importance lay in the fact that not one of the victims made the least acknowledgement of guilt, in thought, word or deed, though it was generally known that they had all been offered a pardon in return for a full confession – or any confession at all.

---

so was Plunket; William Staley was buried at St Paul's, Covent Garden.

Going back to the previous December, twenty-two Catholics had now been barbarously executed, including four laymen; one of them (Coleman) a politique of the lowest type, and two others (Green and Hill) of a very humble station in life and no great reputation for piety. If there had really been a Popish Plot it was against human nature to suppose that one of these men would not have cracked, or if not one of these, then one of the scores of Catholic priests and laymen now in prison, often barely surviving under loathsome conditions and with little prospect of release. As it was, even the arch-renegade Fr John Sargeant, who came over from Holland in November 1679 primed to tell all, would only accuse the Society of Jesus in general terms of inveterate plotting, and the late John Gavan of defending the academic proposition that heretic princes could lawfully be assassinated. Apart perhaps from Miles Prance, only apostates had come forward with 'hard' information on the Plot, and the two principal informers, Oates and Bedloe, had malodorous reputations. It was also clear by this time that Stephen Dugdale, for all his apparent respectability, was little better than they were. The only respectable informer yet to appear was Robert Jenison, and all his protestations to the contrary could not clear him of the suspicion that he had designs on the family estate, which should have descended to his Jesuit brother, now in Newgate.

On top of all this, Wakeman's trial was a shock to thinking people. One of the spectators was that pious *cognoscente*, John Evelyn:

Though it was not my custom and delight to be often present at any capital trials [he wrote primly] ... yet I was inclined to be at this signal one, that by the ocular view of the carriages, and other circumstances of the managers and parties concerned, I might inform myself, and regulate my opinion of a cause that had so alarmed the whole nation.

He was somewhat put out by Oates; the low opinion he had formed of him the previous October was now handsomely confirmed. He was not yet ready to disbelieve in the Plot as a whole, no more than judges like Scroggs were, but he thought Oates was spinning it out:

For my part [he decided] I do look upon Oates as a vain, insolent man, puffed up with the favour of the Commons for having discovered something really true, as more especially detecting the dangerous intrigues of Coleman, proved out of his own letters, and of a general design, which the jesuited part of the papists ever had, and still have, to ruin the Church of England. But that he was trusted with these great secrets he pretended, or had any solid ground for what he accused divers noblemen of, I have many reasons to induce my contrary belief.[19]

Charles tried to take advantage of the new feeling to get the Lords in the Tower tried outside Parliament, but the Judges and the Privy Council again refused. The Council, egged on by Shaftesbury, even refused a petition from Belasyse that he be allowed to retire to the country for a while on bail to recover his health.[20] Even so, the Plot might have collapsed altogether if it had not now merged with the great political struggle over the exclusion of the Duke of York from the succession. Belief in the need for exclusion came to imply belief in the Plot, and vice versa, and the sincerity of the leaders on both sides became distinctly questionable. From now on the government, and conservative forces generally, admitted that there had been some sort of Plot, but argued that the principal offenders had been put down or driven abroad. The opposition continued to insist that the Plot was still in motion, that popery was an aggressive, malignant force which must be scotched. However, in the winter of 1679–80 the tide was running strongly the other way.

The Exclusion Crisis technically began with the introduction of an Exclusion Bill into the House of Commons on 15 May 1679, but what really got it under way was the dissolution of Parliament on 10 July. This was an act of provocation on the King's part, and a blatantly aggressive use of the prerogative. His intervention (as was supposed) in Wakeman's trial was taken as a continuation of this policy; it reached its climax in the last days of August when he fell seriously ill at Windsor and James dramatically returned from Brussels to safeguard his right of succession. It coincided with the opening of one of the most bitter election battles of the century, for the second 'Exclusion Parliament'.

James was the strong man of the royal family; he believed that his brother's conduct hitherto had been distinguished by the same weakness that had brought their father to the scaffold in 1649. For the next two months, while the King lay convalescent, James imposed a strongly conservative and aggressive pattern on English government which survived his subsequent retirement to Edinburgh. On 12 September the Duke of Monmouth was dismissed from the Captain-Generalship of the Army and ordered into exile. On 14 October Shaftesbury was turned off the Privy Council, and next day Parliament was prorogued from October to the following January without a meeting. A reaction was now in progress, fuelled by paranoiac fears of another civil war. This was particularly noticeable in the Church, and clergymen who had been stampeded by the fear of popery the previous winter were now returning to their senses, and offering strong support to the King and his brother, particularly in the elections then in progress.

> They seemed now [wrote Burnet cynically] to lay down all fears and apprehensions of popery; and nothing was so common in their mouths as the year forty-one, in which the late wars began, and which seemed now to be near the being acted over again.[21]

In these circumstances James's appeal to conservative opinion was strikingly successful. On 21 October he presided over a sparsely-attended annual feast of the Honourable Artillery Company, but his words struck home:

> I am the first man that can command property in England [he said], and have the greatest property of any subject in England, and therefore have the greatest reason to defend it. Any other man may have private interests, but I can have none, for I know very well that as long as this nation and this city be well, I shall be so.[22]

A week later he was on his way to Scotland, but he left behind a group of ministers devoted to his interests; the Earl of Sunderland, Sidney Godolphin and Lawrence Hude, who was appointed First Lord of the Treasury in November when the

Earl of Essex resigned and joined Shaftesbury in opposition. The 'forward' policy he had initiated continued. When Monmouth returned to London without permission at the end of November he was promptly dismissed all his remaining offices and forbidden to come to Court. When Shaftesbury organized a series of petitions from London and the Provinces calling for a session of Parliament the answer was two successive proclamations, on 10 and 12 December, the one reinforcing the statute of 1661 against tumultuous and seditious petitioning, the other announcing that, barring emergencies, Parliament would not meet for business until November 1680. At the same time the appearance of pamphlets like *An Appeal from the Country to the City,* and *Great and Weighty considerations touching the point of Succession,* which advocated James's replacement by Monmouth as heir apparent, led to a new campaign against booksellers and publishers under the common law of libel, spearheaded by Scroggs. James returned from Scotland in February 1680 to find the Opposition in considerable disorder, and a powerful Tory reaction under way; his supporters were now bombarding the King with addresses 'abhorring' the unconstitutional practice of petitioning the King in a coercive manner, and 'petitioners' and 'abhorrers' were merging into Whigs and Tories.

It is against this sort of background, then, that the Plot continued to unwind. It degenerated into a tool of the party managers, and on the other side the servants of the government displayed increasing scepticism – in private, at least. The pretence that the informers were the King's evidence wore very thin; Oates, Bedloe, Prance and Jenison all helped Waller to victory in the Westminster election in September, and in January 1680 Oates and Bedloe accompanied Sir Gilbert Gerard to Whitehall with a petition from the inhabitants of Westminster and Southwark calling for a sitting of Parliament.[23] The government's attitude was defined in a royal proclamation of 31 October 1679, which declared that 'the most notorious offenders have been punished, secured or fled from justice'; therefore all those who had further information to give must come forward not later than 28 February 1680, if they were to receive a free pardon for treason or misprision of treason. This was accompanied by a sterner attitude towards recusancy, which found expression in the establishment of the Committee for Suppressing Popery on 1 December.

The reply from the other side was weak. Predictably, Oates and Bedloe mounted a campaign against Scroggs, and in October 1679 submitted a paper to Council accusing him of impugning their evidence. All they secured for the time being was the suspension of the unfortunate Sir Philip Lloyd, who, not content with giving evidence on Wakeman's behalf, had then retired to the *Rainbow* coffee house, where he was heard to declare there was no Plot. Oates had 'four shrewd coffee-drinkers' to support his own testimony, and:

The Board thought fit to advise his Majesty to suspend Sir Philip from his attendance during his Majesty's pleasure, lest his indiscretion against what had been so solemnly voted in two parliaments, about which proclamations had been issued, and a public fast solemnized, should seem to be countenanced here.[24]

But Scroggs was not so easily trapped. He returned from Circuit with a beltful of priestly scalps and full of bounce. He found himself 'highly caressed by all the favourites of both sexes' at Court, and he even dined with the Duchess of Portsmouth.[25] At the beginning of the Michaelmas Term he treated the King's Bench to a reasoned defence of his conduct in Wakeman's trial, and stressed that his belief in the Popish Plot was unaffected. He also gave vent to remarks which, even though they were interlarded with scandalous assaults on the Catholics, show he was not just the brainless bully he is often portrayed as being:

If once our courts of justice come to be awed or swayed by vulgar noise [he said], and if judges and juries should manage themselves so as would best comply with the humours of the times, it is falsely said, that men are tried for their lives or fortunes; they live by chance, and enjoy what they have as the wind blows, and with the same certainty; the giddy multitude have constancy, who condemn or acquit only before the trial, and without proof.

Such a base, fearful compliance made Felix, willing to please the people, have Paul bound, who was apt to tremble, but not to follow his conscience. The people ought to be pleased with public justice, and not justice seek to please the people. Justice should flow like a mighty stream, and if the rabble, like an unruly wind, blow against it, it may make it rough, but the stream will keep its course. Neither, for my part, do I think we live in so corrupted an age that no man can with safety be just, and follow his conscience; if it be otherwise, we must hazard our safety to preserve our integrity.[26]

The times put a premium on courage, a quality notably lacking in the Attorney-General, Sir William Jones. He resigned in November, and Jeffreys, Recorder of London, was strongly tipped to succeed him, because, it was said, 'he hath in great perfection the three chief qualifications of a lawyer: boldness, boldness, boldness'.[27] In fact, his successor was Creswell Levinz. Scroggs continued to delight in his running fight with the Opposition, and he was particularly gratified when he surprised Shaftesbury and a group of Whig peers with the Lord Mayor on 1 December. During dinner Scroggs teased Shaftesbury about his creature Oates, and at the end, when Lord Huntingdon proposed the Duke of Monmouth's health, he joined in. But he then proposed the Duke of York's health, and equably accepted Huntingdon's amendment, 'The Duke of York's health, and confusion to popery!' Lord Howard of Escrick denounced this as a contradiction in terms, but Scroggs replied that 'the Duke might be a papist, but he could not conceive how he might be popery'. At this, 'all the lords, in a great scuffle, rose from the table and went into another room, whither the Lord Chief Justice singly of all the judges followed them', and tackled Shaftesbury direct about Wakeman's trial. Shaftesbury told him 'he was a plain-spoken man', and accepted his assurances that his hands were clean, only he himself had been offered £10,000 to get Wakeman off. Scroggs replied ambiguously that 'he must say what he thought he never should, that then his lordship was in that an honester man than he was, for he, never being proffered any money therein, could not refuse it'.[28]

On 21 January he made merry again at Oates's and Bedloe's expense when their complaints against him were heard before the King in Council. One of the articles of accusation was that he had drunk to excess in the company of a person of quality, who turned out to be, rather surprisingly, Shaftesbury. (Did the Whig lord know his creatures were going to invade his private life in this way?) More seriously, Scroggs said that he was entitled to have doubts of any man's evidence without its being labelled a misdemeanour. Charles at the close 'was pleased to declare that he is well satisfied with the said Lord Chief Justice notwithstanding anything that was alleged against him', and he and Oates were left to pursue their vendetta in the courts.[29]

Another Opposition device was the Pope-Burning Procession, on which a great deal of time was wasted, and has been wasted by historians since. Such processions had been held from time to time earlier in the reign, notably in November 1673, when James had brought his second wife home to St James's. In 1679 they were organized by the Green Ribbon Club, the headquarters of the Exclusionists near Temple Bar, and not on 5 November but 17 November, the anniversary of Elizabeth I's accession.[30]

On the day the bells of the City began to toll about 3 a.m, though it was not until 5 p.m. that the procession got under way from Moorgate, via Aldgate, Leadenhall Street and Cheapside to Temple Bar. It was headed by six whistlers, followed by a bellman crying, 'Remember Justice Godfrey!' Then came:

A dead body representing Sir Edmund Berry Godfrey, in the habit he usually wore, the cravat wherewith he was murdered about his neck, with spots of blood on his wrists, shirt and white gloves that were on his hands, his face pale and wan, riding a white horse, and one of his murderers behind him to keep him from falling, representing the manner how he was carried from Somerset House to Primrose Hill.*

After this awful apparition came representatives of the various Catholic orders: two secular priests, one offering dispensations for murder, the other simply carrying a crucifix; four Carmelites; four Franciscans; and six Jesuits 'with bloody

---

*Notwithstanding Prance's and Bedloe's evidence, in February 1679, that he had been carried first in a sedan chair, then in a hearse.

daggers'; then 'a consort of wind music'; followed by eight popish bishops, and six cardinals in scarlet. A special place was reserved for Wakeman, 'the Pope's doctor', with Jesuits' powder in one hand and a chamber pot in the other. And, of course, the Pope himself:

> In a lofty glorious pageant, representing a chair of state, covered with scarlet, the chair richly embroidered, fringed and bedecked with golden balls and crosses. At his feet a cushion of state, two boys in surplices, with white silk banners and red crosses, and bloody daggers for murdering heretical kings and princes painted on them, with an incense pot before them, sat on either side censing his Holiness, who was arrayed in a rich scarlet gown, lined through with ermine and adorned with gold and silver lace; on his head a triple crown of gold, with a glorious collar of gold and precious stones, St Peter's Keys, a number of beads, *agnus deis*, and other Catholic trumpery. At his back stood his Holiness's Privy Councillor, the Devil, frequently caressing, hugging and whispering and oft-times instructing him aloud.

When they reached the Green Ribbon Club at Temple Bar the Pope was solemnly burnt, while free wine was distributed for toasts of 'No Popery', and 'God Bless the King'.[31]

This was fine public entertainment, clean, and curiously naïve. As one historian points out, the enormous crowds attracted by such displays dispersed peaceably enough under the watchful eye of the city militia, with no recorded damage to property.[32] Moreover, the Duke of York had no place in the procession, which one would have expected if this was a serious demonstration against the Crown. Indeed, Roger North, a Tory scoffer, but an involuntary witness, thought much of the iconography of these processions was confused. In the similar procession of 17 November 1680, the Pope was followed by another cart:

> With a single person upon it, which some said was the pamphleteer Sir Roger l'Estrange, some the King of France, some the Duke of York, but certainly it was a very civil, complaisant gentleman, like the former [l'Estrange], that was what everybody was pleased to have him, and, taking all in good part, he went on his way to the fire.[33]

But there were elements of childishness on both sides. Since Wakeman's acquittal the Catholics had been more 'active and stirring' than was prudent, and James's sudden return to Whitehall galvanized the less responsible elements amongst them. It went to the heads, most notably, of two busy women, the Countess of Powis, no doubt frustrated by her inability to give her imprisoned husband direct assistance, and Mrs Elizabeth Cellier, a well-known Catholic midwife who had catered to the Catholic aristocracy, including the young Duchess of York. She ministered more generally to the many Catholics in the London prisons, and performed such services as providing board and lodging for the witnesses brought over from St Omers on behalf of the five Jesuits in June. John Warner admits that 'Nature had endowed her with a lively, sharp and clear mind, but her powers of judgement were not of the same order; as was to be expected in the weaker sex.'[34]

Certainly she showed very bad judgement in taking into her employ that spring a young man called Thomas Willoughby, *vere* Dangerfield, whom she found lying in the debtors' side of Newgate. Round them both grew up a dangerous and distracted group of conspirators, including Lady Powis, Henry Neville, who had been prosecuted in January for an elegy on his late friend Edward Coleman, and the renegade Whig, Sir Robert Peyton. In September, when Monmouth was dismissed and the King was at death's door, there was much talk of a Presbyterian Plot to seize power. Dangerfield soon fabricated material which implicated Shaftesbury and concealed it in the rooms of Mansell, a leading Whig; at one stage James, with his usual lack of judgement, gave it his approval. Charles's reaction was 'he loved to discover Plots, but not to create any'.[35] By this time the matter had reached Council, but they were sceptical. Dangerfield was clearly an even greater villain than Bedloe, and for once Warner was not exaggerating when he said, 'to record all his iniquities one would have to copy out the whole catalogue of capital crimes' – and this was 1679, not 1678.[36] Denied a search warrant, Dangerfield then organized a bogus customs search of Mansell's rooms, in which he found the treasonable papers he himself had planted there, but the circumstances were still so incredible that the Justice of the Peace before whom he now appeared referred him back to the Council.

The Privy Council met next day to give him a hearing, only to learn that he had been arrested in passing by an official of the Mint on an old charge of coining. When they looked further into his past career they transferred him to Newgate. At the same time, on the morning of 27 October, they ordered a search to be made of Mrs Cellier's house, and found further papers concealed in the famous 'Meal Tub' which gave its name to the whole intrigue. She was arrested, and Dangerfield decided that the time had come to run for cover. On 31 October he confessed that the whole plot had been a sham to incriminate the leading Whigs in an abortive *coup d'état*, and at the same time conceal the real designs of the papists, who were still hell-bent on murdering the King. Arundell, in the Tower, he said, had offered him £2,000 to kill the King, and Powis had offered him £500 for Shaftesbury's head. He went on to detail various unsuccessful attempts on the earl's life, in which he implicated not only Mrs Cellier but Roger Palmer, Earl of Castlemaine, an active and notorious Irish Catholic, who was extraordinarily lucky not to have been more deeply implicated in the Plot from the beginning. He had been sent to the Tower on 31 October 1678, and bailed on 23 January 1679. Dangerfield was duly released from prison, though it is clear that no one really believed him, and he was given a small pension while preparations were made to try Castlemaine, Lady Powis and Mrs Cellier in the New Year.

The Opposition seized on the Meal Tub Plot as evidence that their own leaders, as well as the King, lay under threat of death from the bloodthirsty Catholics. A rumour was put about that Sir William Waller's house had been attacked, and bullets fired into his front door, but it came to nothing. Waller, Justice of the Peace for Westminster and son of the old Parliamentary general, was the most notorious, as well as the most efficient, of the 'priest-takers'; he had personally arrested most of the priests taken in London since October 1678, and he was active as ever in this field. He had also confiscated Catholic books, vestments and regalia and burnt them publicly. To his stupefaction his reputation, and his support from the groundlings, had not been enough to carry him into Parliament in February, perhaps because there was more than a suspicion that confiscated valuables were sticking to his hands. In the second part of Dryden's *Absalom and Achitophel* he appears as 'industrious Arod':

> The labours of this midnight-magistrate
> May vie with Corah's [Oates] to preserve the State.
> In search of arms he failed not to lay hold
> On war's most powerful dangerous weapon, gold.
> And last, to take from Jebusites all odds,
> Their altars pillaged, stole their very gods.
> Oft would he cry, when treasure he surprised,
> 'Tis Baalish gold in David's coin disguised.'
> Which to his house with richer relics came,
> While lumber idols only fed the flame.

He was elected to Parliament in September 1679, but his rage against the Catholics was now of such psychopathic proportions as to reduce his usefulness even to the Whigs. In April 1680 the King felt strong enough to strike him from the list of magistrates, and he fled to Holland to escape his creditors.[37]

Another magistrate whose hatred for Rome had reached psychopathic proportions was John Arnold of Llanfihangel, the man behind the pogrom in South Wales and the Marches, and a notorious character in London, too. He and Bedloe accused Thomas Herbert of Usk of seditious libel in February 1680, but the hearing before the Privy Council was postponed many times because of Arnold's failure to appear. Finally the Council peremptorily ordered Arnold to appear on 16 April, or the accusation would go by default, but the night before he was beaten up and severely wounded in Jackanapes Lane, off Fleet Street. The evidence pointed to John Giles, a friend of Herbert's, who was tried at the Old Bailey on 7 July and found guilty. But Sir John Pollock's careful review of the evidence leaves little room for doubt that this was a 'frame-up', and Arnold's wounds, severe as they were, were self-inflicted.[38] Pollock believed that Arnold hoped to succeed Godfrey as a popular victim-figure; unfortunately he did not have the stature, the time was not ripe, and mad as he undoubtedly was, he was not mad enough actually to kill himself in the Protestant cause.

But in the meanwhile serious and genuine attacks were being made on the authenticity of the King's evidence. Witnesses came forward in October 1679 to testify that Dugdale, who even at this late stage was 'a man of the most unblemished reputation of all the discoverers', had qualms of conscience and was prepared to make a full recantation in return for a sum of money and his fare paid overseas. James rather naïvely swallowed this, as he had swallowed Dangerfield's information, but the story was soon exploded, and Dugdale sued his tormentors, Tasborough and Price, for libel, and won.[39] More serious was an attack on Oates by two of his former servants, Thomas Knox and John Lane. He had had trouble with them before, and in April 1679 he had dismissed Lane and his fellow-servant William Osborn for spying on him, ostensibly on Danby's behalf. After Wakeman's acquittal Knox, Lane and Osborn all turned on him and accused him of sodomy, an offence which carried the death penalty. In November the case was thrown out by a grand jury, Osborn fled abroad, and Oates sued Knox and Lane for heavy damages and won.[40] This may have prompted a mysterious Mrs Le Mare to launch 'a most cursed and complicated conspiracy' against that aged Whig roué the Duke of Buckingham, accusing him of debauching her young son. The bill was thrown out by a grand jury in May 1680, and Mrs Le Mare was convicted of libel by King's Bench. The judges ordered that the proceedings be not printed, but they were wasting their time.[41]

What with pope-burning and petitioning, and scandalous accusations of sodomy and worse ricocheting from one public personage on to another, this was a time of great confusion, well typified by the trial of seven Catholic priests, on a charge of priesthood only, on 17 January 1680 in King's Bench.

They were a very miscellaneous collection, the remaining Jesuits being reserved for better things. They were led by the Benedictines, James Corker and William Marshal, acquitted of treason in July. Lionel Anderson was a renegade Dominican who had signed the Remonstrance of loyalty to the King and had therefore been allowed to reside quietly in England ever since 1671. David Kemish (or Kemys) was another Dominican, a very old man who had been confessor to the dowager Lady Arundell. He had been listed by Oates as one of the London priests involved in the plot, but the date of his arrest is unknown. William Russell was a distinguished Franciscan, Rector of Mount Grace Priory near Thirsk since 1675; he had probably been arrested at the instance of Bolron and Mowbray in Yorkshire. He usually went under the name of Marianus Napper (or Napier). Charles Parris (or Parry) was a straightforward secular priest arrested on Prance's information on 3 May 1679, but a charge of treason against him had not stuck. Henry Starkey was a colourful and quite well-known character; he had lost a leg in the Civil Wars, and was known as 'Old Starkey' or 'Colonel Starkey'. He had been ordained a secular priest in 1649, but there is some suggestion that he subsequently entered the Benedictine Order.[42] Finally there was a Scots Dominican, Alexander Lumsden, who perhaps belonged to the Flemish province, though he had lived and worked in London for more than thirty years.[43]

At the beginning of the proceedings[44] Kemish pleaded that he was too weak to stand, and could scarcely hear or speak. This had not saved Atkins at Stafford Assizes the previous August, but Scroggs had mellowed since then. Having consulted his colleagues on the bench, he announced 'that the world may not say we are grown barbarous and inhuman, we are all contented he should be set by'. (In fact, he died in Newgate ten days later.) This set the tone for the subsequent proceedings, though William Marshal was as irritating as he had ever been, and relations between the Crown's star witness, Oates, and the Lord Chief Justice must have been strained.

Marshal, indeed, was on his feet early, to argue that by the terms of the statute of 27 Elizabeth, 1585, priesthood alone was not treasonable; it was necessary to show intent to seduce the King's subjects from their allegiance. But he was overruled; quite properly, since the phrase in question occurred only in the preamble to the act. Subsequently each of the defendants challenged the prosecution to prove that he had received holy orders, but the Court ruled that this was impossible, and proof that he had said mass or administered the sacraments was enough. The defendants countered this by arguing that a layman could say mass, and in any case they pointed to an embarrassing statute of 1581 which fixed the penalty for saying mass at 200 marks and a year's imprisonment.[45] On the other hand, short of producing a wife, how could a man prove he was *not* a priest? The judges showed great patience in dealing with this and other arguments, but no one in court can have had the least doubt that all these men were in fact Roman priests, and to that extent the prosecution was a formality.

The Court took each in turn, beginning with Anderson, who asserted that he had a licence from the Council to stay in England, since he had taken the oaths. The Court agreed to remind the King of this, but said it must press on regardless. One might be forgiven for supposing that by these exchanges Anderson had admitted his priesthood, but Thomas Dangerfield was produced to testify that Anderson had received his confession and given him absolution in Newgate prison. It was Dangerfield's first appearance in court, and not an auspicious one. Despite feeble protests from the bench, Anderson heaped on the witness every insult he could think of, and called on Captain Richardson, Keeper of Newgate, who stood behind the prisoners, to corroborate that he had asked for a transfer from Newgate simply to avoid this man. In his excitement he even seized Richardson by the shoulders and turned him to face Dangerfield. Richardson, who was clearly amused, demurred: 'I must not witness,' he said. Anderson then asked the court to indulge his 'innocency and infirmity', upon which Mr Justice Pemberton remarked, 'You do not seem to have so much infirmity upon you.'

Oates then testified to seeing Anderson celebrating mass. Anderson denied that this was proof of his priesthood, and said the court must prove that he had received orders from Rome. Scroggs ruled that this was impossible, though Oates, ever-helpful, said 'I have seen his letter of orders'; no one paid him the least attention. Bedloe appeared, and at once made the mistake of saying that Anderson was of a wealthy Oxfordshire family. Not only Anderson himself, but Chief Baron Montague, who knew his father, corrected him, and Anderson remarked offensively, 'And yet this rogue is upon his oath, and indeed all his life is full of such mistakes.'[46] For good measure Prance was also brought in to testify that he had seen him celebrating mass at Wild House, the Spanish ambassador's residence in Covent Garden. Anderson remarked that because he had argued for the oaths he was certainly *persona non grata* there.

After a brief charge to the jury, attention swung on to Corker. Oates, Bedloe and Prance had all seen him celebrating mass, they said, at various places, including the Benedictine house in the Savoy. Corker declined to answer to this last, lest he incriminate himself. Scroggs indicated the witness box, and said, 'Here is one hath sworn it.' 'It is only Oates, my lord,' said Corker, simply. With William Marshal there was a variation. Prance testified that at one stage during his trial for treason in July he had overheard Marshal say to his fellow-prisoners, 'Though we are priests this does not reach us.' Scroggs remarked, 'This is hard evidence, truly,' but he admitted that he had heard the words, too. After a long discussion the matter was left hanging. Russell presented few difficulties in the circumstances; Sir William Waller had found his luggage stuffed with vestments and other priestly gear. The court then heard evidence against Lumsden, Parris, and Starkey, and Scroggs left well before the end, handing over to Chief Baron Montague. Eventually the jury retired for fifteen minutes before returning with verdicts of 'guilty' against all six, except the Scotsman, Lumsden.

The proceedings so far had been conducted with great courtesy, and this was still the case when Jeffreys took over, to pronounce sentence. He allowed each prisoner to have his say, though Corker and Marshal were only repeating at greater length points they had already made, and which had often been ruled out of order. At the end he said to Marshal, 'Now you have been heard,' and Marshal replied, 'Yes, sir, and I thank you for it.'[47] Even then, Jeffreys had to submit to further interruptions before he launched on the terrifying sentence reserved for those found guilty of high treason:

That you be conveyed from hence to the place from whence you came, and that you be conveyed from thence on hurdles to the place of execution, where you are to be hanged by the neck; that you be cut down alive, that your privy members be cut off, your bowels taken out and be burnt in your view; that your head be severed from your body; that your body be divided into four quarters, to be disposed of at the King's pleasure; and the God of infinite mercy have mercy on your soul.[48]

These were the words which Jeffreys was to pronounce many times more, but on this occasion it is doubtful if even he regarded them as more than a formality. None of these condemned priests was in fact ever executed. Lumsden, the Scotsman, disappeared across the border. Anderson, the remonstrant, was banished immediately and forbidden ever to return – the revelations he had made at his trial of the degree of favour he had enjoyed must have been highly embarrassing. (Though the government had none but itself to blame; Anderson had been exhaustively interrogated by the Committee for Examinations on his arrest twelve months before.[49]) The Franciscan William Russell was held in prison until 1684, when he too was exiled; Starkey was still in King's Bench prison in 1683, when he petitioned the King for his release, and Corker was not released from Newgate until 1685; while still in prison, ironically enough, he was elected President of the English Benedictines, the honour Oates had prematurely awarded him in 1678. He acted as confessor to Oliver Plunket in 1681, and went with him to Tyburn. Charles Parris and William Marshal, like so many other priests in this period, simply drop out of sight; it is unlikely that they were released before the end of the reign, but they were certainly not executed.[50]

In fact, as we have seen, no priest convicted under the statute of 1585 after the Council Order of 4 June 1679 was executed. On 28 February 1680, two more priests appeared at Old Bailey Sessions before Sir William Dolben. Against the Benedictine

Jerome Hesketh only one witness appeared; he was acquitted, released and went abroad. Oates swore against Anthony Hunter S.J. (deeply disguised under two aliases, Baker and Gifford), and he was convicted. He died in Newgate on 24 January 1684.

In May, according to the Modenese envoy, an Irish priest, Daniel Macarthy, was condemned at the Old Bailey on Oates's evidence, but nothing further is known about him.[51]

By now belated efforts were being made to extend the Plot geographically. One of the most remarkable things about the Popish Plot is that it found no credence in Scotland, despite Oates's warning that the Jesuits were planning a Presbyterian rising there, and the detailed accusations made against the Scots Catholic nobility by Edmund Everard in December 1678.[52] No attempt was made to capitalize on the Covenanters' Rebellion when it came, in May and June 1679. But Ireland was another matter. Here the waters were muddied, though, by the greater degree of toleration extended to Catholics, inevitable when they comprised a large majority of the population. In particular, the statute of 1585 had never been applied to Ireland, so that priests could only be prosecuted on a *praemunire* under the Henrician statutes for acknowledging a foreign jurisdiction. In fact, the hierarchy was tacitly acknowledged by Dublin Castle, and even in Dublin itself the celebration of mass was widely condoned except in times of acute crisis. A number of clergy, led by the Franciscan Peter Walsh, had even signed a famous remonstrance in 1671 in which they gave their first allegiance to the King. Remonstrant priests seem to have been allowed to pass freely through Ireland and England, even during the Plot. The Irish Franciscans were regarded as a much greater menace than the Jesuits, who were controlled from Madrid, and they were subject to periodic purges and deportations.

The situation was further complicated by the personality and prestige of the Lord Lieutenant, the great James Butler, Duke of Ormonde, a pillar of the Anglo-Irish ascendancy and one of the few men who could always outface Charles II. Oates unwittingly strengthened Ormonde's prestige when he made him the prime target of the new Irish Plot, and as soon as news of his depositions reached Dublin Ormonde anticipated the inevitable orders from Whitehall by ordering all priests to leave the country forthwith, closing the Dublin mass-houses and imprisoning the Archbishop of Dublin, Peter Talbot, a man who enjoyed Charles II's personal regard.

There the matter rested until early 1680, when Shaftesbury dispatched agents to Ireland to ferret out information against Talbot and also against Plunket, Archbishop of Armagh. Behind this move it is easy to trace the hand and mind of Arthur Capel, Earl of Essex, who had now joined Shaftesbury in Opposition; he had briefly replaced Ormonde in the years 1672–7, and hoped to do so again. By 24 March 1680 Shaftesbury had fudged together enough evidence to go to the Privy Council with a harrowing tale of Protestant peril and viceregal neglect. The Council, in conjunction with Ormonde, had no alternative but to undertake a leisurely investigation of the whole matter, which was still proceeding when Parliament reassembled in October.[53]

Meanwhile, ever since October 1679, when the Privy Council had lent them the weight of its authority, Robert Bolron and Lawrence Mowbray, who saw themselves as the Oates and Bedloe of the north, had been uncovering a hellish conspiracy in Yorkshire; they were not discouraged by the evaporation of Bedloe's Plot in the Marches, or Dugdale's in Staffordshire. Bolron, like Dugdale a man of good standing, had been colliery manager to Sir Thomas Gascoigne of Barnborough, a wealthy West Riding baronet; Mowbray had served him in a lesser capacity. They now turned on their former master, his daughter Lady Tempest, and many of his friends amongst the Catholic community in Yorkshire, and they found a new gimmick in 'the Papists' Bloody Oath of Secrecy', supposed to have been forced upon them by Gascoigne.

Like so many designated plotters, Gascoigne did not seem the stuff of which assassins are made; he was eighty-five years old, deaf, half-blind and lame, and he had not been south of the river Trent for thirty years. Nevertheless, he was arrested and brought to London in November 1679, and arraigned for treason before King's Bench the January following. He then demanded a Yorkshire jury, and one was brought down for 11 February. The proceedings were somewhat casual; Scroggs walked out half-way through to preside over another court, and left no designated successor, his role devolving on the puisne judges, Jones, Dolben and Pemberton, apparently in order of seniority. Bolron's and Mowbray's evidence was bloodcurdling, but it was placed in a new light when several Protestant witnesses came forward to testify that at the same time as Gascoigne and his daughter were trying to inveigle these men into the Plot they were under sentence of dismissal for dishonesty. Dolben said uncomfortably:

There is some evidence that makes it a very improbable thing to be true what Mr Bolron has said; and yet Mr Bolron having said it so positively, and Mowbray agreeing to it, probabilities must give way to positive proofs.

Pemberton agreed, but the jury did not. Gascoigne went free, and retired to Germany to spend the remaining years of his life in a monastery.[54]

The government had no greater success with his daughter, Lady Tempest, or Sir Miles Stapleton. After some debate they were sent back to York to be tried at the Assizes there in July, together with Mary Pressicks and a priest called Thomas Thwing. The judges, Dolben and Atkins, directed the jury to acquit Pressicks because the evidence against her was all hearsay, and gave a rather surprising ruling that 'As to what Hutchinson said, that she told him we should never be at peace till we were all of the Roman Catholic religion, and the Duke of York was made king, that will not amount to high treason.'[55] Lady Tempest was also acquitted, though no account of her trial survives, and Thwing was the solitary victim; found guilty and condemned to death, he was executed on 23 October, despite assurances of a reprieve from Whitehall.[56] As for Sir Miles Stapleton, he challenged so many of the jury panel that his trial had to be postponed until the next summer Assizes, on 18 July, before Dolben again, and Baron Gregory. This time unimpeachable Protestant witnesses testified that in his first depositions Bolron had positively sworn that Stapleton had no hand in the Plot, and again the judges were in difficulties. Dolben said:

These things hang not well together; I know not how to make any observations upon it; he denies that he said so, they say he did,

and in the absence of any strong line from the bench, the jury comfortably brought in a verdict of 'not guilty'.[57]

The significant thing about these Yorkshire trials is the way the local Protestant gentry rallied in force to support their Catholic neighbours; seventeen of them took the stand to give evidence on behalf of Gascoigne, including influential leaders of local society like Sir Thomas and Lady Yarborough and William Lowther. The Yarboroughs' evidence was also decisive for Sir Miles Stapleton. Local gentry shied away from jury service, and those who could not escape it were subject to very strong pressure on behalf of the accused. At York the assize judges were in alien territory, and Sir John Reresby tells how one of the jurymen braved Dolben to his face, and made him apologize next day in open court. The other remarkable thing is that, though these men and women were certainly not guilty as charged, they had all been indulging in overt recusant activity on an ambitious scale; Gascoigne had been a patron of the Franciscans at Mount Grace, and Lady Tempest, as appeared at the trials, had been running a nunnery at Dolebank, near Ripon. Apparently their neighbours were quite willing to overlook such conduct on the part of Catholic gentry they knew.[58]

But as the spring of 1680 unwound into summer the Plot seemed to wind down with it, and the attempt to find new witnesses was in vain. On 11 June Mrs Cellier appeared before King's Bench charged with treason, but the result was a remarkable fiasco. She challenged Dangerfield as a convicted felon, still under an outlawry, and therefore disabled from giving evidence in a court of law. His pardon, when produced, contained no mention of felonies, and Scroggs dismissed him with contempt.

It is notorious what a fellow this is [he sneered], he was in Chelmsford Gaol. I will shake all such fellows before I have done with them.

Dangerfield understandably protested:

> 'My lord, this is enough to discourage a man from ever entering into an honest principle.'

'What?' replied Scroggs. 'Do you, with all the mischief that hell hath in you, think to brave it in a court of justice? I wonder at your impudence that you dare look a court of justice in the face, after having been made to appear so notorious a villain!'[59]

The jury was left with no choice but to acquit her without leaving the box. Unfortunately, she then published a triumphant account of the whole affair with the self-explanatory title, *Malice Defeated*. This brought her before King's Bench again in September, this time for a swingeing fine and a session in the pillory.

By this time Dangerfield had repaired the defects in his pardon, and it was decided to try him out against the Earl of Castlemaine. A grand jury had thrown out a similar bill against the Countess of Powis, but Oates had now dredged up some evidence against the Earl from the depths of his capacious memory. The trial opened in King's Bench, before Scroggs, on 23 June. (Special commissions of oyer and terminer were no longer used against the small fry.)

Oates deposed that Castlemaine had been in correspondence in 1677 and 1678 with Spanish Jesuits as well as St Omers about the 'design'; he had also been present at the famous White Horse Tavern Consult in April 1678. Scroggs took him through this with great patience, though he did remark, when Oates was describing letter after letter he had seen and memorized, 'I wish you *had* one that was of moment.'[60] Castlemaine then gave Oates a very searching cross-examination, from which Oates tried to escape by charging that Castlemaine had divorced his wife, Charles's old mistress, now Duchess of Cleveland, and taken priest's orders. This occasioned a protracted argument. Dangerfield was then put up, and sustained an immediate challenge. With some reluctance Scroggs accepted his pardon as now valid. Castlemaine then unexpectedly produced witnesses not only to Oates's previous perjury at Hastings, but to his drunken and 'distracted' conduct as curate of Bobbing. This was obviously another hurdle which Oates would have to get used to.

The new Attorney-General showed an unwise disposition to sum up for Scroggs, but when the Lord Chief Justice took over he was perfectly firm. He played down the evidence on Oates's character (Dangerfield was so consummate a villain that he whitewashed anyone who appeared with him), but he warned the jury, 'You must weigh well with yourselves how probable or not probable what he does swear is.' As for Dangerfield, Scroggs told them he could not discharge his now famous conscience unless he reminded them of this man's remarkable criminal record. He concluded by warning them that if they only believed one of the witnesses they could not convict, a warning repeated by Mr Justice Jones. It took them only a few minutes to find a verdict of 'not guilty'.[61]

So, when Parliament met at last, on 21 October 1680, it found the great Popish Plot in a state of some decrepitude. Bedloe had died at Bristol in August; to the consternation of some and the incredulity of others he had sworn an affidavit on his death-bed confirming all his previous depositions, except those against the Queen. Oates was drawing nearer to Shaftesbury, and the Salamanca Doctor was a familiar figure at the great Earl's Aldersgate house, especially since his weekly allowance had been cut from £12 to £3 in July (apparently as part of a general retrenchment on Crown witnesses). In August, Simpson Tonge had appeared before the Council to testify that his father and Oates had cooked up the Plot with the assistance of Shaftesbury, and the fact that no one really believed him made him no less troublesome. (In fact, he retracted the whole story as soon as Parliament met.) More troublesome still was the Tory journalist Sir Roger l'Estrange, who was patiently exposing the absurdities and internal inconsistencies of Oates's evidence. He was forced to go into exile when Parliament met, but this was only a temporary defeat.[62] Meanwhile, attempts to find a new running mate for Oates had been in vain. Dangerfield had dropped out of sight, to reappear only briefly thereafter. Others were given a trial run, like the aptly-named 'Narrative' Smith, only to be discarded before reaching the courtroom. Since the previous June, 1679, no one had been convicted of complicity in the Plot (except for the wretched Thwing, at York), and this year the prison gates had begun to open. In May 1680, Sir Henry Tichborne, William Roper and John Caryll were all released on bail, followed in June by the first Jesuits, Edward Petre, his brother Robert, and Thomas Fermor.[63]

Parliament lent a sympathetic ear, of course, to all the informers who came before it; including Bedloe from the grave. (It received an affidavit from Chief Justice North concerning his death-bed confession.) Dangerfield gave in a long deposition incriminating the Duke of York in the Plot – an act he was to rue, as did the Speaker, William Williams, who authorized its publication. More surprisingly, the cautious Dugdale took the same line.[64] James was safe in Edinburgh, but his impeachment was in preparation, and another Exclusion Bill was soon brought in.

However, sooner or later the Commons must face up to the embarrassing question of the Catholic Lords in the Tower. They had been impeached two Parliaments ago, in November 1678, and their trial had originally been fixed for May 1679. Since then the scaffolding erected in Westminster Hall to accommodate spectators had 'stood useless, or rather a nuisance, many terms, to the shortening of the promenade of the lawyers, and severe oppression of the shops'.[65] In November 1680, it was at last decided to discard the Earl of Danby, the great stumbling-block, and make a start with William Howard, Viscount Stafford. His trial opened on 29 November in Westminster Hall, with the Lords sitting as judge and jury, under the presidency of the Lord Chancellor as Lord High Steward. The prosecution was managed by the ex-Attorney-General, Sir William Jones, who performed better now than he had ever done for the Crown. Since the Lords were not bound by the curious restrictions acknowledged by the common-law courts this was the only trial for the Plot that lasted more than a day – indeed, it lasted seven, with a Sunday in between.

The choice of Lord Stafford caused surprise in some quarters, but in fact Bedloe's death left the Commons without a strong second witness against Belasyse and Arundell (only Miles Prance) and no second witness at all against Lord Petre. Against Stafford there was not only Oates, but a very powerful witness indeed in Stephen Dugdale, whose evidence had so impressed the King when he first heard it in January 1679. The prosecution had also found a new witness altogether in Edward Turberville of Sker, a Welsh soldier-of-fortune who claimed he had known Stafford in Paris in the 1670s. So, by the accepted conventions of the time, their case was good-looking. Over and above all this Stafford was clearly a quarrelsome and unpopular individual; though a staunch Catholic, he had run with the opposition in the seventies, and even made overtures to Shaftesbury. He had quarrelled bitterly with Lord Arundell in the 1650s, and with the Duke of Norfolk; in the event seven out of eight peers of the Howard family, who could have been forgiven for abstaining, were happy to vote him guilty.[66]

The first day of the trial was taken up by a procesion of witnesses, 'Narrative' Smith, Oates, Dugdale, Robert Jenison, to prove the general existence of a Popish Plot in 1678.[67] Next day, 1 December, opened with Dugdale's evidence of the conversation he had had with Stafford at Tixall in September 1678. Evelyn, watching, thought this 'seemed to press hardest'.[68] Oates for once took second place, with his evidence of letters he had seen from Stafford at St Omers in 1677, and Stafford's commission, which was now as paymaster-general, not secretary of state. He also gave some plausible details of Stafford's negotiations with the Irish Jesuit Con in 1676, in an attempt to heal the breach between the regulars and the seculars.[69]

Then came Edward Turberville, another strange piece of religious flotsam thrown up by the Plot. A member of an old Catholic family, he had first tried being a Dominican, then a Benedictine, before he turned professional soldier and took service in the French Army. He swore that at Paris in 1676 Stafford had tried to enlist him as Charles II's assassin, and indeed, he was a likelier candidate for this role than most others accused of it. The only question he could not sensibly answer was why he had held this back until a few weeks before. He had first approached a magistrate, ostensibly, on 9 November.[70]

Stafford then made a long speech in his own defence, and the next two days (2 and 3 December) were taken up by his defence in detail. He was faced by a difficulty common to all the defendants in these trials (which Corker had expounded to Scroggs at great length at his trial the previous July), that it was almost impossible to prove a negative. He *had* been at Lord Aston's house in September 1678, and although he called several witnesses he could not account for every moment of his time. He *could* have talked treason with Dugdale and Evers. All he could show was that subsequently Dugdale had been dismissed by his employer in highly suspicious circumstances, and that when he was first arrested, at Stafford in December 1678, he had denied all knowledge of a Plot in response to a direct question.[71] As for Turberville, Stafford denied ever having seen him before, but Turberville knew the topography of Paris, and he could name the house where he had met Stafford. Stafford caught him out in the wrong year, but that was a venial sin in a plot witness, speaking of events in the previous decade. (It was now generally accepted that none of these witnesses – Oates, Bedloe, Dugdale, Turberville – had found a proposal to assassinate the King particularly memorable at the time.)

Not a jot of written evidence was given in, so everything hung on the oath of the witnesses. Evelyn had had time by now to digest Titus Oates's peculiar character, and he thought 'such a man's testimony should not be taken against the life of a dog'.[72] Many peers, notably the Earl of Anglesey, thought much the same, but in the peculiar circumstances, in which a vote for Stafford was a vote for popery and James, Duke of York, they found him guilty by fifty-five to thirty-one.[73] Finch, who by general consent had conducted the procedings with urbanity and humanity, pronounced the usual sentence. Charles commuted this to beheading, but otherwise he saw no ground for interference. Stafford was executed on 29 December. Burnet wrote his epitaph: 'He vanished soon out of men's thoughts.'[74]

The following month, January 1681, this Parliament was prorogued, then dissolved. Another was summoned to Oxford in March, but it only lasted seven days. Its successor was never called; instead the King issued a proclamation explaining and justifying his decision to dispense with Parliaments for the time being. Meanwhile the last martyr, and not the least distinguished, was prepared for trial. Oliver Plunket, titular Archbishop of Armagh, had been brought over from Dublin at Shaftesbury's insistence the previous October, with a flock of witnesses – Murphys and Kellys, Banions and O'Tooles – whose brogue could scarcely be comprehended by Englishmen. Jenkins, the new Secretary of State, wrote that it was now not safe to walk across St James's Park for fear of these cut-throats. Ormonde had already denounced them in measured terms:

> The discoveries now on foot in the North and in the West of this kingdom can come to nothing by reason of the extravagant villainy and folly of the discoverers, who are such creatures that no schoolboy would trust them with a design of robbing an orchard. My Lord of Essex's tool is a silly drunken vagabond that cares not for hanging a month hence if in the meantime he may solace himself with brandy and tobacco.[75]

True, but when it came to the point the Duke did nothing, for fear of undermining his influence in London. The prosecution of Plunket had by this time acquired a momentum of its own, and though nobody, not even Shaftesbury, had much interest in continuing it, no one was concerned enough to stop it either. His trial opened in King's Bench on 3 May 1681.[76]

King's Bench was a different world. One era had ended; another just begun. Scroggs was gone, displaced by Pemberton the previous month, and Pemberton was not a man to waste much time in long speeches, or in cross-examining witnesses either. The parade of loathsome Irish passed before the disdainful English without comment; this was a case of Irishmen swearing another Irishman to death. They were all 'wogs'. Jeffreys, who had lost his Recordership, and with it his seat on the bench, led for the Crown as King's Serjeant, and Pemberton left it to him to make the final speech to the jury. At the end the Lord Chief Justice merely said:

I leave it to you. It is a pretty strong evidence. He does not say anything to it, but that his witnesses are not come over.[77]

Found guilty, Plunket was remanded for sentence until 15 June. Then his execution was postponed a week. Many thought that Charles would intervene, but it was not worth it. He declined even to release Peter Talbot, Archbishop of Dublin, who had been imprisoned without trial since October 1678, and died, still in Dublin Castle, in November 1681. He had yet to grasp the strength of his position after the dissolution of the Oxford Parliament, and Plunket was only an Irishman, anyway. To the representations of Louis XIV, conveyed by his ambassador, he agreed quite happily that Plunket was innocent, but 'his enemies were still waiting for him to make a false step, and the moment was not propitious for a counter-attack'. He indignantly rejected the belated plea of the Earl of Essex with the words 'Be his blood on your conscience.'[78] Plunket was executed on 1 July 1681. With him to the scaffold, ironically enough, went Edward Fitzharris, the first victim of the 'Tory Revenge'.

7
The Effects of the Plot

THE obvious question about the Popish Plot is, how much long-term damage did it inflict on the English Catholic community? It is not an easy question to answer; the community was declining anyway, before the Plot, and much of the evidence for its fortunes during the Plot is missing. However, we must beware of exaggerating the damage; the death roll in the Revolution of 1688–9, for instance, was nil, but in terms of disruption and loss of property it weakened the Church much more.

In the period 1678 to 1681 it was the Society of Jesus that suffered most.[1] Nine Jesuits were executed, twelve more died in prison, and the death of three others can be directly attributed to the Plot; Humphrey Evans was thrown downstairs at the Cheshire home of his patron Sir James Pool, and died of his injuries, and Charles Prichard and Francis Bruning died in 1680, after eighteen months on the run, probably of exposure and sheer exhaustion – certainly this was so in Prichard's case. The death of some older priests was also blamed on the Plot: like Francis Parker, the veteran Rector of the Derby district, who arrived at Ghent late in 1678 'broken by suffering, and the fatigue of the long journey', and died the following May. Here the Plot may be said to have merely anticipated the course of nature by a few years or months, but in Edward Mico, who died in Newgate in 1678, and John Gavan the Society lost potential leaders of the next generation, brilliant men not easily replaced. In addition another thirteen Jesuits were imprisoned, in London or the provinces, and only three of them (Edward Petre, his brother Robert, and Thomas Fermor) are known to have been released before 1684.

The plight of the Jesuits was the worse because in the early stages, in late September and October 1678, Catholics and Protestants alike blamed them for the Plot; if they had not actually committed the crimes they were accused of, their general attitude to politics made it seem plausible that they had. On 3 December the General of the Society in Rome, Jean Paul Oliva, wrote to the Rector of St Omers:

I am watching what will be the outcome of that disturbance. Meanwhile my considered judgement on the whole matter is this: that if ours have meddled with politics (which conduct I abominate, though I think it is no less improbable than abominable) I think they deserve to suffer their present calamities.[2]

The distinguished French Jesuit Claude de la Colombière, who was unfortunate enough to be paying a brief visit to England, wrote:

The name of Jesuit is hated above all else, even by priests both secular and regular, and by the Catholic laity as well, because it is said that the Jesuits have caused this raging storm, which is likely to overthrow the whole Catholic religion.

Salvetti, the Modenese Resident in London, heartily agreed:

It is truly deplorable [he wrote], and it grieves me to the heart to see that the ill-governed zeal, not to say insane ambition, of a few priests and lay Catholics, has obliged a king so benign (who up to now has not caused any priests to be executed, or punished Catholics on account of their religion) to proceed with the greatest severity against all of that profession.[3]

By December the Catholics had realized the truth, and swung round to the other extreme, accusing the Protestants generally of fabricating the whole structure of the Plot, but in the meanwhile at least fourteen Jesuits fled abroad, and there might have been more but for the close watch kept on the ports. Actually, there were dangers in moving out of one's home district, and several Jesuits, notably John Gavan, were arrested in London while making arrangements to be smuggled out. The best thing was to travel with a party of lay Catholics; William Aylworth (the 'real' Harcourt, and one of the most sought-after men in England) reached Holland in September 1679 in the company of the Pierrepoints of Holbeck, and John Manners arrived in Ghent the following year with Lady Audley.

Meanwhile the arrest of Thomas Whitbread, the Provincial, had left the whole Province headless – one disadvantage of the Society's tight discipline. In December 1678, Oliva appointed as Vice-Provincial the Rector of Liège, John Warner, but he forbade him absolutely to go to England, and it appears that the prohibition was maintained. Warner was refused permission to make a visitation in October 1680, and he was still in Flanders in 1683. The experience of other Jesuits who tried to return was not encouraging. Richard Prince, who had been ordered by his superiors to retire from England in May 1679, probably because of his ill-health, went back without permission in October; he was arrested at Dover, and died in Newgate the following year. William Morgan was another who made a hazardous escape to the Continent, in February 1679, but when Warner sent him back to reconnoitre in October 1680, he was arrested at the port of entry, and remained in prison the rest of the reign.[4] Some of Warner's replacements got through; Albert Babthorpe, for instance, was sent to Lancashire in February 1679, and remained there unscathed until 1720; but Lambert Boelman, landing in May 1680, was again arrested on the jetty, and it was decided to send no one after him for the time being.[5] By this time Warner was convinced, with some reason, that many of these men were being betrayed by John Sargeant, the renegade secular now in government employ,* and in November 1680, after Morgan's arrest, he took the unusual step of writing direct to Cardinal Howard in Rome, asking him to use his influence on the English Chapter to expel this traitor.[6] One of the worst things was that, apart from the well-publicized treason trials in London, it was difficult to find out what had happened to members of the mission still in England; in July 1680, the government intercepted a coded letter from a Catherine Stacey at Derby, probably one of many, giving lists of priests who had died or were in prison.[7] In these circumstances any attempt to rebuild the central organization for the time being seemed point-

*See p. 265 below.

less. Edward Petre, bailed in June 1680, was experimentally appointed Rector of the London district, though Warner advised him 'to reserve himself for better times, being so well known'. Sure enough, he was re-arrested in October, and stayed in prison until February 1683.

But even in London there is a suggestion of some kind of organization and leadership surviving. In 1679, a Flemish Jesuit long domiciled in England, Cornelius Beagrand, was appointed Procurator of the London district; he was to be found 'At Nathaniel Rich's, glassmaker, next door to Ludgate, at the sign of the Galignani'. Anthony Bruning seems to have remained in London throughout the crisis, too, and in May 1680, he was considered for the post of Rector. (His brother Francis, meanwhile, was being 'hunted to death' through Suffolk.) John Forster was another young Jesuit who stayed on; Whitbread's last act as Provincial had been to summon him to London, and he remained until the end of 1679 before moving out to the comparative safety of the Lincolnshire district.

For it appears from the surviving evidence, which is admittedly sparse, that in some areas of England the Jesuits were scarcely troubled at all. Lincolnshire was one such area, Durham another, and also Derbyshire prior to the arrest of George Busby in March 1681. In Oxfordshire and even in Worcestershire, where the secular priests and the Franciscans suffered considerable persecution and harassment, a Jesuit mission survived. Lancashire, unfortunately, is a mystery. Warner refers enigmatically to disruption in that district in late 1680 or early 1681, and hints that local rivalries led some Catholics to betray their coreligionists to the authorities; but only two seculars were arrested and tried.[8] Edward Scarisbrick continued to labour there from 1678 to 1686, when he came south to be chaplain to James II; yet he was one of the few 'provincial' Jesuits named by Oates.

The main damage suffered outside London was the loss of the Cwm (or Combe) in Herefordshire, the headquarters of the South Wales district, the Residence of St Francis Xavier, and the only one of these Jesuit 'residences' established on their own property. It consisted of two adjoining farmhouses in a secluded valley not far from the Monmouth–Hereford road, managed by a Catholic farmer, Peter Pullen. The then Marquess of Worcester had leased it to William Morgan, S.J., in 1637, for a term of ninety-nine years, and on Morgan's death in 1667 it had passed to Robert Hutton, S.J., thinly disguised as 'Robert Hutton, merchant, of St Giles-in-the-Fields, London'. (Such was the government's ignorance of the Society that this flimsy alias was enough; early in 1679 the Privy Council instituted a search for Hutton the merchant, then gave up.) Its existence had been common knowledge for years, even in London,* but it was not until December 1678 that the Bishop of Hereford, at the instance of the House of Lords, had it raided. He found the priests fled and their lay employees mute, but he did pick up a substantial library of theological works which he transferred to his cathedral library, despite an attempt by Danby to intercept it.[9] Three months later, when poursuivants in search of Anthony Turner, S.J., flushed the Jesuits out of Holbeck Hall in Nottinghamshire, Danby was quicker off the mark; the library was seized and taken to London. But the Jesuits did not lease Holbeck; they were there as semi-permanent guests of the Pierrepoint family, and it is not even clear that it was the 'residence' for the Derby district. The poursuivants recommended that Gervase Pierrepoint be brought before the Council, presumably on a charge of harbouring priests, but when the family went abroad later in the year, as we have seen, they took with them the much-hunted William Aylworth, S.J., alias Harcourt.[10]

Richard Langhorn's betrayal lost the Jesuits their remaining bits and pieces of property in England, though in November 1679, the government, unwilling to believe that this was all, issued a proclamation 'for the further discovery of Jesuits' lands'. But the persecution continued to be sporadic, and the South Wales mission was the only one completely eliminated, with the death of Fathers Lewis, Evans, Lloyd and Prichard in the course of 1679. Even then, John Hugh Owen was still labouring in North Wales, almost certainly not alone, and it is not even clear that the famous shrine of St Winifred at Holywell

* See p. 17 above

was closed. Certainly it was flourishing openly in 1678, and again under James II.[11]* Finally, it should not be forgotten that some of the most 'wanted' Jesuits – Keynes, Conyers, Evers, Strange – were never taken, though at least one of them (Evers) never left England.

In fact, it could be argued that the other religious orders suffered more, bearing in mind the comparative size of their establishments. The discalced Carmelites, for instance, can never have had more than thirteen members on the mission at any one time, and the majority of them located in the Spanish embassy in London. But their only other mission, at Hereford, was broken up, and George Loop and Nicholas Rider were hounded right out of the Marches by the notorious priest-taker Charles Scudamore of Kentchurch. Rider reached London, only to be arrested; but he was bailed by a magistrate and took refuge in the Spanish embassy, which he never left again, dying there in December 1682.† Meanwhile, George Loop got as far as Worcester disguised as a farmer's wife, and, finding the seculars fled, set up a Carmelite mision there; two other friars, George Kemble and John Brett, were later sent to assist him.[12]

Similarly the Franciscans. They maintained a novitiate, and schools of philosophy and theology, at St Bonaventura's College, Douai, and as early as 1647 they had divided the English mission into eight districts. But this was very much on paper, and in 1678 only two districts outside London were manned, Yorkshire and Worcester. Their residence of Mount Grace, at Osmotherley, was sufficiently out of the way to survive even the Yorkshire Plot, though the Rector was taken and tried as a priest in January 1680.[13] But they were driven out of Worcester, and one of their most distinguished members, John Wall, was condemned and executed. Their base in London also suffered;

* There were two missions there, one staffed by the Jesuits, at the 'Old Star', and the other by seculars, at the 'Cross Keys'. In August 1678 Ireland and his party stayed at the 'Old Star', of course.

† According to his own story, the magistrates took sureties from a number of Protestants who happened to be present. An interesting example, and there are others, of the laxity and forbearance that prevailed in some quarters.

indeed, the outbreak of the Plot dispersed a meeting of the English chapter then being held at 'Mr Joll's house in Drury Lane', and the next meeting, in 1680, was held at Bruges. All their papers were seized by the government, but unlike the Jesuits they succeeded in retrieving them under James II.[14] The other orders were so thin on the ground that their sufferings are impossible to assess, except that the Benedictines, who had a large establishment at the Savoy, and were an early target for Oates's accusations, probably suffered quite disproportionately by the execution of Pickering and the long imprisonment of Marshal and Corker who, to judge by their performance in the courtroom, were amongst the most able priests of their generation.[15]

But it is arguable that an equal amount of damage was done to the European bases of the religious orders, their colleges and convents on the Continent which depended almost entirely on alms from the English Catholic community for their continued existence. In the Spanish Netherlands alone there were seven English nunneries, with a total of between 250 and 300 inmates. There was the great college at Douai, of course, for training the secular clergy, and the Jesuit school and seminary at St Omers, as well as smaller Jesuit houses at Liège, Watten and Louvain. (Liège also featured a mysterious college consisting, according to the English government, of 'Jesuitesses, Wardists, Expectatives or galloping girls'.)[16] As early as 22 July 1679,* the Brussels Internuncio wrote to the Secretary of Propaganda at Rome warning him that the condition of these houses and colleges was grievous. The subscriptions they relied on from England had stopped, and instead they were besieged by refugees, lay and clerical. But the heads of the various orders in Rome did not respond, and the Pope only felt able to give a miserly 20,000 florins, spread out over the years 1679–82. However, combined with holy poverty and hard work, this subvention seems to have pulled most of these communities round the corner.[17] More serious was the problem at St Omers, for the great Jesuit school had lost not only its income but its intake of new pupils; a proclamation of 8 January 1679 forbade English subjects to seek

* 12 July, English style dating.

an education abroad, and while adults might brave the difficult Channel passage, they were clearly not going to take risks with their children, and according to Edward Petre this was still so in the autumn of 1680. Warner, promoted to Provincial on Whitbread's death, considered closing St Omers altogether, and he was only deterred by the obstinacy and loyalty of the boys themselves.[18] Had the government but realized it, this was the most effective weapon they had against the Catholics, and if they had persisted in their policy for more than two or three years they must have eliminated the establishments training new priests for the mission. Once closed, it would have been difficult in the then state of Catholic opinion in Europe to get them reopened.

Clearly the history of the religious orders is obscure, and full of gaps, yet we know at least twice as much about them as we do about the secular priesthood. Hundreds of English secular priests are re-created only in the two-line biographies they gave the authorities when they enrolled at Douai; some did not even provide that. Some priests were tried and imprisoned whose real identities cannot now be established with anything like certainty, like William Allison, who died in York prison some time in 1679 or 1680; apart from this nothing is known of him. Some who were executed, and later even canonized, cannot be identified with the precision one would wish, like St John Plessington, who features in the official martyrology as 'John (or William) Plessington (Pleasington), alias Scarisbrick'.

By its proclamation of 20 November 1678, which was the basis of all subsequent persecution, the government implied that all priests arrested should be tried on the spot, at quarter sessions or assizes, but until the end of the year local authorities usually disembarrassed themselves of this problem by dispatching them to London instead, on the excuse that they might know something of the Plot. In December the Privy Council issued orders that unless there was positive evidence to this effect priests were to be arraigned in the localities on a simple charge of being in Roman orders, under the statute of 1585. But very few local authorities complied. Several priests were tried at the winter assizes in Wales, a few at York, and perhaps two at Lancaster, but over the rest of England nothing happened. Nothing happened, for instance, to a priest named Pickering reported as being in Leicester gaol in December 1678; the Council ordered him to be tried at the next assizes, but he was not put up. Nor was another priest, Talbot Constable, who was arrested in Durham the same month, nor was Francis Smith, a suspected Jesuit who was sent up to London from Nottingham early in January 1679. Neither Oates nor Bedloe recognized Smith, so he was sent back to Nottingham for trial; but his trial never took place.[19] The same can be said of Valentine Harcourt, who was brought up from Shrewsbury that same week under the impression that he was William Harcourt, S.J. When the mistake was discovered he was sent back to Shrewsbury for trial, but on his departure from London he disappears from the records.[20] Stranger still was the case of the Dominican William Collins, who took refuge in November 1678 at the Spanish embassy. On the request of the Lords the ambassador surrendered him, and on 16 November he was committed to the Gatehouse prison for 'uttering words of dangerous consequence' – a grave charge to be laid against anyone at this time, and particularly a priest – but nothing more is heard of him.[21] Similarly one Peter Winder, who was arrested with John Birkett in Lancashire early in 1680. Birkett was tried and convicted at Lancaster Assizes in the spring, but Winder drops out of sight.[22] These are just a few instances of a general trend.

In the state of public feeling in the winter of 1678–9, it would be unwise to attribute this trend to a spirit of clemency, or squeamishness. Technically, to convict a priest under the statute of 1585 it was necessary to prove ordination; at the assizes in 1679 a ruling was given, confirmed by King's Bench in January 1680, that it was enough to prove that he had celebrated mass or even heard confession. Even so, this required the testimony of two separate witnesses, who must in the nature of things be Catholics or ex-Catholics, and even the latter were reluctant to come forward in communities which had a strong Catholic minority. So it was never easy to secure a conviction, and several prosecutions failed because one of the witnesses cracked; before the trial of David Lewis, John Arnold of Llanfihangel had several potential witnesses beaten up before two could be induced to take the stand. Finally, the verdict of the jury had to be unanimous, and while the spirit of intolerance and hatred was generally strong, some jurymen still had qualms about the castration and disembowelling of men who were gentle, pious and earnest, however wrongheaded. This was evident at Stafford Assizes in the autumn of 1679.*

In fact, the great majority of priests condemned and executed under the Act of 1585 were tried in South Wales, Monmouthshire and Herefordshire. There were specific reasons for this, which have been established by Margaret O'Keeffe.[23] Since the Civil Wars of the mid-century this area had been torn by a struggle between the Catholics, still led by the Marquess of Worcester though he was now a Protestant, and a powerful consortium of ex-Puritan gentry led by John Arnold of Llanfihangel. These ultra-Protestants were backed by Herbert Croft, Bishop of Hereford, a renegade Catholic with all the convert's hatred of his former co-religionists, and they were probably the motive power behind William Bedloe, who was a native of Chepstow, which he revisited in the summer of 1678, and who was always closely associated with John Arnold thereafter. It is no accident that the depositions Bedloe made about the Plot deeply implicated Worcester's Catholic friends and relatives, though not the Marquess himself.

Indeed, the fight between Worcester and Arnold broke out before the Plot. Arnold sponsored the report made to the House of Commons in April 1678, pointing out that Catholicism was rampant in Monmouthshire, which was Worcester's responsibility as Lord President of the Council of the Marches and Wales.† Worcester's answer was to strike Arnold and seven of his followers from the list of Justices for the county. Sir Edward Mansell of Morgan protested to the King direct; he was reinstated, and so were one or two others, but not Arnold. At the same time Arnold, Mansell and John Scudamore disputed Wor-

*See p. 204 above   †See p. 49 above.

cester's appropriation of common land in Wentworth Chase, but Worcester ordered down troops and cannon from the royal garrison at Chepstow (later described by Bedloe as manned by papists, under a papist governor, Captain Francis Spalding), and tried and fined his adversaries in a kangaroo court. In these circumstances the Plot was a heaven-sent opportunity to harass, if not eliminate, the Catholic community on which Worcester's social power was based.

This is why the campaign against the South Wales priesthood was conducted with a vicious obstinacy unique even at this time, and an ill-feeling exacerbated by the fact that many families were divided between the two religions. For instance, Charles Price of Llanfoist pursued his cousin Walter Price, a secular priest, for two months through the cold of a Welsh winter, until he dropped dead some time between 13 and 16 January 1679 and was secretly buried by friends. But Charles Price did not rest until he had found the grave and disinterred the corpse, to make sure it was indeed his detested relative.[24]

The Catholic laity were undaunted, and when the Lords Committee for Examinations sent down the renegade Edward Turberville in December 1678 with a warrant to arrest certain named priests (amongst them one who was living at the house of his brother, Christopher Turberville of Sker), he was himself arrested by one of Worcester's Deputy Lieutenants. But what with having to explain away incidents like this, and meet Bedloe's accusations, and cope with the folly of his Catholic sister and mother,* it is not surprising that Worcester was hardpressed, nor that in three successive general elections his nominees in the Marches were defeated, though in February 1679 he had the effrontery to bring down troops from Chepstow to overawe the electors.

But it was strictly a political defeat, and a temporary one. Those of his followers and servants accused by Bedloe were all

---

*His sister, the Countess of Powis, was deeply involved in the Meal Tub Plot, and the dowager marchioness married a rather disreputable Irishman who was arrested in November 1679, accused of being one of the four 'Irish ruffians' engaged by Fogarty and Coleman to kill the King at Windsor in 1678.

bailed in the course of 1679, and Arnold's attempt to blame Worcester for the failure to enforce the penal laws in the Marches was at best a qualified success.* The King's confidence in him was unshaken, and as soon as the crisis had subsided, in December 1682, he rewarded him with the dukedom of Beaufort. To John Arnold this was the last straw. There had always been an element of paranoia in his conduct; in August 1678 he had even come to London to call out Edward Coleman, whom he blamed for his dismissal from the Monmouthshire bench, and in April 1680, as we have seen, he almost certainly wounded himself to 'frame' John Giles (a servant of Lord Worcester's, of course). By 1681 he was assaulting strangers in the London streets and hysterically accusing them of popery. Finally, in November 1684, Beaufort nailed him and his friend Trevor Williams of Llangibby for libel against a peer, or *scandalum magnatum*, a device the Duke of York had brought back into fashion. Sentenced to a crushing fine of £10,000, Arnold had to make an abject apology, and after this humiliation he dropped out of sight.

But outside this battle-area on the frontier of Wales, it seems that priests were usually not arraigned without some special reason. Thomas Thwing, as we have seen, was embroiled in the Yorkshire Plot, and it astonished contemporaries that he was condemned and his lay patrons acquitted; they were all either guilty or innocent together. Nicholas Postgate was arrested by an over-zealous Puritan official at Whitby, as a result of incautious words uttered by his Catholic host, but no effort was apparently made to track down the other priests who must have been working in Yorkshire in quite large numbers. One of them, Andrew Jowsie, was in fact arrested at the same time as Postgate, and only a few miles away, at Egton Bridge. He refused the oaths, but denied being a priest, and was apparently released on his bare word.[25] (Some magistrates were clearly prepared to release a man who denied his priesthood; only those who confessed or stood mute were committed.) According to local tradition John Plessington, executed at Chester in July 1679, was arrested at the

*See p. 259 below.

instance of a Protestant landowner because he had forbidden a match between his son and a Catholic heiress.

In all, and excluding the Jesuits and those released after a few days, I have been able to trace the names of forty-two priests arrested in the period 1678–81. Of these only twenty were brought to trial, six of whom were executed. Of the remainder, three are known to have died in prison, and one was remanded to Bedlam as a lunatic.[26] Others may have died in prison, leaving no record; certainly they all remained there for long periods, probably until the accession of James II. Only one is known to have been released before that, in 1681, and early in 1682 Charles II had seven unnamed priests transported to Scilly.[27] But they were certainly not executed.

The attack on the priesthood was almost entirely random. The authorities were confused from the start by the common habit, almost obsessional with the Jesuits, of using one or more aliases, and in general terms they were abysmally ignorant of the most basic facts about the priesthood, which they always imagined to be much better organized than it was. They firmly believed that there was a Catholic bishop in England, for instance, and in 1679 the Privy Council interrogated several prisoners in an attempt to discover his name; some M.P.s even believed that there was a complete 'shadow' hierarchy corresponding to the existing Anglican dioceses.[28] Nor was it easy to distinguish one priest from another, so that the messengers sent to Holbeck in March 1679 to arrest the Jesuit Anthony Turner returned with a secular of the same name; and what was even more irritating, he was so obese that he had to be brought up to London in a coach at considerable expense. Often proclamations were issued for the arrest of men who were then found to have been in one of the London prisons all the time, and in January 1680 even the knowledgeable Sir William Waller made a violent sortie into Buckinghamshire in search of Thomas Bedingfield, S.J., who had died in Newgate back in December 1678.* The search for

* Bedingfield, in fact, enjoyed an active posthumous life; as late as May 1680 a man arrested in mistake for him had the greatest difficulty in proving his identity and securing his release.

the 'real' Harcourt, amongst a multitude of other Harcourts, occupied the authorities for months.[29]

The mendacity of rogues like Oates, and their unwillingness to admit that there were any priests unknown to them, compounded the confusion. In June 1679 he identified one priest in Newgate first as Nicholas Blundell, S.J., then as Jerome Hesketh, O.S.B. Not until 'Hesketh' appeared before the Council was he correctly identified – by Shaftesbury, of all people – as Peter Caryll, O.S.B. (There is a tradition that out of regard for his family, the Carylls of West Grinstead, Shaftesbury unobtrusively ordered his release a few weeks later.) Undeterred, Oates then named Anthony Hunter, S.J., as Hesketh, while Hesketh himself, lodged in the same prison, remained concealed under the alias 'John Nayler'. Hunter was eventually tried in February 1680 under the name 'James Baker, alias Morris Gifford', and many priests went to the grave under their favourite aliases; Thomas Bedingfield's real name was Downes, for instance, and John Fenwick's, Caldwell.[30]

But if the government could not always find the priests it wanted, any and every priest ran the risk of harassment and was now in hiding. Letters from priests are rare, but in June 1680, one of them wrote rather hysterically to Douai:

Sweet Jesus grant us patience in all our adversity, and a resignation of ourselves to his holy will, that we may place all our hopes and confidence in he who alone can grant us consolation for our tribulations, which I doubt not will be ameliorated by all your good prayers, which we never stood more in need of, our small devotions being daily interrupted by frequent alarms and breaking up of our quarters, enough to daunt an old soldier and make such novices as myself sneak into lurking holes.

Nor did there seem any end to it. In December 1679, the Modenese Resident was in despair at the obstinate credulity of the English:

They regard themselves [he wrote] now more than ever as being on the brink of ruin and destruction, on account of a Plot in which there has never been seen, either before or after it was revealed, one single overt act of treason.[31]

As for the organization of the secular priesthood, this was so nebulous that it is difficult to be sure whether it was affected by the Plot at all. Dr Gauden and other leading members of the Chapter fled abroad in 1679 (not surprisingly, since one of Gauden's own servants had now been found guilty of Godfrey's murder). When they returned is not known, but it was certainly before 1683, when they received Cardinal Howard's emissary, Buonaventura Gifford, in London.[32] The proceedings of the Chapter in June 1684, at what was apparently its first general meeting since the Plot, are revealing. Four vicars-general of districts had to be replaced, and one archdeacon, but there was no mention of what lay behind these gaps; it was decided yet again to petition Rome for a bishop, and four names were put forward from which the Pope could choose. For the rest the assembly devoted itself to discussing 'such things as may be expedient for a reformation of manners in our country', and such vexed questions as whether Catholics north of Trent should continue to abstain from eggs on Fridays.[33]

There is no record that the Chapter ever expelled John Sargeant for his betrayal of the Jesuits,* or even reprimanded him. From its foundation down to the present day the Society of Jesus has been viewed with hostility and suspicion by many Catholics; it was Cardinal Manning who said, 'there is only a plank between them and presbyterianism'. Though few Catholics continued to believe them responsible for the Plot, the fact that the Protestants did, almost to a man, was felt to be a grave disadvantage and to some extent their own fault. Even at the Restoration some Catholics had been willing to buy toleration at their expense, and in 1679 or 1680 a paper was put up to James, Duke of York, arguing that he should publicly disown them. The anxious compliments which John Warner paid the secular clergy in his *History of the Presbyterian Plot*, written in the next reign, betray a continuing anxiety.[34]

But, whatever else might divide them, the regular and secular clergy were united in martyrdom. The moral value of the martyrs is not to be calculated according to any objective index.

* See p. 265 below.

They represented the Catholic priesthood in all its aspects. At one extreme stood the cultured and sophisticated Franciscan John Wall, former professor of philosophy at Douai, born of a Norfolk gentry family and once worth £500 a year in his own right, whose acute and academic intelligence was blacked out on the Red Hill at Worcester on 22 August 1679. At the other extreme stood old Nicholas Postgate (or Poskitt), who died on the Knavesmire at York two weeks before. Postgate was born in 1596 of poor parents at Egton Bridge, near Fylingdales; he was arrested in 1678 only five miles away, at Ugglebarnby. When he took up his life's work in 1630 Charles I was safe on his throne, Charles II was at his mother's breast. For nearly half a century he had tramped the high moors of North Yorkshire and the plains of the Holderness, ministering to a scattered flock of small tenants and minor gentry. Around him a whole polity had dissolved, mutated, then re-formed; now it was dissolving again. He explained, rather pathetically, from the scaffold that he could make no speeches, he was simply there to die for the faith in which he had lived.

Cults were quick to form. John Wall's severed head was snatched away by another Franciscan, and after many vicissitudes reached Douai. The Poor Clares at Aire took charge of it, and on the outbreak of the French Revolution it returned with them to England. In 1815 it was brought back to the restored convent at Gravelines, but when the time came for them to return to England for good in 1836 the unfortunate sister responsible for this rather grisly relic felt she could not face the British Customs with it. She buried it in the cloister garden, but subsequently neither she nor anyone else was able to find it.[35] Risible to the ungodly, such anecdotes are a consolation to the faithful.

In this connection it is important that all these martyrdoms were involuntary. Nothing was given away, and the prosecution always had to work for a conviction. As we have seen, Gavan, Ireland and Whitbread all defended themselves against charges of treason with great spirit, and at least dented the prosecution. The Benedictines Marshal and Corker twice put up a remarkable defence, first against charges of treason in July 1679, then against a prosecution under the Act of 1585 the following January; they survived and deserved to. But even men arraigned at provincial assizes, in comparative obscurity, declined to confess, and put the burden of proof on the prosecution. The only exception seems to be Anthony Turner, S.J., who simply gave himself up to the authorities in February 1679.[36] But this was the case of a man absolutely at the end of his tether, perhaps suffering from a temporary nervous breakdown, and he defended himself sensibly enough at his trial in June. Any talk of 'crowns of immortality' was left strictly until after the verdict had been given and sentence pronounced.

The situation in London is difficult to assess. On the one hand the proclamation of 30 October 1678 ordered all Catholics who were not householders or established tradesmen to leave London and Westminster and not return within a twelve-mile radius without special permission from the Council; those who remained were to take the oaths. This proclamation was renewed at intervals of approximately six months throughout the crisis, and some people took it very seriously indeed. For instance, there is a steady trickle of physicians coming before the Privy Council in 1679 and 1680 to testify that their Catholic clients (usually from the nobility or gentry) were too ill to leave London, or so ill that they must come up for treatment. As soon as Parliament rose in December 1678 the King was warned that popish priests might take the opportunity of returning to town, and the Justices of Peace were warned accordingly.[37] On 17 January 1679, even the wealthy and influential Lord Lumley was called before the Committee for Examinations to explain his presence in London without a permit, as was Lord Dunbar, of Burton Constable.[38]

Yet, reading betwen the lines, it is clear that the householders and tradesmen of London formed an active and curiously unconcerned Catholic community, willing to take the oaths, and after that left alone for much of the time.[39] The circumstances surrounding the burial of young Staley, executed for treason in

November 1678, repay study; here was a community which celebrated a series of requiem masses without much attempt at concealment, and which accompanied its dead to the local churchyard in procession, presumably with priests – and this at the height of the Plot fever in London.*

This was in Covent Garden, of course, the centre of a cosmopolitan trading district. The Spanish ambassador's enormous establishment at Wild House, on Wild Street, also bestowed an aura of extra-territoriality on the whole area. Oates had arrested the Jesuits Whitbread and Mico at Mrs Saunders's lodging house in Wild Street on 29 September 1678. Borgomaniero protested that this was part of the embassy, and though in view of the grave charges levelled against the two Jesuits he did not press the matter, he strengthened his case for the future by piercing the dividing walls of a whole row of houses down Wild Street adjacent to the embassy. When Sir William Waller next went to take a priest at Mrs Saunders's he found himself in hot pursuit down a warren of passages which at length brought him into the embassy proper. There were red faces all round. Waller was made to apologize personally to the ambassador, seconded by a letter from the Privy Council; and Williamson, the Secretary of State, was strongly reprimanded by the King for allowing Waller too much initiative. But Borgomaniero's face was red, too, when intercepted letters showed that the priest Waller had been pursuing, Walter Travers, was head of the English Carmelites. He ordered Travers to retire to the Continent.⁴⁰

This cat and mouse game between the foreign ambassadors and the government continued throughout the period.† One of the worst problems was preventing Englishmen attending mass at the embassy chapels, and after a prohibitory proclamation in December 1678 the Privy Council next month ordered constables to be posted outside the embassies every Sunday to chal-

---

* See p. 113 above.

† In fact, the Spanish ambassador was the worst culprit, seconded by the Imperial envoy, when there was one, and to a less extent by the Portuguese ambassador. Despite Louis the XIV's vaunted devotion to Catholicism, the French ambassador was comparatively passive.

lenge English subjects going in or out; if they could give no satisfactory account of themselves, they were to be haled before a magistrate, who would tender the oaths to them. But the oaths had no terrors for London Catholics, and nothing seems to have come of this tactic; moreover, the royal family set the worst possible example. On Good Friday, 1680, the constables had to be temporarily withdrawn from Wild House when the Duke of York himself decided to take mass there under a flimsy incognito. An attempt to tackle the problem from the other end, by restricting the number of chaplains each ambassador was allowed to maintain,* was not very successful. True, when a new Spanish ambassador, Ronquillo, arrived in the spring of 1680, he had the tact to send for a Flemish chaplain, the Carmelite Jean Baptist de Doncher, who had special responsibilities towards the English Catholics; for instance, he prepared Lord Stafford and Oliver Plunket for death, and accompanied them to Tyburn. In 1681 he was joined by another English-speaking Fleming, Father Peter of the Mother of God.[41]

Even so, Ronquillo gave refuge to several English friars, some of them to the end of the reign, and he lent support to the London Catholics whenever he could. For instance, he and his predecessor were associated with one of the most remarkable episodes in English Catholic history, the survival throughout the Plot of the Institute of Mary, the convent of 'les dames Anglaises', established at Hammersmith by Mother Mary Ward soon after the Restoration. Mother Frances Bedingfield, her successor, transferred her attention to York, but the daughter house she established there had to be closed during the Plot; she herself spent some time in York prison, and as soon as she was released she went abroad. Meanwhile the Hammersmith nuns, pedantically obedient to the proclamation of 30 October 1678, retired to the country; however, finding security in a small rural community a more serious problem than they had anticipated, they surreptitiously returned to Hammersmith in 1679. Early in 1680 the house was surrounded by a posse led by none other than Titus Oates himself, but no positive evidence of illegality was

* See p. 122 above.

found, and the officiating priest, the Carmelite George Travers,* declared himself to be a Spanish chaplain at his country's embassy. The Spanish embassy claimed him, and he was released by the Privy Council. The little nunnery continued its anxious existence into the next reign; in fact, it was not suppressed until 1700. Travers, too, led a charmed life, sometimes posing as a Spaniard, sometimes reverting to an English alias. Disguised as Lord Arundell's steward, he regularly ministered to him and the other Catholic prisoners in the Tower.[42]

The investigations which followed the discovery of the Meal Tub Plot in 1679 revealed the continued existence of a large and unsubdued Catholic community in the capital. In January 1680, too, at the trial of six priests at the Old Bailey, there was an interesting exchange between Oates and the bench:

OATES: My lord, the court here is pestered with papists; there are a great many about here.

SCROGGS: If they be witnesses we cannot keep them out.

BEDLOE: Some of them may be witnesses, but all are not; and if they be, they come to catch advantages.

MR JUSTICE DOLBEN: I do not understand why they should be turned out.

MR JUSTICE PEMBERTON: Let them alone. Be at quiet.

SCROGGS: No, no. They will revile us, that they had not an open and fair hearing. We won't have it said that we do anything in hugger-mugger. What we do is done honestly and openly.[43]

At the trial of Lord Stafford in December there was a similar incident, when Sir William Jones protested at the presence of Sir Bernard Gascoigne.

It is not clear that the government was at all concerned at this situation. Certainly it was determined from the beginning of the crisis not to proceed against members of the Catholic landed classes, except under the penal laws, if it could possibly avoid it. Men like John Caryll, William Roper, Sir John Gage and Sir Henry Tichborne were arrested on Oates's or Bedloe's evidence, but they were released as soon as the climate of opinion began to

---

*Not to be confused with his half-brother, Walter Joseph Travers, who was also a Carmelite. (See p. 252 above.)

change; sometimes, one feels, before it began to change. The lucky ones were bailed as early as February 1679, and all but a few were out by July 1680. In January 1679, as we have seen, the Council released a number of Staffordshire gentry accused by Dugdale, though they admitted they had been sending money to support the Catholic seminaries abroad, contrary to statute. In the case of the five Catholic peers the government's hand was forced by Parliament, and Charles too might have felt there was a case to answer, against Stafford at least. But apart from Stafford, Castlemaine, Sir Miles Stapleton and Sir Thomas Gascoigne, no member of the landed classes was tried for treason. (Coleman, Wakeman and Langhorn were members of the professions.) Similarly, though priests were as often as not arrested at the homes of their lay patrons – the notorious Ireland was arrested at the town house of Sir John Southcote – none of these laymen was charged with the offence of harbouring a priest, though the public were twice reminded by proclamation that it carried the death penalty.

Even the judges made a clear distinction between the priesthood and the laity. Scroggs told Ireland at his trial in December 1678:

There are honest gentlemen, I believe hundreds, of that communion who could not be openly won upon to engage in such a design;

and later the same day, pronouncing sentence, Jeffreys said;

I do not speak this to you, as intending thereby to inveigh against all persons that profess the Romish religion; for there are many of that persuasion that do abhor those base principles of murdering kings and subverting governments. There are many honest gentlemen in England, I dare say, of that communion, whom none of the most impudent Jesuits durst undertake to tempt into such designs; these are only to be imposed upon silly men, not upon men of conscience and understanding.[44]

The case of Sir Francis Ratcliffe is instructive. This wealthy northern landowner was named by Bedloe as well as Oates, and one of his former servants also came forward to accuse him of seditious speeches in the 1670s. The evidence against him at this stage was quite as strong as it was against the Lords in the

Tower. Yet, on the production of a medical certificate that he was unfit for travel, and affidavits swearing that he had not left his home in Northumberland for two years, he was left in peace. Not until the new Parliament met in March 1679 was he troubled again, but when he reached town at last, on 12 May 1679, escorted by a sergeant-at-arms, there is no indication that he was put in prison.[45]

Similarly Lord Aston. He was sent to the Tower in January 1679, under very serious charges levelled against him by Dugdale. In June he petitioned the Council for his release, and when they refused he sued out a writ of *habeas corpus*, only to see this rejected, too. He is next heard of on 20 May 1680, when he was formally indicted before King's Bench, and his trial fixed for 22 June. On 22 June the trial was adjourned for three days because of the difficulty of finding a key witness, but it was finally decided to hold it over until the Michaelmas term, and he was bailed until September. In fact he never returned to prison, nor faced trial.[46]

As for the English peers, their position was still jealously safeguarded. In April 1679, the Lords Committee of Privileges, headed by Shaftesbury, went against all precedent when it ruled in the case of Lady Abergavenny's servants that privilege did not extend to recusancy. But the same Committee in the same session protected the dowager Countess of Portland* against a defaulting steward who was trying to take legal advantage of her recusancy, and forced the constables of Westminster to apologize to the Countess of Powis for searching her house without permission.[47] There is no evidence of any peer – even the Lords in the Tower – being proceeded against for recusancy, except the Duke of Norfolk. His case is baffling, especially since his eldest son had now conformed to the church and been summoned to the House of Lords as Lord Mowbray.†

---

*Another Catholic family in decline. This was the mother of the 4th Earl, who had retired abroad, penniless, soon after the death of his wife in 1668. He died in a monastery at Louvain in 1688, leaving no heirs.

†He was presented at Norwich Assizes in August 1680, and returned from the Continent to answer the charge at Thetford on 14 October. He was in London for the trial of his cousin Stafford, then went abroad again.

However, in the panic days of October 1678, all this was in the future. Their compulsory disarming was a traumatic shock to the Catholics in a society without police, where the right to bear arms was a means of protection as well as a mark of gentility. The proclamations of 30 October and 6 November, ordering Catholics out of London and forbidding them to travel more than five miles from their homes, were even more ominous. Suddenly they were all at their servants' mercy, and such servants did not lack encouragement. When the Staffordshire magistrates arrested Stephen Dugdale in December 1678 and found he was Lord Aston's steward, they hung on to him, though he had voluntarily taken the oaths, and pressed him to make a deposition. William Blundell of Crosby wrote gloomily:

Here we do all lie like people shut up for the pestilence, expecting the King's pleasure and the blessed will of God. As for myself, in this scandalous plotting age I have no other support but my innocence, which only God doth know, and him I do appeal to as my witness, although it will not avail me in case I be falsely accused before any tribunal but his.[48]

In these circumstances many Catholic gentry simply asked for a pass from a Secretary of State and went abroad. The expense and upheaval involved was perhaps the most severe burden imposed on the Catholic community by the Plot. Not surprisingly, in view of recent events, the nobility led the exodus in November 1678: the Earl of Cardigan on the 12th, followed by the Earl of Berkshire on the 19th and Viscount Montagu ten days later.[49] In December the trickle became a flood. Dame Mary Scrope, Sir Edward and Lady Mostyn, Lord and Lady Teynham, Sir Charles Shelly of Michelgrove, the dowager Lady Abergavenny and the young lord, her son; Elizabeth Plowden, Margaret Stafford and Elizabeth Blunt, travelling together; John Petre of Ingatestone, one of the Essex Petres; Francis Pointz, James Porter and Henry Audley travelling together; Richard Walmesly of Duncan Hall, Lancashire; Lord Carrington; and so on throughout the month. By the end of the year thirty-four parties had left, most of them presumably bound for the Spanish Low Countries. In January 1679 the rush continued, with another thirty-one parties leaving, and this is a minimum figure; some received passes from the House of Lords, no doubt others did not apply for passes at all.[50]

The government's attitude was that these people were better out of the country. In the long run the Catholic community might go into voluntary liquidation; in the short term it was a means of getting rid of potential nuisances. In January 1679, for instance, Francis Gage, son of Sir Edward Gage, was brought before the Privy Council for being in London in defiance of the King's proclamation, and for slandering the King's witness, Stephen Dugdale. We next hear of him being given a pass to go abroad in March.[51] The form of pass soon became standardized. The recipient swore not to consort with the King's enemies, not to visit the city of Rome, not to enter a foreign seminary, nor place his children there. In the case of a grandee like the Duke of Norfolk, his large retinue also had to submit to interrogation by a magistrate, to detect fugitive priests.[52] In February sixteen more Catholics took out passes; in March another sixteen; the flood was slackening. In April nineteen left, in May only ten, and in June eleven. A further thirteen left in July, but after that the flood subsided to a trickle of one or two a month. It is difficult not to associate this with the dissolution of the first Exclusion Parliament and Wakeman's acquittal.

One advantage of going abroad was that in most cases it frustrated a presentation for recusancy. On 10 March 1679, Philip Constable of Everingham was committed to York Castle for refusing the oath of allegiance, but on the 26th the House of Lords gave him a pass to go overseas.[53] The penal laws, as interpreted by the courts, depended on the personal presence of the accused; a man could not be said to have refused the oaths if they had not been tendered to him.

Government policy towards the Catholic laity was set out in the proclamation of 17 November 1678, which ordered the constables in each parish to draw up lists of papists or suspected papists and hand them to the nearest magistrate. He would summon the persons concerned before him and tender the oaths to them. If they refused they were to be bound over to the next assizes or quarter sessions, where they would be prosecuted for recusancy under the Elizabethan statutes. But it is doubtful if it was obeyed; on 31 January 1679, a further proclamation threatened with dismissal those Justices who did not carry out the first, and this is suggestive in itself. Moreover, there is positive evidence to show that the procedure was not being followed in precisely those areas in which it was most needed, where there was a large Catholic minority.

In Monmouthshire, for instance, the enforcement of the penal laws was just one facet of the Arnold–Worcester feud.* Early in the new year, Arnold complained to the Council, through his relative the Earl of Anglesey, Lord Privy Seal, that the majority of the Monmouth bench (Worcester's nominees, of course) were not summoning Catholics before them to take the oaths, and were not taking recognizances from the few who appeared voluntarily. The Privy Council and the Committee for Examinations each sent strong letters to the Marquess of Worcester (a member of both bodies), but on 26 February the Council found it necessary to write direct to the Justices in the most magnificent and awe-inspiring terms it could command:

We have long before this expected to have received from you some effectual testimony of your diligence in the execution of the orders his Majesty was pleased to transmit unto you under the Great Seal of England. But instead of such a compliance with the service which is incumbent on you in a time of so great and public danger, we are sorry to find a return from you where the marks only of great animosities and differences amongst yourselves appear unto us, without any tendency or inclination towards such methods as can only answer the ends of his Majesty's great care to prevent those mischiefs which are apprehended from popish recusants, according to the plain direction of the law. We have therefore thought fit, before there be any further proceeding in the examination of your respective complaints against each other, to acquaint you with the great dissatis-

* See p. 244 above.

faction his Majesty has conceived at the neglect of your duties, and in his Majesty's name to require you to lay aside all those differences which have been so manifestly prejudicial to his royal service, and given great scandal to his government, advising you before all things heartily and unanimously to pursue those rules and orders which from time to time his Majesty has been pleased to prescribe unto you for your better guidance and direction in putting those laws into execution against popish recusants which the wisdom of Parliament hath established as absolutely necessary for the public safety. And so, not doubting of your ready obedience to his Majesty's commands herein, we bid you heartily farewell.[54]

Unfortunately, these embattled Welsh gentry cared not a fig for the distant displeasure of King and Council, and Worcester was strong enough to prevent the obvious remedy being used, that of throwing his nominees off the bench; they even survived the purge initiated by the Council under Shaftesbury in April. But perhaps Worcester himself realized it was time he put his house in order; at the Monmouth spring assizes only one Catholic was presented, but in the summer fourteen were bound over for refusing to take the oaths, and another nine were sent to prison. At the next spring assizes, in 1680, sixteen were presented and eight bound over, though only two of these eight in fact appeared at the summer assizes, and when they were asked why judgement should not be given against them, 'they put on their hats and went laughing out of court'. The Justices, Sir James Herbert, Sir William Herbert and Captain Wolseley, declined to proceed further; nor would the Deputy Sheriff, Francis Jenkins. As soon as Parliament met in October, John Arnold complained to the Lords Committee for Examinations, who ordered Jenkins's arrest and summoned the Justices before them. But they were defended by Sir Robert Sawyer, King's Serjeant, and after a full hearing the Committee recommended to the House that they be released with an admonition. Jenkins was not even admonished. The schedule to the Papists (Removal and Disarming) Bill brought in later that session shows the dimensions of the problem; it listed the names of 189 important Catholics in Monmouthshire, of whom seventy were brought within the scope of the bill – both figures being far in excess of those for any other county.[55]

The pattern of Monmouth was repeated elsewhere. Local magnates and justices were reluctant to proceed against their neighbours, and in counties with large recusant minorities their reluctance was greater, not less. The Lord Lieutenant of the North Riding was so naïve as to advise the Council that the large number of Catholics under his jurisdiction made it unwise to proceed against them – for which poltroonery he was sharply reprimanded. The Committee for Examinations was even more distressed to find that on the news of the prorogation of Parliament in December 1678, some Catholics at Wigan had

made bonfires for joy, assembling themselves and using many seditious and dangerous expressions in relation to the peace of the government, and in contempt of all prosecutions made for the discovery of the Plot and detecting of the conspirators;

which it considered 'an insolence not fit to be borne'. The dissolution in January and the subsequent elections caused further trouble. In March the Commons investigated a complaint that the Sheriff of Durham had released a large number of Catholics at election time; released them, that is, from the five-mile limit on travel. Certainly this limit may have contributed to the defeat of government candidates in some areas; William Blundell of Crosby wrote to the Earl of Derby in February to explain that he could not vote for his candidates in the county election because Lancaster was more than five miles from home.[56]

By 28 January, the Committee for Examinations was so irritated at the general conduct of local officials that it decided 'that a warm order be drawn [up], and such as may be printed, for the reprehension of those that be slack and the bringing into their rooms men of integrity and vigour'. This resulted in the Proclamation of 31 January ordering them to enforce the law on pain of dismissal. Nothing further was done until 21 May, when the new Council ordered the lists of justices to be reviewed; even then, the councillors appointed to act for each county – Hereford, the Marquess of Worcester and Lord Cavendish, for instance; Monmouth, Worcester again, with the Duke of Monmouth; Berkshire, Prince Rupert and Henry Powle – were so neatly balanced between Court and Opposition as to inhibit any decisive result.[57]

But even if resolute magistrates did decide to proceed, the delays allowed by English law were numberless, and the failure of the defendant to appear could be paralysing. In the latter event it was not clear what the magistrates should do next. If they impounded the defendant's recognizances he would escape with a comparatively slight fine, yet not all magistrates were prepared to do that much. The alternative was to send out the sheriff (if he would act) to arrest men who were usually substantial members of country society, with formidable gangs of servants and dependants and houses which were often still semi-fortified. And if the worst came to the worst the offender could usually evade the consequences merely by slipping over the border into the next county. Moreover, the government's decision to create a new category of 'suspected papists', or papists unless proved otherwise, created another category of men 'proved otherwise'.* In other words, what were the authorities supposed to do with a Catholic who took the oaths?[58]

It is noticeable that though the suggestion was discussed in two successive parliaments, magistrates were never ordered to tender the anti-papal test to suspected Catholics, only the oaths of allegiance and supremacy. And it was quite clear that most Catholics would take the first, and many the second, despite the anxious *démentis* of Catholic apologists then and since. Even Sir Thomas Strickland, who had grave doubts about the oath of supremacy, because it would oblige him as a loyalist to follow the King's religion, 'whatever it might be', willingly swore 'to defend the King against all enemies, domestic and foreign, and against the Pope no less than against a pagan, should he invade

*It was not quite new: the Long Parliament's Sequestration Ordinance (1643) gave several definitions of a recusant, one of which was any person who refused to take a drastically strengthened oath of allegiance. (See Kenyon, *Stuart Constitution*, p. 460.) But before 1643 and after 1660 the term 'suspected recusant' had no strict legal meaning.

the King's dominions', and few were as scrupulous as he.[59] There are examples of Catholics taking both oaths simply to regain a cherished piece of weaponry, like a pair of duelling pistols, and it is clear that though the net thrown out by the Justices of London and Westminster no doubt had many gaps, most of the Catholic householders and tradesmen within their jurisdiction must have been challenged, and taken the oaths, at one time or another during the crisis. The laity seem to have taken the matter much less seriously than the clergy, and they had a clear if unobtrusive lead from the Duke of York, who had taken the oath of allegiance to his brother, as had other Catholic noblemen and courtiers. When Buonaventura Gifford came to England in 1683 he tried to take the matter up with James, but the Duke rebuffed him, saying that now the nation was at peace again it was not the time to look for fresh causes of disagreement.[60]

Nor were the clergy in fact united on this question. The Blackloist wing of the Chapter, represented in Charles II's reign by John Sargeant, had always argued that Catholics could take the oaths with a clear conscience, and others regarded the practice as permissible in an emergency. Of the comparatively few priests brought to trial at this time it is worth noting that two, Charles Carne and Andrew Bromwich, had taken the oaths themselves, and a third, John Plessington, had never forbidden his communicants to do so. Under the stress of persecution others followed suit, and one priest, writing to Douai in the summer of 1680, remarked matter-of-factly: 'The oath of allegiance we here allow of generally; the other meets with a stop until it be better examined.' By 1681 the English Benedictines admitted that only one third of the English Catholics were against taking the oath of allegiance.[61]

The truth is that the supporters of this oath had a strong case, and they could argue that the Pope's obduracy in clinging to his theoretical power to depose princes was causing his followers unnecessary suffering. Nor was it a position he was allowed to maintain in Catholic countries; the first Gallican Article, passed by the French bishops in 1682, stated:

Kings and sovereigns are therefore not by God's command subject to any ecclesiastical dominion in things temporal; they cannot be deposed, whether directly or indirectly, by the authority of the rulers of the Church, their subjects cannot be dispensed from that submission and obedience which they owe, or from the oath of allegiance.[62]

It is significant that the Papacy never felt strong enough to reject this article, even in 1870, whereas it has never withdrawn the bull *Regnans in Excelsis* of 1570,* and even in the seventeenth century some priests felt strongly enough about the matter to defy papal authority openly. In 1671, a number of Irish clergy, led by the Franciscan Peter Walsh, subscribed to a Remonstrance in which they disowned the power of Rome in all temporal matters, and swore allegiance to the Crown; in return they were granted immunity from arrest, and some freedom of action. A few English priests signed this Remonstrance; one of them was Lionel Anderson,† and another was almost certainly John Sargeant, a controversialist of European repute and a member of the English Chapter.[63] However, in January 1679, Anderson was arrested on an accusation of treason by Oates,‡ and Sargeant thought it best to retire to the Continent. Rumours began to fly about that he intended to take a public stand against the oaths, though he denied it strongly, and on 1 June at Paris, Dr Gauden and three other members of the exiled Chapter put out a statement absolutely forbidding Catholics to take the oath of supremacy. But they were silent on the oath of allegiance, and when Cardinal Howard took them up on this point, the following April, their answer was to seek a ruling from the Sorbonne, which was in their favour.[64] It is not certain that the Chapter was ever forced into line – certainly Sargeant continued as a member of it – but the Franciscans, meeting at Bruges in 1680, the Jesuits at Liège in 1681, and the Benedictines at Paris, also in 1681, passed resolutions firmly adhering to the papal line.[65]

* See footnote to p. 3 above.

† See pp. 220–21 above.

‡ Rawl. A. 136, ff. 91–2, 229. The Council was reluctant, but Oates insisted, though the charge of treason broke down because of the lack of a second witness. Twelve months later Anderson was tried under the statute of 1585.

Meanwhile Sargeant allowed his hatred for the Jesuits to get the better of his discretion and good faith. In November 1679, he contacted the English ambassador in Holland, who arranged for him to come over and give evidence before the Privy Council.[66] The information he gave was unimportant; he denied all knowledge of the Plot, and the only persons he incriminated, Gavan and Coleman, were already dead. But, combined with the fact that he then settled down in London under the protection of the government (in fact he enjoyed a small pension), and was strongly suspected of betraying individual Jesuits to the authorities, it naturally blackened not only his own reputation but that of his followers amongst the clergy.

Nevertheless, the fact that the Jesuits, the Franciscans and the Benedictines should all have felt it necessary to issue public statements on the matter in 1680 and 1681 betrays the continuing anxiety they felt. Warner admitted in a letter to Rome that in Yorkshire, Staffordshire and Huntingdonshire a majority of Catholics had taken the oaths, and Cardinal Howard remarked in a letter to the Chapter:

It is not to be wondered if in a numerous flock some be found who do not hear their pastor's voice, or, which is worse, refuse to obey it.[67]

Clearly the Earl of Castlemaine was not hearkening to his pastor's voice, for he thought it perfectly legitimate for anyone to take the oath of allegiance, the Pope's power of deposing princes having lapsed, and the Benedictine James Corker took much the same line in his influential tract *Roman Catholic Principles in Reference to God and the King* (1680), though he was contradicted by the Chapter of his own order the following year.[68] In the Westminster Cathedral Archives there is a rare broadsheet, probably published abroad, entitled *The Case of Several English Catholics in Communion with the Church of Rome*. The anonymous authors protested their complete loyalty to the King and their abhorrence of the doctrine that the Pope could depose princes, or exercise any temporal jurisdiction, and in return, subject to certain safeguards, they asked to be taken back into positions of trust.[69] Catholic opinion was on the move, and not all the clergy were lagging behind. One Yorkshireman, told that a priest at the head of forty gentlemen had taken the oaths at Winchester Assizes, made the wry comment: 'My opinion is, Sir Thomas More and Bishop Fisher died much mistaken.'[70]

Finally, how many Catholics not only took the oaths but left the church altogether we simply do not know. Common sense would suggest a few, at least. Three peers, Lumley, Shrewsbury and Mowbray, the heir to the Norfolk dukedom, publicly conformed, but I have come across no similar examples amongst the gentry. According to David Mathew there was 'something of a landslide' in the towns, especially in the south of England, but he offers no evidence in support.[71]

Parliament certainly hoped to eliminate Catholicism altogether, and though there was a general feeling that the existing laws were adequate enough if only they could be enforced, this did not prevent their looking at possible alternatives. On 3 April 1679, the Commons were bored by 'a long, long bill brought in by Sir Thomas Clarges against popery, of so prodigious a length the very reading of it lost above an hour, and the reporting or summing of it by the Speaker spent above half an hour more'. Naturally it made slow progress, and it did not go up to the Lords in time for them to deal with it that session. Meanwhile, the Lords had sent down a much shorter bill, 'for the better discovery and speedy conviction of popish recusants', which was presumably much the same as a bill they had sponsored the previous session, which would have empowered magistrates to tender the test to any person over sixteen, refusal branding the offender as a 'constructive' recusant. While the Commons chewed this over the Lords went on, and 'wound themselves into a kind of labyrinth, coveting to secure England in general from popery, and the City of London from papists, by expelling all, even tradesmen, out of it who should refuse the oaths and test'; in other words, the 'Papists (removal from London) Bill' introduced on 31 March. Unfortunately, the peers were promptly warned that this would 'shake the very trade of the City': an interesting commentary on the number of Catholic tradesmen and merchants in London.[72] In May they discussed a drastic 'final solution', the compulsory exile of the Catholic landowning classes, which was later echoed in the 'Papists (Removal and Disarming) Bill' introduced in the Lords in December 1680, which listed the leading Catholics in each county and proposed to destroy their influence by forcibly transferring them to other parts of the country.[73]

It was perhaps fortunate that Parliament passed none of these bills, for the government was still having difficulty enforcing the laws already on the statute book. In fact, the main government drive in 1679 was against the clergy, with empty reminders from time to time that harbouring priests was a capital offence. Not a great deal further was even attempted against the laity until December, when the King, anxious to rebut the accusation that he still secretly favoured the Catholics, instituted a new Committee of Council 'for Suppressing Popery'.

This Committee began by ordering the trial of all priests still in custody. More constructively, it then appropriated the lists of papists and suspected papists submitted by M.P.s to the Speaker in December 1678, and ordered the Lord Chancellor to prepare special commissions empowering and enjoining magistrates to tender the oaths to those listed, and prosecute those who refused. The Assize Judges were to supervise the operation, and lest there should be any misunderstanding a new proclamation was issued on 21 December, rehearsing the relevant Elizabethan and Jacobean statutes. The King let it be known that he himself was prepared to go further, and offer the Catholics the choice of going into exile or surrendering two thirds of their property.[74]

There were now some signs that for once the Privy Council's orders were to be taken seriously. On 9 February, Henry Guy, Secretary to the Treasury, wrote to the Barons of the Exchequer asking them to prepare a more efficient (which meant quicker) method of convicting recusants; exact copies were taken of the Commons lists; the Attorney-General was called in to give advice; and finally the three Chief Justices, Scroggs, North and Montague, were ordered to attend the Lords of the Treasury on their return from the Assize Circuits in April.[75] There is also a certain amount of literary evidence to suggest that from about April 1680, when the lists of magistrates were thoroughly revised, the new procedure began to bite. By that time the Judges had begun to return further lists of obstinate recusants, and the government was considering how best to proceed: whether to levy a £20 a month fine, or sequester two thirds of the offenders' estates.[76] In May a Mr Bedford was appointed Receiver of Recusant Revenues for the counties of Berkshire, Buckinghamshire, Oxford, Bedfordshire and Hertfordshire, and the sheriffs of those counties were ordered to levy the £20 fine for the financial year September 1678 to September 1679. A warrant of 30 June from Henry Guy shows that such receivers had in fact been appointed over the whole country, and there were complaints from some Catholics that they had been better off when a persecuting Parliament was in session.[77]

But the procedure was still spotty. On 24 January the Council complained to the Wiltshire justices that no 'men of note' appeared on the lists for their county, while in Lancashire, reputed to have one of the largest Catholic populations in the country, the whole of 1680 was taken up by an argument between the Justices and the Lords of the Council on the vexed question of recognizances.[78] On 8 January, in fact, the Council was so displeased by the conduct of the Lancashire Justices that it took the unusual step of ordering them to appear before them *en bloc*. The issue here was whether they should take recognizances at all from Catholics who refused to take the oaths. But in May the Justices shifted their ground slightly; they reported that they simply could not find some prominent Catholics who had already appeared before them, and all they could do was confiscate their recognizances. They inquired as to the possibility of prosecuting them under a *praemunire* – clearly the remodelling of the bench that spring had had an effect – but they added significantly:

Most of them are already presented of recusancy, and such as by pleading have deferred their convictions cannot escape above one Quarter Sessions longer.

The implementation of the law was still, obviously, a step to be deferred as long as possible. Yet in October the same Justices were worrying the Privy Council again, this time inquiring whether they ought to confiscate the recognizances of papists who had presented themselves at sessions and had taken the oath of allegiance, but still balked at the oath of supremacy. The Council was adamant. After a detailed review of the whole question, it ordered them to confiscate the recognizances, and then proceed against the offenders under the Elizabethan statutes.[79]

So by now there were two lines of attack. First, the Catholics were to be coerced into political conformity by being forced to take the oaths. The lengths to which this could go were shown by a petition to the House of Lords in March 1679 from the widow of Sir Thomas Smith of Sproxton, Leicestershire, who had been thrown into gaol with her three children for refusing the oaths.[80] The Lords ordered Lady Smith's immediate release, but others were not so lucky. As late as March 1683, six Catholics from Newcastle were committed to gaol for refusing the oaths, and in July no less than sixty-five from Northumberland.[81]* In 1680, thirty-two Catholics were sent to York Castle for the same offence, and in March 1685 there were still twenty-eight imprisoned there, seven of them women.[82] Nor was York unusual in this respect; indeed, in September 1684, when the Lord Chief Justice returned from circuit, he submitted a report to the Privy Council which portrayed it as a national problem. He was ordered to report back with exact and detailed lists.[83]

The other prong of the government's fork was still the enforcement of the old penal laws. Here, ironically enough, the full weight of the government's campaign was not felt until after the dissolution of the Oxford Parliament in March 1681, when the lists of magistrates were again revised, and they were

---

*It should be remembered that this was unusual; imprisonment was not a normal punishment, and gaols were usually reserved for those awaiting trial. The normal punishments were death, mutilation, the pillory, a fine or confiscation of goods.

ordered to enforce the penal laws against Dissenters as well as Catholics. Such work as has been undertaken in this field, by J. Anthony Williams and John Miller, suggests that persecution reached its height in 1682, and predictably declined after the return of the Duke of York from exile in Scotland in 1683.[84] Even then, some counties lagged behind the others; Dr Miller shows that in Norfolk, for instance, persecution went on mounting into 1684. In Derbyshire the Plot did not begin to bite at all until March 1681, when the Jesuit George Busby was arrested in the county, and tried for his priesthood at the summer assizes. Documents found on him led to an investigation into lands devoted to 'superstitious uses' which lasted into 1682, and involved the Eyres of Hassopp and several other prominent county families.[85]

Some of the fines sustained by wealthy Catholics in this period seem comparatively trifling. Thomas Eyre, for instance, was only paying a 'rent' of £25 14s. 5½d. a year on his Derbyshire estates in 1679, and £20 2s. 3d. on his Leicestershire estates.[86] The influence of Protestant friends and relatives was still operative, and on 7 November 1682, hearing that Roger Kenyon, a J.P., was holding an inquisition on recusant estates in Lancashire, Edward Fleetwood asked him to treat 'Cousin Anderton of Exton' leniently, for 'he has a great many children, and the estate but small'.[87]

But whatever the level of fines, the degree of harassment could be severe. Take the case of the Constables of Everingham, near Market Weighton. Philip Constable went abroad in 1679, as we have seen*; he returned the following year and tried to remain inconspicuous on his Leicestershire estates. But he was arrested and committed to York Castle until 1683, and at the same time amerced of £120 a year in fines. Careful estate management was needed to offset this kind of drain, and such management was not easy in the absence of the head of the family.[88] Some lesser Catholics, refusing to pay their fines, were thrown into prison and their property confiscated, though they protested that this was 'not agreeable to the course of the Exchequer, nor

* See p. 258 above.

prescribed or allowed by the laws against recusants'. The Carylls of West Grinstead had to forfeit one of their manors, which was handed over to their neighbour Edward Guildford, and they paid heavy fines until the end of the reign. On the other hand, the correspondence of old William Blundell of Crosby is silent on such matters, though he was bound over for refusing the oaths, was taking steps early in 1679 to transfer some of his property to Protestant friends, and was refused a pass to go abroad until April 1680, and then for one year only.[89]

In other words, persecution could be severe, but it was decidedly erratic, and there is no evidence of a substantial land-owner being ruined by the implementation of the penal laws.* Any drift there was away from the Catholic Church had begun much earlier in the century, and if it was accelerated by outside factors, it was by the Test Acts of 1673 and 1678 and the Revolution of 1688, followed by the imposition of a double land tax on Catholics after 1692. This, plus the general growth of scepticism and free-thinking throughout Europe, reduced the eighteenth-century Catholic community in England to an attenuated remnant.

The main penalty inflicted on Catholics was always imprisonment for refusing to take the oaths, and such imprisonment could be indefinite. The Lord Chief Justice's protest in 1684 eventually bore fruit in a warrant of pardon issued on 15 January 1685 to no less than 730 named recusants, though whether they were all in prison, and, if so, whether they comprised all who were in prison, is not clear. There were 228 in Durham alone, 239 in Hereford, 'mostly women', 78 in Lincolnshire and 75 in Northumberland; yet neither Durham nor Lincolnshire were counties which apparently suffered a great deal during the actual crisis of the Plot.[90]

Three weeks later Charles II was dead, and on 27 February the new king, James II, dispatched letters to the Assize Judges and the Lords of the Treasury informing them that in pursuance of a policy initiated by his late brother in the last weeks of his life, it

* Except for the unverifiable case of one Sir Ralph Babthorpe. See Courson, p. 187.

was his will and pleasure that all persecution of his Catholic subjects should forthwith cease.[91]

The effect of the Plot on the Protestant community is in some ways easier to assess. The superficial nature of the panic which gripped London in the winter of 1678–9 is shown by the fact that six years later, in February 1685, the City was prepared to accept and even welcome the Duke of York as King James II. On the other hand, the basic instability of the situation is also betrayed by the fact that in December 1688 a briefer but much more damaging panic engulfed London in the wild excesses of the 'Irish Night', during which public order completely collapsed.[92]

The situation in the London of 1678 is one familiar to modern sociologists and social psychologists.[93] The 'structural strain' implicit in a panic atmosphere existed not only horizontally (Protestant versus Catholic) but vertically (the government versus the governed). Indeed, all the classic factors isolated by Strauss were present to an unusual degree:

Psychological factors are surprise, uncertainty, anxiety, feeling of isolation, consciousness of powerlessness before the inevitable expectancy of danger. Sociological factors include lack of group solidarity, crowd conditions, lack of regimented leadership in the group.[94]

The situation was further aggravated by the unnatural size of London in proportion to the total population of the country, and the fact that its inhabitants were still concentrated on a remarkably small area, creating a situation of social pressure and confinement without any obvious or easy means of escape. Add to this almost total ignorance. Throughout the crisis the *London Gazette*, the only official newspaper, adhered to its usual policy, which meant that it took no notice of the Plot at all except to print royal proclamations and factual notices of such events as executions. Opposition newspapers, like *The Protestant Domestick Intelligence* and the *Weekly Pacquet of Advice from Rome*, did not start up until after the expiry of the Press Licensing Act in May 1679, though it is true that had they appeared earlier they would probably only have encouraged panic. But in the absence of newspapers, or any real alternative at all, news had to circulate by letter or by word of mouth, with inevitable distortions and exaggerations. One may reasonably compare seventeenth-century London to a huge theatre or sports arena crammed to capacity, with no public-address system: at the mercy of panic in case of fire or structural collapse.

Moreover, the information which the government did decide to issue that winter was just sufficient to create ambiguity without resolving it, and its actions partook of the kind of panic it was its duty to discourage; in fact its conduct was what Smelser calls a 'value-added factor' in the precipitation of panic.[95] Told nothing except the fact that there had been a conspiracy against the King's life, the people can be forgiven for thinking, first, that it was entirely proved, and, second, that it was much more serious than it was. The government's successive decisions thereafter, to disarm the Catholics, to order them out of London, to confine them within a five-mile radius of their homes, to order the arrest of all priests – all without any but the vaguest explanatory gloss – confirmed the truth of the premises. In this context the death of Godfrey was another 'value-added' factor, and so was the conviction of Edward Coleman. (Remember that Coleman's trial gave the public at large the first 'hard' information about the Plot.)

But if the government displayed what Strauss calls 'lack of regimented leadership in the group', so did Parliament. Not only did a majority of both Houses swallow Oates's and Bedloe's evidence whole, they were as negligent as the government in releasing it.* (This is in contrast to the next Parliament, which at least ordered the printing of Oates's *Narrative*, though it was then rather out of date. The Parliament of 1680 may even be said to have published too much.) No information was released at all, nor did the King make a move, and the result was a 'classic' panic, which in November 1678 bellied out into the provinces.

---

*Nor was this for fear of contempt of court. The concept was almost unknown, and in any case Parliament, as the highest court in the land, would have been exempt.

The phenomenon of the 'night riders' is a typical example of mass hysteria on a national scale.* Of course, this panic never reached a climax; if it had done the whole structure of society and government must have collapsed; and in the provinces, where the pressure was not so intense as in London, there are signs of returning sanity as early as December 1678, in the wake of the Purbeck invasion scare.† Indeed, it could be argued that the Plot was a metropolitan phenomenon which never took hold in the provinces, except in areas where local leaders were in close touch with the opposition in London (Wales and the Marches), or which were stirred up by emissaries and informers sent down from London (Yorkshire).

In London, too, chronic unemployment and under-employment heightened the tension amongst the working classes; too many men had too little to do, and were hungry and apprehensive in their idleness. The London apprentices had been riot-prone the whole reign, arguing a condition of instability caused by poor working conditions, insufficient work, and fear of unemployment when their training was completed. The watermen were another notoriously restless element, feeling their livelihood threatened by the hackney coachmen. Even well-established workmen suffered in the financial recession of 1678 and 1679, brought on by the end of the war in Europe and the unstable political situation at home. Several London firms failed altogether in 1679, and by July the King was in such dire straits he had to cancel the free dinner customarily offered the Privy Council after its weekly meeting.

The parliamentary Opposition took advantage of the situation, of course, but the government played into their hands. Charles's delay in executing Ireland, Grove and Pickering, however correct on humanitarian grounds, was politically disastrous. While the tension over this issue was at its height, in January 1679, there came the sudden dissolution of Parliament – the first for eighteen years – and a serious fire which destroyed most of the Temple. This fire, followed by lesser outbreaks over the next

*See pp. 115–16 above.
†See p. 123 above.

few months, generated fresh hysteria. Here London's likeness to a theatre or an arena is explicitly worked out. The *idea* of fire was inextricably connected with Rome; the physical *fact* of fire was inexpressibly alarming in an overcrowded, tinder-dry urban area, especially after the Great Fire of 1666. The obsession of Londoners with fire, even Londoners of the highest social class, is impressive,. At the end of Lord Stafford's trial, which he had conducted with notable fairness, Lord Chancellor Finch, with no relevance at all to what had passed, said: 'Who can doubt any longer that London was burnt by papists?'[96]

The seventeenth-century English were notorious thoughout Europe for their fickleness and lack of political stability. Some of the blame for this must be placed on the unnatural position assumed by London in the national polity, and the unnatural state in which most of its citizens lived.

8

The Reckoning

In the summer of 1681, Charles II at last began to turn on the informers. Stephen College, one of the Whigs' unsavoury hangers-on, and an intimate of many Plot witnesses, was arraigned for high treason, in that he had conspired to levy war against the King by appearing in arms at the Oxford Parliament. This thin charge was thrown out by a London grand jury, but he was brought to trial at Oxford on 17 August. Dugdale, ever pliant, appeared as chief witness for the Crown, followed by Turberville and John 'Narrative' Smith, but Oates, more consistent, gave evidence in defence. This produced the first of many exchanges between him and Jeffreys, who was now, it will be remembered, a King's Serjeant:

ATTORNEY-GENERAL: Mr Oates is a thorough-paced witness against the King's evidence.

JEFFREYS: And yet Dr Oates had been alone in some matters, had it not been for some of these witnesses.

OATES: I had been alone, perhaps, and perhaps not; but, yet, Mr Serjeant, I had always a better reputation than to need theirs to strengthen it.

JEFFREYS: Does any man speak of your reputation? I know nobody does meddle with it, but you are so tender.

The Solicitor-General was not so amused, and observed balefully:

This looks as if the Doctor were again returning to St Omers, that he is thus going about to disparage the testimony of Mr Dugdale, which in great measure verified the truth of the discovery he himself first made of the Popish Plot.

Oates was not on oath now, and the piquancy of the situation was not lost on Jeffreys: 'Here is Dugdale's oath,' he said at one

276

point, 'against Dr Oates's saying.' (He was offensively punctilious in giving Oates his Salamanca D.D.) He was delighted when Bolron and Mowbray appeared on behalf of College, and so was the Solicitor-General; as Finch tactfully explained, 'They have been so unfortunate as never to gain credit with any jury.'[1]

College was found guilty, and duly executed, and a week later, on 2 September, Oates's allowance from the King finally ceased, and with it his last contact with the government. (On 27 July 1680, it had been reduced from £12 a week to £3, then raised to £10 on 29 October, obviously at the instance of Parliament. From 14 May 1681, it was reduced to £2.)[2]

As with all the informers in the Popish Plot, his pecuniary reward was disproportionately small. His weekly allowance was for maintenance, and living as he did in Whitehall Palace there is no reason to doubt that he needed every penny of it; he often claimed it in advance. He also received a total of £116 17s. for expenses, and these were probably genuine enough; the Secretary to the Treasury noted that some of this money was disbursed 'against bills', and the greater part of it (£84 17s.) was earmarked for the legal expenses incurred in defending himself against Knox and Lane. In addition, over the period 1678 to 1681 he received various small sums described simply as 'royal bounty'; this made up a further £297 10s. The value of the Whitehall apartments he shared with Tonge (the Crown paid Sir Edward Carteret £1 a week for them) cannot be estimated, but they were a temporary provision. Everything was temporary; at the height of his prestige he continued to be paid out of the 'secret service money'; he never received a funded pension for life. Still less was he offered a government sinecure, or a living in the Church, though he angled for one, and later said Archbishop Sancroft had promised him one.

Of course, he may have received something from Shaftesbury; we have no proof one way or the other; but it should be remembered that none of the Opposition lords was magnificently, splendidly rich (this was partly why they were in opposition). Undoubtedly he also made some money as an author; from his famous *Narrative*, and from such effusions as *The Cabinet of the Jesuits' Secrets Open'd, An Exact Discovery of the Mystery of Iniquity as it is now in Practice amongst the Jesuits*, and *The Pope's Warehouse, or the merchandise of the Whore of Rome*, all published in 1679. But it should be remembered that royalties were then unknown; an author simply sold his manuscript to a printer-publisher for a lump sum.

Israel Tonge probably made more out of books than Oates did, if only because he was more prolific. In 1679, he flooded the market with all his previously unsaleable material: *Jesuitical Aphorismes, or a Summary Account of the Doctrines of the Jesuits*; *The New Design of the Papists Detected*; *An Account of the Romish Doctrine in case of Conspiracy and Rebellion*; *Popish Mercy and Justice*; and (dottiest of all) *The Northern Star: the British Monarchy, or the Northern the Fourth Universal Monarchy . . . being a Collection of many choice Ancient and Modern Prophecies*. Apart from this and his lodgings at Whitehall he also received a surprisingly large amount of bounty, considering the fact that he was never a direct witness at all. In 1679 he received two gifts of £50 each, and in January 1680 another £50 'towards enabling him to settle himself and his family in such accommodation as may be most suitable to their condition', and later that year another £50 with no strings attached. The Parliament of 1680 even got him a small pension of £2 a week, but he died on 18 December. The King then gave his brother a further £50 to pay for his funeral.

Bedloe received much the same as Oates – an allowance of £10 a week and lodgings at Whitehall (Sir Paul Neale's, rented from him by the government for £1 a week). This allowance was reduced to £2 a week on 30 June 1680, and in August he died. In April 1679 he received the reward of £500 offered for the discovery of Godfrey's murderers, but an unspecified proportion of this was earmarked for Prance and others. Apart from this he received no bounty as such, but he did receive the suspiciously large sum of £187 for expenses, £150 of it on 19 September 1679, 'for maintaining witnesses in town'. What witnesses?

But the 'expenses king' was Dugdale. In 1679 and 1680 he

received the massive total of £475 under this head, usually just for 'disbursements'. It may have been disguised bounty, to pay his notorious debts in Staffordshire, but in 1681 he presented another bill, for £251 15s. 6d. up to January of that year; this was scrutinized and approved by the Attorney-General and paid off in five instalments, ending in June 1682. Apart from all this he also received two free gifts of £100 each in 1679, and another of £30 in January 1680. His modest allowance of £5 a week was cut to £3 a week on 18 July 1680, and again to £2 on 17 April 1681, but at this reduced figure it continued to be paid right up to his death in 1683. So, with £230 in bounty, plus £726 in highly questionable expenses, and a small weekly allowance for life, Dugdale emerges as the best paid of all the informers – perhaps a tribute to his superior respectability and intelligence.

The payments to other informers are not significant. Bolron and Mowbray received large amounts in expenses, but they were in constant motion between York and London, with troops of witnesses. They received no pension until as late as 1682, when Bolron was given a paltry £2 a week for his wife and himself, and Mowbray £1 a week for himself. These terminated in December 1682 and September 1683, when the holders probably died. However, Bolron's pension may have been terminated as the result of an inquiry instituted by the Lords of the Treasury in August 1682; they sent the Attorney-General a list of witnesses still on pension, and asked if he had any further use for them. The total then being disbursed to these wretches was £21 14s. a week.[3] The only pension which continued to be paid until the end of the reign was £3 a week to the renegade priest, John Sargeant, which began as £5 a week on 29 October 1679, and was reduced on 14 July 1680. Dangerfield's allowance of £2 a week was one of the first to be terminated, on 1 April 1681.

Edward Turberville died in December 1681, confirming on his death-bed all the evidence he had given against Lord Stafford. Burnet was baffled: 'In this mist,' he wrote, 'matters must be left till the great revelation of all secrets.'[4] Dugdale died two years later, supposedly haunted in his closing months by Stafford's ghost. Oates was still a comparatively young man, in his early thirties, but fate was now catching up with him. His financial needs were already acute – he was presumably living on charity – and in 1682 and 1683 he unsuccessfully claimed a share of the Jesuit property confiscated during the Plot. In his occasional periodical *The Observator* the great Tory journalist Sir Roger l'Estrange was relentlessly exposing the absurdities and inconsistencies of his original evidence.

In February 1684 he had the effrontery to request an audience with the King, and when this was refused he sent in a petition complaining about L'Estrange. He also wrote to the Bishop of London.[5] There was pertinence in his query how the government could in good conscience license denials of a Plot in which it had several times announced its belief, but by now public opinion, and political influence, had deserted the Whigs. Stephen College and Edward Fitzharris had been executed for treason in 1681, and only the notorious '*ignoramus*' juries, the grand juries of London and Middlesex empanelled by the Whig sheriffs, saved Shaftesbury himself from the same fate.* In 1682 the King first put in a Tory Lord Mayor, and then a new set of Tory sheriffs, and Shaftesbury fled to Holland, where he died early in 1683. In the summer of 1683 the discovery of the Rye House Plot, a Whig–Radical conspiracy to assassinate the King and James, finally destroyed some of Oates's most powerful supporters. Lord Russell and Algernon Sydney went to the scaffold, the Earl of Essex committed suicide in the Tower, and Monmouth fled abroad. A wave of unquestioning loyalism swept over the whole country, and the Duke of York was back from Scotland, looking for vengeance.

One of James's first triumphs was to secure the release of the Catholic lords. On 5 January 1684, Lord Petre died in the Tower, and James insisted that his fellow-prisoners, Powis, Arundell and Belasyse, be brought before the next session of King's Bench, on 18 February, and bailed. Jeffreys, now Lord Chief Justice, remarked 'that impeached or not impeached he

---

*A grand jury could either return a 'true bill' (*billa vera*) and send the accused on for trial, or dismiss the accusation with the statement '*ignoramus*'.

thought it all one, and that it was not a favour to bail them, but that in justice and conscience they ought to be [*sic*] bailed long since'.* On 10 May Oates was suddenly arrested at the Amsterdam coffee house on a writ of *scandalum magnatum*, for referring to the Duke as 'that traitor James, Duke of York', at the Bishop of Ely's dinner-table in April 1680. There could be no defence, and King's Bench awarded James the enormous sum of £100,000 damages; in default of payment he was cast into the debtors' side of King's Bench prison, where it seemed he would remain for life.[6]

However, James was by no means finished with him; on 28 October and 12 December two grand juries presented him on separate counts of perjury for his evidence against Ireland in 1678, and he was promptly put in chains. Sir Roger l'Estrange began collecting evidence against him, with the aid of the Secretary of State, Lord Sunderland, one of James's closest associates, and on 23 January 1685 he had a preliminary hearing at King's Bench bar, when 'very hot words' passed between him and Jeffreys. His trial was fixed for 8 February, and James thought the fact worth retailing in a letter to his nephew William of Orange.[7]

Charles II died on 6 February, but Oates was arraigned two days later, as planned. However, it was then discovered that no barrister would undertake his defence, not even ultra-Whig lawyers like Sir George Treby and William Williams. The trial had to be postponed, and the prisoner complained once more about his irons. Rather unexpectedly, Jeffreys told the Deputy Marshal that imprisonment ought not to be an execution, but it seems the irons stayed until 8 May, when his trial on the first count of perjury finally opened.[8]

All the Plot trials partook of the nature of baroque entertainment, and the judges, defendants and witnesses all displayed characters of surpassing richness. In the trial of Oates for the

---

* Luttrell, i, 301. As soon as he came to the throne James entered a *nolle prosequi* against their further prosecution, without waiting for the Lords to cancel their impeachments, which they did in May 1685.

first time our enjoyment is not flawed by the consciousness that the defendant was wrongfully charged or that his life was at stake. His eventual punishment was ferocious, but it was no more, and arguably less, than he deserved.

The main question was, whether Oates's trial for perjury was to be used to undermine the whole structure of the Plot, and establish the innocence of all those convicted of treason in 1678 and 1679. At first it seemed not. The first indictment accused him of swearing that he had been at the Jesuit Consult in London on 24 April 1678, when in fact he was at St Omers, and it was confined to the trial of Ireland, Grove and Pickering on 17 December 1678. So only one trial out of several was in question, and only part of the evidence given at that trial; if the rest of Oates's evidence was not challenged, then it was still possible to imagine that the defendants had been guilty as charged. Jeffreys showed that this was probably his own view quite early in the proceedings, when Oates argued that the fact that Ireland and his associates were still attainted confirmed his evidence. Jeffreys replied: 'God forbid, if a verdict be obtained by perjury, that that verdict should protect the perjured party ... There is no justice in that.'[9]

But the logic of the situation proved to be inescapable, and it was the Earl of Huntingdon who drove the point home. When he opened his defence, Oates began by calling a whole string of eminent politicians and judges in an attempt to show that in 1678 and 1679 Parliament and the Courts had readily accepted his evidence as true. But very few of these witnesses had answered their *subpoenas*, and those who had were afflicted by crippling amnesia. John Maynard said, 'I know nothing truly, nor can I remember anything of it now'; the Earl of Devonshire confessed: 'I cannot remember any particular, it is so long ago'; and the Earl of Clare and William Williams were in a similar state.[10] Then Oates caught sight of Lord Huntingdon in the well of the court, recognized him as an old associate of Shaftesbury's, and in desperation implored him to take the stand. The Earl complied, and Jeffreys asked him if he remembered how the House of Lords had received Oates's evidence in 1678.

His answer was a cold blast of realism, which whirled away all the evasions and hypocrisies that had gone before.

I do believe, my lord [said he], Mr Oates's discovery found a good reception in the House of Lords, but it was grounded upon the opinion that what he said was true, and that he was an honest man, for so the House then accounted him to be, and upon this it was their lordships gave credit to his testimony. And indeed, had the matter been true, it was of high importance to have it thoroughly examined. But since that time, it being apparent that there were so many and great contradictions, falsities and perjuries in his evidence, upon which so much innocent blood had been shed, I believe a great many persons who were concerned in the trials of those unfortunate men are heartily afflicted and sorry for their share in it, and I do believe that most of the House of Peers have altered their opinion as to this man's credit, and look upon his evidence, as I do, to be very false.[11]

Jeffreys and Sir Francis Wythens were moved to indecent mirth at this (throughout the trial Wythens was even more hostile to the defendant than Jeffreys), but they soon sobered up, and Jeffreys was ready to second Huntingdon's remarks. He told Oates: 'This is in truth the same answer that must be given for the judges and juries that tried the people upon your evidence.' Turning to the court, he went on: 'I now believe in my conscience he is actually forsworn, and has drawn innocent blood upon the nation, and nobody will believe a word he says.'[12] A few minutes later another judge who had sat on the special commissions for the plot, Chief Baron Montague, took the stand. Jeffreys asked him about the trial of the five Jesuits in June 1679, and he replied: 'My lord, I cannot charge my memory with it.' But before Jeffreys could go on he added:

No, not in particular, but in general I remember there were a great many persons that gave evidence in those trials on the one side and the other. There were a great many persons that came from St Omers that gave evidence there of Mr Oates being in St Omers when he said he was in town.

Oates intervened with a question: 'And what credit were they of, at that time, pray my lord?' Montague replied: 'I think they were persons of very good credit; they were gentlemen of good families, many of them.' Oates came back: 'Did the jury believe them at that time?' 'I cannot tell what the jury did,' said Montague. 'Nor is it any matter at all what they did,' added Jeffreys. 'I ask you, my lord, but one question,' he went on. 'Have you heard this evidence that has been given here today?' Montague said he had not, and Jeffreys said: 'If you had, I would then have asked you whether you believe him now or not.' Montague replied simply: 'Truly, my lord, I never had any great faith in him, I do assure you, as to myself.'[13]

The Solicitor-General, Heneage Finch, summed up the evidence for the Crown. He, too, had sat under Scroggs on the special commission which had tried Whitbread and Langhorn in June 1679. His peroration was reasoned, dignified and specific:

Gentlemen [he said], when we consider the circumstances of this case now, I do verily think it will appear to be a very strange and wonderful thing to us, that ever any man should have believed him. And it is a strange consideration to reflect upon, to think what credit he had at that time. But withal consider, gentlemen, could anyone imagine that it were possible for any man on earth to become so impudent, as to dare expose himself before the high court of Parliament, the great courts of justice, and there tell a most infamous lie for the taking away of lives of men? The greatness of the attempt was a great inducement to the belief of it, because no man could be presumed to dare the doing of such a thing, if he had not a foundation of truth to build upon.

Therefore, he went on, the gullibility of Parliament was excusable and the very measures they took to stifle the conspiracy which Oates so confidently described created a climate of opinion in which it was difficult for those accused by him to obtain a fair trial. Finally, he said, with a glance at the Whigs:

There were ill men at work, that laboured to improve those fears and jealousies that had already possessed men's minds.

But if Parliament and the Courts of Law could be exculpated, so too could the Protestant religion.

Nor is this prosecution [he concluded] any reflection on the Protestant religion, whose cause he falsely assumed to himself. No, gentlemen, the Protestant religion had no share in that invention. It needs not the support of a lie, no, not the most plausible lie, much less of one so infamous as this does now appear to be. It is rather a vindication of our religion to punish such offenders as they deserve, and the proper way to maintain the justice of the nation, and wipe off that reproach this man's perjury has brought upon it.[14]

When it came to Jeffreys's turn he was lost in wonder at Oates's monstrous effrontery, not so much then as now:

Is it not a prodigious thing [he said] to have such actions as these today defended in a court of justice, with that impudence and unconcernedness as though he would challenge even God Almighty to punish his wickedness, and blasphemously blesses God, that he has lived to do such wonderful service to the Protestant religion, and is so obstinate in his villainy as to declare he would venture his blood for the confirmation of so impious a falsehood? And, indeed, he makes no great venture in it, for when he has pawned his immortal soul by so perjured a testimony, he may very easily proffer the venturing of his vile carcase to maintain it.

However, he then remembered that the case was not decided until the verdict was in, and he solemnly told the jury:

The justice of the nation lies under a very great reproach abroad, for this particular thing, and we must be, all of us that have any concern for the honour and good of our country, uneasy till this matter be thoroughly searched into and impartially determined, and I take it to be a case of the greatest importance to the settlement of the kingdom, for the credit of our laws, for the honour and justice of our kingdom, that ever came in judgement in any of our courts of justice.

So he exhorted them:

Take care to examine strictly and impartially into the merits of this cause and weigh evidence which has been given on all sides. Be not at all dismayed with the apprehension of clamour or calumny, from any sort of people whatsoever, for doing your duty; neither be led away by the insinuations of what was believed formerly.[15]

The evidence the jury had to consider was formidable. The prosecution brought twenty-one witnesses who had been living at St Omers in 1677 and 1678, and they all swore that Oates had never left the seminary until June of the latter year. Only two were survivors of that forlorn group which had given evidence for the five Jesuits in June 1679, but their evidence was little changed. Oates argued that since they were Catholics their evidence was of inferior value and cited a decision of the great Sir Edward Coke to this effect. Jeffreys dismissed this as 'clamorous and idle extravagancies', and in his summing-up he firmly told the jury that other things being equal a Catholic's evidence was on all fours with a Protestant's.[16]

In fact, this was nothing new; Scroggs had told the jury much the same in the case of the five Jesuits. Since then the climate of opinion had changed; also these Catholic witnesses were now on oath. The jury may also have been swayed by the fact that the boys who had been with Oates at St Omers had now grown into men. Oates, not unnaturally, pointed out that by attending a Catholic seminary abroad all the witnesses had broken the law; to which Jeffreys made the remarkable reply: 'I hope a man may be at St Omers and yet not be punished for it, Mr Oates.'[17] (Obviously he was referring to Oates's own sojourn at St Omers, forgetting that he had a royal pardon for that and worse offences.) More remarkably, Jeffreys must have known that at least five of these witnesses were not only Catholics but Jesuits, having taken orders since they graduated from St Omers.* But when Oates tried to ask one of them the date on which he entered the Society of Jesus, Jeffreys was furious.

I will not ask him that question [he said]. How often have I told you no such questions are to be asked? Must I make him liable to penalty? No, ask questions that are fair, and you shall have a fair answer.[18]

In rebuttal Oates called a group of witnesses somewhat shrunken in numbers since 1679. The court was treated to some interesting evidence as to why this should be so. They heard how the old priest Clay had been bullied into perjury by being threatened with a charge of treason; and William Smith, Oates's old schoolmaster, was ready to take the stand to swear that he had

---

* William Conway, Robert Beeston, John Haggerston (or his brother Henry), Clement Smith and William Garrard were definitely full members of the Society. There may have been others, appearing under aliases.

been forsworn on previous occasions. (To the great irritation of the Attorney-General, Jeffreys ruled that his evidence was inadmissible, since he was a confessed perjurer.) Most serious, Oates could still not produce anyone with whom he had stayed in London in April 1678 (a Mrs Grove had been named before, but at Langhorn's trial she had denied it point-blank). Jeffreys pressed him on this point, but he was evasive, and Jeffreys's comment – 'I perceived it is a secret, and let anybody judge why' – was for once perfectly fair. In desperation Oates then said he had stayed with Whitbread and Mico: 'I believe', he added, 'that Mr Whitbread, if asked at his death, would have justified and stood by it.' This left even Jeffreys at a loss for words.[19]

Two other witnesses who had met Oates casually in the street in 1678 were now not all sure whether the year was 1678 or 1677, and one of them did not even know what month it was; they could safely be dismissed. This left Cecilia Mayo and John Butler, servants of Sir Richard Barker, who still firmly deposed that Oates had dined with their master one night towards the end of April 1678. On these two was bent the full weight of Jeffreys's formidable technique: he was a master of the art of cross-examination, and Finch showed himself only marginally inferior. Jeffreys's method was simple; he bombarded Butler with question after question after question, at rapid rate, designed to elicit why he remembered so particularly the time, the place and the person. The wretched man could produce no reasons at all, and under inexorable pressure from the bench he even moved into the first week of May 1678, raising questions in the jury's mind as to whether it might not have been June or July. By this time, Butler had been in the box at least half an hour, and Oates protested: 'My lord, he is my witness, and I desire I may examine him.' 'Hold there, Mr Oates,' said Jeffreys wolfishly, 'he is mine, too. All the witnesses are mine, to satisfy me in the truth of the fact.'[20]

Finch then took over, to grill Butler further. Mayo was recalled and her evidence compared with his. Minor inconsistencies were triumphantly discovered, and the evidence of both was then carefully compared with the evidence they had given in

1679, exposing further inconsistencies. Oates again protested: 'After six years' time, to ask such poor ignorant people such trifling questions!' but it was no use.[21] Jeffreys resumed, and soon discovered that the two witnesses could not agree on what colour wig Oates had been wearing on that far-off day. Oates angrily remarked: 'These things are lean stuff to perjure a witness on!' But Jeffreys affected to be shocked and disgusted: 'Here are I know not how many contradictions in these witnesses' testimonies,' he said. Oates replied:

Truly, my lord, I do not find in the examination of the St Omers witnesses you were so strict, or bore half so hard upon them, as you do upon my witnesses. What does it signify, my lord, whether the wig were long or short, black or brown?

Jeffreys took refuge in an obscure reference to Susannah and the Elders, but in fact he and Finch had done most of what they had set out to do; they had been unable to break the witnesses down, but they had reduced them to a pitiable state of confusion, and in that state had forced them into errors which might reasonably leave the jury to conclude that their powers of observation were poor and their memory weak.[22]

Obviously Jeffreys and his colleagues were violently prejudiced against Oates from the start, and he received a trial every bit as unfair as those of any of his victims. Jeffreys retained his temper until the afternoon, then it blazed forth. When Oates objected to the St Omers witnesses as Roman Catholics, he remarked: 'I wonder to see any man that has the face of a man carry it at this rate, when he hears such an evidence brought in against him.' Oates interrupted him and said: 'I wonder that Mr Attorney will offer to bring this evidence, men that must have malice against me.' 'Hold your tongue,' roared Jeffreys. 'You are a shame to mankind. Such impudence and impiety were never known in any Christian nation.'[23] But a little later Oates burst out again: 'I appeal to all the hearers', he said, 'whether I have justice done me.' Jeffreys exploded. 'What's that?' he bellowed. 'Why, you impudent fellow, do you know where you are? You are in a court of justice, and must appeal to none but the court and the jury. We'll suffer none of your commonwealth appeals to your *mobile*.'[24] Towards the end the proceedings degenerated into an exchange of insults between Jeffreys and the defendant which made it questionable whether the trial could continue, even in seventeenth-century conditions. Jeffreys pulled himself together at last, but, as we have seen, some of the most powerful sections of his summing-up were devoted to the defendant's character. By this time Oates had given up, pleaded illness, and retired, but this did not inhibit Jeffreys one bit.

My blood does curdle [he told the jury], and my spirits are raised, that after the discoveries made, I think, to the satisfaction of all that have attended this day, to see a fellow continue so impudent as to brazen it out as he has done this day; and that there should appear no confusion and shame than what was seen in the face of that monstrous villain that stood but now at the bar. The pretended infirmity of his body made him remove out of court, but the infirmity of his depraved mind, the blackness of his soul, the baseness of his actions, ought to be looked upon with such horror and detestation as to think him unworthy any longer to tread upon the face of God's earth.[25]

The verdict was 'guilty', of course, but judgement was reserved, for next day, 9 May, Oates appeared again at King's Bench bar to answer a second count of perjury, in that he had falsely sworn that he had met Ireland in London between 8 and 12 August 1678, and again on 1 or 2 September, Ireland in fact being in Staffordshire on both occasions. The evidence was flawlessly mustered. This had not been so the previous day, and at one stage Jeffreys had told Finch: 'Mr Solicitor, if you take this confused method we shall never be at an end, and for my part I cannot make anything of it'; to which Finch could only reply: 'We beg your lordship's patience but a little while, and we shall have it in very good order.'[26]

But now Finch and Sawyer paraded forty witnesses, in chronological order, to prove in detail Ireland's every movement from 3 August 1678, when he left London for Staffordshire, until 13 September, when he left Wolverhampton for London. (There was one blank day, 8 September, but that was not material to the case.)[27] Oates seemed remarkably unconcerned, though his only defence could be that many of these witnesses had given evidence in December 1678, and had not been believed. This produced, early on, the following exchange:

OATES: My lord, there was a time when it was not believed.

LORD CHIEF JUSTICE: Ay, Mr Oates, we know there was a time when there were *ignoramus* juries, and things were believed, or not believed, as the humour went.* What can you, Mr Oates, say to it? I must needs tell you, *prima facie*, it is so strong an evidence, that if you have any sense in the world you must be concerned at it.

OATES: Not at all, my lord. I know who they are, and what is the end of it all.

LORD CHIEF JUSTICE: Upon my faith, I have so much charity for you, as my fellow creature, to be concerned for you.

OATES: It is not two straws' matter whether you be or no. I know my own innocency.

LORD CHIEF JUSTICE: Thou art the most obstinately hardened wretch that ever I saw.[28]

Oates continued to object that most of the witnesses against him were Catholics, but none of them were priests, and most of them were substantial gentry – Lord Aston, Sir James Symons and their like. Moreover, their Protestant servants were ready to support their testimony to the full. Jeffreys was delighted when Oates asked Frances Allen, one of Lord Aston's servants, his usual question and she replied, 'I am a Protestant of the Church of England; so I was christened, so I have lived, and so I hope to die before you all.' Jeffreys affected alarm. 'Upon my word,' he said, 'she is very kind; she has a mind to die before us. It is a sign she lives a good life, she's so ready to die.'[29]

But Oates never gave in, and his closing speech in his own defence was combative and closely reasoned.[30] He made a good point when he reminded the court that 'Ireland was convicted for a treasonable resolution to murder the late king, and not for being in town in August or September 1678, or elsewhere'. He went on to argue that Ireland's presence in Staffordshire had been attested at his trial, and Lord Chief Justice Scroggs had then dismissed this evidence as 'punctilios of time', or 'catching

* See p. 280 above.

in point of time'. He and the jury had readily accepted Oates's counter-evidence, and it had been supported by Bedloe. For further corroboration he tried to cite the evidence Robert Jenison had given at Wakeman's trial in 1679, but unfortunately he was nowhere to be found (in fact, he had fled to Holland), nor was Sarah Paine, the mysterious servant girl who had been the only witness at Ireland's trial to confirm his presence in London after 3 August 1678. After the usual sterile argument as to what could or could not be produced in evidence Oates was reduced to summarizing Jenison's and Paine's evidence for the benefit of the jury, but he finished strongly with a fluent, if biased, analysis of the history of English Catholicism since the Reformation. He argued that the Gunpowder Plot showed the Catholics' propensity for conspiracy and assassination, and that Coleman's letters proved to the hilt the existence of a Plot in the 1670s. There *had* been a Popish Plot, irrespective of whether every single piece of evidence for it was technically watertight or not. Finally he sneered at the hypocrisy of Jeffreys, and others who had been concerned in the Plot trials.

My lord [he said], as they would now fling the Popish Plot upon me, so there is an evident design to fling the murder of Godfrey upon a Protestant peer [Shaftesbury] . . . And so they will go on, step by step, if they be let alone, and think at length to wipe their mouths with Solomon's whore,* and say, they have done no mischief.[31]

Oates then retired, having secured an arrest of judgement for one week while he sought legal advice. So he again missed the Lord Chief Justice's summing-up. Jeffrey's had got his second wind by now, and overnight he had thought of other adjectives for the defendant.

I cannot but bewail [he said] that so many innocent persons (to the reproach of our nation be it spoken) have suffered death upon this account. God deliver me from having the least stain of innocent blood imputed to me! And it is more to be lamented, when we see that impudence which has brought that infamy upon our land continues with a brazen face, defying all shame to this day. But by this

*An obscure reference (to 1 Kings 11.11?). By 'with' he meant 'like', of course.

we may be informed how some men's consciences are seared, and that there are some people that do indeed live without the fear of God in the world.

But Oates's reference to Bedloe reminded him of one who was even worse:

I cannot but lament likewise the wickedness of our age, when I reflect upon the testimony of that other wretch (indeed, I cannot use terms severe enough for him) that, when he was going into another world, should persist in such gross falsities. I mean Bedloe, infamous Bedloe, and let his name be for ever infamous to all mankind that have any regard or deference for the truth: That he should with his latest breath dare to affirm that every word he had said of the Popish Plot was true, when it is as clear as the sun, by the testimony of this day, that every word he swore about Ireland was utterly false. Good God of Heaven! What an age have we lived in, to see innocence suffer punishment, and impudent falsity reign so long!

Gentlemen [he went on], I hope all eyes are opened (I wish they had been so long since). Let us lay the burden, the infamy and reproach of these things upon them that deserve it, for we cannot but know, we are reckoned as a by-word to all our neighbours, and shall remain monuments of ignominy to all succeeding ages and times, if we do not endeavour to discharge ourselves and our religion, and the justice of our nation, from these scandals.[32]

The only difficulty was that the law did not prescribe a sufficient penalty for perjury. And why? Because such monstrous and unnatural crimes had never been foreseen in less decadent ages.

How could it be imagined [he lamented] that there should be such horrid villains, as should attempt the destruction of the government of three kingdoms? Good Lord! What times do we live in! Surely it is such an age as was never known from the creation of the world to this day!

Moreover, the crimes of Oates and Bedloe were exacerbated by the fact that they had acted under the forms of law, and perverted the cause of justice for their own ends. In this respect they were comparable with those who had tried and executed 'our late blessed sovereign, King Charles the Martyr, of ever happy memory'. Hanging was too good for them, for:

The destruction of poor innocent persons by false accusations, by the pernicious evidence of perjured witnesses in a court of justice, makes their crime infinitely more odious than common murder.[33]

After reviewing the evidence, he apologized to the jury for the length of his address:

Gentlemen [he said], I have taken up much of your time, and detained you the longer in this matter, because I cannot but say, with a grief of heart, our nation was too long besotted, and of innocent blood there has been too much spilt. It is high time to have some account of it. It is a mercy that we ought to bless Almighty God for, that we were prevented from spilling more of innocent blood! God be blessed, our eyes are opened, and let us have a care for the future, that we be not so suddenly imposed upon by such prejudices and jealousies as we have reason to fear such villains have too much filled our heads with of late.[34]

The jury brought in a verdict of guilty, and received the congratulations of all four judges individually; then the proceedings were adjourned for a week. When they resumed on the 16th, Oates tried to raise some technical points of law, which were brushed aside by Jeffreys. Jeffreys then proceeded to discuss the punishment appropriate in this case. In the interval, he told the court, he had consulted the other judges on this point. He said wistfully that in olden days perjury was punishable by death, and later by the cutting-out of the offender's tongue, but his colleagues had ruled that sentence of death or mutilation was no longer legal. Yet, he went on:

When a person shall be convicted of such a foul and malicious perjury as the defendant is, I think it is impossible for the court, as the law now stands, to put a punishment upon him any way proportionable to the offence, that has drawn after it so many horrid and dreadful consequences. We do therefore think fit to inflict an exemplary punishment upon this villainous, perjured wretch, to terrify others for the future.[35]

Sir Francis Wythens then handed down the sentence, with the prefatory remark: 'I do not know how I can say but that the law is defective that such a one is not to be hanged.' However, if they could not execute him formally, they were clearly intent on killing him all the same. Oates was fined 1,000 marks on each count, and unfrocked. On Monday next, 18 May, he was to be paraded through the Courts of Justice in Westminster Hall with a notice proclaiming his offence, then he was to stand in the pillory outside for an hour. Next day the process was to be repeated at the Royal Exchange in the City. On Wednesday, 20 May, he was to be whipped from Aldgate to Newgate (about a mile and a half), and on Friday, after a day's rest, he was to be whipped from Newgate to Tyburn (another two miles). He was then to be imprisoned for life, but every year on 24 April, 9, 10 and 11 August and 2 September he was to stand in the pillory for an hour at Tyburn, Westminster Hall, Charing Cross, Temple Bar and the Royal Exchange, respectively. 'And', said Wythens, in conclusion, 'I must tell you plainly, if it had been in my power to have carried it further, I should not have been unwilling to have given judgement of death upon you, for I am sure you deserve it.'[36]

Sentence was duly carried out. On Monday morning, Oates was paraded through the Courts of Justice, and when he came to King's Bench he told Jeffreys 'that he was to stand in the pillory for truth'. (Unfortunately, Jeffreys's reply is not recorded.) Outside was a crowd estimated at ten thousand, and he was pelted with rotten eggs. But next day Sunderland wrote to the sheriffs conveying the King's displeasure that 'some disorder' had occurred, and ordering them to prevent a repetition.[37] Since it is unlikely that James would have been displeased at rioting prejudicial to Oates it must be presumed that his supporters were out. On the Tuesday, indeed, they overturned the pillory outside the Royal Exchange and nearly rescued him. On Wednesday and Friday he received the prescribed whipping at the hands of Ketch, the King refusing a petition that he remit the second half. He was not expected to survive, but survive he did, though he was dragged most of the way to Tyburn unconscious on a sled. He then retired into prison for the rest of James's reign, emerging only on the prescribed dates to stand in the pillory.

However, he was luckier than Thomas Dangerfield. In August 1684, hearing that James's lawyers were preparing a writ of *scandalum magnatum* against him, Dangerfield went into hiding. As soon as James came to the throne a thorough search was instituted, and he was arrested in March 1685. His performance in the courts had been so inept that he could not very well be indicted for perjury, instead he was prosecuted for seditious libel on the evidence of his *Narrative*, published in 1680, in which he had accused James of complicity in the Plot. (In defiance of parliamentary privilege the former Speaker, William Williams, was also convicted and heavily fined for authorizing its publication, though he had done so on the orders of the House of Commons.) He was tried in King's Bench on 30 May, found guilty, and sentenced to the same savage whipping as Oates. He survived it, but on his way back from Tyburn by coach he got involved in an altercation with one Robert Francis, a Tory barrister in Hatton Garden. Francis struck him on the face with his cane, and by a fluke it pierced his brain and killed him. On the King's orders Francis was tried for murder, convicted and executed.

The last remaining perjurer, Miles Prance, was arraigned in King's Bench in the Easter Term 1686, but he pleaded guilty. On 15 June he was fined £100, given three sessions in the pillory, and ordered to be whipped from Newgate to Tyburn. The King remitted the last part of the sentence. The delay in bringing him to justice and the lightness of his sentence confirmed Sir John Pollock in his belief that there was collusion between him and the Jesuits from the beginning, but in fact there were many strong factors working in his favour. Obviously he had been subjected to a very strong pressure in 1679, and he blamed this on Lord Shaftesbury, a popular whipping-boy; his victims were of a very low social status, he had made scarcely any money from their deaths, he expressed deep regret for his conduct, and he was still a practising Roman Catholic.[38] It is unnecessary to seek more sinister explanations.

On the evening of 8 May 1685, at Whitehall, King James told Sir John Reresby 'that now Oates was thus convicted the Popish Plot was dead'. Reresby's reply was that 'it was long since dead, and now it would be buried'. The King was charmed, and later repeated this *bon mot* to the Princess Anne.[39] However, the refusal of the House of Commons to reverse Lord Stafford's attainder soon showed that it was far from true.

On 27 May, by special command of the King, a bill was introduced in the House of Lords to reverse Stafford's attainder. On 3 June a Committee of the Whole House heard the record of Oates's trial read out, but still voted to excise from the preamble to the bill all reference to him or any of the other witnesses, and substitute a less explicit formula: 'It is now manifest that the said Viscount Stafford was innocent of the treasons laid to his charge, and that the testimony whereupon he was convicted was false.' Next day it was passed by the House and sent down to the Commons. There is no division list, of course, so all we know of the voting is that three unrepentant Whigs, Stamford, Clare and Eure, entered their dissent on the grounds that an attainder could only be reversed because of a technical legal fault. Of the fifty-five peers who had voted Stafford guilty on 7 December 1680, twenty-nine were present on 4 June 1685, and it is reasonable to suppose that at least some of them reversed their vote. However, of the remaining twenty-six only six had died in the interval or are definitely known to have been elsewhere, so some probably absented themselves deliberately.[40]

When the bill reached the Commons – and it must be remembered that this was the most royalist House of Commons of the century – they objected to what the French ambassador called 'some words inserted in the preamble which seemed to favour the Catholic religion', and laid it aside. In fact, in the bill as printed from the Lords archives no such words can be detected, and the simple fact seems to be that this Tory House of Commons was not ready to give its Whig predecessors the lie.[41] For if the Lords had sentenced Stafford, it was the Commons which had prosecuted him. From then on James's relations with Parliament deteriorated so badly that no second attempt was possible. On 5 October 1688, acting on a premonition that he would not have the power to do so much longer, he made Stafford's widow Countess of Stafford *suo jure*, and his eldest son Earl of Stafford. The attainder on the barony and the viscountcy was not lifted until 1824, by a private bill which merely stated that Lords and Commons thought it 'just and proper that the said attainder should be reversed'.[42] In any case, being a private bill, it was not printed. Parliament does not admit its mistakes easily.

This uncharitable spirit was even more evident in the Parliament of 1689, elected in the wake of the Revolution. Oates was unofficially released from prison in December 1688, and on 11 March 1689, with King James deposed and King William on the throne, he petitioned Parliament for redress. Naturally he portrayed himself as the victim of a dastardly conspiracy, and castigated the 'partial behaviour' of Jeffreys, now safely lodged in the Tower, awaiting trial himself; but, the merits of his conviction apart, there was justifiable doubt whether his sentence had been good in law, and the Lords gave him permission to proceed by writ of error. This had the very considerable merit of making an inquiry into the validity of his conviction unnecessary.[43]

But, whether because of prejudice against him (as he thought), or because of the press of business at this time (the details of the Revolution Settlement were still under discussion, and the country was at war with France), the hearing was constantly postponed, and it was not until 17 May that Wythens and Holloway, two of the judges who had sat with Jeffreys in 1685, were brought before the House to justify their proceedings; this they did by arguing that this was an unprecedented case; five people had died as a result of Oates's perjury, and they had tried to make the punishment fit the crime. The new Lord Chief Justice, Sir John Holt, was asked to give an opinion on 25 May.

However, when the House assembled on the twenty-fifth they were informed that the day before Oates had sent a petition to the Commons. The Lords took grave exception to his appealing to the lower House on a case pending before themselves; they also objected to the language he used of Charles II and James, and, more important, one of their own number, the Bishop of St Asaph. When he was asked to enlarge on the vague term 'persons' used in the petition he showed that he had changed not a bit since 1678; his reply was 'When I am in a condition to justify what I say against any man, I will name persons and names.'[44] He was found guilty of a serious breach of privilege, and remanded to the King's Bench prison once again, though six Whig peers entered their dissent. On 30 May he petitioned to be released, but the Lords now objected to his continued use of the degree of D.D. (Salamanca), and since he obstinately refused to abandon it, in prison he remained. Next day the Lords heard the considered opinion of the judges, Holt, Pollexfen, Atkins, Nevill and Lechmere, that the judgement on Oates was 'erroneous in all points': the King's courts could not unfrock a clergyman, nor could they impose perpetual imprisonment, and the rest of the sentence was illegal in the case of a gentleman, as well as being 'barbarous, inhuman and unjust'. Having listened to all this, the House then voted to reaffirm the judgements of 1685, fifteen peers dissenting. Clearly there was an unwillingness to do anything which might throw doubt on his conviction for perjury, and a House of Lords which had a solid conservative majority was unlikely to pay much attention to William III's new Whig judges. On 6 June they tried to close the whole matter by requesting the King to give Oates a free pardon, which he promptly did.[45]

But the Commons were not prepared to leave the matter there. The hidden question was, did Parliament still believe in the Popish Plot, and on 11 June the Commons affirmed that they at least did. This is particularly interesting in that the House as a whole did not possess a Whig majority. John Maynard and William Williams, the leading Whig barristers surviving, told the House that the judges were right; the punishment inflicted on Oates was illegal, and an infringement of the clause voted into the Bill of Rights in February forbidding 'cruel and unusual' punishments.* But Maynard also hinted that behind the Lords' action was an attempt to disown the Plot, and Sir Robert Howard, a member of the government, said: 'I am zealous in one thing, not to blacken all things relating to Protestants, and whiten Papists.' Colonel Birch, who had been Chairman of the

---

* This was not inserted in Oates's honour alone; it also referred to the whipping imposed on a clergyman named Samuel Johnson in 1886 for publishing a pamphlet inciting the Army to mutiny.

Commons Committee for Examinations in 1679, was understandably still a believer:

> We all know [he said] who they were that did what they could to make this Plot a ridicule, but when a jesting business would not do, they took all the ways they could to suppress it.

He went on to argue that a vote against the Plot was a vote for popery and King James, and Sir Henry Capel, another Whig veteran of 1679, wholeheartedly agreed. On Capel's motion the House resolved:

> That the prosecution of Titus Oates upon two indictments of perjury in the Court of King's Bench was a design to stifle the Popish Plot, and that the verdicts given there were corrupt, and that the judgements given thereon were cruel and illegal,

and ordered a bill to be brought in to reverse the convictions as well as the sentence.[46]

This bill reached the Lords on 6 July, and they speedily produced a whole series of amendments. Unfortunately, it seems that no copy of the bill survives, but from the record of the amendments, and the conference between the two Houses on 30 July, much can be deduced. The Lords, naturally, refused to go back on their previous decision to affirm that the punishment inflicted on Oates was legal, and they were even less willing to declare his conviction void; they were impatient with the Commons' wild accusation that the juries had been bribed, and called for proof (which was never forthcoming, of course). In whatever form the bill finally passed, they wanted to insert a clause barring Oates from appearing as a witness in any court of law thereafter.

On this last point the Commons threw down a direct challenge:

> The business of the Popish Plot had great examinations in several parliaments, and in several courts of justice, in all which Oates stood a good witness, and though his testimony did not stand alone, but was confirmed by other witnesses, and by papers and letters (evidence which could not be mistaken), yet it did deserve to be considered if the declaring him to be an incompetent witness by Act of Parliament would not be interpreted [as] a great step towards dis-

avowing the Popish Plot, it being certain that what had been done by the Lords in affirming the judgements against him had already had such an interpretation beyond sea. It was therefore fit to have it plainly known whether that was intended, and to have it well weighed whether the thing will be so much for the honour of our nation, or our religion, that we should go out of the way, and do an extraordinary thing to come at it.

The Lords replied that Oates had not only committed the perjuries for which he was convicted, but many others; for instance, he had accused the then Queen of conspiring to poison the King, 'which nobody could believe of her'. When he had appeared before them recently it was apparent that the patronage of the Commons had 'made him fancy himself to have a right of creating evidence rather than delivering it'. They argued 'that it was not fit to encourage such witnesses, that his brain seemed to be turned'. They admitted 'that this was a matter of great expectation, that the eyes of all Europe were upon it', but that only meant 'that it would be the occasion of great censures if he should be set up as a witness again without a full examination of the whole affair'.[47]

This was defeat, but John Somers, the future Whig Lord Chancellor, salvaged something by persuading the House on 13 August to throw over any talk of the Plot, or Oates's conviction, and send up a closely reasoned Address on the strictly legal aspects of the case. For the rest the Commons could only accept the royal pardon already issued, and on 20 August, the last day of the session, they sent a request to the King that he give Oates 'some allowance for his maintenance'.[48] William granted him the least he decently could: £10 a week from the secret service money. The martyr had to content himself with writing a long account of his treatment, published under the title *A Display of Tyranny*. His case was not raised again, and I can find no record thereafter of the British Government or the British Parliament making any public pronouncement on the Plot; the preambles to the Catholic Relief Acts of 1778, 1791 and 1829 are absolutely non-committal. But the last of the Penal Laws, the Act of 1700 'for the further preventing the Growth of Popery', referred ominously to 'such treasonable and execrable designs and conspiracies against his Majesty's person and government and the established religion as have lately, as well as frequently heretofore, been brought to light and happily defeated by the wonderful Providence of God' – a phrase which can be construed as applying primarily to the Assassination Plot of 1696, but which had other implications.[49]

As for Oates, he settled down in Axe Yard, Westminster, and pursued his two hobbies of writing religious tracts and attending the courts of law in Westminster Hall as a spectator.[50] He was still friendly with old Whig extremists like Aaron Smith and John Arnold. Appropriately enough, he was also a friend of William Fuller, the chief exponent of the theory that James II's son had been an impostor smuggled in in a warming-pan. In August 1693 he improved his fortunes by marrying a wealthy city widow. (He seems to have abandoned his homosexuality, or perhaps he had always been bi-sexual; there is a well-attested story that he fathered a bastard in the King's Bench prison in 1688.) But even with his wife's assistance he ran heavily into debt, and in 1698 he was granted a lump sum of £500, and £300 a year on the post office, in place of his allowance. So he received from William III what Charles II had disdained to give him, a funded pension.

In the same year this extraordinary man was admitted to the Baptist community after long negotiations stretching over years. There is no reason to doubt his sincerity, he was only returning to the ways of his father; and he was a popular and effective preacher at the Baptist chapel in Wapping. But not all the congregation were happy with him, and in 1701 he was expelled after a discreditable intrigue to set aside the will of a wealthy female member. These various scandals were faithfully reported in the gutter press, and his standing seems to have declined even with the old-fashioned Whigs, most of whom had died or lost their seats in Parliament anyway. A brief revival of anti-Catholic feeling in 1700 seems to have passed him by; there is no record of his being re-introduced as an expert on popery. He died on 12 July 1705, almost unnoticed. Though he had outlived almost everyone else of note connected with the Popish Plot he was still only fifty-six.

APPENDIX A

The Murder of
Sir Edmund Berry Godfrey

In Chapter Four I purposely refrained from speculating on the identity of Godfrey's murderers. A great deal has been written on the matter, and I have nothing constructive to add to it. Moreover, Sir John Pollock's *The Popish Plot* is a warning of what can happen when a man setting out to write a book on the Plot as a whole becomes obsessed by the murder of Godfrey.

For I am not sure that Godfrey's murder is central to a study of the Plot. I am not even sure that the agitation which swept England in November and December 1678 would not have been just as hysterical without it. Certainly outside London the crime made little impression; it was essentially a metropolitan event, just as Godfrey was a strictly metropolitan figure, and in a sense, therefore, parochial. By February 1679, his 'murderers' had been tried and executed, to the satisfaction of most people, but the general uproar continued with very little diminution. However this may be, clearly anyone writing a book on the Plot must at least express an opinion on the matter – but I must stress that what follows is merely an expression of opinion.*

First of all, was Godfrey murdered at all, or did he just commit suicide? Many contemporaries clearly thought this, including his own brothers and his servants; in other words, the people best qualified to judge. So did the journalist Sir Roger

---

* There is no book on Godfrey which can be wholeheartedly recommended (if there were this appendix would be unnecessary), but *The Murder of Sir Edmund Godfrey*, by the Amercian detective story writer John Dickson Carr (New York, 1936), is not to be despised. It contains some bad history and some very doubtful characterization, but it sets out the facts as they are known, and gives an exhaustive review of the possible culprits.

l'Estrange, who investigated the matter thoroughly in the years immediately following, and had the advantage over us of being able to talk to many of the participants. Moreover, in a radio programme on Godfrey broadcast in 1952,* an eminent psychologist, the late Alexander Kennedy, after studying the available evidence, concluded that he 'was suffering at that time from an acute state of morbid depression'. He had a tradition of insanity in the family, as a young man he gave up his studies at the bar for undisclosed reasons, and his conversation in the first week of October 1678 was often far from rational. His conviction that he was to be 'the first martyr' is characterized by Kennedy as a typical hallucination; he even remarked to one friend, 'Have you heard that I am to be hanged?'

So the theory is that he hanged himself, and that he was found by men to whom his death was embarrassing, dangerous or possibly advantageous. These could have been his brothers, bearing in mind that a suicide's estate was forfeit to the Crown; or his Catholic friends, who would fear to be blamed; or some ultra-Protestants, who at once saw in the corpse a means of incriminating the Catholics. These people, whoever they were, kept the body hidden for several days, while they laid their plans, then they took it out to Primrose Hill and drove a sword through it, in a clumsy attempt to make it look like a case of murder. The bruising on Godfrey's chest was merely the result of extravasation, the draining of blood to the underlying parts of the body after death.

However, in the same programme in which Kennedy lent his support to the suicide theory, the distinguished pathologist and forensic scientist Keith Simpson categorically declared that the medical evidence ruled suicide out. The bruises on the chest, he said, could only have been caused by heavy blows with the fist or the boot *before* death, and, most important, the detailed description of the marks on his throat made it clear that he could not have hanged himself; the marks were too low down. So he could only have been strangled with a ligature, a thin cloth or

* 'Who killed Sir Edmund Berry Godfrey?', written and produced by Nesta Pain, B.B.C. Home Service, 16 September 1952.

cord, as contemporaries thought. He added that the sword thrust was certainly inflicted after death, but it could just as well have been inflicted half an hour after death instead of days later.

This is unfortunate, because there has never seemed to be any strong motive for murdering Godfrey, as distinct from making his accomplished suicide look like murder. And this question of motive is crucial; if we only knew *why* he was murdered we would know with some certainty *who* did it.

Obviously most contemporaries blamed the Catholics, but none of them could explain why they should commit a crime which would almost certainly be laid at their door. Bedloe's explanation, that they wanted to get hold of Oates's original depositions, to expose the inconsistencies between these and his later testimony, is just ridiculous. Oates's narrative in eighty-one articles, which he showed Godfrey the morning Tonge first went before the Council, can be shown to be identical with what he swore to the Council.* But in any case, no contemporary judge would accept previous depositions as evidence in criminal cases, or even a record of evidence given by the same witness at a previous trial; this was confirmed again and again in 1678 and 1679. The witness stood or fell by the evidence he gave in that court on that day. Prance's explanation, that Godfrey had been harassing a mysterious priest called Fitzgerald, or Gerald, is even less likely, in view of Godfrey's known leniency towards Catholics and Protestant Dissenters alike.

Pollock believed that Godfrey was murdered because his friend, Coleman, in an unguarded moment, had betrayed to him the fact that the Jesuit Consult of 24 April 1678 had been held in St James's Palace. He also concluded that the Jesuits did in fact commit the murder, and that Prance's confession was a 'cover-

---

* In fact, the deposition sworn by Oates before Godfrey on 28 September 1678 is in the Bodleian Library (Rawl. D. 720, ff. 172–91), though I did not discover it until a late stage in the preparation of this book. It is a summary, in continuous prose, of the eighty-one articles, to which it refers by number; this confirms that the full version of these articles already existed then in much the same state as they were given to the Lords in November.

up story' designed to protect them. This is a remarkable display of anti-Catholic prejudice from an educated and cultivated man in the reign of Edward VII: almost worthy of Charles II's reign. It is also most perverse. The fact that the Jesuits had met at St James's Palace could not hurt them (Oates had already accused them of treason ten times over), only the Duke of York. It is ludicrous to suppose that in such an emergency James would have turned to a group of priests to do his business, when around him he had any number of unscrupulous Catholic 'swordsmen' and professional soldiers, like Richard Talbot, Bernard Howard, Justin Maccarty, and Henry Jermyn.

Men like this would have killed Godfrey with few qualms, if James had ordered it, and they would surely have done it much more skilfully. The strange thing about this murder is that it was so badly bungled. If the Catholics had really done it, surely they would have had the sense to disguise it more thoroughly, or plant evidence incriminating others? The best way to get rid of Godfrey was simply to club him to death, strip him of all his valuables down to his shirt, and leave him in the nearest side-alley, in which case a common footpad would almost certainly have got the blame. Whoever killed Godfrey had several days to plan the disposal of the body, but he still bungled it.

Or did he? Certainly the circumstances of Godfrey's murder threw suspicion on the Catholics, and for this reason Oates or Shaftesbury, or both of them, or associates of theirs, were favourite targets of Tory politicians and writers, then and later.* But it does not really fit the character of either. Oates was a most despicable villain, but he was not a physically violent man, rather the opposite. Nor was he a known associate of thugs and killers, like Bedloe. Bedloe is a much more promising murderer, either directly or indirectly, but if he was guilty, why did he wait a fortnight to collect his reward, and why did he give such a complicated and implausible story when he did appear? As a skilled confidence trickster of years' standing, he ought to have been able to do better than that. As for Shaftesbury, with all his faults he was a man of considerable nobility of character; he was

* For example, Roger North, *Examen*, pp. 197 ff.

not a killer, nor a hirer of killers, especially when the killing was to be done in cold blood, as an outrageous gamble. For nobody could be certain before the event that the Catholics would be blamed for the murder, or that it would rouse the degree of panic and fury that it did. This, too, would rule out any of Shaftesbury's young associates; the risk was too great, the gain too speculative, for them to act without orders from above.

The only exception is the Whig Earl of Pembroke. In 1924 J. G. Muddiman brought forward some new evidence which certainly points to his guilt.* This young peer – he was twenty-five – had long been recognized as a homicidal maniac, when drunk, at least. In earlier years he had been guilty of several unprovoked attacks which could easily have ended in death, and in January 1678 Charles II sent him to the Tower 'for blasphemy, abuse of the celebration of the sacrament of the Lord's Supper, and other misdemeanours altogether unfit to be named'. The House of Lords soon let him out, but in February they had to bind him over for making an unprovoked attack on a passer-by in the street. Finally in March 1678 he made another unprovoked attack on another stranger, a Mr Cony, in a tavern, knocked him down, jumped on him, and then kicked him to death. The foreman of the grand jury which promptly found a verdict of 'wilful murder' was Sir Edmund Berry Godfrey.

He was tried by the House of Lords on 4 April 1678, and found guilty not of murder but manslaughter, and for this peers were allowed to plead benefit of clergy for the first offence. To a man of Pembroke's cast of mind Godfrey had probably done enough to earn his bitter enmity. We know that he did not change; in November 1678 he even made a savage attack on a fellow-peer, the Earl of Dorset, with whom he was involved in a lawsuit, and in August 1680 he committed another unprovoked murder, at Turnham Green, and had to flee abroad. There are a few other scraps of information which point in his direction, such as the fact that the three men who found Godfrey's body on Primrose Hill were all from St Giles's Fields, near Leicester Fields, where Pembroke had his town house.

* *National Review*, lxxxiv (1924–5), 138 ff.

On these grounds Muddiman concluded that Pembroke summoned Godfrey to an interview on some pretext – Godfrey did receive a mysterious letter the day he disappeared – beat him up, jumped on his chest, then strangled him. Later his hirelings thrust the sword through the body and took it off to Primrose Hill. This is an attractive theory, and it is the only one which features a plausible motive. But there are flaws in it, apart from the fact that all the evidence is entirely circumstantial. Like all the other theories of Godfrey's murder, it does not explain how he was kept, where or why, from 12 October, when he disappeared, until the 17th, when he was found on Primrose Hill, clearly having just been dumped there. It would have been very difficult for Pembroke to hide him at his house in Leicester Fields without his servant knowing or suspecting something, and in that case why not use them to dispose of the body, instead of a butcher, a baker and a farrier, all independent men with their own businesses, from the next parish? Pembroke may have made a rendezvous with Godfrey elsewhere, and kept the body there, but all this implies a degree of planning inconsistent with his manic temperament. In either case, there seems no reason to keep the body for four or five days; having emerged from delirium to find he had committed another murder, Pembroke's first instinct, surely, would have been to get rid of the body as soon as possible.

However, the case of Pembroke has significant implications. He was a peer of the realm and a leading member of Court and Society; his wife was sister to the King's favourite mistress, the Duchess of Portsmouth. Yet he left no papers for posterity, and because he did not take a leading part in politics or government contemporaries scarcely ever mention him, though his crimes were a nine-day wonder in the newsletters. Now he survives only as a brief entry in *The Complete Peerage*, and the same can be said of many peers: the Earl of Scarsdale, the Earl of Thanet, Lord Ossulston, Lord North and Grey, are a few examples taken at random. No contemporary seems to have made the connection which Muddiman makes between him and Godfrey, though, of course, some may have suspected it.

The point is that, if this can be said of a man of Pembroke's eminence, how much more can it be said of the lower orders? As I have remarked above,* the Plot gives us occasional glimpses, through men like Bedloe and Dangerfield, of a metropolitan underworld of crime and vice of which we know scarcely anything. For that matter we know next to nothing of the more respectable world of a skilled craftsman like Miles Prance. Yet Godfrey, as an active and conscientious magistrate, perhaps the best in London, must have known that underworld well, and it would be strange if he had not made scores of enemies amongst its inhabitants. The murder of a magistrate was an unusual thing, but assaults on them were not; Godfrey usually walked the streets with a servant to act as a bodyguard. It is perfectly likely that some unknown criminal, uncaring of the Plot and perhaps not even realizing Godfrey's connection with it, gave him a thorough beating-up, then realized that Godfrey had recognized him, and strangled him. He then thrust the sword through the body in a clumsy attempt at mystification, and dumped it as far from the city centre as he could get. It is true that a lower-class criminal would have been sorely tempted by the magistrate's personal valuables. But if he had taken them it could have altered the whole complexion of the crime, and set the authorities looking amongst the criminal classes from the start. As it was, it does not seem to have occurred to any contemporary that Godfrey was the victim of a footpad; the fact that he had not been robbed was enough.

There are two frail inferential arguments in favour of this 'unknown criminal' theory. The first is the fact that, apart from Bedloe and Prance, no one came forward to claim the £500 reward offered for information leading to the conviction of Godfrey's murderers. Yet £500 was a vast sum to any ordinary man; worth at least £5,000 and probably more in modern money, and even more desirable bait in an age which did not offer large windfalls from football pools or state lotteries. The failure of any witness to come forward whose evidence we are still prepared to accept is usually explained away by saying that the murderers

*See p. 152 above.

were united by a religious or ideological motive, whether Protestant or Catholic. The alternative explanation is that this was a one-man venture; and it has the added attraction that a man living alone, or with a loyal wife, would have had no difficulty in hiding the body in his house for four days.

Secondly, this theory could explain those mysterious four days. The delay is much easier to explain if we visualize a poor man working alone, who would find it difficult to borrow a cart and horse at short notice without rousing suspicion, and had to wait for some plausible occasion. In the meanwhile, the alarm raised in the City for the missing magistrate would have made him realize the unusual danger he was in.

All this is the merest speculation, of course, and no one could call it a contribution towards solving the murder. I am suggesting, in fact, that up to now the circle of suspects has been kept unnecessarily narrow, and confined to people and parties we happen to know. The crime could just as easily have been committed by an unknown man who is now quite undiscoverable.

APPENDIX B

The Catholic Nobility

BECAUSE several Catholic peers conformed under Charles II, and the rest were not indicted for recusancy in his reign, it is difficult to be certain how many there were on 30 November 1678. The list which follows is more accurate than Magee's,* but apart from that I would make no claims for it.

There were at least twenty-one Catholic peers, made up of the following:

1 Duke:	Norfolk†
5 Earls:	Berkshire, Cardigan, Portland, Powis, Shrewsbury.
2 Viscounts:	Montague, Stafford.
13 Barons:	Abergavenny, Arundell of Wardour, Audley, Belasyse, Carrington, Clifford, Gerard of Bromley, Hunsdon, Langdale, Petre, Stourton, Teynham, Widdrington.

But of those, three were minors (Abergavenny, Clifford and Shrewsbury), two are known to have fled abroad (Berkshire and Cardigan), and six were in gaol and likely to remain there. So the number available to vote in November 1678 was a mere ten.

In addition, de Courson says that three Catholics took the Test and continued to attend.‡ On the face of it this is a contradiction in terms, but she may have had in mind Lord Morley and Mounteagle, or Henry Jermyn, Earl of St Albans, who was often accused of being a secret papist. Morley's family had been

---

* *English Recusants*, pp. 127 ff.

† His eldest son was called to the Lords in 1678, in the family barony of Mowbray, but he took the oaths on 11 April, 1679 (*L.J.*, xiii, 511).

‡ Courson, p. 51.

Catholics for generations, and though he seems to have conformed, his way of life was so dissipated, indeed deranged, that no church would be anxious to claim him.

It should be remembered that other Catholic peers, like Aston, Dunbar and Lumley, held Scots or Irish peerages. Outside Parliament, Lord Audley was usually known by his Irish title, Earl of Castlehaven.

APPENDIX C

The Canonization of the Martyrs

ALL those Catholics executed as a result of the Plot were granted the status of 'Venerabile' by Pope Leo XIII in 1886, with the exception of William Staley, Lawrence Hill and Robert Green. However, Green and Hill do appear in the ranks of the 'Dilati', those whose cause has been postponed 'until further evidence of their martyrdom is forthcoming'. Amongst the Dilati are also nine priests who died in prison (five Jesuits, two Benedictines and two seculars). On the other hand three Jesuits (Edward Mico, Thomas Bedingfield and Francis Nevill) and one Franciscan (Francis Levison), who also died in prison, are 'Venerabile'. This distinction cannot be explained by reference to historical sources.

Furthermore, on 15 December 1929, Pope Pius XI beatified all those actually executed, with the exception, again inexplicable, of Nicholas Postgate, executed at York on 7 August 1679, and Charles Mahoney, the Irish Franciscan, executed at Ruthin on 12 August in the same year. On the other hand, Edward Coleman was included.

Finally, on 25 October 1970, Pope Paul VI canonized forty English martyrs, who may therefore be invoked as Saints, and these include six from the Plot period: John Plessington, Philip Evans, John Lloyd, John Wall, John Kemble and David Lewis.

Since it has always been acknowledged that these forty martyrs are representative of the whole body, and were also chosen partly as representing the various orders of the priesthood, the Catholic laity and the various regions of England, further comment would be irrelevant. It is just worth noting that the English Hierarchy and the Holy See have avoided canonizing any who were condemned for overt acts of treason, as distinct from treason under the Elizabethan penal statutes.

This may possibly have resulted in an injustice being done to the Jesuits and others condemned and executed in London. However, in this context the use of the term 'injustice' is perhaps impertinent, or in another sense superogatory.

List of Works Cited

Akerman, J. W. (ed.), *Moneys received and paid for secret services of Charles II and James II*, Camden Society (London, 1851).

Aveling, Hugh, 'The Catholic Recusants of the West Riding of Yorkshire 1558–1790', *Proceedings of the Leeds Philosophical and Literary Society*, x (1963), 191 ff.; *Northern Catholics* (London, 1966); *Post-Reformation Catholicism in East Yorkshire* (East Yorks Local History Society, 1960); 'Some aspects of Yorkshire Catholic recusant history 1568–1791', in *Studies in Church History IV*, ed. G. J. Cuming (Leiden, 1967).

Beales, A. C. F., *Education Under Penalty: English Catholic Education from the Reformation to the Fall of James II* (London, 1963).

Blundell, Margaret, *Cavalier: Letters of William Blundell and his friends 1620–1698* (London, 1933).

Bowler, Hugh, 'The Caryll Letter', *The Month*, clxi (1933), 256 ff.

Brady, W. M., *Annals of the Catholic Hierarchy in England and Scotland 1585–1876* (Rome, 1883).

Browning, Andrew, *Thomas Osborne Earl of Danby*, 3 vols. (Glasgow, 1944–51).

Burke, W. P., *The Irish priests in penal times* (Waterford, 1914).

Burnet, Gilbert, *History of my own time*, ed. J. Routh, 6 vols. (Oxford, 1833).

Camm, Bede, *Forgotten Shrines* (London, 1910).

Cavelli, La marquise Campana da, *Les derniers Stuarts à St Germain*, 2 vols. (Paris, 1871).

Challoner, Richard, *Memoirs of Missionary Priests*, ed. J. H. Pollen (London, 1924).

Clarke, J. S. (ed), *The Life of James II*, 2 vols. (London, 1816).

Coleridge, H. J., *St Mary's Convent, York* (London, 1887).

Courson, R. de, *The Condition of English Catholics under Charles II* (London, 1899).

Crinò, Anna Maria (ed.), *Il Popish Plot nelle relazioni inedite dei residenti Granducali alla Corte di Londra* (Rome, 1954).

Davey, Frank, *John Wall* (London, 1962).

Dodd, Charles, *The Church of England chiefly with regard to Catholics*, 3 vols. (Brussels, 1737–42).

Evelyn, John, *Diary*, ed. E. S. de Beer, 6 vols, London, 1955).

Foley, Henry, *Records of the English Province of the Society of Jesus*, 7 vols. including *Collecteana* (London, 1877–83).

Gillow, Joseph, *Bibliographical Dictionary of the English Catholics*, 5 vols. (London, 1885–1902).

Grey, Anchitel, *Debates of the House of Commons*, 10 vols. (London, 1769).

Guilday, Peter, *The English Catholic Refugees on the Continent 1558–1795: Volume I: The English Colleges and Convents in the Low Countries* (London, 1914).

Haley, K. H. D., *The First Earl of Shaftesbury* (London, 1968).

Harting, J. H., *Catholic London Missions* (London, 1903).

Hatton, Correspondence of the family of, ed. E. M. Thompson, 2 vols., Camden Society (London, 1878).

Hay, M. V., *The Jesuits and the Popish Plot* (London, 1934).

Kenyon, J. P., *Robert Spencer Earl of Sunderland* (London, 1958); *The Stuart Constitution* (London, 1966).

Kitchin, George, *Sir Roger l'Estrange* (London, 1912).

Lane, Jane, *Titus Oates* (London, 1949).

Lingard, John, *History of England*, 10 vols., 6th edition (London, 1854–5).

Lovejoy, M. V., *Bl. John Kemble* (London, n.d.).

Luttrell, Narcissus, *A brief historical relation of state affairs*, 6 vols. (Oxford, 1857).

Magee, Brian, *The English Recusants: A study of the post-Reformation Catholic survival* (London, 1938).

Mathew, David, *Catholicism in England* (London, 1955).

Miller, J. L., 'The Catholic Factor in English Politics 1660–1688', Ph.D. dissertation, Cambridge, 1971.

North, Roger, *Examen: or an enquiry into the credit and veracity of a pretended complete history* ... [Kennett's] (London, 1740); *The lives of Francis North, Baron Guilford, Sir Dudley North and Dr John North*, 3 vols. (London, 1826).

O'Keeffe, Mary Margaret Cusack, 'The Popish Plot in South Wales and the Marches of Hereford and Gloucester', M.A. dissertation, University College, Galway, 1969.

Oliver, George, *Collections illustrating the history of the Catholic religion in the counties of Cornwall, Devon* ..., etc. (London, 1857).

Poems on Affairs of State, Vol. II, 1678–81, ed. E. F. Mengel (New Haven, 1965), Vol. III, 1682–5, ed. H. H. Schless (New Haven, 1968).

Pollock, John, *The Popish Plot* (London, 1903).

Quinlan, David, *Ven. Nicholas Postgate* (London, 1961).

Raine, J., *York Castle Depositions*, Surtees Soc. Pubs., Vol. xl (York, 1861).

Ralph, James, *The History of England*, 3 vols. (London, 1744–6).

Reresby, The memoirs of Sir John, ed. Andrew Browning (Glasgow, 1936).

State Tracts, 2 pts (London, 1692–3).

Thaddeus (pseud.), *The Franciscans in England 1600–1850* (London, 1898).

Treby, Sir George, *A collection of letters and other writings relating to the horrid Popish Plot* (London, 1681); *The second part of the collection of letters* ... [etc.] (London, 1681).

Warcup, The Journal of Edmund, ed. Keith Feiling, *English Historical Review*, xl (1925).

Warner, John, *The History of the English Persecution of Catholics and the Presbyterian Plot*, ed. T. A. Birrell, 2 vols., *C.R.S.*, xlvii, xlviii (1953).

Waugh, Margaret, *Bl. John Plessington* (London, 1960).

Weldon, Bennet, *Chronological notes containing the rise, growth and present state of the English congregation of the Order of St Benedict* [1709] (Stanbrook, Worcs., 1881).

Williams, J. A., *Catholic Recusancy in Wiltshire 1660–1791* (London, 1968).

Zimmerman, B., *Carmel in England: A history of the English mission of the discalced Carmelites* (London, 1899).

Notes

Chapter 1: The Catholic Problem

1 Grey, vii, 148 (27 April 1679); Marvell, in *State Tracts*, i, 70.
2 Tillotson, Sermon to House of Commons, 5 November 1678; *State Tracts*, i, 70–73.
3 Grey, vii, 149 (27 April 1679).
4 See Brian Manning, in *The English Civil War and After*, ed. R. H. Parry (London, 1970), pp. 4–6.
5 William Haller, *Foxe's Book of Martyrs* (London, 1963), *passim.*
6 Halifax's Notebook, Chatsworth MSS, *sub* 'E'; 'An Appeal from the Country to the City', qu. Kenyon, *Stuart Constitution*, p. 467.
7 *The Trial of Edward Coleman, Gent.* (London, 1678), pp. 93–4.
8 Foley, vii, 532.
9 Qu. Sr Joseph Damien, 'These be but women', in *From the Renaissance to the Counter-Reformation*, ed. Charles H. Carter (London, 1966), p. 373.
10 *C.S.P.D. 1675–6*, p. 51 (3 April 1675).
11 J. A. Williams, 'Some Sidelights on Recusancy Finance', *Dublin Review*, Autumn 1959, pp. 248–9.
12 See Rosamund Meredith, note 69 below.
13 Anstruther, *Vaux of Harrowden*, pp. 395–6, 402, 419. (See note 67 below.)
14 Kenyon, *Stuart Constitution*, p. 403.
15 *ibid.*, p. 451, *C.S.P.D. 1666–7*, p. 124 (14 September 1666).
16 *Autobiography of William Taswell* (Camden Misc. 1853), p. 11.
17 *C.S.P.D. 1666–7*, p. 110.
18 ibid., p. 127.
19 *State Tracts*, ii, 41.
20 ibid., pp. 40–41; *C.S.P.D.*, loc. cit.
21 *State Tracts*, ii, 43.
22 W. G. Bell, *The Great Fire* (London, 1920), pp. 191–5.
23 Undated memo by Sir Joseph Williamson, then Clerk to the Council, *C.S.P.D. 1666–7*, p. 175.
24 Bell, op. cit., pp. 200–201.
25 *State Tracts*, ii, 29–39 (Note that it was only eleven pages).
26 Bell, op. cit., p. 203.
27 *C.S.P.D. 1667–8*, p. 413.

28 *C.S.P.D. 1667*, p. 447; J. A. Williams, 'English Catholicism under Charles II', *Recusant History*, vii (1963), 132.

29 *C.S.P.D. 1667–8*, pp. 53, 54, 108, 110; *C.S.P.D. 1668–9*, p. 130

30 *C.S.P. Venetian 1669–70*, p. 294; Brady, pp. 119 ff.

31 *C.J.*, ix, 206.

32 ibid., 218 (13 March).

33 *C.S.P.D. 1667–8*, p. 414; *State Tracts*, ii, 63.

34 Grey, iii, 136.

35 *C.S.P.D. 1673–5*, pp. 27, 57.

36 *H.M.C. Rept IX*, ii, 42; *C.J.*, ix 303; *C.S.P.D. 1673–5*, pp. 136–7, 150–51.

37 *C.S.P. Venetian 1673–5*, pp. 257, 281, 291.

38 *C.S.P.D. 1673–5*, pp. 548–51.

39 Wi'liams, *Dublin Review, ut supra*, p. 250.

40 *C.S.P.D. 1675–6*, pp. 51, 87; Williams, loc. cit., and in *Recusant History*, vii, 134–5.

41 *Catalogue of the MSS of Alfred Morrison*, 2nd Series (London, 1893–6), ii, 247 (2 April 1675).

42 *C.T.B.*, v. 58–9.

43 Grey, iii, 136.

44 *H.M.C. Rept XI*, vii, 17. See *C.S.P.D. 1675–6*, p. 389.

45 'Verbum Sapienti', *C.S.P.D. 1673–5*, pp. 131–2.

46 Raine, pp. 222, 225; Richard Greene, *The Popish Massacre* (London, 1679); Coventry MSS (Longleat), XI, ff. 117–40; Aveling, *Northern Catholics*, p. 327.

47 *C.S.P.D. 1676–7*, p. 255.

48 See in genera', Browning, *Danby*, Vol. i, Ch. 10.

49 *C.S.P.D. 1676–7*, p. 542 (10 February 1677).

50 The bill is printed in *State Tracts*, i, 98.

51 ibid., i, 69 ff.

52 Philip Hughes, *Rome and the Counter Reformation in England* (London, 1942), p. 276.

53 Robert Bradley, 'Blacklo and the Counter Reformation', in *From the Renaissance to the Counter-Reformation, ut supra*, pp. 348 ff.

54 Hay, pp. 78–92.

55 *C.R.S.*, xxv (1925), 271, 273, 276–7; Brady, pp. 105–29 *passim*.

56 For a list of the Chapter, see W.A.(A.) 34, f. 211.

57 Summarized in Philip Hughes, op. cit., pp. 408 ff.

58 *C.R.S.*, ix (1911), p. 106.

59 26 July 1674, qu. Hay, p. 118. See Brady, p. 125.

60 *C.R.S.*, ix, loc. cit.

61 Foley, vii, pp. xcix-vi.

62 Aveling, *West Riding*, p. 191.

63 Foley, vii, 590, 619.

64 John Bossy, 'The Character of Elizabethan Catholicism', in *Crisis in Europe 1560–1660*, ed. Trevor Aston (London, 1965), p. 223.

65 Mathew, *Catholicism in England*, p. 93.

66 R. J. Stonor, *Stonor* (London, 1951).

67 G. Anstruther, *Vaux of Harrowden* (Newport, 1953).

68 Joan Wake, *The Brudenells of Deene* (London, 1954).

69 Rosamund Meredith, 'The Eyres of Hassopp 1470–1640', *Derbys. Arch. Journal*, lxxxiv (1964), 1, and lxxxv (1965), 44; 'The Eyres of Hassopp and their forfeited estates', *Recusant History*, viii (1965), 12; 'The Eyres of Hassopp from the Test Act to Emancipation', ibid., ix (1967–8), 5, 267 (2 pts).

70 Peter Roebuck, *Four Yorkshire Landowning Families 1640–1760* (Ph.D. dissertation, Hull, 1969), Ch. 3.

71 For Yorkshire, see the works listed under 'Aveling' in the bibliography; for Wiltshire, J. A. Williams, *Catholic Recusancy in Wiltshire 1660–1791* (C.R.S., 1968).

72 G.E.C., *Complete Peerage*, i, 286n.

73 *C.J.*, ix, 467a.

74 *C.R.S.*, v (1909), 76. These figures include women. The figure for Staffordshire is almost certainly too low; Cromwell's government identified 1,019 Catholics there in 1657, *Staffs Record Soc. Pubs.*, 4th Ser., ii (1958), 71.

75 *V.C.H. Oxon.*, ii, 43–5; Stonor, op. cit.

76 *V.C.H. Leics.*, ii, 67–8; *V.C.H. Wilts.*, iii, 92; Williams, *Wiltshire*, p. 149; *Staffs Record Soc., ut supra*, pp. 71, 81–2.

77 Bryan Little, *The City and County of Bristol* (London, 1967), p. 201; J. A. Williams, *Bath and Rome* (Bath, 1963), *passim*.

78 Mathew, p. 93.

79 Lords Papers, 3 December 1678.

80 *C.R.S.*, xxxviii (1941), pp. xxix ff., 2–28.

81 *C.S.P.D. 1679–80*, p. 250.

82 *H.M.C. Rept XI*, vii, 17.

83 Aveling, *West Riding*, p. 246.

84 *Complete Works*, ed. J. P. Kenyon (London, 1969), p. 84.

85 *L.J.*, xii, 556; *Parl. Hist.*, ii, 564.

Chapter 2: James and Coleman

1 Foley, i, 272n.; *H.M.C. Fitzherbert*, p. 102; Brady, p. 122.

2 Aveling, *Northern Catholics*, p. 334.

3 Qu. J. R. Jones, *The First Whigs* (London, 1961), pp. 67–8.

4 *D.N.B..*, *sub* 'Coleman'; Dodd, iii, 254; Venn, *Alumni Cantabrigienses*, i, 369; *H.M.C. Ormonde N.S.*, iv, 482–3.

5 All this is summarized in a letter to La Chaise, 29 September 1675,

Treby, pp. 109–10. See also Treby, pp. 1–4, 6, and *H.M.C. Fitzherbert*, pp. 57–8.

6 Treby, p. 111. Also Coleman to Ferrier, 29 June 1674, ibid., pp. 1–2.

7 ibid., pp. 111–12. Also Ferrier to Coleman, 15 September 1674, ibid., p. 6; Coleman to Ferrier, September 1674, ibid., pp. 3–4.

8 In date order: *H.M.C. Fitzherbert*, p. 105; Treby, p. 6; Treby, pt 2, p. 4; Treby, pp. 21, 7–8; *H.M.C. Fitzherbert*, p. 106; Treby, pp. 9–10, 28, 11–12, 22; Treby, pt 2, pp. 4–6; Treby, pp. 23, 12–13, 24. Also an undated letter in *H.M.C. Fitzherbert*, pp. 57–8, to which Treby (p. 65) assigns the incorrect date 15 December.

9 Treby, pp. 3–4, 112.

10 28 November 1674, *H.M.C. Fitzherbert*, p. 50; 1 December, Treby, p. 57; 1 February 1675, Treby, pt 2, pp. 1–2.

11 6 February 1675, Treby, p. 70.

12 ibid., pp. 75–6 (20 February 1675).

13 Coleman to Internuncio, 30 August 1675, Treby, p. 17; F. A. M. Mignet, *Négociations relatives à la succession d'Espagne* (Paris, 1835–42), iv, 365.

14 Treby, p. 53; Mignet, op. cit., iv, 367–70.

15 Treby, pp. 109–19.

16 *H.M.C. Fitzherbert*, p. 111 (11/21 December 1675); Treby, p. 72 (9/19 February 1676).

17 *H.M.C. Fitzherbert*, p. 83 (18 April 1676); Treby, pt 2, p. 16 (6/16 May).

18 *H.M.C. Fitzherbert*, pp. 87, 88 (15/25 June, 21 June/1 July 1676).

19 ibid., p. 89 (24 June/1 July), p. 95 (4/15 November).

20 Coventry MSS (Longleat), XI, ff. 245–6.

21 ibid., ff. 247–8.

22 ibid., f. 247.

23 *H.M.C. Ormonde N.S.*, iv, 485–6; North, *Lives*, i, 298; North, *Examen*, pp. 133–4.

24 Pollock, pp. 51 ff.

25 Coventry MSS (Longleat), XI, ff. 245, 246.

26 Treby, pp. 78–97.

27 ibid., p. 60.

28 ibid., p. 76.

29 ibid., p. 116.

30 *H.M.C. Fitzherbert*, p. 107; Treby, pp. 50, 82–3.

31 Pollock, pp. 61 ff.

32 Treby, pp. 98 ff.

33 *L.P.*, pp. 4, 8–9; *H.M.C. Fitzherbert*, p. 93.

34 Arthur Bryant, *Samuel Pepys: Years of Peril* (London, 1935), pp. 203–9, 275. cf. Pollock, pp. 61–4, 376–7.

35 *L.P.*, p. 44.

36 Rawl. A. 136, ff. 116, 119 (21 January 1679).

37 Kenyon, *Stuart Constitution*, pp. 396, 413, 419.
38 *H.M.C. Ormonde N.S.*, iv, 462 (Southwell, 26 October 1678); Evelyn, *Diary*, iv, 154.
39 *C.J.*, ix, 466–71.
40 Cobbett's *Parliamentary History*, iv, 990.
41 ibid., App., pp. xxi–ii.
42 Richard Greene, *The Popish Massacre, as it was discovered to the Honourable House of Commons in the month of June 1678* (London, 1679).
43 Warner, i, 194–5; Courson, pp. 77–8.
44 Rawl. A. 136, ff. 125–30; *S.T.*, x, 1263–80.

Chapter 3 : Titus Oates

1 Simpson Tonge's narrative, S.P.29/409, preface.
2 See Greene, *Popish Massacre, ut supra*.
3 Foley, vii, 54.
4 Warner, ii, 415. cf. North, *Examen*, p. 225.
5 *Vindication of the English Catholics* (1681), qu. Lane, p. 65.
6 Greene, ut supra.
7 S.P. 29/409, f. 29.
8 Warner, i, 196.
9 Burnet, ii, 149.
10 Coventry MSS (Longleat), XI, ff. 19–49.
11 ibid., ff. 183, 191–202.
12 J. G. Muddiman, *The King's Journalist* (London, 1923), p. 208; J. B. Williams, 'The Genesis of Oates's Plot', *The Month* (1912); W. C. Abbott, 'The Origins of Titus Oates's Story', *English Historical Review*, xxv (1910), 126.
13 cf. S.P.29/409, f. 55, and Oates's evidence, art. 44.
14 Ralph, i, 384n.
15 Lane, p. 85.
16 P.C.2/66, 392 (27 September).
17 S.P.29/409, f. 112.
18 ibid., ff. 135–40.
19 ibid., f. 145.
20 Burnet, ii, 147–8.
21 S.P.29/409, f. 152; *C.S.P.D. 1678*, p. 425.
22 P.C.2/66, 392.
23 Ralph, i, 385.
24 *H.M.C. Ormonde N.S.*, iv, 455.
25 Clarke, ii, 517–18.
26 P.C.2/66, 396, 400.
27 *C.S.P.D. 1678*, p. 427.
28 Add. 38015, f. 278.

29 ibid., and P.C.2/66, 396.
30 *C.S.P.D. 1678*, pp. 431–2; Clarke, ii, 520–21.
31 P.C.2/66, 396.
32 ibid., 398 ff.
33 *L.J.*, xiii, 307.
34 Add. 38015, f. 283; P.C.2/66, 404.
35 *H.M.C. Ormonde N.S.*, v, 457; Barillon, 10 October (NS), P.R.O. 31/3/141, 574–5.
36 *H.M.C. Ormonde N.S.*, iv, 207; Barillon, ibid.
37 Burnet, ii, 153; Evelyn, *Diary*, iv, 154.
38 *H.M.C. Ormonde N.S.*, iv, 207.
39 Finch MSS (Leicestershire Record Office), box 56.
40 P.C.2/66, 421; *H.M.C. Ormonde N.S.*, v, 458; Add. 25124, f. 155.
41 Finch MSS, *ut supra*.
42 *H.M.C. Ormonde N.S.*, v, 459; Rawl. A. 136, f. 299.
43 P.C.2/66, 427–8.

Chapter 4: Godfrey's Autumn

1 Grey, vi, 295 (28 November).
2 *C.S.P.D. 1678*, pp. 464, 466.
3 For example: *H.M.C. Ormonde N.S.*, iv, 206–7 (1 October); *H.M.C. Le Fleming*, p. 148 (5 October); *C.S.P.D. 1678*, p. 453 (9 October).
4 ibid., p. 462.
5 *L.J.*, xiii, 294–5; *C.J.*, ix, 516.
6 *H.M.C. Ormonde N.S.*, iv, 461
7 *C.J.*, ix, 517–18; North, *Examen*, p. 206.
8 *C.J.*, ix, 519; *C.S.P.D. 1678*, p. 480.
9 ibid., pp. 511–12, 517.
10 *L.J.*, xiii, 299, 301.
11 ibid., pp. 335, 346; *L.P.*, pp. 16–17, 18; *C.J.*, ix, 531. The information on the militia I owe to Mr D. F. Allen.
12 *L.J.*, xiii, 311.
13 *C.J.*, ix, 530, 531.
14 *L.J.*, xiii, 308.
15 North, *Examen*, pp. 177–8.
16 *C.S.P.D. 1678*, p. 615; *H.M.C. Ormonde N.S.*, iv, 244–5.
17 *L.P.*, pp. 3–16 (esp. 5–6, 15); *L.J.*, xiii, 354; *H.M.C. Ormonde N.S.*, iv, 465; Coventry MSS (Longleat), XI, f. 263.
18 *C.J.*, ix, 534 (7 November).
19 29 September 1675, Treby, p. 116.
20 ibid., pp. 119–20; Treby, pt 2, pp. 18–19; *H.M.C. Ormonde, ut supra*; *C.J.*, ix, 523 (30 October).
21 *L.J.*, xiii, 307–8.
22 Treby, pp. 7, 76; Treby, pt 2, p. 5; *H.M.C. Fitzherbert*, p. 56.

23 Treby, pp. 78–97 *passim*. cf. Grey, vii, 141, 142, 152 (27 April 1679), 236 ff. (11 May).

24 Treby, p. 8; *C.J.*, ix, 523 (30 October).

25 Treby, pp. 117–18.

26 ibid., p. 116; *L.P.*, p. 11.

27 *L.J.*, xiii, 309.

28 Haley, pp. 471–2.

29 Grey, vi, 142, 144.

30 *C.J.*, ix, 536.

31 *H.M.C. Ormonde N.S.*, iv, 467, 470, 473.

32 *L.J.*, xiii, 340; *H.M.C. Ormonde N.S.*, iv, 473; Burnet, ii, 272. cf. Grey, vi, 188.

33 *H.M.C. Ormonde N.S.* iv, 470; *C.J.*, ix, 539, 540; *C.S.P.D. 1678*, p. 529; Grey, vi, 206, 209; Burnet, ii, 168.

34 Grey, vi, 240–53.

35 *L.J.*, xiii, 310 (31 October).

36 *Autobiography of Sir John Bramston* (London, 1845), p. 194. cf. Warner, i, 214–15.

37 *L.J.*, xiii, 350–53.

38 *H.M.C. Beaufort*, pp. 71, 72.

39 *H.M.C. Ormonde N.S.*, iv, 470.

40 *L.J.*, xiii, 356–7, 362, 364; *C.S.P.D. 1678*, pp. 540–41; Warner, i, 205.

41 Add. 32059, ff. 47–8 (North Papers).

42 *L.P.*, p. 64; *L.J.*, xiii, 370; *C.S.P.D. 1678*, pp. 482, 514, 516, 518; *H.M.C. Ormonde N.S.*, iv, 473; *H.M.C. Beaufort*, p. 72.

43 *C.S.P.D. 1678*, pp. 475, 480, cf. *L.P.*, pp. 54–5, 56.

44 *S.T.*, vi, 1501–12.

45 *L.P.*, pp. 21–2; P.C.2/66, 432.

46 *H.M.C. Beaufort*, pp. 71, 73 (12, 23 November).

47 *L.P.*, p. 20; Coventry MSS (Longleat), XI, f. 299.

48 *C.S.P.D. 1678*, pp. 463, 521; P.C.2/66, 442, 446, 447, 449.

49 P.C.2/66, 443; *C.S.P.D. 1678*, pp. 517, 541–3; *L.J.*, xiii, 357, 377, 378; Grey, vi, 212–13; *H.M.C. Ormonde N.S.*, iv, 485; Coventry MSS (Longleat), XI, f. 295.

50 Grey, vi, 192, 204, 213, 243; *H.M.C. Ormonde N.S.*, iv, 474.

51 *L.J.*, xiii, 354; *C.J.*, ix, 541.

52 Grey, vi, 167; P.C.2/66, 443; *C.S.P.D. 1678*, pp. 511, 512, 518.

53 Grey, vi, 225–7; *H.M.C. Ormonde N.S.*, iv, 475–7.

54 ibid., 478–9. cf. Grey, vi, 262–8.

55 *C.S.P.D. 1678*, p. 523.

56 Grey, vi, 268, 274, 300–301.

57 *C.S.P.D. 1678*, pp. 525, 547, 550, 615–21 *passim*; Clarke, i, 523.

58 *L.P.*, p. 64. For the proclamation see *London Gazette*, 18/21 November.

59 *C.J.*, ix, 552; *L.J.*, xiii, 405.

60 P.C.2/66, 469, 470.
61 *L.J.*, xiii, 398, 404; *H.M.C. Beaufort*, pp. 72, 75, 81; P.C.2/66, 505.
62 O'Keeffe, p. 69.
63 Bryant, *Pepys: Years of Peril*, pp. 235–8.
64 *L.J.*, xiii, 396: D.W.L.: E.B./1., 191.
65 Rawl A. 136, ff. 456, 569–70; *C.S.P.D. 1678*, p. 569; *H.M.C. Beaufort*, p. 77; Luttrell, i, 5.
66 *C.S.P.D. 1678*, pp. 562–3 (9 December).
67 *H.M.C. Le Fleming*, p. 154; P.C.2/66, 446 (15 November).
68 *C.S.P.D. 1678*, p. 583.
69 *H.M.C. Beaufort*, p. 76. cf. Coventry MSS (Longleat), XI, f. 291.
70 Burnet, ii, 171. cf. Haley, pp. 462–7, 483–4.
71 *L.J.*, xiii, 310–11.
72 *C.S.P.D. 1678*, p. 519.
73 *H.M.C. Ormonde N.S.*, iv, 481; Clarke, i, 529.
74 Rawl. A. 136, ff. 212–18 (has some details missing from *L.J.*, xiii, 390).
75 *L.J.*, loc. cit.
76 Burnet, ii, 173; *H.M.C. Ormonde N.S.*, iv, 481; North, *Examen*, p. 186.
77 *C.J.*, ix, 547; *Grey*, vi, 274 ff.; *H.M.C. Ormonde*, loc. cit.
78 *L.J.*, xiii, 391–2.
79 *C.S.P.D. 1678*, p. 550; *H.M.C. Ormonde N.S.*, iv, 484.
80 ibid., 483–4; *Grey*, vi, 287–300; *C.J.*, ix, 549.
81 *L.J.*, xiii, 388–92; *L.P.*, p. 66; *H.M.C. Beaufort*, p. 74; Ralph, i, 398; *H.M.C. Ormonde*, loc. cit.
82 *H.M.C. Ormonde N.S.*, iv, 486–7; *C.J.*, ix, 551; *Grey*, vi, 298, 314–15.
83 Luttrell, i, 4; Burnet, ii, 170–71.
84 Pollock, pt iv; Sir James Stephen, *History of the Criminal Law* (1883), i, Ch. xi.
85 *Political Testament*, ed. Henry B. Hill (Madison, 1961), p. 89.
86 See J. P. Kenyon, 'The Acquittal of Sir George Wakeman', *Historical Journal*, xiv (1971), 693.
87 North, *Examen*, pp. 206, 507–8.
88 I have used the contemporary trial record, published in December 1678, and I have not provided detailed page references.
89 *London Gazette*, 30 December 1678 (No. 1368).
90 *H.M.C. Rept IV*, p. 243 (1/11 February 1679); Warner, i, 221–2.
91 *S.T.*, vii, 79 ff.
92 *L.J.*, xiii, 394; *H.M.C. Ormonde N.S.*, iv, 486.
93 *C.J.*, ix, 551; *Grey*, vi, 308–11.
94 Rawl. A. 136, ff. 1–2, 439.
95 *Grey*, vi, 349.
96 Browning, ii, 75.

97 *L.J.*, xiii, 441; *L.P.*, p. 85.
98 Grey, vi, 400.

Chapter 5 : The High Tide of the Plot

1 Ralph, i, 480 ff.; *L.J.*, xiii, 431, 436–9; *L.P.*, pp. 51–2; *S.T.*, vii, 183, 191.
2 Pollock, pp. 139 ff.
3 P.C.2/66, 503; *H.M.C. Ormonde N.S.*, iv, 494.
4 ibid., 492, 495; *C.S.P.D. 1679–80*, p. 68.
5 *H.M.C. Ormonde N.S.*, iv, 495; *S.T.*, x, 1264.
6 S.P.29/336, 719 (partly transcribed *C.S.P.D. 1679–80*, pp. 6–8).
7 Salvetti, 20 January (N.S.), Crinò, p. 58; Barillon, 5 January (N.S.), P.R.O. 31/3/142; *H.M.C. Ormonde N.S.*, iv, 295; *C.S.P.D. 1679–80*, pp. 15, 21, 22, 24.
8 Rawl. A. 136, ff. 1–2, 81.
9 Kitchin, p. 324; *C.S.P.D. 1679–80*, pp. 76–7, 83; P.C.2/67, 15; Rawl. A. 136, ff. 17–18, 132–3.
10 Rawl. A. 136, ff. 176, 507.
11 ibid., ff. 13, 295; *L.J.*, xii, 442.
12 Burnet, ii, 183–4.
13 Almost all his depositions are printed in *H.M.C. Fitzherbert*, pp. 118–38.
14 S.P.29/366, 743–4; *C.S.P.D. 1679–80*, p. 13; Rawl. A. 136, f. 29; Rawl. A. 135, f. 411; P.C.2/67, 15; *H.M.C. Fitzherbert*, pp. 119–22.
15 Rawl. A. 136, ff. 49, 116, 119; *C.S.P.D. 1679–80*, pp. 27–8, 44; Grey, vii, 57.
16 Foley, v, 41.
17 *C.S.P.D. 1679–80*, p. 41.
18 Rawl. A. 135, ff. 127–9, 172–7; Foley, v, 862–3.
19 *H.M.C. Fitzherbert*, p. 122; *C.S.P.D. 1679–80*, p. 44.
20 P.C.2/67, 61.
21 *H.M.C. Fitzherbert*, p. 122; *C.S.P.D. 1679–80*, p. 54.
22 Foley, v, 49, 434–5.
23 *C.S.P.D. 1679–80*, p. 52; Foley, vi, 40.
24 *Hatton Corr.*, i, 173–4; *S.T.*, vii, 159 ff.
25 ibid., 231–2.
26 *C.S.P.D. 1679–80*, p. 81.
27 Rawl. A. 136, f. 185.
28 *H.M.C. Fitzherbert*, pp. 145–6.
29 ibid., p. 133.
30 ibid., pp. 134, 135–6.
31 Rawl. A. 136, ff. 16–18; *C.S.P.D. 1679–80*, pp. 10–11; Foley, vi, 36–7; *L.J.*, xiii, 558, 559.
32 *C.S.P.D. 1679–80*, p 77.

33 *H.M.C. Ormonde N.S.*, iv, 340 (1 March). For the figures, see J. R. Jones, *The First Whigs* (London, 1961), p. 71, and 'Shaftesbury's Worthy Men', *Bulletin Institute Historical Research*, xxx (1957), 232.

34 Shaftesbury Papers, P.R.O. 30/24/6A, 334.

35 *H.M.C. Ormonde N.S.*, v, 69, 91; *Hatton Corr.*, i, 171; Evelyn, *Diary*, iv, 161; Salvetti, 3 March (N.S.), Crinò, p. 63.

36 *S.T.*, vi, 1429–34; *C.J.*, ix, 573, 576.

37 Grey, vii, 10, 63; *H.M.C. Ormonde N.S.*, v, 55 (22 April).

38 ibid., pp. 31–2; *S.T.*, vii, 271–2.

39 Grey, vii, 14 (21 March).

40 Warner, i, 302; *L.P.*, p. 105; *C.J.*, ix, 571; *L.J.* xiii, 534.

41 *C.J.*, ix, 605, 606, 612; *H.M.C. Ormonde N.S.*, v, 33, 36.

42 *L.P.*, p. 145; *H.M.C. Ormonde N.S.*, v, 68–9.

43 Browning, i, 325–9.

44 *H.M.C. Fitzherbert*, pp. 135–7.

45 *C.J.*, ix, 605; Grey, vii, 141, 147.

46 *C.J.*, ix, 607; Grey, vii, 159; *H.M.C. Ormonde N.S.*, v. 74. See Jones, *First Whigs*, p. 65.

47 Grey, vii, 215 (9 May).

48 *L.J.*, xiii, 595; *H.M.C. Ormonde N.S.*, iv, p. xx; ibid., v, 103, 116. See in general, Haley, pp. 522–5.

49 2 June (N.S.), Crinò, p. 72.

50 D.W.L.: E.B.1/196.

51 For the trial, see *S.T.*, vii, 311 ff.

52 *H.M.C. Fitzherbert*, p. 149 (28 April); Luttrell, i, 11; Foley, v, 342, vi, 66–7.

53 Warner, i, 263; Foley, v, 44 ff.; Hugh Bowler, 'The Caryll Letter', *The Month*, clxi (1933), 265 ff. For the means by which Oates secured his witnesses, see Lane, pp. 52–4, 180–81.

54 Warner, i, 262. cf. *S.T.*, vii, 377–90.

55 *S.T.*, vii, 431 ff.

56 Sir William Temple, *Memoirs Part III* (London, 1709), pp. 48–9; Foley, v, 93–4; Salvetti, 26 June (N.S.), Crinò, p. 77; Barillon, 5 January (N.S.), 26 June (N.S.), P.R.O. 31/3/142.

57 P.C.2/68, 75, 173; Barillon, 12 June (N.S.), *ut supra; H.M.C. Ormonde N.S.*, v, 110.

58 *S.T.*, vii, 580 ff.; Warner, ii, 484.

59 *H.M.C. Ormonde N.S.*, iv, 526.

60 ibid., p. 527; Rawl. A. 135, f. 424, A. 136, ff. 237–40, 359–65.

61 For a thorough examination of this subject, see my article in *Historical Journal*, xiv (1971).

62 Kenyon, *Sunderland*, pp. 27–9.

63 *S.T.*, vii, 595 ff.

64 Foley, v, 614-16.

65 Quoted in *Historical Journal, ut supra*, p. 705.

Chapter 6: The Tide Ebbs

1 *Poems on Affairs of State*, ii, 290–91; Ralph, i, 407n.; D.W.L.: E.B.1/302, 304; Luttrell, i, 15; Evelyn, *Diary*, iv, 169; Crinò, pp. 82–5.

2 *H.M.C. Le Fleming*, p. 162; Luttrell, i, 19–20; *C.S.P.D. 1679–80*, p. 214.

3 Warner, i, 306–7.

4 O'Keeffe, p. 130; Grey, ix, 308 (14 June 1689). The time-table of the assizes is in *London Gazette*, no. 1422.

5 Foley, v, 919.

6 Lovejoy, p. 15.

7 *S.T.*, vii, 715.

8 Warner, i, 308; *S.T.*, vii, 715, 725 ff.

9 Foley, v, 450–52, vi, 21–2.

10 Thaddeus, pp. 70–71, 310: Davey, *passim*; Warner, i, 292.

11 Raine, pp. 230 ff.; Foley, v, 757 ff.; Quinlan, *passim*.

12 Waugh, *passim*; Warner, i, 295–7; Foley, v, 882–9.

13 *C.J.*, ix, 541; Thaddeus, pp. 71–2; *L.J.*, xiii, 585, *English Reports*, 83:197.

14 Warner, ii, 416–17.

15 ibid., i, 270.

16 *The Month*, clxi (1933), 270.

17 Lovejoy, p. 16; Davey, p. 16.

18 Burnet, ii, 196–7.

19 Evelyn, *Diary*, iv, 174–6.

20 Crinò, pp. 81–22, 86.

21 Burnet, ii, 215–16.

22 *H.M.C. Le Fleming*, p. 163. For a general review of events, see Kenyon, *Sunderland*, pp. 32 ff.

23 *Hatton Corr.*, i, 215; Crinò, p. 88 (Salvetti, 12/22 September).

24 *H.M.C. Ormonde N.S.*, iv, 546.

25 *Hatton Corr.*, i, 196.

26 *S.T.*, vii, 702–3.

27 *Hatton Corr.*, i, 199.

28 ibid., pp. 207–10; *C.S.P.D. 1679–80*, p. 296; Luttrell, i, 29; D.W.L.: E.B.1/240.

29 *S.T.*, viii, 172–4; P.C.2/68, 359; *C.S.P.D. 1679–80*, p. 376.

30 J. E. Neale, 'November 17th', in *Essays in Elizabethan History* (London, 1958), p. 15.

31 Sheila Williams, *Jnl Warburg & Courtauld Institutes*, xxi (1958), 104, and O. W. Furley, *History*, xliv (1959), 16. These articles overlap, and both are regrettably slight.

32 Haley, p. 454.

33 *Examen*, p. 578.

34 Warner, i, 314; Burnet, ii, 240.

35 Warcup's Journal, p. 245.

36 Warner, i, 314; *D.N.B.*, xiv, 16.

37 D.W.L.: E.B.1/237; *Hatton Corr.*, i, 203; Coventry MSS (Longleat), XI, f. 443; Crinò, pp. 62, 64, 114; *Poems on Affairs of State*, iii, 310–11.

38 Pollock, pp. 394–9.

39 Rawl. A. 135, f. 526; *The Pythouse Papers* (London, 1879), p. 75; D.W.L.: E.B.1/212, 227, 228, 237, 249.

40 Rawl. A. 136, ff. 262–70; D.W.L.: E.B.1/236–7; *S.T.*, vii, 763 ff.

41 D.W.L.: E.B.1/256–60 *passim*; Ralph, i, 507; *English Reports*, 83:218.

42 Warner, ii 324n.

43 ibid., ii, 325n.

44 *S.T.*, vii, 811 ff. Also, *A Brief Account of the Proceedings against the Six Popish Priests*, B.M. T3*(89).

45 23 Eliz.c.1 (sect. III). See G. R. Elton, *The Tudor Constitution* (London, 1960), p. 423.

46 *S.T.*, vii, 839.

47 ibid., 875.

48 ibid., 882.

49 Rawl. A. 136, ff. 91–2.

50 Warner, ii, 325n.; Thaddeus, p. 76; *C.S.P.D. January–June 1683*, p. 159.

51 Terriesi, 13 May (N.S.), Crinò, p. 114; *Downside Review*, July 1933, pp. 464 ff.

52 *H.M.C. Fitzherbert*, pp. 141–5.

53 *C.S.P.D.* 1679–80, p. 426.

54 *S.T.*, vii, 959 ff. (cf. ibid, 1041); *English Reports*, 83:191.

55 *S.T.*, vii, 1179.

56 Warner, ii, 427; Dodd, iii, 252–4; *S.T.*, vii, 1162 ff.

57 *S.T.*, viii, 501 ff. (cf. ibid., 524).

58 Aveling, *West Riding*, pp. 235–6; *C.S.P.D. 1679–80*, p. 391; Raine, p. 242; P.C.2/68, 234; Reresby, p. 198; Courson, p. 190; Coleridge, Ch. 2. Also Agnes Stewart, *Sir Thomas Gascoigne* (London, 1880), *passim*.

59 *S.T.*, vii, 1053.

60 ibid., 1078.

61 ibid., 1109–11.

62 Kitchin, Ch. viii; *C.S.P.D. 1680*, pp. 597, 628–9, L.P., pp. 246 ff.

63 Luttrell, i, 45.

64 *The Information of Stephen Dugdale, Gent.*, 1 November 1680; *The Information of Thomas Dangerfield, Gent*, 20 October 1680.

65 North, *Examen*, p. 217.

66 Burnet, ii, 262–3; Stafford's deposition, 21 January 1679, Rawl. A. 136, f. 116.

67 *S.T.*, vii, 1310–33.

68 ibid., 1341 ff.; Evelyn, *Diary*, iv, 230.

69 *S.T.*, vii, 1347 ff.

70 ibid., 1351 ff. (cf. ibid., 1425 ff.).

71 ibid., 1398–9.

72 Evelyn, *Diary*, iv, 230–31.

73 Burnet, ii, 268; North, *Lives*, i, 328.

74 Burnet, ii, 263.

75 *H.M.C. Ormonde N.S.*, v, 302 (12 April 1680). cf. W. P. Burke, *passim*.

76 *S.T.*, viii, 447 ff.

77 ibid., 488.

78 Barillon, 10 July (N.S.), P.R.O. 31/3/149: Burnet, ii, 286–7; Terriesi, 7 July (N.S.), Crinò, p. 199.

Chapter 7: The Effects of the Plot

1 This examination of the Society of Jesus is principally based on Foley's *Records*.

2 Warner, i, 203.

3 ibid., 214; Coventry MSS (Longleat), XI, f. 483; *L.J.*, xiii, 367; Crinò, p. 51.

4 Rawl. A. 136, ff. 283–9; Warner, i, 258.

5 Foley, vii, 70.

6 Cambridge University Library, MS.Ll.i.19, f. 24. Also Warner, i, pp. xii–xiii.

7 Rawl. A. 135, f. 357.

8 Warner, ii, 451. cf. Foley, v, 319.

9 O'Keeffe, pp. 27–9; Foley, iv, 462 ff.; Rawl. A. 136, ff. 7, 13, 501–3; P.C.2/67, 116.

10 Foley, v, 479, 486; *L.J.*, xiii, 484, 486; Rawl. A. 135, ff. 172–6.

11 Margaret and Agnes Blundell, *St Winifred and her Holy Well* (London, 1954), *passim*; Waugh, pp. 6–7; *S.T.*, x, 1250–54; Foley, iv, 528 ff.

12 Zimmerman, pp. 342, 358–61, 364–5.

13 Thaddeus, pp. 56–8, 100, 101–3, 193.

14 ibid., 169–70.

15 Guilday, p. 249; *Downside Review*, xvii (1898), 279 ff

16 Guilday, pp. 28–9, 31–2.

17 ibid., pp. 33n., 52–3, 226n.

18 Warner, i, 234.

19 Rawl. A. 136, ff. 192, 444, 446.

20 ibid., f. 16.
21 *L.J.*, xiii, 357, 359, 360; C. F. R. Palmer, *Cardinal Howard* (London, 1867), pp. 185–6.
22 *C.T.B.*, v, 587.
23 In her M.A. dissertation; see 'List of Works Cited', p. 315 above. See also A. H. Dodd, *Studies in Stuart Wales* (Cardiff, 1952), pp. 201 ff.
24 O'Keeffe, pp. 89–90, 95.
25 Raine, p. 232.
26 John Morgan. See P.C.2/68, 98.
27 Warner, ii, 378n., 482; Akerman, p. 44.
28 Grey, vii, 150; Rawl. A. 136, ff. 138–9.
29 Crinò, p. 118; Rawl. A. 135, ff. 174–7.
30 *Downside Review, ut supra,* and July 1933, pp. 453 ff. Also *The Month,* clxi (1933), 265.
31 Rawl. A. 135, f. 353; Crinò, p. 98.
32 Warner, i, 81, ii, 527 ff.
33 W. A. (A.) 34, ff. 819–41.
34 ibid., f. 705; Hay, p. 69. See T. A. Birrell's note to Warner, i, 81.
35 Davey, p. 6.
36 Rawl. A. 136, ff. 463–4.
37 ibid., ff. 8, 9, 12, 47; Rawl. A. 135, f. 494.
38 Rawl. A. 136, ff. 80, 90.
39 *C.S.P.D. 1679–80*, pp. 35–6.
40 Rawl. A. 136, ff. 59–60, 77–80, 72; Zimmerman, p. 324; Salvetti, 20 January (N.S.), Crinò, p. 58.
41 Zimmerman, pp. 338, 343, 346, 357; Barillon, 22 April (N.S.) 1680, Cavelli, i, 319.
42 Zimmerman, pp. 157–60, 225, 231, 316–17, 322; Coleridge, Ch. 3; Lane, p. 359.
43 *S.T.*, vii, 860.
44 ibid., 135, 138–9.
45 Rawl. A. 135, f. 1; Add. 47840, ff. 14–53; *L.J.*, xiii, 568.
46 D.W.L.: E.B.1/197, 206–7, 259, 261, 262; Terriesi, 1 July (N.S.), Crinò, p. 120. *The Complete Peerage* states that he was imprisoned until 1686, but this is impossible; he gave evidence against Oates in May 1685 and later that year was granted an army commission. His name disappears from the Tower bills in September 1680; *C.R.S.*, iv (1907), 245.
47 *L.J.*, xiii, 493, 530; MS. Minute Book of the Committee of Privileges 1664–85 (Lords MSS), p. 158; *English Reports*, 83:546; *C.S.P.D. 1679–80*, p. 143.
48 Blundell, p. 208; *S.T.*, vii, 1398–9.
49 This and what follows is taken from the lists in *C.S.P.D. 1678*, pp.

615–21, and *C.S.P.D. 1679–80*, pp. 326–9. I am grateful to Mr J. A. Williams for confirming my tentative identification of these families as Catholic.

50 *C.S.P.D. 1679–80*, p. 3, gives a pass to Henry Nevill of Holt which is not listed at the end of the volume. When Parliament met in March many members of noble families were given passes by the Lords.

51 P.C.2/67, 16; *L.J.*, xiii, 480.

52 *C.S.P.D. 1679–80*, p. 82; P.C.2/67, 47.

53 Aveling, *Northern Catholics*, p. 330.

54 P.C.2/67, 58; Rawl. A. 136, ff. 144, 163, 164.

55 Rawl. A. 136, ff. 497–8; O'Keeffe, pp. 155, 161; *L.P.*, pp. 207–9, 229–30, *L.J.*, xiii, 675, 681; P.C.2/67, 112.

56 Rawl. A. 136, ff. 131, 478; *C.J.*, ix, 576; Blundell, pp. 187–8.

57 P.C.2/68, 47; Rawl. A. 136, f. 144.

58 *H.M.C. Kenyon*, pp. 112–13; *C.S.P.D. 1679–80*, pp. 114–15.

59 *H.M.C. Le Fleming*, p. 154.

60 W. A. (A.) 34, ff. 784–5 (3 July 1683).

61 Foley, v, 81n.; Rawl. A. 135, f. 353.

62 Qu. Hay, p. 51.

63 Warner, i, 230 ff., ii, 527 ff.

64 ibid., i, 73n., 224–6; W. A. (A.) 34, ff. 513–636, 651–4, 709–18, 751, 783–6; Add. 47840, f. 55; Dodd, iii, 383–7; Hay, pp. 140 ff.

65 Foley, v, 80–81nn.

66 Hay, Ch. iv, *passim*.

67 Dodd, iii, 386; Warner, 15 September (N.S.) 1679, Vatican Sega de Stato 20, ff. 44–5 (Mount St photocopy).

68 T. A. Birrell, *Catholic Allegiance and the Popish Plot* (Nijmegen, 1950), pp. 6–7, 11; Warner, ii, 226; Dodd, iii, 386.

69 W. A. (A.) 34, f. 585.

70 Aveling, *Northern Catholics*, p. 329.

71 *Catholicism in England*, p. 128.

72 *H.M.C. Ormonde N.S.*, v, 31, 66–7, 75; *L.P.*, pp. 63, 105.

73 Grey, vii, 241; *H.M.C. Ormonde N.S.*, v, 89; *L.P.*, p. 222.

74 P.C.2/68, 327 ff.; *H.M.C. Ormonde N.S.*, v, 252–3, 282–3.

75 *C.T.B.*, v, 426, 442, 470, 502.

76 *H.M.C. Ormonde N.S.*, v, 306; *H.M.C. Le Fleming*, p. 165; Terriesi, 1 July (N.S.), Crinò, p. 120.

77 *C.T.B.*, v, 529–30, 553–4, 601–3.

78 Williams, *Wiltshire*, p. 30.

79 *H.M.C. Kenyon*, pp. 114, 117–22; *H.M.C. Le Fleming*, pp. 167, 171–3.

80 *L.P.*, p. 102; *L.J.*, xiii, 485.

81 Raine, pp. 238–9.

82 ibid., pp. 269–72.
83 North, *Lives*, i, 309 ff.; Barillon, 16 October (N.S.) 1684, P.R.O. 31/3/159.
84 J. A. Williams, 'English Catholicism under Charles II', *Recusant History*, vii (1963–4), 123 ff.; J. L. Miller, 'The Catholic Factor in English Politics 1660–1688', Cambridge Ph.D. dissertation, 1971, appendixes I–II.
85 Rosamund Meredith, *Recusant History*, ix (1967–8), 9 ff.
86 ibid., p. 9.
87 *H.M.C. Kenyon*, p. 152.
88 Peter Roebuck, 'Four Yorkshire Landowning Families 1640–1760', Hull Ph.D. dissertation, 1970, pp. 261 ff.
89 *C.T.B.*, vii, 382 (27 January 1682); Courson, pp. 184, 187; M. de Trenqualéon, *West Grinstead et les Carylls* (Paris, 1893), i, 449, ii, 420; Blundell, pp. 186–7, 209, 210, 214, 222.
90 *C.S.P.D. 1684–5*, p. 287.
91 *C.S.P.D. 1685*, pp. 52–3; *C.T.B.*, viii, 176.
92 W. L. Sachse, 'The Mob in the Revolution of 1688', *Journal of British Studies*, iv (1964), 23 ff. (Rather slight, but all there is.)
93 Neil J. Smelser, *Theory of Collective Behaviour* (London, 1962), esp. Ch. vi, 'The Panic', and Ch. viii, 'The Hostile Outburst'.
94 Qu. ibid., p. 12.
95 ibid., pp. 132–3.
96 Burnet, ii, 269.

Chapter 8: The Reckoning

1 *S.T.*, viii, 640, 641, 701, 702.
2 Unless otherwise stated, what follows is based on Akerman and *C.T.B.*
3 *C.T.B.*, vii, 572–3.
4 Burnet, ii, 298–300.
5 *C.T.B.*, vii, 786–7.
6 *S.T.*, x, 126 ff.
7 *C.S.P.D. 1684–5*, pp. 118, 210–11, 230–31, 251, 293, 294; Luttrell, i, 326; Kitchin, p. 346.
8 *C.S.P.D. 1685*, p. 8.
9 *S.T.*, x, 1136–7.
10 ibid., 1162, 1165, 1166, 1167.
11 ibid., 1168.
12 loc. cit.
13 ibid., 1169.
14 ibid., 1209–10.
15 ibid., 1212, 1214–15.
16 ibid., 1192–3, 1213.

17 ibid., 1105.
18 ibid., 1114.
19 ibid., 1154.
20 ibid., 1153.
21 ibid., 1157.
22 ibid., 1158.
23 ibid., 1177.
24 ibid., 1193.
25 ibid., 1212.
26 ibid., 1181.
27 ibid., 1243–81.
28 ibid., 1257.
29 ibid., 1262.
30 ibid., 1282–91.
31 ibid., 1290–91.
32 ibid., 1298–9.
33 ibid., 1299–1300.
34 ibid., 1309.
35 ibid., 1315.
36 ibid., 1316–17.
37 *C.S.P.D. 1684–5*, pp. 156, 157.
38 *S.T.*, vii, 228–9; Pollock, pp. 163–4.
39 Reresby, p. 365.
40 *L.P.*, pp. 292–3; *L.J.*, xiv, 30; *S.T.*, vii, 1552–3.
41 *L.P.*, loc. cit.; Barillon, 16 July (N.S.), in Charles James Fox, *History of the early part of the reign of James II* (London, 1808), app., p. cvi. See also Henry Hallam, *Constitutional History of England* (Everyman ed.), iii, 50n.
42 5 Geo. IV c.46 (House of Lords Record Office).
43 *Lords Manuscripts 1689–90*, *(H.M.C.)*, pp. 47–9, 75–6.
44 ibid., pp. 76–8; *L.J.*, xiv, 219–21.
45 *Lords Manuscripts 1689–90*, pp. 78–80; *L.J.*, xiv, 228, 234, 236.
46 *C.J.*, x, 177; Grey, ix, 288 ff.
47 *C.J.*, x, 247 ff.; *Lords Manuscripts 1689–90*, pp. 259–71.
48 *C.J.*, x, 263–4.
49 11 Will. III, c.4, printed E. N. Williams, *The Eighteenth Century Constitution* (London, 1960), pp. 331–4.
50 What follows is based on Lane, pp. 329 ff.

Index

Index

Southcote, Sir John, 50, 82, 145, 255
Southwell, Sir Robert, 43–4, 48, 79, 84, 85, 103, 119, 139, 161, 191
Spalding, Capt. Francis, 108, 122, 245
Stacey, Catherine, 237
Stafford, Margaret, 257
Stafford, William Howard, 1st Viscount, 33, 36, 46, 47, 93, 94, 107, 158, 159–60, 162, 164, 169, 176, 230 ff., 231, 253, 255, 275, 279, 310;
  posthumous earldom, 276;
  reversal of attainder, 296–7
Staley, William, 112–13, 191, 206 n., 251–2, 312
Stamford, Thomas Grey, 2nd Earl of, 296
Stapleton, Fr, 129
Stapleton, Miles, 198
Stapleton, Sir Miles, 226, 255
Starkey, Henry, 220, 222, 223
Stephen, Sir James, 131
Stephenson, Mr, 124
Stevens, Lieut., 82
Stillingfleet, Edward, 64
Stonor, Thomas, 30
Stourton, William, 12th Lord, 310
Strafford: Thomas Wentworth, 1st Earl of, 142–3, 154;
  William Wentworth, 2nd Earl of, 77
Strange, Richard, 43, 55–6, 58, 63, 66, 240
Strickland, Sir Thomas, 124, 262
Stubbs, Mr, 172
Suffolk, James Howard, 3rd Earl of, 55
Sunderland, Robert Spencer, 2nd Earl of, 120, 155, 210, 281
Swiman, Hierom, 74
Symons, Sir James, 163, 290

Talbot, Peter, 225, 234

Talbot, Richard, 38, 305
Tasborough, Mr, 219
Tempest, Lady, 225, 227
Test Acts, 1, 9, 18, 35–6, 39, 118, 120, 147, 171, 271
Teynham, Christopher Roper, 5th Lord, 115, 257, 310
Teynham, Elizabeth, Lady, 257
Thimbleby, Mr, 108
Thimbleby, Richard: see Ashby
Thomas, Ely, 112
Throckmorton, Sir William, 40, 41, 45, 98
Thwing, Thomas, 226, 230, 246
Tichborne, Sir Henry, 94, 115, 230, 254
Tilden, Mary, 165
Tillotson, John, 1, 102, 112
Titus, Silas, 116, 131
Tonge, Israel, 50, 52 ff., 55, 57, 58 ff., 65, 67, 68 ff., 75, 76–7, 78, 80, 85, 95, 97, 229, 277, 278
Tonge, Simpson, 229
Tonge, Thomas, 62
Travers, George, 254
Travers, Walter, 252
Treby, Sir George, 281
Trelawney, Sir Jonathan, 105
Trials:
  for treason, 131–43, 144–6, 154, 178–9, 180–88, 192–201, 230–32, 276–7;
  for treason under Act of 1585, 177 ff., 219 ff., 242–4;
  for murder, 164 ff.;
  for perjury, 281 ff.
Turberville, Christopher, 245
Turberville, Edward, 231–2, 245, 276, 279
Turenne, Henri, vicomte de, 37
Turner, Anthony, 162, 180, 181, 239, 247, 251
Turner, Edward, 162

Vaughan, John, 122, 144

345

More about Penguins
and Pelicans

Penguinews, which appears every month, contains details of all the new books issued by Penguin as they are published. From time to time it is supplemented by *Penguins in Print*, which is a complete list of all titles available. (There are some five thousand of these.)

A specimen copy of *Penguinews* will be sent to you free on request. For a year's issues (including the complete lists) please send 50p if you live in the British Isles, or 75p if you live elsewhere. Just write to Dept EP, Penguin Books Ltd, Harmondsworth, Middlesex, enclosing a cheque or postal order, and your name will be added to the mailing list.

In the U.S.A.: For a complete list of books available from Penguin in the United States write to Dept CS, Penguin Books Inc., 7110 Ambassador Road, Baltimore, Maryland 21207.

In Canada: For a complete list of books available from Penguin in Canada write to Penguin Books Canada Ltd, 41 Steelcase Road West, Markham, Ontario.

PENGUIN UNIVERSITY BOOKS

The Growth of Political Stability in England 1675-1725

J. H. PLUMB

'By providing this illuminating introduction to the political scene when Walpole first entered the Commons he has done much to clear up the complexities of a very confusing period and lay the basis for a new interpretation of it. Future students of these years cannot afford to disregard *The Growth of Political Stability in England*' – Dorothy Marshall in the *Cambridge Review*

In the seventeenth-century England experienced civil war, revolution and constant turbulence; yet by 1725 the stability of her institutions was the envy of Europe. In this series of lectures Professor J. H. Plumb examines the question of how – almost abruptly – England achieved political peace in the early eighteenth century.

'Particularly impressive is the study of the grass-roots of politics – the parliamentary constituencies... Yet, new as much of the detail is, it is the thinking that commands most attention' – *New Statesman*

The Pelican History of England: Volume 6

England in the Seventeenth Century

MAURICE ASHLEY

'A closely packed portmanteau of varied knowledge and mature thought, which travellers setting out on a voyage of discovery in the seventeenth century would do well to carry with them' – C. V. Wedgwood in *Time and Tide*

The political and constitutional changes in this epoch were remarkable. Thus when King James I came to the throne in 1603 he exercised wide and undefined powers, including the right to suspend the law. When Queen Anne died in 1714, the powers of the Crown had been reduced by statute, the monarch had ceased to be his own first Minister, and the House of Commons had become pre-eminent in the State.

In the author's opinion, the Interregnum in the middle of the century, far from being a backwater in our history, marked a turn in the river. With the rise of science, the gradual acceptance of the idea of liberty of conscience, the invention of realist political theories by Hobbes and Harrington, and the spread of Puritan nonconformity, the whole field of thought and complexion of life was transformed. Dr Ashley discusses the movements not only in politics and common history, but in the arts and in literature, and their fore-shadowings of our world of today.